THE CULT OF DIVINE BIRTH
IN ANCIENT GREECE

THE CULT OF DIVINE BIRTH IN ANCIENT GREECE

Marguerite Rigoglioso

First published in hardcover in 2009 by PALGRAVE MACMILLAN® in the United States — a division of St. Martin's Press LLC, 175 Fifth Avenue, New York, NY 10010.

Where this book is distributed in the UK, Europe and the rest of the world, this is by Palgrave Macmillan, a division of Macmillan Publishers Limited, registered in England, company number 785998, of Houndmills, Basingstoke, Hampshire RG21 6XS.

Palgrave Macmillan is the global academic imprint of the above companies and has companies and representatives throughout the world.

Palgrave® and Macmillan® are registered trademarks in the United States, the United Kingdom, Europe and other countries.

ISBN: 978-0-230-11132-5

Library of Congress Cataloging-in-Publication Data

Rigoglioso, Marguerite.
    The cult of divine birth in ancient Greece/Marguerite Rigoglioso.
       p. cm.
    Includes bibliographical references and index.
    ISBN 0-230-61477-9
    1. Greece—Religion.   2. Women priests—Greece.   3. Virgin birth (Mythology)   4. Goddesses, Greek.   5. Women and religion—Greece.   I. Title.

    BL795.P7R54 2009
    292.2'114—dc22   2008043015

A catalogue record of the book is available from the British Library.

Design by Macmillan Publishing Solutions

First PALGRAVE MACMILLAN paperback edition: March 2011

10 9 8 7 6 5 4 3 2 1

Printed in the United States of America.

Transferred to Digital Printing in 2011

To Robert, with profound gratitude

CONTENTS

ACKNOWLEDGMENTS

I would like to thank many people for their support in association with this book. First, my dissertation committee members, who read earlier versions of this manuscript as it was birthed into my doctoral dissertation at the California Institute of Integral Studies (CIIS): my chairperson, Associate Professor Jorge Ferrer, Professor Lucia Chiavola Birnbaum, and Marvin Meyer, Griset Professor of Bible and Christian Studies at Chapman University, for their openness and wise guidance, and Dr. Birnbaum, especially, for her loving mentorship during the eight years of my graduate studies; Professor Janis Phelps, my doctoral advisor, for her encouragement of my research topic; Professor Charlene Spretnak, for her helpful feedback on an earlier draft and her visionary guidance in the field of feminist studies in religion; Mara Keller and Arisika Razak, former and current (respectively) directors of the Women's Spirituality Program at CIIS, for, along with the institute's other faculty and staff, providing a wonderful program and graduate school in which nontraditional ontologies, epistemologies, and methodologies may be explored with seriousness, rigor, and creativity; Deborah Grenn, Dianne Jennet, and Judy Grahn, codirectors of the Women's Spirituality Program at the Institute of Transpersonal Psychology, as well as faculty member Vicki Noble, for their inspirational research and encouragement of my own; Pamela Eakins, for her enthusiastic feedback on a preliminary paper that led to this book; Farideh Koohi-Kamali, Brigitte Shull, and Christopher Chappell at Palgrave Macmillan, for their professional editorial support and guidance; Angeleen Campra, Tom Hassett, and the staff of Macmillan Publishing Solutions for editing and proofreading; Suzanne Sherman Aboulfadl for her indexing skills; librarians Fawzia Campana and Cindy Mattison (CIIS), and Lisa Wendell, Adolfo ("AJ") Real, Jr., Kenneth Fish, and Shaun Barger (Dominican University of California), for their patient assistance with my relentless interlibrary loan requests; Jerry L. Hall, for assistance and clarification regarding the scientific aspects of parthenogenesis in humans and animals; astronomer Conrad Jung at the Chabot

Space and Science Center in Oakland, CA, for his generous time showing me computer simulations of the trajectory of the Pleiades in the heavens; Walter Tanner, for his spirited help with Greek tutoring and translations and his support in making my work available to others; Joan Marler, for assistance with pesky details regarding citations; Miriam Robbins Dexter, for guidance on linguistic queries; MaShiAat Oloya Tyehimba, for meaningful background information; the Venerable Dyhani Ywahoo for helpful correspondence; Joe Burull, for his excellent photography and dedicated help with the cover image; friends and family members, for their listening ears and helpful insights as I shared the unfolding of my research with them; Teague Owings, for her excitement and appreciation for this topic, and her provocative drawing gracing the cover; and, above all, Robert Owings, for unconditional support, scholarly references, abundant insights, and teachings that have been critical to this process.

NOTE ABOUT CITATION STYLE

For this book, *The Chicago Manual of Style*'s author-date system of documentation has been used so that the reader may discern the sources being referenced without having to flip back constantly to the endnotes. This should be particularly helpful for the classical citations. Where citations contain more than two sources, are otherwise visually cumbersome, or require further commentary, however, they have been reverted to endnotes.

INTRODUCTION

Now is come the last age of the Cumaean prophecy:
The great cycle of periods is born anew.
Now returns the [Virgin] . . .
Now from high heaven a new generation comes down.

—Virgil *Fourth Eclogue* (4–7)[1]

"The daughter becomes identical with the mother." This statement of Erich Neumann (1963, 309), providing what may well be the key to the mystery of the cult to Demeter and Persephone in antiquity, haunted me for months as I wrote my master's thesis on these two goddesses in central Sicily. There was a depth to it, fascinating and unplumbable, that kept me traveling ever further inward.

I remember standing in my brother's apartment in Brooklyn, New York, in January 2001 when I had the insight that was the starting point of this book. I had been reading Sicilian scholar Anna Maria Corradini's book *Meteres: Il Mito del Matriarchato in Sicilia* (Mothers: The Myth of Matriarchy in Sicily). Corradini stated for me what seemed a sudden and profound truth: the Demeter/Persephone mystery was, at core, a *female-only* mystery. Stripping off the layers that the Greeks had added on through the violent intrusion of Hades and other male gods into the story, she suggested that Demeter was a pre-Hellenic *parthenogenetic* goddess who produced the natural world—and her daughter, Persephone—spontaneously out of her own body (1997, 12–4; 81–3).

Parthenogenesis. Self-conception. Virgin birth. Mothers and identical daughters. As I stood in my brother's small office, I had the strange sensation of a foreign thought suddenly illuminating my mind: Were holy women of ancient Greece once engaged in attempting to conceive children miraculously?

Since that time, shards of a Greek history seeming to link women and divine birth have continuously presented themselves to me, glinting through obscure passages in ancient texts and in the prose of unsuspecting contemporary scholars. I have collected these pieces, and in this book I have assembled them. The result is a vessel that may still have many missing parts, but one that begins to reveal an integral form and shape, nonetheless.

During the course of this research I have come to realize there have been so many artifacts staring at us for 2,000 years, in fact, that it is truly stunning no one has put them together before as evidence of possible female cultic practice.[2] Practically all of the legendary heroes who came to head the great genealogical tribes of early Greece, as well as various historical political and spiritual leaders and a handful of humans turned divine, were said to have been born of mortal women through sexual union with gods. Not only were Heracles, Perseus, Theseus, and a host of other legendary heroes associated with divine birth stories, but so were historical figures such as Pythagoras, Plato, and Alexander the Great. In certain corners of the Graeco-Roman world, it was believed that miraculous conception could occur through the influence of snakes and celestial rays of light. The healing cult of Asclepius held that women could be impregnated with supernatural assistance—a belief that was the basis for the entire nearby Egyptian civilization. The *basilinna,* the "queen archon" of classical Athens, was even attested to conduct a secret and presumably sexual rite with the god Dionysus every year. Are such stories and practices—and many, many more—to be dismissed as mere remnants of mythology—that is, fiction—alone? Or do they point to something important about the actual beliefs and rites of ancient Greece?

VIRGIN BIRTH AS A HOLY PRACTICE IN GREECE

This book argues for the latter. In doing so, it offers what amounts to a radical reinterpretation of ancient Greek religion, one that suggests priestly women—and the figure of the "holy virgin"—may have been considered far more central to the founding of Greek civilization than previously understood. Specifically, this book makes the case that certain specialized priestesshoods in ancient Greece may have endeavored to conceive children in various non-ordinary ways as an elevated form of spiritual practice. It demonstrates that the intended purpose of this practice was to give birth to a hero or heroine, gifted spiritual leader, or what was considered to be a supernatural being—an individual it was thought could not enter into the human stream through the "normal" sexual channels. This miraculously born individual, as the following chapters show, was considered a special soul capable of benefitting humanity significantly in some way, or of heralding or reinforcing particular value systems for the human race. The book proposes that attempting to produce offspring through various asexual and/or magical methods was thought to be a specialized sacerdotal activity for women. Although some Greek writers, such as Herodotus, were reportedly skeptical about women's capacity for virgin birth, there were many who apparently believed it was possible—including some in the highest intellectual echelons, such as certain followers of Pythagoras and Plato. This book argues that Greeks who believed in the reality of such a phenomenon held miraculous conception and birthing of a child to be the most advanced form of magico-spiritual achievement possible. At its best, divine birthing was considered a feat that could transport the human race to a new level of functioning and awareness through the influence of the incarnated individual. The evidence shows that the purported birth of a specially conceived child was thought to result in the apotheosis, or literal divinization of the priestess herself—a "promotion" from human to goddess—and led to her corresponding veneration. Similarly, the child of this conception was considered to be of a divine nature and likewise the focus of worship.

WHAT THIS BOOK IS NOT ABOUT

To be clear, the task of this book is not to argue whether birth through miraculous means is or ever was possible. It is also not to argue whether any assumed practice by women in ancient Greece to conceive and give birth miraculously to a special category of children was successful or not. Rather, the work is to present and analyze a vast array of information from history, legend, and myth suggesting that groups of priestly women in ancient Greece who at the very least *attempted* divine birth as a spiritual discipline *and who were believed at the time to have been successful* may have formally existed. In doing so, this book brings into relief an aspect of Greek religion that has been obscured in the patriarchal era through the relegation of divine birth stories to the status of quaint and frivolous fable.

It is also important to note that in presenting evidence for the existence of what I am calling *divine birth priestesshoods* in Greece, the aim is not to make a scientific case that parthenogenesis—that is, conception and birth without the participation of the male—ever may have existed as a method intended to eclipse sexual procreation and do away with men.[3] Nor is it to suggest that parthenogenesis should be explored as a means of doing so in future. The study discusses parthenogenesis in the religious context only, as a possible spiritual practice that would have had a specialized purpose.

FROM PARTHENOGENESIS TO SACRED MARRIAGE

As I elaborate shortly, the aforementioned thesis has enormous heuristic utility in explaining and clarifying numerous paradoxical and puzzling characteristics of ancient Greek religion and mythology. First, it must be emphasized that a key theoretical perspective underpinning this work is the assumption that an earlier cultural substratum underlay all Greek (and related Roman) mythology as it was conveyed in archaic, classical, and post-classical periods. In this, I am in alignment with a number of prominent scholars of ancient Greek religion, as I explain further in Chapter 1. Of particular importance is the fact that such scholars, among them Jane Ellen Harrison, Karl Kerenyi, and Lewis Farnell, posit that this older system was matriarchal. According to this theoretical view, the religion most of us identify with ancient Greece, which is based on the Olympian myths, was a later—and patriarchal—development, the result of invasions to the Greek peninsula throughout the second millennium B.C.E. Although classicists originally thought such newcomers came from the North, subsequent archaeological data has revealed that they arrived from the East and Northeast (Dergachev 2007; Gimbutas 1989, 1991).

There are plentiful indicators in the archaeological, historical, and literary record to support the theory that female deities enjoyed a far greater prominence and stature in pre-Greek culture than they did in Olympian religion[4]—and that nearly all such pre-Greek goddesses were understood to be generative mothers *and* virgins simultaneously. That is, they were parthenogenetic, producing the cosmos and all earthly creatures, including humans, out of their own essence without need for a male partner. This book offers basic evidence to support this idea, a theme that will be developed more fully in a second volume, titled *Virgin Mother Goddesses of Antiquity*.

This book provides extensive support for the proposition that the cults of these Divine Virgins generated priesthoods that aspired to replicating the parthenogenetic abilities of the goddesses.

Thus, it posits that in its pre-Olympian form, the cult of divine birth was exclusively a female enterprise, dedicated to attempting to produce special *female* children. The evidence suggests that as early Greece transitioned to patriarchy, the divine birth priestesshoods experienced a corresponding disruption. No longer were priestesses focused on replicating the exclusive parthenogenetic abilities of the goddess/es, rather they were conscripted to give birth to what were considered the children of male gods—usually, but not always, sons. This book thus offers a fresh perspective on the much-contested religious concept of "sacred marriage," or *hieros gamos*. It not only provides evidence to support the theory that a sexual ritual was indeed conducted in antiquity between a human figure and what was believed to be a divinity, but it also places the rite in what I contend is its correct historical position as a patriarchal revision of a custom whose intended purpose was the achievement of divine birth.[5]

NEW INSIGHTS THIS BOOK OFFERS ABOUT GREEK RELIGION

This is the first scholarly book to explore the theme of divine birth in ancient Greece in an in-depth and comprehensive fashion.[6] While other writers have suggested that parthenogenesis may have been an attribute of certain ancient goddesses or that women in different cultures and time periods may have attempted non-ordinary methods of reproduction for various purposes, no one has discussed these topics at length in relation to priestess groups in Greek antiquity.[7] Thus this book articulates an entire thematic complex that has been given only cursory attention.

This book brings a number of new understandings to the study of Greek religion and women's leadership roles in Greek cult. The preliminary analysis offered here of the parthenogenetic aspects of various Greek goddesses, for example, should begin to provide a fresh angle on our understanding of the nature, attributes, and agency of these deities as they were originally conceived. One point it clarifies is the fact that in the ancient world virginity and motherhood were originally understood to be simultaneously possible, coexisting as two complementary aspects of both feminine divinity and the human female in their most exalted, empowered manifestations. Correspondingly, it resolves the seeming paradox of Artemis's serving as a goddess who rejected heterosexual eroticism but who protected women's birthing process. Similarly, it explains why the "married" Hera periodically needed to "renew" her virginity in cultic rites.

In its abundantly detailed argument that various Greek priest-esshoods patterned themselves after parthenogenetic goddesses in attempting to conceive children through divine conception and that they later capitulated to *hieros gamos* unions with gods under the pressure of patriarchy, this book helps coalesce disparate motifs and resolve paradoxes in a larger matrix. It brings into a meaningful whole the numerous legends of women's unions with gods that once seemed fanciful and unrelated. Moreover, in reframing the many "rapes" by gods as instances of male intrusion into the female divine birth mysteries, it provides the missing discourse about female agency in divine/human congress. It subsequently renders understandable the goddesses' "mythological" rage toward such legendary women as representative of conflict that occurred within the divine birth cult during this transitional period. It also retrieves from the realm of "fiction" the identities and practices of women who may well have been historical priestesses.

The thesis of this book similarly renders sensible a number of previously indecipherable female-related rituals. The rite reported by Herodotus in which Ause girls fought each other with sticks and stones to the death in ancient Libya, for example, suddenly becomes understandable as a method the tribe used to divine which maidens the goddess Athena/Neith favored to become holy virgins dedicated to attempting divine birth, as discussed in Chapter 3. The work explicates other previously confounding rituals as propitiation rites—means of circumventing the rage of parthenogenetic goddesses who were believed to be severely displeased over their virgin priesthoods reverting to *hieros gamos* unions with gods. Among them is the mysterious ritual in which young priestesses on the Acropolis of Athens (Athena's domain) were ceremonially required to transport "secret things" in baskets to the "garden of Aphrodite," but were expressly forbidden to peek into their bundles, as also explored in Chapter 3. Another is the practice by which young girls at Brauron were required to "mimic" bears as a curious means of honoring Artemis, a topic elaborated upon in Chapter 4. Moreover, in Chapter 5, this book explores the possibility that the Olympic Games originated in the female-only foot races dedicated to Hera at Olympia, leading to the stunning discovery that this famed athletic contest may have emerged from the cult of divine birth associated with this goddess.

In Chapters 6 and 7, this book draws together interesting or typically overlooked details regarding the oracles at Dodona and Delphi, particularly as they relate to women and the feminine. It provides a more comprehensive feminist analysis of the goddess Dione at Dodona, and of the female oracular functionaries at both sites, than has been attempted before. The discussion of the possible connection between these cultic locales and the astral realms of Taurus and the Pleiades opens the window to an expanded understanding of the significance of such star systems in Greek religion and of their relation to the feminine, as well as of prophetesses' likely engagement with not only the chthonic but also the celestial mysteries.

In bringing to light the fact that the dove and the bee were symbols of divine birth, this book further explains why oracular priestesses at Dodona and Delphi were identified with such totems. Similarly, it renders plain why the lore of such places was replete with stories of virgin birth. It explicates the Delphic Pythia's "spousal" relationship with Apollo and, by elucidating the dual understanding of the concept of "conception" as both a physical and mental/oracular process, makes clear why the same verb, *anaireô*, "to take up," would have meant both "to give an oracle" and "to conceive in the womb." In so doing, this book provides a coherent rationale as to why oracular and parthenogenetic aspirations would have been understood as the province, in many cases, of prophetesses.

In its thesis that terms such as *parthenos* (variously but unsuccessfully defined by classics scholars as "maiden" or "virgin") as well as *heroine* and *nymph* were titles originally used to denote the priestess of divine birth, articulated in Chapter 2, the theory detailed here allows for the resolution of contradictory meanings and characteristics associated with such words, and lends to a new interpretation of Homer's "cave of the nymphs" as symbol of virgin birth. This book foregrounds the importance of virginity as a requirement in certain priesthoods, as well, but clarifies that celibacy originally was a specialized practice, not a burden imposed on all young women with its later moral connotations. The theory likewise eases the apparent contradictions associated with the possible linguistic relationship between the Greek *parthenos* and the Egyptian *Pr ṯ hn*, allowing for a conjectural definition of the term as the poetic and apt "holy vessel for the divine star being who has descended from the heavenly cow/Hathor/Neith."

In short, this book places focus on those figures usually ignored or glossed over in discussions of divine birth: the female participants. It moreover suggests new ways of looking at Greek priestesses as not mere ritual technicians, but as holy women who were deeply connected with the esoteric—the hidden and mysterious aspects—of Greek religion. In positioning virgin priestesses as they once may have been seen in the ancient world—as active and purposeful agents in the divine birth process rather than passive bystanders or rape victims—this book also has tremendous implications for the future study of the most famous virgin mother of all, Mary.

METHODOLOGICAL APPROACHES

For this book, I have approached ancient and secondary texts and iconography using a number of methodologies, which, given the provocative nature of what is being proposed, bear some attention. I first and foremost utilize a feminist hermeneutical approach. That is, I recast written records applying what Schüssler Fiorenza calls "a feminist hermeneutics of suspicion that understands texts as ideological articulations of men expressing, as well as maintaining, patriarchal historical conditions" (1983, 60).[8] Moreover, I follow Goff's approach (2004, 25) of reading texts "against the grain," or reading them "for other than their ostensible significance" to recover where and how historical women may have had agency and autonomy in an attempt to create what I hope is a more complete and accurate picture of the ancient Greek priesthood.

Another methodological approach I employ is neo-euhemerism. That is, I look to mythology and legends as sources of important clues about historical events and actual ancient cultural and cultic practices. The term *neo-euhemerism* derives from the name of the fourth century B.C.E. writer Euhemerus, who, by investigating the actions and places of birth and burial of the divinities of popular religion, claimed the gods were simply deified human beings, great heroes who were revered because they had benefited mankind in some important way. His rationalizing method of interpreting Greek myths, known as classical euhemerism, was revived in the nineteenth century by scholars such as Spencer ([1876] 1969). In more recent works, Nilsson (1932, 1964), for example, argues that the Greek epics originated in the aristocratic society of Bronze Age Mycenaean culture, reflected the deeds of historical men, and described contemporary events while mixing mythical and folktale elements. Harrison ([1903] 1957, [1912] 1963) similarly assumes that myth reflects broad historical contours of Greek and pre-Greek culture. Farnell, too, throughout his classic five-volume work *Cults of the Greek States* ([1896–1909] 1977), conjectures that various myths may have been indicators of actual custom and ritual.

It should be noted that reading myth as history violates the injunctions of scholars who assume myth is predominantly fictional in nature (see, e.g., Dowden 1995, 44). It is also to be acknowledged that mythology may have suffered at the hands of certain families who attempted to connect themselves with an ancestry that could be traced back to an Olympian god (Guthrie 1967, 55). Still, I concur with Nilsson (1932, 3–4) that there may be at least some measure of reliability to myths as representations of genealogies and chronology. As he notes (2), "The glory and fame of ancient poets depended not, like that of modern poets, on their invention of something new and original, but rather on their presentation of the old traditional material in new and original fashion." Cook (1914–40, 1:675), too, comments, "Even Ovid, facile though he was and frivolous though he may have been, did not invent his *Metamorphoses* wholesale. Recent research is in fact tending toward the conclusion that he did not invent them at all."

The position I take is that myths are not always or necessarily purely of the realm of fiction, but may contain genuine relics or traces of historical events and cultural practices. I also follow Birnbaum (1993, 3–35), who provides an amplified theoretical discussion of folklore as a repository for secret, subversive, and often subjugated and repressed religious beliefs, particularly as regards women, the feminine, and the subaltern. I would extend this theoretical terrain to include material found not just in folklore, but in the biographies of the goddesses and gods. My aim in examining the ancient stories from such perspectives is not, as in classical euhemerism, to attempt to "demote" the gods to human status in what has been called the "faded god" approach (Lyons 1997, 72). I give but an occasional mention to the idea that many of the deities, notably Hermes, Dionysus, and Apollo, but also Zeus and Athena, to name a few, also have rationalizing myths associated with them. Rather, my aim is simply to bring into consideration the possibility that many of the figures in mythology such as heroes, heroines, "nymphs," and so forth, may have been historical figures. Hence my modified approach is more strictly known as "neo-euhemerism," one also embraced to some extent by Farnell (1921). It is this that really forms the crux of my analysis, as I propose it is to the great religious myths and legends—by the latter, I mean unsubstantiated stories local peoples believed were historical[9]—that information about the cult of divine birth has been relegated. I contend that the rewards of this approach in terms of what it may reveal about priestly women of Greece outweigh the potential dangers.

I should note that starting from the position that heroines and "nymphs" may represent historical women leads to a different interpretation of myth than that of scholars who assume female figures who consorted with gods were in fact demoted local goddesses. Cook (1914–40, 1:524), for example, conjectures that the Phoenician princess Europa, who is said to have borne a son named Dodon or Dodonus to Zeus, "was at first a great earth-mother, who sent up vegetation from her home in the ground." I argue, instead, that the divine status of women such as Europa was granted *as a result* of their supposed union with gods. Indeed, I suggest that the assumption that such women represented downgraded forms of earlier goddesses is in part what has obscured the recognition of the divine birth priestesshood by scholars. My work of discerning certain female figures in Greek text to be priestesses rather than goddesses parallels work being done by Connelly (2007, 108–36) and others in the area of vase painting, cult implements, and sculpture.

I should also note that in reading myths as history, for the most part I do not distinguish between myths in terms of their dating or the "reliability" of their systematizers, except to comment on instances of what I discern may have been androcentric revisions to an original story. To do otherwise would be beyond the scope of this book and would, I believe, bog the arguments down with unnecessary tedium. Whether one particular myth or another may be suspect as a source of historical information becomes, to my mind, irrelevant in the face of the sheer number of myths I have laid out that point in similar directions. I also maintain that repetitive myth typologies (such as the theme of the "hero slaying the python/serpent"), far from proving the ahistorical nature of such stories, affirm general trends and events in human experience across a variety of locales and time periods. I suggest they may even be survivals of historical events that took place prior to particular diffusions of various pockets of our human ancestors into new cultural groups.[10]

Ultimately, I also approach myths intuitively. As Drewermann (1994, 125) observes, "The symbolism of the myths has to be read like expressionistic works of art in order to grasp their existential code language." Just as myths are what I would argue a pastiche of histories, hidden codes, and politico-religious programs and propaganda, so they require multiple methods in their decipherment and analysis. I am not content to approach them from one vantage point only. Sometimes I apply a feminist hermeneutics of suspicion, sometimes a neo-euhemeristic reading. And sometimes I apply what I would call a "gnostic lens" to the story. That is, I take myths to be expressions of mystical concepts corresponding with what I contend were the more esoteric aspects of Greek religion.[11]

CONCLUDING THOUGHTS

The words of Guthrie (1967, 23) may serve as fitting beacon for what is to follow:

> The classics live only because each generation sees in them something a little different from the last, and to try to see them through the eyes of the last generation would be unwise even if it were possible.

It is to be acknowledged that this book is highly provocative. Clearly this project takes the patchwork that is ancient Greek religion and puts it together in new combinations to make unconventional assertions about the way things might have been in the ancient Mediterranean world. As the reader will hopefully discern in the following chapters, I attempt to make such claims as responsibly as possible by supporting them with carefully compiled data. It should be noted that the argument I make herein is *cumulative*. No one piece of evidence alone is likely to "prove" that a cult of divine birth existed in ancient Greece. The persuasiveness of the thesis, I propose, lies in the sheer volume of suggestive details that point in this direction—the full impact of which cannot be felt without reading through to the very end, where many of the threads come together at last. Whether all may agree with my assumptions, methods, interpretations, and conclusions or not, I can only but proceed ahead, bearing forth the fruits of what has amounted to seven years of gestation and labor with the hope that this project will be meaningful in the larger scheme of things.

CHAPTER 1

A TAXONOMY OF DIVINE
BIRTH PRIESTESSHOODS

The intuitive flash I had that wintry New York day in January 2001—that specialized women in ancient Greece may have actively participated in attempts to produce children in non-ordinary ways as part of a spiritual calling—stimulated me to approach my research on ancient Greek history and religion from new angles. In my studies, I began to notice data that seemed to cluster around and verify this idea, which inspired me to seek out supporting information more actively. As I made sense of the data I was collecting, further and unanticipated patterns began to emerge. New insights were sparked, as well, which subsequently stimulated ever new cycles of mining ancient texts and secondary literature in search of validating details. The process thus was both deductive and inductive.

I soon discerned in the ancient literature that there was more than one method by which women were credited with achieving divine birth. A theoretical structure began to emerge that seemed to allow the data to speak in the most coherent way possible. In this chapter I present that structure—what I am calling a taxonomy of divine birth priestesshoods. This taxonomy serves as the theoretical reference point for the rest of this book.

KEY TERMS IN THIS BOOK

First, some preliminary details are in order. Throughout this book, I use a number of terms to denote what may be more generally referred to as miraculous or divine birth. By both *miraculous* and *divine birth,* I mean any kind of conception and birth of a child in which either (1) male sperm was believed not to be involved or (2) male sperm may have been involved, but the conception was thought in fact to be the result of impregnation by a male god. I will expound upon the latter more fully shortly.

Another term I use to refer to the phenomenon of birth through non-ordinary means is *parthenogenetic birth.* The word *parthenogenesis* derives from the Greek *parthenos,*[1] essentially "virgin, maiden," and *gignesthai,* or "to be born." Scientifically, it refers to the conception and birth of offspring without fertilization by male sperm.[2] A third important term I occasionally use is *autogenesis.* This is generally reserved for deities, and refers to the process of self-generation, that is, deities' creation of themselves out of themselves/the void/nothingness/the All.

THE MATRIARCHAL UNDERPINNINGS OF GREEK RELIGION

It is also important for me to elaborate here upon the theoretical assumption that pre-Olympian Greek culture was woman centered to a far greater degree than Olympian culture was. Various scholars have posited that before the Greeks as we know them existed, a series of invading peoples from the East and Northeast successively overran and took over the Greek peninsula throughout the second millennium B.C.E.[3] Such invasions culminated with the Indo-European Dorians, who entered Greece about 1100 B.C.E., bringing the tongue that became the language of Greece. It is thought that these various invaders brought a patriarchal theology with them, as well. Guthrie (1967, 52–3), for example, writes that

> the contrast between [the earlier] Aegean and [the later] Homeric cults was, generally speaking, a contrast between a religion of the soil, a worship of the fertility of the earth [Ge/Gaia] not unmixed with magical practices to secure its continuance, and a religion of the sky, whose chief god [Zeus] was the sender of thunder and lightning upon those who displeased him.

The idea that Greek mythology preserves hints of the older religious substratum in which a Great Goddess was the primary deity prior to the installation of the Olympian pantheon, as codified by Hesiod and Homer, forms the basis of much twentieth-century scholarly interpretation. It is this line of reasoning that I draw upon for my analyses in this book. Critical to my argument is the related concept that pre-Greek goddess-venerating culture was not only theologically matriarchal, but socially matriarchal as well—a position that is also embraced by a number of classicists.[4] Harrison ([1903] 1957, 261), for example, notes,

> In historical days in Greece, descent was for the most part traced through the father . . . [P]rimitive goddesses reflect another condition of things, a relationship traced through the mother, the state of society known by the awkward term matriarchal, a state echoed in the lost *Catalogues of Women*, the *Eoiai* of Hesiod, and in the Boeotian heroines of the *Nekuia*.

Similarly, Kerenyi observes that the ancient Greek title for "king," *basileus*, which appears widely throughout Homer and, in an earlier form, on Mycenaean-age tablets, was, in fact, a derivative of *basile*, an ancient queen's title and the name of a goddess.[5] He writes (1975, 44–5),

> The linguistic evidence is that the source of the rank borne by these "kings" was a "queen," and the system of law in which both titles were originally valid was a different one from the Greek. In it the "queen" stood higher than a "king." The title *basileus*, which in Homer is borne neither by Zeus nor by any other god, is likely a key fossil opening the way back into a still more ancient time than that of the Mycenaean kingdom. If it is really the case that the supremacy of Zeus over all the gods reflects the position of the Mycenaean high king, then in Mycenae a patriarchal order of society, no longer a matriarchal one, must have been in force.

Harrison and Kerenyi thus affirm that the early Greece of the Mycenaean period, to which the exploits of the heroes and the Olympian gods are generally assigned, emerged out of a matriarchal culture upon which a patriarchal social structure had been laid. In the matriarchal period, as Kerenyi comments, the queen had in fact possessed greater power and status than any male. The title *basile* becomes important in Chapter 2, when I discuss the derivative term *basilinna* held by the wife of the *archon basileus*. The *basilinna* annually engaged in a historically attested "sacred marriage" ritual with the god Dionysus in classical Athens.

Gimbutas (1982, 1989, 1991, 1999) has provided archaeological evidence to support the theory that a civilization based on a Great Goddess, in which women held high positions of cultural leadership in tandem with men, predated the patriarchal civilization in Old Europe and surrounding regions. She dates the beginnings of the transition between the late fifth and early fourth millennia B.C.E. Following Gimbutas (1989, xx–xvi), I assume that the patriarchal peoples whom Guthrie, Harrison, and others posit invaded the Greek peninsula from the East/Northeast throughout the second millennium B.C.E. to create the beginnings of Greek civilization encountered hybrid societies in which matriarchal traits were still prominent.[6] The second millennium invasions would have served to intensify the patriarchal nature of such societies and systematically erase vestiges of matriarchy, as was discussed earlier. Throughout this book, as part of the larger discussion on the historical trajectory of the hypothesized divine birth priestesshoods, I present what I believe is evidence attesting to this phenomenon in Greece.

THE ROLE OF TRANCE IN DIVINE BIRTH PRACTICE

Before proceeding with a discussion of the various types of practices to achieve divine birth, I should also note that regardless of the type of reproductive method attempted, the practice as a whole most likely required that the priestess enter into a profound non-ordinary state of consciousness, or "trance." This finds support in Lezzi-Haftner (1988a, b), who similarly theorizes that such a state was part of the *hieros gamos*, or sacred sexual union, that purportedly took place between the historical *basilinna* and the god Dionysus. She bases this on her interpretation of images on ancient ceramics thought to portray the *basilinna* (or possibly her mythic prototype, Ariadne) in a ritualized "drowsy" or "sleep" state waiting for her union with the god. I contend it is indeed only through a hypnagogic state that a priestess would have been thought capable of fully accessing her special skills as well as the spiritual forces believed necessary to guide her in this most extraordinary of activities.

Iamblichus (*Theurgia [Letter of Porphyry]* 1.3, 1911, trans. Wilder) describes various ways in which the spiritual adept was thought to enter into non-ordinary states of consciousness in the ancient world:

Certain . . . of these ecstatics become enthusiast or inspired when they hear cymbals, drums, or some other choral chant; as for example, those who are engaged in the Corybantic Rites, those who are possessed at the Sabazian festivals, and those who are celebrating the Rites of the Divine Mother. Others, also, are inspired when drinking water, like the priest of the Clarian Apollo at Colophon; others when sitting over cavities in the earth, like the women who deliver oracles at Delphi; others when affected by vapor from the water, like the prophetess at Branchiae; and others when standing in indented marks like those who have been filled from an imperceptible inflowing of the divine plerome.

Others who understand themselves in other respects become inspired through Fancy: some taking darkness as accessory, others employing certain potions, and others depending on singing and magic figures. Some are affected by means of water, others by gazing on a wall, others by the hypethral air, and others by the sun or in some other of the heavenly luminaries.

His remarks are echoed by Lewis, former London School of Economics anthropology professor:

Trance states can be readily induced in most normal people by a wide range of stimuli, applied either separately or in combination. Time-honored techniques include the use of alcoholic spirits, hypnotic suggestion, rapid over-breathing, the inhalation of smoke and vapours, music, and dancing; and the ingestion of such drugs as mescaline or lysergic acid and other psychotropic alkaloids. Even without these aids, much the same effect can be produced, although usually in the nature of things more slowly, by such self-inflicted externally imposed mortifications and privations as fasting and ascetic contemplation (e.g., "transcendental meditation").

(1971, 39)

Iamblichus's "potions" are no doubt the "psychotropic alkaloids" of Lewis, or what are today known as *entheogens*. This term, introduced into the English language by Ruck et al. (1979), derives from *entheos*,[7] which in Greek means "full of the god," "inspired," or "possessed," and connotes a state in which the practitioner was "in the god" and the god was "in the practitioner" (Cook 1914–40, 1:673).[8] *Entheos*, then, anciently referred to a state of "oneness" with the deity, and an *entheogen* is thus a substance, usually plant based in the ancient world, thought to engender such a state.[9] I suggest that while engaging in a meditative state may have been enough for some divine birth priestesses to enter into what was believed to be the requisite deep state for their task, imbibing entheogens may have been a particularly effective means of doing so. In Chapter 5, I point to literary evidence attesting to the presence of one entheogenic plant, asterion (cannabis), in connection with the cult of Hera at Argos, for example, and, in Chapter 7, I discuss the probable use of various entheogenic compounds by the prophetesses of Apollo at Delphi.

The mention of the use of plant-based medicines also brings up the question as to whether attempts at non-ordinary conception were thought to have been aided by the ingestion or vaginal insertion of certain herbs, or by the practice of vaginal fumigation, which I discuss in Chapter 7. Such a possibility is lent credence by the scientific fact that human eggs have been observed to begin division spontaneously under the influence of various chemicals.[10]

THE ROLE OF VIRGINITY IN DIVINE BIRTH PRACTICE

Another important preliminary point is that it appears that in many cases virginity was thought to have been a biological and spiritual precondition necessary to render non-ordinary conception possible. Greek myths and legends of women conceiving the children of gods indicate that such women were generally virgins in the younger years of their lives. Some seem to have been dedicated virgins from the time of menarche or earlier. I discuss the virginity requirement in ancient Greek priestesshoods more fully in Chapter 2.

TAXONOMY OF DIVINE BIRTH PRIESTESSES

I now turn to the taxonomy. In reviewing it, I ask that the reader bear with me as I lay out the ideas in broad and, for the most part, unsubstantiated theoretical strokes. I discussed the underlying assumptions and the methodologies I have used to arrive at such a theoretical picture earlier and in the introduction. The myths, legends, and history from which I have drawn this picture naturally form the substance of the rest of this book.

In exploring Greek myths and history, I have discerned what appear to have been a number of non-ordinary ways by which women were thought to conceive divine or divinely endowed children. I suggest that the method used depended upon the ontological framework with which the particular cults that the priestesses served viewed the universe. Thus, in general, gynocentric (female/goddess-centered) theologies corresponded with priestesshoods in which women attempted to mimic the ultimate parthenogenetic capacity of the creator goddess in generating divine children.[11] Androcentric (male/god-centered) theologies corresponded with priestesshoods in which non-ordinary reproduction was thought possible through the sexual union of the priestesses with gods.

Pure Parthenogenetic Priestesshoods

The first category in my proposed taxonomy of divine birth priestesshoods is what I call the *pure parthenogenetic priestesshood*. I propose that this priestesshood was dedicated to attempting conception without the participation of a male in any form whatsoever—either human or divine. I subdivide this priestesshood into two categories: *pure daughter-bearing parthenogenetic priestesshoods* and *pure son-bearing parthenogenetic priestesshoods*.

The Pure Daughter-Bearing Parthenogenetic Priestesshood

I hypothesize that this priestesshood was dedicated to producing female offspring and that it marked the original and first stage of the practice, carried out when social structures were matriarchal. This would have been a period well before the advent of the Olympian cults, when, as I argue in forthcoming chapters, various Greek goddesses, among them Ge/Gaia, Athena, Artemis, and Hera, were conceived of as creator divinities who generated the cosmos, the earth, and all life without male consorts—that is, they were virgin mothers.

Given my theory that priestesses patterned themselves after their goddesses, I submit that one class of sacerdotal women of this time consisted of virgins whose holy reproductive rituals were aimed at generating the spontaneous meiosis of their ova. This type of activity would have corresponded with biological parthenogenesis in the animal and insect world. There, given that progeny conceived parthenogenetically share the same genetic material as their mothers, such offspring are generally female.[12] On the symbolic level, the parthenogenetic creation of the human daughter would have been understood as a process whereby the mother essentially "replicated" herself. The holy daughter born in this unusual way would have been seen as an earthly manifestation of the Great Goddess, and the mother would have been thought to achieve divinity herself for having accomplished the birth of such a being. That is, in being able to generate life spontaneously from her body in the *manner* of the goddess, she was thought to *become* the living embodiment of the goddess. We can think of the parthenogenetic mother and daughter "goddesses" as "twins,"[13] a motif that I suggest formed the basis of the earliest layer of the cult of the mother/daughter goddesses Demeter and Persephone.[14]

The Pure Son-Bearing Parthenogenetic Priestesshood

I propose that with the development of patriarchy and the increasing domination of cultural institutions by men, the male god came into theological ascendancy. Pure parthenogenesis at this secondary stage was modified to bring in a child who served as a human manifestation of this male god. Thus, we have the creation of what I am calling the *pure son-bearing parthenogenetic priestesshood.*

The "birth of the divine son," I contend, was considered a special kind of numinous event that expressed, to borrow Neumann's (1963, 309) words, "the miracle of the male's containment in the female." The priestess now was exalted for having incarnated one "other than" herself, yet still without the benefit of a male fecundator, a feat that may have been seen as even more challenging than bringing in a female. The male holy child—an expression of the newly ascendant male godhead—was rendered "king," and was expected to agree to a ritual death to benefit humanity. His death served, in the words of Pindar (in Plato *Meno* 81b), as "requital for ancient wrong" (*penthos*);[15] that is, it was believed to release the community from negativity associated with the transgressions of their living and deceased members.[16] In undergoing this ordeal, the miraculously born individual was thought to be apotheosized on the ontological level—that is, to achieve godhead—which resulted in his subsequently being worshipped as a divinity.

Although a detailed analysis of parthenogenetic themes in Gnostic texts is beyond the scope of this book, it is important to mention here one Gnostic passage that contains a stunning testament to the existence of an ancient esoteric belief in women's capacity for pure parthenogenesis in a religious context. The passage appears in *The Revelation [or Apocalypse] of Adam*, the last tractate of Nag Hammadi Codex V. It describes one of the means by which "the illuminator of knowledge," the salvific figure known as Seth (of whom Jesus was considered by some to be a manifestation), was thought to have been brought to humanity:

> From the nine muses one separated. She came to a high mountain and spent some time seated there, so that she desired her own body in order to become androgynous. She fulfilled her desire and became pregnant from her desire. He [the illuminator] was born. The angels who were over the desire nourished him. And he received glory there and power.
>
> (Barnstone and Meyer 2003, 186–7)

The text, ascribed to the end of the first century or the beginning of the second (Meyer 2007, 345), contains the most direct ancient reference I have located to date of an episode of pure parthenogenetic conception. The excerpt even affirms the method by which the woman supposedly achieved this feat: by "sitting on a mountain" for some time, that is, through a non-ordinary state of consciousness likely brought about through an extended period of meditation. The identification of the female as a "muse" suggests a priestly connection with the Greek tradition, where muses and nymphs, as I explain throughout this book, were related figures frequently associated with divine birth stories. Although the child believed to have arisen from this particular miraculous conception was male, it is not unreasonable to suggest that such a self-generative mechanism would have been considered a valid method for producing holy female children as well.

Evidence in Greek cult for pure daughter-bearing and son-bearing parthenogenetic priestesshoods, as well as of their sequential emergence, hypothesized above, is otherwise mainly suggestive. In several chapters, I discuss myths that may point to the existence of pure parthenogenetic priestesshoods of the daughter-bearing kind in relationship to the cults of Ge/Gaia, particularly in the earliest days of the oracular cults at Dodona and Delphi. The story of Hera's parthenogenetic birthing of Ares, Typhon, and Hephaestus, which I elaborate upon in Chapter 5, may be an allusion to son-bearing parthenogenesis. The mystical formula—"Brimo has given birth to Brimos!"—recited by the high priest at the conclusion of the Eleusinian Mysteries and possibly referring to the birth of the divine male child, also may have been an allusion to son-bearing parthenogenesis.[17]

Hieros Gamos Divine Birth Priestesshoods

As patriarchy continued to develop, male and female deities came to be conceived of in sexual relationship to one another. This phenomenon finds expression in myths such as that of the goddess Cybele and her fecundating consort, Attis, in Phrygia. Still later, as patriarchy eclipsed matriarchy nearly completely as the dominant social form, the universal deity came to be seen as primarily *male,* sometimes with shadow female attendants who assisted in the generative process in a much reduced and passive role. This is expressed in myths of deities such as Zeus and Hera, explored in Chapter 5.

This transition marked what I propose was a concomitant shift to what I term the *hieros gamos,* that is, *"sacred marriage" divine birth priestesshood.*[18] In the condition of the *hieros gamos,* a woman was thought to conceive a child as the result of "sexual intercourse" with a male supernatural entity or god, without the involvement of a human male in the earliest stage of the practice. The numerous stories of unions between women and gods in Greek mythology and legend, to be explored throughout this book, indicate that this form of *hieros gamos* became the most widespread method for achieving what was believed to be miraculous birth in the incipient days of Greek culture.[19] The women involved are depicted as either mortals or "nymphs." Mortal women who engaged in such unions were generally honored as "heroines," a status that afforded them divine honors upon their death. The term *nymph* referred to a low-level female divinity, generally a nature spirit. Many such nymphs were also honored in cult. Throughout much of this book, particularly in Chapters 2 and 4, I discuss what I believe to be evidence indicating that "heroine" or "nymph" status in fact was a posthumous cultic marker for the priestess who was believed to have borne the child of a god.

The influence of patriarchy on the divine birth cult of this era can be seen in the fact that women's supposed unions with gods resulted nearly always in the production of male figures who promoted the patriarchal values of the Greek state and of Zeus-centered Olympian religion. Often these purported children grew to become founders of a lineage or a city-state—that is, they were "heroes," which means they were generally warriors in service to the patriarchy. Indeed, such male figures were seen to be the very incarnations of the patriarchal Olympian gods themselves. Speaking of the phenomenon of father/ son divine pairs a bit further afield in Phrygia, Ramsay (1895) illuminates this phenomenon noting that "the father and the son . . . are merely complementary forms of the single ultimate form of the divinity as male" (1.34) and "the character and personality of the God-father and God-son pass into one another in such a way in the divine tale or drama, that no clear line can be drawn to separate them" (1.40). We see this exemplified in the story of Heracles, the supposed son of Zeus by the mortal woman Alcmene, whom I discuss in Chapter 5. The rare female progeny of purported *hieros gamos* couplings are often depicted as themselves later engaging in *hieros gamos* unions with gods, indicating that they may have been considered part of hereditary lineages of divine birth priestesses.

Stories of unions between mortals/"nymphs" and gods also frequently express a common theme: the encounter with the god was often considered a violation or rape. Sometimes the union was also violently opposed by the "goddess" to whom the priestess was in service—frequently Athena, Artemis, or Hera, who I argue in the coming chapters were originally considered parthenogenetic beings themselves. That is, union with male gods was strictly forbidden from the perspective of the old order. Yet such stories occurred in liminal contexts in which the goddess had already become subsumed into the Olympian pantheon, no longer as an independent parthenogenetic being, but as a daughter or wife of the new male creator god, Zeus. I thus suggest that these stories indicate a time of transition and conflict during which priestesses from the pure parthenogenetic tradition may have been pressured into performing *hieros gamos* to produce what were believed to be the holy progeny who would advance the cause of Zeus and the other male gods. It was a pressure that at times these priestesses apparently vehemently resisted.

But there was, in some cases, ambivalence. The stories hint that engaging in *hieros gamos* with a god was thought to be a profoundly pleasurable sexual experience, one that many priestesses may have had trouble resisting. Moreover, great social status seems to have accrued to women considered to be the mothers of heroes born miraculously, as evidenced by the fact that virgin mothers frequently served as the eponyms of city-states and of topographical features such as springs and mountains. Thus the period of transition to *hieros gamos* divine birth seems to have been a time of confusion, conflict, and broken virginal vows to virgin goddesses. I explore this trajectory in many of the coming chapters.

One specific mythological detail that may provide further information about the sexual proclivities of certain divine birth priestesses is worth mentioning here. According to one legend, Zeus seduced Artemis's "nymph" Callisto (again, a title possibly indicating that Callisto was a divine birth priestess in service to Artemis) by transforming himself into the goddess herself (Apollodorus 3.8.2; Hyginus *Poetic Astronomy* 2.1). This may hint that some Artemisian priestesses were associated with lesbian love, an idea that is also strongly implied in the numerous sensual and quasi-erotic mythological depictions of Artemis bathing and otherwise consorting with her "nymph" companions (see, e.g., Callimachus *Hymn 3 to Artemis* 1–20, 160–225). A sexual preference for women no doubt would have made it easier for certain priestesses not to fall victim to sexual temptation with men and hence to maintain the "virginal" bodily condition possibly thought necessary to engender children parthenogenetically. It may be, then, that the divine birth priestesshood tended naturally to be populated in large part by lesbians, particularly during the earliest phase of pure parthenogenesis hypothesized above. The "rage" of the goddesses toward priestesses succumbing to the lure of sexual union with the "phallus" of the god thus also may have related to a change in priestly personnel to include more heterosexual women.

Priestesshoods of *Hieros Gamos* by Surrogate

In *hieros gamos* stories, I have discerned a secondary non-ordinary reproductive process whereby the priestess engaged in what was believed to be sacred union with a god using a human male as a "surrogate" for the male deity. As in all phases, this no doubt was thought to take place when both the male and female actors were in a profound trance state such that the deity was believed to manifest and impregnate the priestess through the body of the human male. Under such conditions the child was still considered the progeny of the god rather than the man; yet this development allowed for the securing of the lineage through the paternal line. I propose that a number of Greek myths I discuss in which priestesses were said to have had intercourse simultaneously with a "god" and a mortal in the same night are indicative of this practice.

Support for this idea also can be found in the *Testament of Reuben* (5:5–6), one of the books of the *Testaments of the Twelve Patriarchs*. The *Testament of Reuben* (5:5–6), which dates to the second or third century C.E. (Collins 2008, 265), explains how it is thought that angelic beings known as "the Watchers" could copulate with women and beget children:

> As [the Watchers] continued looking at the women, they were filled with desire for them and perpetrated the act in their minds. Then they were transformed into human males, and while the women were cohabitating with their husbands they appeared to them. Since the women's minds were filled with lust for these apparitions, they gave birth to giants. For the Watchers were disclosed to them as being as high as the heavens.
>
> (Collins 2008, 266)

Although this work is mainly Jewish and Christian in nature (265), it is useful to the present argument in that it affirms the existence of an esoteric belief in antiquity that women could be "visited" in the trance state by male beings who possessed the power to impregnate them. What is described here is the mechanism by which this was thought to take place: the male beings "mentally" transformed themselves into the images of human males and inserted themselves into the women's erotic fantasies activated during intercourse. It is these incorporeal beings, not the human males, who were understood to be the "true" fathers of children conceived in this way. This suggests that such beings were also understood to insert themselves into the precise physical substances exchanged during the conception process.[20]

Hieros gamos by surrogate fully put the practice of divine birth under the control of the patriarchy, as it placed the benefits associated with claims of divine birth in the male lineage. That is, in the earlier condition of *hieros gamos* divine birth, when no human male was involved, the prestige presumably would have rested with the purported mother alone. In this new situation, however, the divine child was arrogated to the sphere of the "father." The mother involved thereby also was made the property of this male. Moreover, the new arrangement guaranteed the retention of privileges associated with the "divine child" even if somehow the human performers believed they had failed in their mission to evoke the god. In other words, even if the male actor believed he had not been able to incorporate the god during sexual union—which would mean that the child was merely humanly, not divinely conceived—the claim of divine impregnation would have been maintained. Thus both the male surrogate and his male progeny still would have enjoyed sacred status and its associated political privileges.

DIVINE CONCEPTION AS AN EROTIC ACT

I conclude this chapter by addressing a possible feminist concern about the nature of this taxonomy. In at least three of the four types of divine birth practices hypothesized above, I have discerned that virginity was a strict requirement. Given that virginity has come to be equated with sexual abstinence, the repression of erotic feelings, and moral "purity," one might argue that the case I am making thus subtly perpetuates the dualism between flesh and spirit, the sexual and the spiritual, that recent feminist critics have identified as one of the most problematic aspects of patriarchy (see, e.g., Eisler 1995). One might argue that promoting the idea that a woman was required to eschew sexuality and sexual pleasure to bring in the "holy" undermines the emancipatory intention of this project.

I propose, however, that my argument does not necessarily perpetuate the sex/spirit split. In fact, it may well bring in a new understanding of both elements as being even more interconnected than previously considered. Such an idea requires further elaboration of the perceived nature of the act of divine conception.

My reflections on this material have led me to conjecture that, in their essence, all types of attempted pure parthenogenesis and *hieros gamos* divine birth must have been considered to be profoundly erotic experiences. I posit that in the case of pure parthenogenesis, conception was thought to be a condition achieved through the most true form of *entheos* possible: *the literal becoming as one with the goddess*. This, I contend, was thought to be a powerful sensual/ sexual experience in which the woman aligned herself with what was arguably considered to be the ontologically sexual nature of the cosmos itself. I will even go so far as to speculate that the orgasm was considered the critical event thought to instigate the meiosis of the woman's ovum.

We find evidence for this line of reasoning in the aforementioned excerpt from the Gnostic *Revelation of Adam*. There we see affirmation of an ancient belief that women's practice of pure parthenogenesis involved a highly erotic component. As we will recall from that tractate, the woman who sat on the mountain to conceive the savior entered into a state in which she "desired her own body in order to become androgynous." The text goes on to tell us that "she fulfilled her desire and became pregnant from her desire" (in Barnstone and Meyer 2003, 187). In other words, it is indeed autoerotic desire that is the critical element believed to have created the condition in which parthenogenetic conception could occur. But what is described here is much more than mere masturbation. Rather, the process is one whereby the woman must become *as one* with the generative power of the universe, as I suggested above: as the text conveys, she must "become androgynous." That process, according to the author of this description, involves the "fulfilling" of desire—the experience of sexual ecstasy.

In cases of *hieros gamos* divine birth, the idea of impregnation by a god implies some form of sexual contact between human female and divine male, as the numerous myths to be explored make plain. Anthropologically, the intensely sexual nature of women priestesses' relationships in situations of so-called spirit possession by male deities has been amply attested across a wide array of cultures in contemporary times, for example, by Lewis (1971, 57–64). Quoting Jones (1949), he writes, "The notion that 'sexual intercourse can occur between mortals and supernatural beings is one of the most widespread of human beliefs.'"[21]

I furthermore propose that the attempt at achieving *hieros gamos* with a god may have involved the use of an artificial phallus to facilitate the encounter and particularly the orgasm that may have been considered necessary to spark fertilization/division of the ovum. I derive this hypothesis from the following. Rhys (1922, 148) reports that "in some of the numerous ancient forms of phallic worship, virgins were deflowered by a priapus [phallus] made of stone or some other kind of hard material." In one of the legends connected with this custom, Ocresia, a slave of Tanaquil, the wife of Tarquinius Priscus, became pregnant with the future king Servius when she "sat down" (*sedet*) at the hearth where the likeness of a phallus appeared. The father was deemed either the household Lar, that is, the spirit of the family forefather who was buried under the hearth (Cook 1905, 295), or the god Vulcan (Pliny *Natural History* 36.70; Ovid *Fasti* 6.629). Rhys (148n3) further notes that phalli and other stones "were often credited with the actual parentage" of children. Although I do not discuss the myth of the Egyptian goddess Isis in this book, I here merely mention that the motif of her constructing an artificial phallus for her dismembered husband, Osiris, after his death (Plutarch *On Isis and Osiris* 18) may be a reference to the priestesses' use of a priapus in divine conception rituals.[22] In examining the sexual rite between the historical *basilinna* and Dionysus in classical Athens, other theorists have similarly posited the use of a priapus, or "herm," in such a ritual (see Avagianou 1991, 180–1). As to *hieros gamos* by surrogate, in which an actual human male may have been involved, the erotic element is clear.

Thus I am proposing that divine conception, far from having been considered a non-erotic act, may have been thought to include an embodied dimension, indeed, in which matter and spirit, human and divine, sexuality and the sacred were thought to be related and to interact in ways that are, by and large, no longer considered possible or viable outside of certain esoteric circles. In this way, my argument may provide new theoretical avenues for resolving the spirit/sex dualism more fully than before. Rather than emphasizing restrictive and polarized ideas of sexuality, then, this book may in fact lead to more expansive ideas about the nature of sexuality and the erotic capacities of women.

CHAPTER 2

DIVINITY, BIRTH, AND VIRGINITY:
THE GREEK WORLDVIEW

To begin this exploration of divine birth in ancient Greece, we must first consider beliefs about the nature of divinity and the human being in antiquity. For the Greeks, deities were not only "up there," they were also, in many cases, "down here"—or they could readily get here. Moreover, the dividing line between humans and deities was hardly clear-cut. Such perceptions enabled, and were enabled by, a belief in divine birth—even while Greek science held that such a phenomenon was not possible.

THE ORDERS OF SPIRITUAL BEINGS AND THEIR RELATIONSHIP TO DIVINE BIRTH

The ancients classified beings into several ontological orders. According to Diogenes Laertius (*Pythagoras* 8.23), Pythagoras spoke of four such orders: gods (*theoi*), demigods (*daimones*), heroes, and men. In a play on the same idea, the Pythagoreans held that beings could be subdivided into "god, man, and such as Pythagoras" (Aristotle in Iamblichus *Life of Pythagoras* 6), the latter referring to a holy person who was considered to have divine parentage.[1]

The categories of god and *daimon* were not rigidly and permanently demarked. Some beings, such as Isis and Osiris, were said to have been elevated from good *daimones,* that is, semidivine entities with supernatural powers, to the rank of gods (Plutarch *On Isis and Osiris* 27/361E). Many of the great gods of old themselves were originally considered human beings. Both Plato (*Philebus* 18b) and, much later,

Iamblichus (*Life of Pythagoras* 11.56) express a general uncertainty as to whether Hermes (Thoth), for example, was a god, *daimon,* or divine man. Diodorus Siculus (3.68–71) treats Zeus Ammon as a living king and Athena as an African warrior. In his second and third books of *De Natura Deorum,* Cicero notes euhemeristically that divine status was conferred upon distinguished benefactors of humanity and relates beliefs that there was more than one version of several of the deities—among them, Zeus (Jupiter), Apollo, Hephaestus (Vulcan), Athena (Minerva), and Artemis (Diana)—each with a different parentage and set of characteristics. Pliny (*Natural History* 7.57) says that Demeter (Ceres) came to be regarded as a divinity because she introduced grain as a food, as well as the arts of grain grinding and bread making.

The boundary between humans, heroes, and *daimones* was also semipermeable. The category anciently identified as "heroes" (sing. *hêrôs*) cannot be defined precisely, but generally refers to legendary males who were thought to be outstanding in some way, by virtue of their divine parentage, their founding of city-states and family lineages, their prowess in warfare or athletics, or a combination thereof.[2] In Hesiod's myth of the world ages (*Works and Days* 156–773), the heroes are a special divine generation antecedent to the present (and devolved) "iron race" of humankind. Some have met their deaths in the battles for Thebes and Troy, while others have gone on to live "in the islands of the blessed." In the Hesiodic *Catalogue of Women,* also known as the *Ehoiai,* the heroes are those men who came to head the great genealogical tribes of early Greece. Practically all such epic heroes appear in the pages of Homer.

What is significant is that these Hesiodic heroes were supposedly born of numerous mortal women through sexual union with gods. All purported sons of gods were acknowledged as heroes, even though divine parentage was not a condition for being made a hero (Burkert 1985, 207–8). Divine parentage was rather a condition for being raised from a hero to a full-fledged god, as in the cases of Heracles, Dionysus, and Asclepius (Rhode [1925] 1966, 141n23). Again, however, the ontological position of heroes was somewhat amorphous, with all heroes enjoying some kind of semidivine status. This is attested by the widespread cult honoring heroes at their graves as individuals who could exert power among the living. Such a cult is traceable in Greece at least from the last quarter of the eighth century B.C.E. (Burkert 1985, 203).

Thus it is clear that at varying stages in their history and to varying degrees, Greeks held that deities, demigods, and the children of gods could all walk the earth in human form. Those figures (including, in some cases, females, as I discuss later in this book) were believed to be the progeny of human women and immortal gods. The belief that women and gods could consort together sexually to produce children persisted on the levels of both myth and historical legend until the Roman era, as I show in the coming chapters. Clearly, not all Greeks and Romans believed such a thing was possible; for example, Plutarch gives unclear messages about his view in this regard[3] and Herodotus (1.181.5–182) expresses skepticism that in Assyria the god Bel actually came into the temple at night to consort with a priestess. However, in numerous quarters of Greek society, even the highest intellectual spheres, the belief was alive and well. Not only was Pythagoras believed to have a divine father, but so were Plato (Apollo) and Alexander the Great (Zeus Ammon), among others.[4]

It is perhaps important to note that, at least as recorded during the patriarchal era, heroes could achieve elevated status without maintaining a saintly existence on earth, as is clear in the numerous myths explored throughout this book. They were not necessarily expected to be "morally good," in the modern sense. Indeed, in the Greek lore, heroes were frequently rapists, murderers, and even rivals or enemies of the gods themselves. What made such individuals stand out were their special powers, not the manner in which they used them.

As noted, heroes with divine parentage achieved full-fledged divinity in some cases. It is significant that those who attained such status—namely Heracles, Dionysus, and Asclepius—all experienced particularly unusual deaths. Dionysus was cut up and boiled in a cauldron, only to be reconstituted (Pausanias 8.37.3; Diodorus Siculus 3.62.6–7). Asclepius died from a "bolt of lighting" delivered by Zeus (Apollodorus 3.10.4; Diodorus Siculus 4.71). I propose these are veiled references to ritualized murders each agreed to undergo willingly during the time they were believed to walk the earth, fated events that were based on the ancient understanding that full apotheosis could not be accomplished without self-sacrifice.[5] This would explain why Heracles insisted on throwing himself on a funeral pyre before the poison secretly administered by his jealous wife could vanquish him (Apollodorus 2.7.7): only purposeful, not accidental, death would allow him to ascend to Olympus as a god.

HESIOD'S *KOURAI* AS PRIESTESSES OF DIVINE BIRTH?

In light of this discussion, it is significant that in the genealogy of the Greek deities known as *Theogony* (346–8), Hesiod calls the first 41 of the female offspring of Tethys and Oceanus "a holy race of

Kourai who on earth raise youths to manhood, with Lord Apollo and the Rivers" (Hesiod 1987, 48, trans. Caldwell). This charge, the poet asserts, was given them by Zeus. What Hesiod implies here is that these holy *Kourai*—that is, "maidens," or, more to the point, "virgins"—either took earthly form or had human counterparts; in either case, the task of the holy daughters was to rear boys. I suggest their charges were not just *any* boys, but the progeny of male deities, among them Zeus and Apollo. I also suggest that the *Kourai* were tasked not only with raising these boys, but also mating with the gods so as to bring such boys onto the earth plane.[6]

Indeed, an examination of the names of these *Kourai* reveals that quite a number of them are identical with those of female figures who, as I show in coming chapters, were depicted in myth as being associated with divine birth or with parthenogenetic goddesses. Among them are Admete, a priestess of Hera (Chapter 5); Kallirhoe, whose name was interchangeable with that of Io, another priestess of Hera, who bore Epaphus through union with Zeus (Chapter 5); Dione, the primary female deity at Dodona, where I argue a divine birth priestesshood was located (Chapter 6); and Europa, who, also by Zeus, bore both the namesake of Dodona, Dodon, and other important male heroes (Chapter 6). Thus, I propose that Hesiod is referring to figures believed to be the legendary ancestresses of the Greeks and that his lines therefore serve as the oldest extant reference to the divine birth priestesshood. Although the poet describes this priestesshood in androcentric terms—as being at the bidding of male gods and presumably involving *hieros gamos* unions—we can read with a feminist hermeneutics of suspicion that this may be a patriarchal gloss over what was probably originally conceived of as a pure parthenogenetic function on the part of goddesses and their earthly priestesses, as I elaborate in the chapters that follow.

THE MOBILE DIVINITY AND THE DUAL NATURE OF "CONCEPTION"

To the Greeks, the amorphous boundary between the human and divine realms corresponded with a general belief that the souls of the gods were mobile and could lodge in different manifestations of physical matter. An entire esoteric practice emerged from this belief: the animating of statues. The Greek philosopher Plotinus, born in southern Egypt in 205 C.E., purportedly possessed knowledge of this art. In the third tractate of *The Fourth Ennead* (11), he writes,

> I think, therefore, that those ancient sages, who sought to secure the presence of divine beings by the erection of shrines and statues, showed insight into the nature of All; they perceived that, though this Soul is everywhere tractable, its presence will be secured all the more readily when an appropriate receptacle is elaborated, a place especially capable of receiving some portion or phase of it, something reproducing it, or representing it, and serving like a mirror to catch an image of it.
>
> (1952, 148, trans. MacKenna)

A similar passage in the Hermetic tract known as *Asclepius,* a late Latin text, may reveal a much earlier philosophy:

> Because [our ancestors] could not create souls, they evoked the souls of daemons [divinities] or angels and introduced them into the holy images and the divine mysteries; and from those the idols acquired the power of acting well and badly.
>
> (in Shumaker 1972, 206)

The scholiast on Plato's *Phaedrus* also alludes to the "telestic art" of animating statues with divine spirit (in Iamblichus [1821] 1968, 353, trans. Taylor):

> But how are statues said to have an enthusiastic energy? May we not say, that a statue being inanimate, does not itself energize about divinity, but the telestic art, purifying the matter of which the statue consists, and placing round it certain characters and symbols, in the first place renders it, through these means, animated, and causes it to receive a certain life from the world; and, in the next place, after this, it prepares the statue to be illuminated by a divine nature, through which it always delivers oracles, as long as it is properly adapted.

It is noteworthy, as this excerpt indicates, that statues imbued with divine spirit were thought to become "oracular." We see the living example of this phenomenon in the oracular priestesses of Delphi, where, as I describe in Chapter 7, the prophetess was thought to bring the deity directly into her body and speak as the god. I suggest that the ultimate process of bringing the "mobile" divinity into matter, however, was considered to be the priestess's divine incarnation of that being through her womb.

This idea is strengthened by the fact that, to the Greeks, the verb *anaireô* meant (1) "to give an oracle," (2) "to take up," and (3) "to conceive in the womb." It was specifically used to describe the Delphic priestesses' delivery of Apollo's oracles (Parke 1939, 13). I propose that these multiple connotations indicate that the Greeks indeed understood the double nature of conception as the process of both "taking the god into the mind" and "taking the god up into the womb."[7] As I show in Chapter 7, the Delphic prophetess was believed to "take up" vapors thought to induce her prophetic state through her vagina. Moreover, her encounter with the god was seen as a sexual union.

The understanding of the dual nature of conception as both a mental and reproductive process indicates that the Greeks saw an ontological correspondence between the womb and what they referred to as the "third eye," which in contemporary thought corresponds with the pituitary gland behind the forehead and which in the occult tradition is considered the organ by which one receives oracular information.[8] It is because of the perceived esoteric connection between these two regions of the female body, I propose, that both oracular and parthenogenetic aspirations would have been understood as the province of prophetesses.[9] For the secrets of the gods—delivered in the form of either divine/oracular knowledge or souls to be born—were all a part of the same mysterious territory. Again, I suggest that the "sexual intercourse with" and "conception by means of" the god, in what was considered to be the highest level of the practice, was seen as more than just a vivid trance experience: it was thought to result in a literal, physical conception.[10]

This exploration of Greek beliefs suggests that the idea of a sacerdotal group dedicated to divine birth would not have been a foreign one to Greek consciousness. Moreover, it seems clear that the Greeks would have seen women as the primary carriers of such a tradition. Plutarch (*Numa* 4.4) points to Egyptian beliefs in this regard:

> The Egyptians make a distinction here which is thought plausible, namely, that while a woman can be approached by a divine spirit and made pregnant, there is no such thing as carnal intercourse and communion between a man and a divinity.
>
> (1914, 319, trans. Perrin)

That the Greeks too, by and large, held to such a distinction[11] is indicated by the fact that stories of goddesses having sexual relations with mortal men and bearing children by them are much more rare and that aspiring to sex with a goddess was a classic example of hubris.[12] The far greater number of legends attesting to mortal women's unions with gods suggest that what was being described was indeed considered a terrestrial phenomenon, one that required the female womb space for its accomplishment.

THE "HEROINE" AS PRIESTESS OF DIVINE BIRTH

The women who were said to have engaged in sexual unions with gods fall into two primary (and frequently overlapping) categories in the ancient literature: "nymphs" and "heroines" (see Larson 1995, 18–21, 23). I discuss nymphs at length in Chapter 4 as probable historical priestesses of divine birth. I focus to a lesser degree on heroines in this book, except as they relate to the parthenogenetic goddesses I explore, namely, Athena, Artemis, and Hera, as well as to the cultic locations of Dodona and Delphi. Given that heroines are important figures in Greece's divine birth literature, however, a few words of general discussion about them are in order.

The "heroine" category, as identified by contemporary scholars, is a broad one, applying, according to some interpretations, to nearly every female protagonist who appears in myth.[13] In certain cases, such figures were apotheosized and worshipped. The term *heroine* makes its first appearance in Pindar (*Pythian Ode* 11.7) as *hêrôis,* which is generally taken to be the earliest female equivalent of *hero* (*hêrôs*). While all words used to indicate the female equivalent of *hero* are derived from this masculine form (Lyons 1997, 13), the term *hero* likely in fact derives from the goddess name *Hera* (Spretnak 1982, 87; O'Brien 1993, 113–9). As I discuss in Chapter 5, heroes were closely associated with Hera in epic and cult, and Hera, I argue, was originally a parthenogenetic goddess. Thus, I contend that, both cultically and etymologically, the terms *hero* and *heroine* have a female-oriented origin that centers on the concept of divine birth. Moreover, as I show in subsequent chapters, heroines, like nymphs, were frequently, if not exclusively, virgins.

I thus posit that, in contrast to the contemporary understanding of the term, the ancient terms for *heroine* (among them also *hêrôinê* [Lyons 1997, 14–5]) originally referred to the priestess who gave birth to the child of a god. That the term designated such a specialized class of women is indirectly indicated in various references. For example, in its first appearance in Pindar, mentioned earlier, the poet uses the word to identify Semele, Ino, and Alcmene. That both

Semele and Alcmene were mortals who conceived sons (Dionysus and Heracles, respectively) through sexual union with the god Zeus (*Iliad* 14.323–5; Apollodorus 2.4.8) indeed puts them in the category of virgin mothers. Ino was entrusted with the care of Dionysus after the death of her sister Semele, thereby incurring the wrath of Hera, and was herself eventually apotheosized (Apollodorus 3.4.3). As the "nurse" of a miraculously born child, Ino played a role that, as I discuss in Chapter 7, seems to have been an integral part of divine birth priestesseshoods, thereby indicating that she too was possibly one in a line of priestesses who aspired to miraculous conception.

A related piece of evidence to support my conjecture about the meaning of the term *heroine* is that one form of the word, *hêrôis,* gave its name to a Delphic festival, *Heroïs,* held in honor of Semele. Her identification with *hieros gamos* divine birth and the fact that her festival involved women's mysteries (Plutarch *Greek Questions* 12c–d/293) strengthen the idea that *hêrôis* was understood as a marker for women associated with miraculous conception. That names of festivals are usually of great antiquity further suggests that the word in fact predated Pindar by many generations (Lyons 1997, 14).

On an urn in northern Greece dating to the Hellenistic period, the form *hêrôissa* is used in an inscription honoring the "Founding Heroines" (*Herôissôn Ktistôn*) (14). I suggest this intriguing reference again harkens to the female ancestors who were considered to have founded lineages through their unions with gods, given that, as I show in Chapter 4, "nymphs," who were similarly credited as lineage "founders," are frequently recorded as having done so through supernatural unions.

Aristophanes uses the word *hêrôinai* in his play *Nephelai,* or "Clouds." In the comedy, the *Nephelai*/Clouds appear and speak as a chorus of female entities. The character Strepsiades asks Socrates whether such figures might be heroines (*hêrôinai*) (line 315), but the sage responds that they are instead "great goddesses" (*megalai theai*) who provide humankind with all manner of thought and speech. The fact that Strepsiades believes such heavenly females could be "heroines" affirms that *heroine* was no casual marker for a woman, but designated a special class of individuals who could achieve divine status.[14]

Further, the title of the Hesiodic *Catalogue of Women* as translated by the *Suda* is *Gunaikôn hêrôinôn katalogos,* "Catalogue of Heroine Women" (in Lyons 1997, 16 and n33). That it is a reckoning of the foundations of lineages by women via their conceptions through gods underscores what I am proposing was the original meaning of the term *heroine.*[15] Again, a full analysis of the divine birth lore associated with heroines will not be accomplished here, but my analysis of the so-called nymphs in Chapter 4 indicates the general directions in which such a study would proceed. In short, I propose that both the terms *nymph* and *heroine*, in their true archaic sense,[16] were markers for the priestess of divine birth who, having achieved what was believed to be the birth of a god's child, was thought to attain divinity herself. As in the case of "nymphs," however, heroines' stories include numerous episodes of sexual resistance to, refusal of, and rape by gods, as well as of ostracizing by their fathers in cases of pregnancy. They even sometimes include the theme of the ritual sacrifice of the heroine or her wrongful death. I discuss a number of such stories in coming chapters (see also Larson 1995, 96–110, 131–44). Such phenomena have helped to inform my hypothesis that a transition from pure parthenogenesis to *hieros gamos* divine birth occurred under patriarchy, and that this was not met with favorably by the old matriarchal guard.

GREEK MEDICAL VIEWS ON CONCEPTION

With the rise of natural philosophy in Ionia in the sixth century B.C.E., scientific views began superseding mythology in explaining the workings of the natural world, including the functioning of women's bodies (Dean-Jones 1994, 43). In contrast to Greek religion, Greek science did not particularly support the idea that human pregnancy could be achieved parthenogenetically. Texts such as the Hippocratic Corpus, Aristotle's biological canon, and Roman era sources indicate that the ancients had reasonably adequate knowledge of the shape and functions of the human uterus in conception, although they held varying views on women's contribution to the embryo.

Such views were, in some cases, based on patriarchal ideology. Certain early men of science, such as Diogenes, Hippon, Anaxagoras, some Pythagoreans, and Aristotle, for example, asserted that only men, and not women, contributed seed to the embryo (Dean-Jones 1994, 149, 184–7). However, from the earliest Greek periods, there were those who claimed that women also contributed seed, among them Empedocles, Parmenides, and Democritus. Given that the latter point of view informs most of the Hippocratic Corpus, it is likely that it served as the predominant theory in the archaic and classical periods (149). At least as far back as the Hippocratics, women were correctly understood to conceive in the midpoint of their menstrual cycle (98–9). Yet, the Hippocratics did not seem to be able to explain exactly why seed was needed from the father if the woman could provide both seed and the nurturing womb (149–50, 161).

History of Animals, most of which has been attributed to Aristotle (14) directly addresses the issue of parthenogenesis by stating that when such a phenomenon took place in humans it resulted in an undifferentiated fleshy lump rather than a fetus, analogous to a "wind-egg," an egg produced by a bird that has not been impregnated by a male (Dean-Jones 1994, 161). Plutarch also refers to such a fleshy mass in his *Advice to Bride and Groom* (48/145D–E):

> It is said that no woman ever produced a child without the cooperation of a man, yet there are misshapen, fleshlike, uterine growths originating in some infection, which develop of themselves and acquire firmness and solidity, and are commonly called "moles" [*mulai*].
> (1927–69, 2:339, trans. Babbitt)

Both authors are referring here to what scientists today call *dermoid cysts* or *benign teratomas,* jumbled masses of embryonic tissue that contain teeth, bones, hair, skin, and other recognizable human features. These strange interior growths in women are indeed the result of the spontaneous parthenogenetic division of the egg within the ovary. That is, they are failed parthenogenetic "issue" (deGrouchy 1980). In *History of Animals,* mentioned above, after referring to such "lumps" the author immediately poses the question, "Why don't women reproduce parthenogenetically?" The subsequent text is missing in the original, leaving us with some ambiguity as to what the precise medical view was on the matter (Dean-Jones 1994, 161–2). Plutarch's comment, however, that "no woman can make a child without the cooperation of a man" may represent the general consensus from the biological standpoint. Moreover, his remark makes it clear that in the Greek medical mind, the parthenogenetic process was anomalous and inevitably resulted in the production of something abnormal.[17]

At first glance, then, it seems that ancient Greek men of science by and large did not believe that parthenogenesis in humans was possible. However, they held that asexual conception was possible in certain cases for animals. The theory of wind impregnation of animals, for example, was accepted by Aristotle (*History of Animals* 6.2.559b–560a), and we see references to it in Homer (*Iliad* 16.149–51, 20.223–5), Virgil (*Georgics* 3.271–6), Aelian (*On Animals* 4.7), Pliny (*Natural History* 8.67, 4.35), and Plutarch (*Table-Talk* 8.1.3). As Guthrie ([1952] 1993, 94–5) points out, the Greek word for "soul," *psyche,* means breath, reflecting the Greek belief that the soul or life principle was identified with air. Hence, "wind impregnation" can be read as a marker for parthenogenetic conception, the process whereby the female takes the wind/breath of life into herself spontaneously without the action of a human male. I discuss a reference to wind impregnation in the case of Athena's legendary priestess Oreithyia in Chapter 3, which I suggest may have been a parthenogenetic allusion.

More important, the concept of miraculous impregnation seems to have been alive and well in the healing cult of Asclepius, the legendary son of Artemis's priestess Coronis via the god Apollo.[18] Asclepius himself was apotheosized and worshipped as a god of medicine. Stelae found at his sanctuary at Epidaurus, where men and women slept to receive dreams thought to effect various bodily cures, attribute a number of pregnancies to the influence of this god. One memorial records the experience of Andromache from Epirus, who dreamt that a beautiful boy undressed her and that the god Asclepius touched her with his hand. As a result, she was made pregnant by her husband and later gave birth to a son. Another tablet reports that Agameda of Ceus dreamt that a snake lay on her belly and that afterward she produced five children (Blundell, 1995, 106). Yet another reports a pregnancy having taken place as a result of the woman engaging in sexual intercourse with the snake in her dream (Demand 1994, 92). Aristodema, the mother of the third-century B.C.E. general Aratus, claimed to have become pregnant with Asclepius's assistance. She was portrayed in statue form on the roof of Asclepius's temple at Sicyon riding a serpent, and the Sicyonians publicly considered Aratus the son of the god (Pausanias 2.10.3, 4.14.8). Thus, the implication was that the god was believed capable of causing pregnancy separate and apart from human coition and that the snake was an instrument of such divine conception. The snake returns again and again in connection with parthenogenetic legends associated with Ge/Gaia, Hera, and the Pythia of Delphi, as I discuss throughout this book. Thus, although Greek "science" in its contemporary sense seems to have held a different view from religion about whether parthenogenetic birth was possible, the Greek healing tradition embraced the concept.

VIRGINITY IN ANCIENT GREECE AND THE PROBLEM OF THE TERM *PARTHENOS*

As I discuss in Chapter 7, virginity was an important requirement at Delphi, where the prophetesses were thought to embody the spirit of the god in giving oracles. Given my argument that the Delphic priesthood was involved in attempting divine birth at some point during the history of the oracle, I contend that virginity was stressed in this and other priestess cults precisely because chastity was considered a bio-spiritual requirement necessary to prepare the woman for engagement with her reproductive functions on a seemingly counter-biological level. Dexter (1990, 164–9) has provided a prelude to this idea in her discussion of the concept of virginity in ancient Graeco-Roman myth. She conjectures that remaining in a state of celibacy was thought to allow a woman to store up her vital energies so that she could transmit them in holy ways to others without a loss of vitality. She posits that, in myth, females avoided sexual intercourse with human males because the act was thought to dissipate this energy, while "cohabitation with a divine spirit" was thought not to result in such a diminishment (164).[19] I propose that such concepts underlie the term *parthenos,* a word commonly thought to denote "virgin" or "maiden," but whose multiple and contradictory meanings have long confounded classicists. In short, I propose that the term *parthenos* at some point and in some cases specifically denoted a priestess who was dedicated to retaining her vital energies in order to use them to attempt divine birth. I elaborate upon this in what follows.

Parthenos[20] (pl. *parthenoi*), a word typically used in ancient Greece to describe a young, unmarried girl, has indeed proven difficult to define precisely. Attempts to equate it with "virgin" and "maiden" inevitably become problematic, as textual evidence reveals that a *parthenos* was sometimes one but not the other and sometimes neither. While the term frequently refers to a girl who has not yet had sexual relations (in *Iliad* 2.514, for example), *parthenos* is also used to designate an unmarried woman who is *not* a virgin, as I show below. Moreover, the conventionally accepted definition of *parthenos* as "maiden"—that is, a young, prepubescent girl—is contradicted in the expression employed by Euripides, *polia partheneuetai,* "grows gray in maidenhood" (Liddell and Scott, 7th ed., s.v. *partheneuô*). *Nature of Women* 3 of the Hippocratic Corpus also refers to "aged *parthenoi,*" and the adjective used, *palaios,* has the connotations of extreme age (Dean-Jones 1994, 53).

The definition of *parthenos* as "virgin" is also problematic. For a *parthenos* was in some cases a woman who gave birth, as indicated by the derivative *parthenios* (or *partheneias;* pl. *partheniai*), which means "child of a *parthenos.*" *Partheniai,* in particular, was a term referring to "illegitimate" children born to young Spartan women by soldiers during the First Messenian War (Ephorus in Strabo 6.3.3). Farnell ([1896–1909] 1977, 2:448) thus posits, "The oldest sense of

Parthenos was not 'virginal' but 'unmarried.'" The word may, he suggests, have emerged from the early matriarchal peoples of the lands
the Greeks came to occupy, among whom settled marriage was not a
custom, descent was reckoned through the female line, and "women
were proportionately powerful."

Although a definition of *parthenos* as "unmarried woman" is com-
pelling, I contend that the real clue to the meaning of *parthenos* lies
in Pindar. In *Pythian Ode* 3.34, the poet persists in calling Coronis
a *parthenos* despite the fact that she already had sexual relations with
both Apollo and a mortal man and that she carried Apollo's child
Asclepius within her. He similarly refers to the pregnancy of Pitana
by Poseidon as a case of "virgin birth (pain)" (*partheneian ôdina*)
(*Olympian Ode* 31). Clearly, here we have at least one instance in
which the term *parthenos* cannot mean "woman who refrains from
sexual intercourse," since Coronis lay with a man. What is important
in both cases is that the word refers specifically to women who bear
the children of gods. I maintain that the poet's continued use of the
term *parthenos* in these instances indicates that the title denoted a
"holy priestess of divine birth." That the term *parthenos* may have
been, as Farnell suggests, an artifact of matriarchy is in line with this
idea, particularly given my hypothesis, as outlined in Chapter 1, that
divine birth cults likely had their most pure expression during the
pre-patriarchal period.

The case of the priestess Herophile, a possibly historical virgin
prophetess of Apollo, provides further information about the meaning of *parthenos*. Pausanias (10.12.1–6), who accords Herophile great
antiquity (she was "born before the Trojan War"), says she was the
first to prophesy from "Sibyl's Rock" at Delphi. He quotes an epitaph
on her tomb in which she was referred to as a *parthenos,* indicating
that she had carried this moniker throughout what seems to have
been a long life. This emphasizes, as I argued earlier, that the term
parthenos did not necessarily mean "youthful woman" or "maiden."
Moreover, the term is used here specifically to identify not only an
oracular priestess, but one who, when in a state of oracular possession by the god, claimed that she was the "wedded wife" of Apollo.
I contend that while Herophile is not credited in ancient texts with
having borne Apollo's child, she was in the tradition of other oracular
parthenoi who were believed to have preserved their virginity to be in
sexual partnership with the god, as I discuss in Chapter 7.

Like the term *parthenos,* the related noun *partheneia* has been
translated as "virginity." But, once again, *partheneia* could not merely
have meant "the state of not yet having had sexual relations," for

partheneia was apparently *renewable*. We see this no more clearly than in one legend concerning the goddess Hera: the Argives said that every year she recovered her *partheneia* by bathing in the Canathus spring at Nauplia. Pausanias (2.38.2) emphasizes that the event recognized a great "mystery" about which he could not speak. Guthrie (1967, 102) notes that this legend indicates that "the distinction between pure maiden [i.e., virgin] and mother, which seems to us a logical necessity, was no stumbling block to the Greeks." I propose this is because Greek religion held that the virgin/celibate was capable, under special circumstances, of becoming a mother without having intercourse with a human male. *Partheneia,* then, I suggest, was the state of ritual purity and preparedness thought necessary for a priestess to attempt divine conception. A state of virginity—or perhaps simply a state of celibacy for the period of time in which divine conception was attempted—may have aided it. Hera's story suggests that, for the priestess, *partheneia* was a form of ritual readiness that could be reentered as needed, possibly even if she at some point had had sexual relations with a human male.

I propose that, originally, the priestess's *partheneia* was seen as a homolog of the "virgin motherhood"—that is, the parthenogenetic creative ability—of the Great Goddess. As I discuss in Chapters 3 through 5, the title *Parthenos* persisted for the Greek goddesses Athena, Artemis, and Hera as a remnant of their original parthenogenetic status.[21] I contend, moreover, that it was believed that only priestesses who were able to achieve extraordinary powers, most likely through rigorous spiritual training, were capable of producing children miraculously. Virginity was one requisite condition for the work, indeed, but it had to be accompanied by various hard-won qualities—ideally, purity of heart and the most profound level of spiritual maturity and wisdom possible. I suggest that in the earliest stages of the cult of divine birth, celibacy was not simply equated with "spiritual purity"; rather, celibacy and moral purity were considered to be separate elements. In addition, as I discussed in Chapter 1, I propose that the celibate state of the divine birth priestess was likely not characterized by sexual repression, but instead by highly charged eroticism that was inwardly directed—or, later, directed toward what were believed to be non-corporeal entities. I suggest it was from the template of the priestess of divine birth that "virginity" came to be associated in the ancient mind with "moral purity" by virtue of the fact that the *parthenos* was both celibate *and* morally elevated. However, I submit that it was not until the advent of patriarchy, when women's bodies—and perhaps also the divine birth cult as a whole—came under male control, that virginity came to be oppressively equated with asexuality/noneroticism and that the entire bundle came to be linked with "moral purity." It is at that point, I contend, that a commitment to virginity, which was once the province and responsibility primarily of the divine birth priestess, or holy *parthenos*, was imposed on all non-married women. Women's chastity became equated with their moral goodness—and, by extension, their very worth. Women thus became trapped by a standard that was misinterpreted, and never meant for the masses to begin with. In summary, I propose that, originally, *partheneia*, "holy virginity," was not something required of all women, not an onerous burden to be borne by the ordinary girl, but rather a state freely chosen by certain female cult participants who wished to attempt the miraculous and become divine themselves.

VIRGIN PRIESTESSHOODS OF GREECE

Virginity or celibacy was an important requirement in numerous Greek priestesshoods, particularly those devoted to virgin goddesses such as Athena and Artemis, as well as those in which the female priests appear to have been in *hieros gamos* relationships with gods. I posit that the virginity requirement persisted as a vestige of the divine birth priestesshoods of old into historical times, even though in most instances the original purpose of virginity was either forgotten or no longer acted upon and the virginity requirement had become temporary or was transferred to postmenopausal women.

Before discussing the virginity requirement as it operated in various documented priestesshoods of the historical period, I should comment on the widespread importance of the priestesshood in the ancient world in general. In a fragment of the play *Melanippe Desmotis* (in Dillon 2001, 1), one of Euripides' female characters remarks that in religious matters, women were the dominant figures in Greece. The oracular sites and religious rituals, she notes, all "flourish[ed] in the hands of women." Indeed, while women were barred from political leadership, they thrived in the sacerdotal quarter as prominent functionaries, performing public and private rites, serving as oracular priestesses, making offerings to the deities, punishing those who infringed on cultic regulations, and taking care of temples and their precincts, among other duties. Priestesses sometimes held special cultic privileges such as permission to enter forbidden places or see forbidden things associated with rites. They also often enjoyed payment in the form of money and food items. Some owned property.[22]

Women priests generally served goddesses, including Artemis, Athena, Hera, and Aphrodite, while men generally served gods such as Zeus, Poseidon, and Asclepius, with some notable exceptions (Turner 1983, 175). Some of the exceptions are the *basilinna*, who served Dionysus; the priestess at Thespiai of Heracles; the priestess at Calaurea of Poseidon; the priestess at Elis of Sosipolis; the *peleiades*, or oracular dove priestesses of Zeus at Dodona; the Pythia, or oracular priestess of Apollo at Delphi; and the oracular priestess of Apollo at Patara. I am in agreement with Fehrle (1910), who explains these particular exceptions as examples of *hieros gamos* unions between the priestesses and their gods.

Herodotus specifically describes virginity in association with the *hieros gamos* role in a number of cases. In discussing the topography and history of Babylon, he remarks,

> On the summit of the topmost tower stands a great temple with a fine large couch upon it, richly covered, and a golden table beside it. The shrine contains no image and no one spends the night there except (if we may believe the Chaldaeans who are the priests of Bel) an Assyrian woman, all alone, whoever it may be that the god has chosen. The Chaldaeans also say—though I do not believe them—that the god enters the temple in person and takes his rest upon the bed. There is a similar story told by the Egyptians at Thebes, where a woman always passes the night in the temple of the Theban Zeus [that is, Amun] and is forbidden, so they say, like the woman in the temple at Babylon, to have any intercourse with men; and there is yet another instance in the Lycian town of Patara, where the priestess who delivers the oracles [of Apollo] when required (for there is not always an oracle there) is shut up in the temple during the night.
>
> (Herodotus 1.181–2, 1972, trans. Sélincourt 114)

Thus, Herodotus is describing similar customs of his day in Egyptian Thebes, Babylon, and Lycian Patara in which (the historian's own skepticism aside) oracular virgin priestesses were believed to engage in sexual relations with their respective gods. He attests to the purported practice not only in association with Apollo, which will be significant to the discussion in Chapter 7 of Delphi, but also with Theban Zeus, which will be relevant to the discussion in Chapter 6 of the foundation of Dodona by an Egyptian priestess of this god.[23]

Lifelong virginity was a requirement of various priestesshoods, and the following examples of those devoted to permanent or temporary chastity by no means form a complete list. The priestess at the sanctuary of Heracles at Thespiae was bound to a life of celibacy

(Pausanias 9.27.6). At Sicyon, one of the two priestesses of Aphrodite was a woman who lived in permanent chastity after her appointment (the other was a virgin woman priest serving for a year) (Pausanias 2.10.4). A group of priestesses at Eleusis known as the *hiereiai panageis* never had sexual intercourse with men (Hesychius s.v. *hiereiai panageis*, in Turner 1983, 185).

Other priestesshoods required celibacy of women, but in some cases only during the period of service. In Achaia, the priestess in the sanctuary of Ge/Gaia had to maintain chastity after taking up her role and was allowed to have had intercourse with only one man before (Pausanias 7.25.13). Similarly, at Larisa, the prophetess of Apollo was also a woman "debarred from intercourse with a man" (Pausanias 2.24.1), although it is not clear whether she assumed her position when she was a young girl or after she had raised a family. The same was true of priestesses of two cults of Demeter at Cos (Turner 1983, 180).

For some women priests, membership in older age groups may have meant that at the time of their service they were living chaste lives, although they may not have been lifelong virgins. The *hestiades*, the women who kept perpetual fires burning at sacred sites such as Athens and Delphi, were "widows past the age of marriage" (Plutarch *Numa* 9.5).[24] The celibate female priest who tended the sanctuary of Sosipolis was also an old woman (Pausanias 6.20.2). As I discuss further in Chapter 7, the Pythia at Delphi, who in the earliest days of the oracle was a young virgin, in later times, after the rape of one of the priestesses, was a woman over 50 who could not be sexually active while serving Apollo (Plutarch *Obsolescence of Oracles* 45/435D, 51/438C; Diodorus Siculus 16.26.6).

Numerous other priestesshoods also maintained virginity requirements, particularly those that were in service to Athena and Artemis.[25] More evidence exists for virgin priestesses of Artemis, in fact, than for other goddesses (Turner 1983, 181). By the late first century B.C.E. and the first and second centuries C.E., virginity requirements were frequently temporary, however, given that many such priestesshoods were filled by girls only until they became eligible for marriage. Among them were the priestess of Poseidon on the island of Calaurea (Pausanias 2.33.2), the priestess of Artemis Triclaria at Patras (7.19.1), the priestess of Artemis at Aegeira (7.26.5), and, in the earliest days of the cult, the priestess of Artemis Hymnia at Mantineia (8.5.11–3, 8.13.1, 5).[26]

Various sub-sacerdotal females with cultic duties who were not full-scale priestesses were also usually virgin, prepubescent girls.

These included the *agretai* at Cos; the *aletrides, arrephoroi, ergas-tinai, lykiades korai,* and *plynterides* at Athens; the *anthesphoroi* in Magna Grecia; the *anthesteriades* at Camiros; the *arktoi* at Brauron; the *bacchantes* and *tragephoroi* of Dionysus; the *Dionysiades* and *leukippides* at Sparta; the *hersephoroi* at Agrai; the *hydrophoros* of the Dipolieia; and the *kanephoroi* at Athens and elsewhere (Turner 1983, 189–97).

Such titles generally referred to the various cultic roles these young women performed, such as preparing offering cakes, tending the cult, carrying water and sacred objects in procession, weaving the sacred *peplos* to Athena, running cult-associated races, and so forth.

Thus, virgins, particularly young girls around the age of puberty, played a major role in Greek religious life. Indeed, they were held in great honor as a foundation stone of the *polis* itself. It is young virgin women, as we shall see in future chapters, who feature almost exclusively in the legends of *hieros gamos* unions with gods. Connelly (2007, 44) conjectures that many priestesshoods for young women may once have required perpetual chastity, but that the requirement was ultimately abandoned because it was "untenable." I, too, contend that many young priestesses were, indeed, once dedicated to a life of virginity. My conjecture, however, is that such women were part of priestess groups dedicated to attempting miraculous birth, for which a celibate state was a necessity. I suggest that the historical priestesshoods and sub-sacerdotal groups in which virginity was a temporary assignment represent a vestige of the older divine birth priestesshoods.

THE *BASILINNA* AS HOLY *PARTHENOS*

One striking survival of what I suggest may have originally been a child-bearing divine birth priestesshood was the office of the *basi-linna*.[27] According to Demosthenes (*Against Neaira* 59.73–8, 85), the *basilinna* was the wife of the *archon basileus*, the king archon of Athens, a city official whose duties included presiding at various ceremonies. The *basilinna* "carried out as the city's representative the many ceremonies, holy and secret, which were handed down by [the] ancestors," and which it was "not permitted for people even to hear of" (Demosthenes 1992, 61–5, trans. Carey). She was required to be a *parthenos* at the time of her marriage so that the "unspoken" sacrifices could be made on behalf of the city according to ancestral practice "without any excision or innovation" (*mêden katalumetai mêde kainotomêtai*). At the Great Dionysia in fifth-century Athens, a solemn marriage, a *hieros gamos*, was conducted between the *basilinna* and the god Dionysus every year in a building called the *Boukoleion*, "Ox-stall," which at an earlier time had been the residence of the king (Aristotle *Constitution of Athens* 3.5). No further details about the nature of the rite are given, but mention is made of a cadre of sacerdotal women who were cultically related to the *basilinna*. These were the *gerarai*, or "venerable priestesses" (Demosthenes *Against Neaira* 59.78–9). They were 14 older women who oversaw matters in Dionysus's cult at Athens and assisted in the sacrifices of animals involved in Dionysian rituals. The *basilinna* led the *gerarai* in an oath by which each woman swore that she was living a chaste and pure life and that, according to ancestral practice, she would serve as a *gerara* at two other festivals of Dionysus. Nowhere else does Greek literature speak so unequivocally of a sacred marriage ritual (Burkert 1985, 239). Goff (2004, 38) presents the generally accepted view that the god was represented by the *basilinna*'s husband, although there is no evidence that such was the case. Assuming a similar view, Guthrie (1967, 57) posits that such a *hieros gamos* may have symbolized the fertilizing of the earth by the moisture of the sky and served as a means of sympathetic magic to ensure earthly fertility.

Given that "fertility" ultimately, by logic, has to do with the creation of new life, I would go further in suggesting that the entire schema of the *basilinna* and the *gerarai* represents an ancient group of priestesses whose purpose was to conceive and raise offspring—specifically, the children of Dionysus. I suggest that out of that group, one woman was selected in remote times to conduct the rite that was believed to result in miraculous conception—the individual who later came to be known as the *basilinna*. The allusion to the "Ox-stall" may indicate that this woman was thought to consort with Dionysus in his form as a bull, a motif we see repeated in the story of Europa's *hieros gamos* with Zeus, and one that, as I discuss in Chapter 6, may reference the constellation of Taurus and the Pleiades as the presumed source of divine souls. By the time of Demosthenes' writing, no mention is made of the *basilinna*'s ritual resulting in the birth of a child, but the fact that the rites are specifically referred to as "secret" indicates that aspects were shrouded from public view even in antiquity. It is not known how many children any of the women who served as the *basilinna* had, or whether the timing of their conceptions related in any way to the *hieros gamos* ritual. It is interesting to consider, however, whether there may have been a correspondence between such events. Were they to have been synchronized, this might suggest that the children born of the *basilinna* in historical times were understood by the cognoscenti of the inner sanctum to be progeny of the god himself.

Dillon (2001, 101) affirms, "The rites must have been ancient, going back to when Athens had a king whose wife would have been equivalent to a high priest." Indeed, as I noted in Chapter 1, the title *basileus* derived from *basile*, a queen's title—and name of a goddess— that dated back to the pre-Mycenaean period. The linguistic precedence of the female title *basile* indicates that the female who held this office "stood higher than the king" (Kerenyi 1975, 44–5). Thus, the term *basilinna* was in fact an unnecessary and later feminization of *basileus*, one that indicates that the *basile*/queen's status was probably diminished under patriarchy. It is very likely, then, that the ritual of the *basilinna* originated under matriarchal conditions when she was called the *basile*.

The Athenians' firm insistence that the rite of the sacred marriage be conducted in the most ancient manner is a further clue in this direction. As Demonsthenes comments (*Against Neaira* 59.75–6), the requirement that the king-archon marry a *parthenos* was established to ensure that the rite be carried out according to ancient custom "without any excision or innovation" (*mêden katalumetai mêde kainotomêtai*). The Athenians even went so far as to make this requirement into a law, which they inscribed into a stone column in the temple of Dionysus. Having a non-*parthenos* participate in the ritual, then, would have marked a grave departure from the original practice.

What, then, did the Greeks mean by *parthenos* in this case? I contend that the critical factor in the selection of this woman was not simply her virginity, for even if she had been a virgin at the time of her marriage with the *archon basileus*, she presumably did not remain one from her wedding night on. The *basilinna's* "marriage" with Dionysus took place yearly, well after she had been in sexual relationship with her husband. Thus, if we take *parthenos* to mean "virgin" here, we are lost, for what would have been the point of presenting the god with a "virgin" who was no longer a virgin? Even if the *basilinna* had abstained from intercourse with her husband initially so that she could perform the first *hieros gamos* with the god in a celibate state, would the ritual not have lost its meaning and power if in subsequent years she went to Dionysus's bed as a nonvirgin? We are faced with a problem if we take *parthenos* to mean "unmarried woman," as well, as the *basilinna* ceased to be unmarried once she was betrothed to the *archon basileus*, and thus she would have gone to the god as the wife of someone else. Moreover, defining *parthenos* as "maiden" is similarly problematic, in that presumably the *basilinna* held her office after she was well beyond her postpubescent years. What, then, would have been the religious import of having the *archon basileus* simply marry a "virgin" or "maiden," if such a status really did not enter into the ritual arena in any significant way? Why the extreme anxiety over this requirement on the part of the Greeks?

These problems are resolved if we consider the possibility that, in requiring that the *basilinna* be a *parthenos,* the ancient Greeks had in mind the most ancient meaning of the title, as I proposed earlier: "priestess of divine birth." If we accept that the *archon basileus* had to marry a woman who was not *just* a virgin, but rather a holy *parthenos,* a special priestess who was knowledgeable about the practice of uniting with a god, then the requirement makes sense in light of the entire ritual program being described. I propose that even in the classical period, by which time the rite may no longer have been carried out with the intention of literally impregnating the *basilinna* with the god's issue, the *parthenos* requirement was an occult reference to the original purpose of the rite as a divine conception ritual, one perhaps not unlike those performed by the queens of Egypt, who were thought to give birth to divine pharaohs (again, see Rigoglioso 2007, 70–94).

I further propose that although by the classical period the *basilinna* was subsequently yoked in marital union with the *archon basileus,* originally, in the much older role as *basile,* she was not tied to the male religious hierarchy and the institution of marriage. I submit that beyond being the "equal" of any male authority, to refer to Dillon's comment above, she was in fact an independently sovereign queen/priestess who was considered to be the manifestation of the goddess herself. It was she, as holy *parthenos,* who attempted divine conception in the earliest, matriarchal, layer of cult. According to the taxonomy I presented in Chapter 1, the earliest cult of divine birth associated with her thus may well at first have involved attempts at pure parthenogenesis, and may have undergone a change in type and focus over time as the Greeks transitioned to patriarchal social order. The anxious requirement that the *archon basileus* "marry" the *basilinna* is likely indicative of the capture, domestication, appropriation of the queen's divine birth priestesshood for the purposes of the Greek state.

The documented existence of the rite of the *basilinna* indicates that *hieros gamos,* or sacred marriage, arrangements between priestesses and gods were not merely the stuff of myth and legend in ancient Greece. Still, the question arises as to why more such direct references do not survive in Greek historical accounts. Perhaps the paucity of such records is the result of the fact that, ultimately, divine birth was considered an aspect of the mystery traditions—specifically, women-only mysteries. I draw here on Burkert's definition (1987, 8) of *mysteries* as "initiation ceremonies, cults in which admission and participation depend[ed] upon some personal ritual to be performed on the initiand." Speaking of the general attitude toward the mysteries in the ancient world, Origen comments (*Contra Celsum* 1.7),

> The existence of certain doctrines, which are beyond those [that] are exoteric and do not reach the multitude . . . is shared by the philosophers. For they had some doctrines which were exoteric and some esoteric . . . [Some] were taught in secret doctrines which could not deservedly reach ears that were uninitiated and not yet purified.

Thus, I posit that women's "parthenogenetic mysteries" were secret and ongoing rituals to induce what was believed to be miraculous conception, rituals requiring special initiation, a special calling, and intense dedication. Following on Origen, the secrets of the holy *parthenoi* may have been kept to the fewest number of "ears" possible. Initially, this would have been a means of protecting the institution of divine birth. Later, as women's power was increasingly eroded, such secrecy would have made the demotion of the cult of divine birth to the level of "fiction" much easier as part of a process of dismantling it. The hidden information, as I attempt to demonstrate in the following chapters, may have been deposited for safekeeping in those great repositories of the forbidden—myth and folklore—where they have remained veiled in plain sight for two millennia.[28]

CHAPTER 3

ATHENA'S DIVINE BIRTH
PRIESTESSHOOD

I begin the exploration of what I propose were specific divine birth priestesshoods with an analysis of Athena and her female priests. In the Greek tradition, Athena was the goddess who most famously bore the cult title *Parthenos*. This is attested, for example, by the self-same epithet that accompanied her massive sculpture housed in the Parthenon at Athens in the classical period. I propose that this title points to an understanding of Athena's original nature as a Virgin Mother and that this aspect of the goddess served as the model for the fertility practices of her specialized virgin priestesses.

A number of myths associated with Athena speak of figures who may be identified as her female priests engaging in *hieros gamos* unions with gods. I suggest that the resulting "anger" of the goddess indicates this type of activity marked a grave transgression on the part of women in the inner sanctum of her cult, thereby serving as a clue to an earlier, pre-patriarchal practice in which priestesses were devoted to attempting pure parthenogenesis. The goddess's mythological outrage and the punishments she meted out to her virgin servants for their sexual transgressions with male gods may symbolize the internal conflict that ensued among holy *parthenoi* dedicated to Athena during this transition period. In this chapter, I explore some of the relevant myths and aspects of cult to make the case for these ideas.

ATHENA'S ORIGINS IN THE NORTH AFRICAN NEITH

To understand Athena as a Virgin Mother, we must first understand
the North African goddess Neith, whom the Greeks widely acknowl-
edged was identical with Athena.[1] It is important to emphasize that
Athena was not just the Greek "version" of Neith; rather, she *was*
Neith. This is attested by Herodotus (2.62), Plato (*Timaeus* 21e),
Plutarch (*On Isis and Osiris* 9/354C), Diodorus Siculus (5.58), and
Pausanias (2.36.8, 9.12.2). Correspondingly, according to Origen
(*Contra Celsum* 5.29), the Egyptians themselves also believed that
the goddess the Greeks knew as Athena in Attica was also the goddess
of Saïs, Neith's most holy city in Egypt. On Mt. Potinus in Argolis,
Athena was known as Athena Saïtis (Pausanias 2.36.8), probably in
recognition of her North African origins.

Neith was a parthenogenetic goddess par excellence. A text from
the Ramesside period of the New Kingdom in Egypt (1304–1075
B.C.E.) calls her "the eldest, the Mother of the gods, who shone on
the first face," implying that she was considered the original, primordial deity who predated all others (Lesko 1999, 57). Analyzing
this and other similar references, Griffis-Greenberg (1999, para. 7)
identifies Neith as Egypt's "deity of the First Principle," the highest
and unmoved mover. As such, she was in fact *autogenetic,* having
created herself out of her own being. We see this aspect echoed in
both Egyptian and Greek texts. Plutarch (*On Isis and Osiris* 9), for
example, refers to an inscription on her statue in Saïs,[2] where, as
Herodotus affirms (2.59–62), a great and mystical annual festival was
held to honor her:

> I am everything that has been, and that is, and that shall be, and no
> one has ever lifted my garment (*peplos*).

That in the above-noted Saïtic inscription Neith's "garment"
remained perpetually "unlifted" is also a sexual reference (Plutarch
1970, 284–5, ed. Griffiths), as the Greek word used is *peplos,* a robe
typically worn by women. The inscription therefore communicates
that Neith never engaged in any kind of sexual union, that is, she was
eternally a virgin.[3] Yet, as the primordial Being, she was also generative. Thus, in Neith we have one of the earliest appearances of the
archetype of the Virgin Mother, the Holy *Parthenos,* in her original,
unadulterated form.

According to Budge ([1904] 1969, 1:451), Neith's name may
have derived from the root of the Egyptian *netet,* "to knit, to weave."

She was indeed thought to have invented weaving (Sayed 1982, 1:17–8). The Neoplatonist Porphyry (*On the Cave of the Nymphs* 14) notes that in the esoteric Pythagorean tradition, weaving was understood to symbolize the process of incarnation of the soul. Given Neith's preeminence as an autogenetic/parthenogenetic goddess, I suggest that the "weaving" aspect associated with her—a symbol of manifestation and "becoming," itself—was by definition a parthenogenetic reference, a point that will be significant as we proceed throughout this book.

Another parthenogenetic symbol associated with Neith was the bee. I discuss the parthenogenetic aspects of the bee more fully in Chapter 7 on Delphi, but for now it is important to note that bees were associated with parthenogenesis by virtue of the fact that they were believed to be born spontaneously from the carcasses of bulls.[4] Neith's temple at Saïs was sometimes known as the House of the Bee (Lesko 1999, 48). The earliest symbol associated with Neith, two click beetles head to head, also may well have had parthenogenetic meaning. Click beetles were most likely seen by the Egyptians as parthenogenetic given that their young appear to emerge in full adult form "spontaneously" from the earth (in fact, they arise there from eggs laid by the female) (Hollis 1994–5, 49).

We see Athena's identification with Neith in a number of historical and mythological references. The very story of Athena's "birth"—which in the Greek account results from her emergence from the god Zeus's head (Hesiod *Theogony* 924)—in some traditions takes place at the river Triton (e.g., Apollodorus 1.3.6), a North African locale. Apollonius Rhodius (*Argonautica* 4.1310) affirms that the pre-Hellenic peoples in Greece, the Pelasgians, believed that Athena was born beside Lake Tritonis/River Triton in ancient Libya (i.e., North Africa).[5] Writing about the geography of his day, Herodotus (4.175–80) confirms the existence of a large river called "Triton," which flowed into "the great lake of Tritonis" in North Africa far west of Egypt. Apollonius Rhodius (4.1307) further records a legend that Athena was found and nurtured at the river Triton by three nymphs dressed in goat skins, which Herodotus (4.188) reports was the typical garment worn by Libyan women. Herodotus (4.180) notes a specifically Libyan tradition that Athena/Neith was the daughter of Poseidon and Lake Tritonis itself. A possibly older genealogy for Athena in North Africa, however, is related by Diodorus Siculus (3.70.2–3). The historian confirms the tradition that Athena was born beside the river Triton, but relates an ancient belief that she was "born of the earth," Ge/Gaia herself. Not only does this mythologem stress Athena's affiliation with Africa, it also connects her, once again, with a *pure daughter-bearing* parthenogenetic story, to relate back to the taxonomy I outlined in Chapter 1.

The African provenance for the birth of Athena supports her identification with the Libyo-Egyptian Neith, as well as the implication in the ancient texts that she was brought to Greece by Egyptian or Libyan colonizers, which I discuss later in this chapter. Athena's probable African origins are further underscored by the fact that the first coins to show her head portrayed her as a black African woman (Bernal 1987–2006, 3:548).

ATHENA AS VIRGIN MOTHER

Athena was, like Neith, widely acknowledged to be a virgin (e.g., Diodorus Siculus 5.3.4; Ovid *Metamorphoses* 5.375). Various other elements associated with her suggest that she retained hints of autogeneity, as well. Plutarch (*On Isis and Osiris* 62/376A) claims that the name *Athena* signified "I have come from myself" (*'élthon 'ap' 'emautês*), an unequivocal autogenetic reference. The Orphic *Hymn to Pallas* (Athena) begins by addressing Athena as *monogenês*, which is generally translated as "only-begotten" (Liddell and Scott, 7th edition, s.v.), but which can also mean "only born sole offspring," "unique in kind," and "singly born" (Long 1992, 49). In short, it connotes a self-born, self-created being, which corresponds perfectly with Athena's identification with the autogenetic Neith.[6] Athena also wore the lizard or crocodile on her breast in certain gems and statues (Elworthy 1958, 320). This is likely a vestige of her association with Neith, whose mythology included a story that she gave birth to the crocodile god Sobek (see Lesko 1999, 50–1). What is particularly interesting here is that the lizard was believed to conceive by the ear and bring forth its young from the mouth (King 1887, 107). Thus, Athena's wearing of the lizard/crocodile would further connect her with both Neith and parthenogenesis.

Athena also retained Neith's function as goddess of weaving (e.g., Hesiod *Works and Days* 63–4; Aelian *On Animals* 6.57), which, as I have argued, was symbolic of parthenogenetic creation. Athena's role as virgin patron of weaving was acknowledged during her most important festival at Athens, the Panathenaia, which was held in the summer and celebrated as the new year. As part of this event, four females wove the goddess's woolen *peplos*, or ceremonial robe, and presented it to her statue at the Acropolis at the culminating moment of the grand procession (Suda, s.v., *arrephorein; peplos*). The *peplos* motif vividly calls to mind the inscription to Neith mentioned earlier, "No one has ever lifted my *peplos*," a direct reference to Neith's parthenogenetic nature. I suggest that in the context of the Panathenaia, then, the *peplos* similarly was a symbol of Athena's original capacity as virginal creatrix. I discuss the Panathenaia and its parthenogenetic associations more fully later in this chapter.

Athena's Virgin Mother aspect was perhaps most fully retained in one of her most celebrated cults, located in Tegea in southeastern Arcadia, where she was known as Athena Alea ("shelter," "asylum"). Archaeological evidence from the oldest layers at this site reveals that Athena was once identified with fertility symbols (Deacy 2008, 131). As Deacy (131) affirms, such symbolism raises the possibility that, early on, Athena had more in common with a mother goddess such as Demeter than she did with her later pan-Hellenic character as sterile virgin. The symbol that emerges as preeminent in this regard was the pomegranate. As I argue in Chapter 5, this motif was associated not only with fertility, but also with virgin motherhood, specifically.

DIVINE BIRTH PRIESTESSES ASSOCIATED WITH ATHENA/NEITH

Apollonius Rhodius (4.1493) speaks of a "Tritonian nymph" who gave birth to Nasamon, the eponym of the Nasamonians of North Africa. A connection is thus implied between this "Tritonian nymph" and the "nymphs" of Lake Tritonis/River Triton who, as we will recall, also are said to have helped rear Athena. As I argue more fully in Chapter 4 in relation to Artemis, the "nymph" epithet was often a posthumous marker for a parthenogenetic priestess, a sign of her apotheosis for having achieved what was believed to have been a successful divine birth. Thus, I contend that the myth fragments regarding the birth and homeland of Athena point to the existence of a divine birth priestesshood associated with Athena/Neith at Lake Tritonis in ancient North Africa.

We see the first signs of support for this idea in a detail in Apollodorus (3.12.3): the Pelasgians maintained that while engaged in combat as a girl, Athena killed her playmate, Pallas, the "daughter" of the river god Triton. As a "daughter" of a river, Pallas herself would have had "nymph" status, given that, as Larson (2001 passim) demonstrates, legendary daughters of waterways were always nymphs. Thus we are at once alerted to the possibility that Pallas was a priestess of divine birth. Apollodorus goes on to report that the Pelasgians contended that Zeus intervened to prevent Pallas from striking Athena, thereby causing Athena to wound her comrade mortally. As a token of her grief, Athena placed Pallas's name before her own, becoming Pallas Athena. She is said to have carved from a tree trunk a statue of Pallas known as the Palladium, which in Greek legend was venerated as an image of the goddess herself.

The story of Athena battling her friend Pallas in Libya suggests a tradition of armed female combat in North Africa. According to the Suda (s.v. *Pallas*), the very name *Pallas* comes from *pallein*, "to brandish," as in a spear. Kerenyi (1978, 26) also notes that "it was once the name for robust maidens and implied the meaning of the masculine word *pallas* . . . 'robust young man.'" Thus, the name *Pallas* itself connoted a robust, masculine, fighting woman: in short, an Amazon.

A tradition of women warriors in prehistoric North Africa is affirmed archaeologically in the ancient rock art of the Tassili mountains, located in contemporary Algeria. One scene depicted at Sefar, dating approximately 3550 to 2500 B.C.E., is clearly one of pitched battle in which female combatants with small breasts attack with bows and arrows opponents of ambiguous gender (Lajoux 1963, 164–8). This image supports the claims of Diodorus Siculus (3.52–5) that historical warrior women known as the Amazons dwelt in the region of Lake Tritonis and had a significant influence on North African geopolitics many generations before the Trojan War (i.e., before 1275 B.C.E.).[7]

Female warriorhood is furthermore documented ethnographically by Herodotus (4.180). Writing in the fifth century B.C.E., the historian reports that Libyan girls of the Ause tribe, who lived on the shores of Lake Tritonis near the river Triton, engaged in armed ritual combat. It is noteworthy that the Auses and this festival in particular were specifically associated with Athena/Neith. As the historian relates,

> They hold an annual festival in honor of Athena [Neith], at which the girls divide themselves into two groups and fight each other with stones and sticks; they say this rite had come down to them from time immemorial, and by its performance they pay honor to their native deity [Neith]—which is the same as our Greek Athena. If any girl, during the course of the battle, is fatally injured and dies, they say it is a proof that she is no maiden [*pseudoparthenos*]. Before setting them to fight, they pick out the best-looking girl and dress her up publicly in a full suit of Greek armor and a Corinthian helmet; then they put her in a chariot and drive her round the lake.

Herodotus then describes the nature of Ausean social structure:

> The women of the tribe are common property; there are no married couples living together, and intercourse is casual—like that of animals.

When a child is fully grown, the men hold a meeting, and it is considered to belong to the one it most closely resembles.
(Herodotus 1972, 331, trans. Sélincourt)

If we penetrate through the androcentric and derogatory tone
in this passage (e.g., portraying women as "common property,"
presumably *of men,* and likening members' sexual habits to that of
animals), it becomes apparent that what Herodotus is describing is
a classical matriarchal society in which childrearing was communal,
monogamous marriage was not practiced, lineage was reckoned
through the mother's line, and paternity was of little consequence.[8]
The Auses also retained memory of a tradition of female warriorhood, as suggested by the maidens fighting *to the death* and the
custom of parading a maiden around the lake in full combat gear.
That they held the rite was a survival "from time immemorial" further supports the idea of a probable deep history of female military
tradition in their culture and in the larger North African region.
I posit, in short, that the Auses were a remnant of the Amazon
tribes of North Africa written about by Diodorus and depicted in
the rock art. I also posit that their maidenly combat ritual echoes
the myth of Athena slaying her friend Pallas in Libya. That the
Auses carried out their old ritual specifically in honor of Neith, and
that Athena and Pallas were associated with the rite, suggests that
Neith/Athena was most likely the primary deity of the Libyan Amazons more broadly, dating from the remotest of times. I propose
that the symbols of the crossed arrows and the bow and arrows that
appear in Neith's early iconography reference her connection with
the ancient Amazons (see, e.g., Budge [1904] 1969, 1:31; Hollis
1994–95, 47). In short, I propose that originally Neith was no
generic "warrior goddess," but rather the goddess of the Libyan
Amazons, specifically.

Bates (1970, 104) suggests that the armed maiden who mounted
the chariot in fact "represented" the goddess Neith/Athena herself.
I agree and add that the criteria for her selection probably had to do
with more than beauty. I submit, in fact, that the young woman may
have been a victorious combatant from the previous year who had
been selected for the position of high virgin priestess for a special
reason. The clue to that—and its full meaning—may be found in the
detail that the maidens who died in combat were considered *pseu-
doparthenoi,* false virgins. I propose that for the Auses, the opposite
of a *pseudoparthenos,* that is, an *authentic parthenos,* was not simply
a girl who had not engaged in sexual intercourse. From Herodotus's
description of the Auses as a people among whom sex was casual and

unfettered, it is clear that this tribe was not interested in virginity in a moralistic sense as a measure of a girl's purity and "value" in the brokering of marriage. Indeed, in this tribe, there was no marriage, certainly not in the monogamous sense that the Greeks had in mind. This was clearly a people for whom sex was a natural act that had few taboos attached to it.

I propose instead that the Ause ritual originally may have served as a means of divining which maidens among them were fit to become priestesses of divine birth in the manner of their parthenogenetic goddess Neith/Athena. Not having engaged in sexual intercourse may have been one physical criterion for the priestesshood, but there was undoubtedly much more required on the spiritual level. I submit that those who perished in the combat were considered "false virgins" in that they were assumed to be the ones the goddess herself had determined as unfit for the role of holy *parthenos*.[9] Thus, I suggest that the ritual originally served as a divinatory "test" to determine which girls had the proper constitution to participate in the greatest mystery practice of their religion.

I propose that in the earliest phase of Ausean culture, the *parthenos* who was crowned with the helmet of Neith/Athena prior to the battle may have been considered a particularly worthy priestess. Perhaps this was so by virtue of the courage and physical prowess she had displayed in the combat ritual the year before. Perhaps, also, at some remote period she was a *parthenos* who it was believed had conceived in a miraculous fashion. Whether the Auses were attempting divine birth in Herodotus's day (fifth century B.C.E.) remains an open question. I suspect it is more likely that by that late period the rite had become merely a symbolic one, which preserved the memory of an original cultic practice.

That divine birth may have been the actual or symbolic focus of the ritual is further suggested by a detail related some four centuries after Herodotus by the Roman geographer Pomponius Mela (1.35). The annual festival, he writes, was celebrated on Neith/Athena's birthday. As we will recall, the earliest substratum of Neith's story related that the goddess gave birth to herself out of herself, that is, autogenetically. Although, according to Herodotus, the Auses believed Neith/Athena to have been the child of Poseidon and the river Triton, I submit that the motif of celebrating the day of Neith's "birth" was a remnant of an archaic memory of the goddess's autogenetic origins.

If it is true that the Ause ritual centered around the selection of maidens for the divine birth priestesshood associated with Neith/Athena, the fact that combat was an integral part of the rite may signal that divine birth was originally practiced by the earlier Libyan Amazons, as well. Furthermore, given that the primary familial relationship in a cultural condition of Amazony, the one imbued with the greatest importance and sacrality, was the mother/daughter bond,[10] it may be that the cult of the earlier Amazons was dedicated to pure daughter-bearing parthenogenesis, in particular. I suggest it may even be the case that the "quarrel" the Auseans reported between Athena and Poseidon reflected the imposition of the Poseidon cult onto their culture. Given that, in the Greek tradition, Poseidon fathered numerous children by way of mortal women, it may be that the advent of the Poseidon cult to the region involved what I indicated in Chapter 1 was a transition from pure parthenogenesis to *hieros gamos* divine birth, and a corresponding power struggle between the clergy involved.

ATHENA AND HER DIVINE BIRTH CULT IN ATHENS

Cecrops, the legendary first king of Attica, is said to have introduced the cult of Athena in Athens, probably from Egypt: Diodorus Siculus (1:28.4–5) affirms that the Athenians believed they themselves were "colonists from Saïs in Egypt," Neith's primary cult center, and that Cecrops was Egyptian. The twelfth-century Byzantine scholar Tzetzes quotes Charax of Pergamon, a priest and historian of the earlier centuries of the common era, as echoing that Cecrops colonized Athens from Saïs (in Bernal 1987–2006, 3:566). I propose that these stories reflect an actual history in which Cecrops was a bona fide leader who brought the worship of Neith with him from Africa to Greece, where the goddess took on the name *Athena*. Bernal (571) plausibly dates Athens' first foundation to the first half of the nineteenth century B.C.E.

Cecrops's establishment of the cult of Athena at Athens is further indicated in legends relating that he was the first to erect a statue to Athena (Eusebius *Preparation for the Gospel* 10.9.22), that he was "called upon" by Athena to witness her planting the olive tree there, and that his testimony persuaded the Olympian gods to grant the goddess supremacy in Attica over Poseidon (Apollodorus 3.14.1). According to Varro (in St. Augustine *City of God* 18.9), Cecrops is said to have called the citizens together to cast their vote in favor of one deity or another. As women of that period participated in civic affairs (in contrast to later Greek women, who were barred from such participation), they all voted for Athena. Given that the women outnumbered the men by one, they won the vote for the goddess. Shortly after this event, Athena laid down the large "rock" on which the Acropolis was to be built in the city that was to bear her name, Athens (Callimachus *Hecale* frag. 260.18–29 [Trypanis]).

I suggest, then, that Cecrops's "establishment" of the Athena cult reflects the period in which the Neith cult of Africa was made part of the "official" state religion on Greek soil. Yet I also agree with Cook (1914–40, 3.1: 189–226), who believes that Athena was a pre-Greek divinity of the Athenian Acropolis, and that she was antecedent to Zeus. Thus I suggest that the legend of Cecrops depicts the moment in which Athena was theologically "demoted" from Virgin Mother in her own right to "daughter" of Zeus. For Cecrops was also credited as the first to apply the name *Zeus* to the masculine god (Eusebius *Preparation for the Gospel* 10.9) and the first to give him the epithet *Hypatos,* "Highest," indicating that under his rule Zeus was established as supreme deity (Kerenyi 1978, 19). The once powerful genetrix of Africa thus was made to come into subordinate relation with this god. Perhaps the corresponding Ausean legend reported by Herodotus that Athena broke with Poseidon and was made Zeus's "daughter" reflected a political bargain whereby the Athena cult was able to reign with supremacy over the Poseidon cult in Attica on the condition that it remain secondary to that of the religion of the "father," that is, Zeus.

PARTHENOGENETIC ASPECTS OF THE PANATHENAIA

The Panathenaia was an important festival with parthenogenetic associations that was held in honor of Athena at Athens in antiquity. As part of this event, four women were elected from those of noble birth to weave the goddess's woolen *peplos,* or ceremonial robe, and present it to her statue at the Acropolis at the culminating moment of the grand procession (Suda, s.v. *arrêphorein; peplos*).[11] It seems that two of the women were married, while two were maidens between the ages of 7 and 11. These latter were priestesses known as *arrephoroi,* or "Bearers of the Sacred/Secret Things," who lived on the Acropolis along with possibly two additional girls who bore that title and who served the goddess in a related capacity that I discuss later.[12] Thus, as in the case of the Auses, the priestesshood of Athena in Greece involved virgin girls, that is, *parthenoi,* here in relation to the weaving function.

As did the Ausean combat ritual, the Panathenaia celebrated the day of Athena's birth. Although the Greeks held the goddess to have been born from the head of Zeus, the androgenetic (male parthenogenesis) aspect of this Zeusian motif may well point to Athena/Neith's

earlier autogenetic story and to the cosmological arrogation of parthenogenetic power to the sphere of the masculine. Furthermore,
that the interval between the beginning of the weaving of the *peplos*
and the presentation to Athena was nine months is significant, in that
it may well have mirrored the period of human gestation (Kerenyi
1978, 29, 58). The birthday of the goddess and the day of the reception of the *peplos* were also specifically timed according with the new
moon. The *peplos* was presented to the goddess on the day of the
hidden moon (Suda, s.v. *tritogenes*, in Kerenyi 40). The birthday
of the goddess was assigned to the night when the first sliver of the
moon appeared, which allows for the conclusion that there was a
correspondence between the mythological "rebirth" of the goddess
and the "renewal" of this luminary body (40–1, 58). That the Greeks
believed the female menstrual period took place during the new, or
waning, moon affirms that they associated the moon with women's
fertility cycle.[13] These related motifs point to the specifically female
nature of the birth process expressed in the Panathenaia, underscoring the idea that the male Zeusian birth element had no real place in
the most archaic level of the story associated with Athena.

The "nine months" element also suggests a reference to an actual
human birth. One could imagine that the Panathenaia originally may
have been a celebration of a virgin priestess who, like Athena, was
thought to give birth to a divine child, as Athena had given birth
to ("recreated her *peplos*") herself. It may be that the timing of the
ritual with the "hidden" aspect of the moon was an occult reference
to the most "secret" of women's blood mysteries—parthenogenesis.
Perhaps the sexual status of the two sets of weavers of the *peplos* in
the Hellenistic period—on the one hand, virgins who were non-fertile
(prepubescent), and on the other, fertile mothers who were nonvir-
gins—was understood to constitute, in their totality, the symbol of
the Virgin Mother.

If achieving parthenogenetic conception was indeed an aspiration
of Athena's priestesshood at Athens, presumably young virgins would
have been trained for the role and retained in the priestesshood after
puberty. The fact that by the time of the Hellenistic writers virgin
priestesses were dismissed from service after a year (Pausanias 1.27.3)
suggests that a divine birth priestesshood in association with Athena
ceased to function at some point. However, numerous legends and
certain latter-day cult practices suggest that such a priestesshood may
have operated prior to the historical period, that is, in the Bronze Age
or even earlier. I now turn my attention to such stories and accounts
of such practices.

DAUGHTERS OF CECROPS AS PARTHENOGENETIC TRANSGRESSORS

One such story involves the daughters of the legendary Attic king Cecrops, who, I posit, mark three of the earliest priestesses of Athena on Greek soil. Aside from the following legends suggesting these daughters were priestesses of Athena is the fact that two of them, Pandrosos and Aglaurus, were commemorated with their own special sacred precincts on the Acropolis in historical times. Both were also equated with the goddess herself, as can be seen by Athena's epithets Athena *Aglaurus* and Athena *Pandrosos*.[14] I propose that such identification of mortal women with goddesses generally indicates that these women served as "hypostases," or "proxies," that is, priestly living manifestations of the goddess, a theme I return to more fully in Chapter 4.[15] Moreover, mystery rites and initiations are attested in honor of these two daughters in association with Athena's Plynteria festival (Athenagoras *Plea on Behalf of the Christians* 1). This celebration involved secret rites that accompanied the removal of the *peplos* from the statue of Athena and the covering of her image (Plutarch *Alcibiades* 23); additionally, it commemorated the death of Aglaurus. That she and Pandrosos were associated with such mystery rites further stresses their likely original sacerdotal role with the Athena cult.

Already a transgression of some sort involving parthenogenetic birth was attached to these virgin daughters. The story centers on the birth of Erichthonius, who would become the legendary king of Athens. In Callimachus (*Hecale* frag. 24, ed. Trypanis) and Pausanias (1.2.6), we hear that it was Ge/Gaia who gave birth to Erichthonius via the god Hephaestus. In a slightly expanded version, Erichthonius was said to have sprung up from the ground when Athena disgustedly threw down the wool wiped with Hephaestus's semen, which the god had ejaculated onto her leg in an attempt to rape her (Apollodorus 3.14.6).

These two narratives essentially show the "true" mother of Erichthonius to be Ge/Gaia. I discuss more fully the profoundly parthenogenetic nature of the earth goddess in the forthcoming *Virgin Mother Goddesses of Antiquity*. For now, I will merely mention that in Hesiod's *Theogony* (126–32) Ge/Gaia bears the god of the Heavens (Uranus), as well as the mountains, nymphs, and Pontus Sea without a male partner. The aforementioned stories thus indicate that Erichthonius's birth essentially was a parthenogenetic one. They also point to a problem, from the perspective of the Athena cult, in the motif of the intrusion of a male god into the proceedings, and even possibly a sexual violation. Given the strong possibility that in Greek cult priestesses were considered to be the earthly proxies of the goddesses they served, the mythologem of Athena's being "raped" may suggest some sort of attempted—and transgressive—union between a priestess of Athena and the god Hephaestus to create Erichthonius, the "divine" child who would rule Athens. This idea is supported by another myth in which the birth of Erichthonius was indeed attributed to the union of an earthly woman named Atthis and the god Hephaestus (Apollodorus 3.14.6). That Atthis, the daughter of the Attic king Cranaus, who ruled after Cecrops, was an important ancestress in the region is revealed by the fact that she was the eponym for Attica itself (Pausanias 1.2.6). Her commemoration in this regard—what I suggest was a form of immortalization—is, I propose, an indicator that she was indeed considered a divine birth priestess, a holy *parthenos,* and her status as a princess of the royal house of early Athens suggests that she was a priestess of Athena, in particular.

Although in these legendary fragments it is Atthis who is named mother of Erichthonius, I propose this may reflect a transfer of the parthenogenetic element in the story, which should more appropriately be associated with the daughters of Cecrops. It is they who are the central figures in this legend, one that occupied an important place in Athenian lore. According to the ancient accounts, after the birth of Erichthonius, Athena, although unhappy with the entire situation, decided to enclose the infant for secret rearing in a special wooden chest in order to help the boy achieve "immortality."[16] She entrusted the chest to Cecrops's "maiden" daughters (i.e., *parthenoi*), Aglaurus, Pandrosos, and Herse, giving them strict orders not to open it. The goddess then went off to establish the rock on which the Acropolis was to be built. Thus the timing of the event was, as we will recall, the moment in which Cecrops officially linked Athena/Neith's cult to the city-state of Athens. According to Pausanias (1.18.2), Pandrosos obeyed the goddess's command, but the other two, Aglaurus and Herse, opened the chest out of curiosity. Depending on the tradition, upon seeing the child they were either destroyed by a serpent that lay coiled around the babe, or driven mad by Athena, causing them to commit suicide by throwing themselves off the Acropolis (Apollodorus 3.14.6). In Hyginus's account (*Fabulae* 166), all three daughters peeked, were driven mad by Athena, and threw themselves into the sea. Hyginus adds the curious detail that the "snake" they witnessed was in fact the lower part of Erichthonius's body itself, a feature that Apollodorus (3.14.1) reports was also said to characterize Cecrops.

It is significant that two of the daughters of Cecrops specifically have *hieros gamos* stories associated with them. In Ovid (*Metamorphoses* 2.550–830), Hermes desired to lie with Herse and agreed to pay Aglaurus (in this account the only sister to look into Erichthonius's basket) a handsome fee in exchange for her granting sexual access to the girl. Athena subsequently cursed Aglaurus with jealousy toward her sister, however, and Aglaurus was "turned to stone" by the god when she reneged on their agreement and forbade him access. Yet, in another tradition, Aglaurus also had her opportunity to be with a god: with Ares she bore a daughter, Alcippe (Apollodorus 3.14.2).

Who, then, was responsible for conceiving Erichthonius, the legendary first king of mighty Athens? Callimachus (*Hecale* frag. 21, 1975, trans. Trypanis) calls his birth "mysterious and secret" (*lathrion arrêton*). Philostrates (*Life of Apollonius of Tyana* 7.24) quotes the great seer Apollonius of Tyana as remarking that it was Athena herself who "bore" Erichthonius, whom he calls a "dragon" (*drakonta*), referring to the boy's reptilian lower half. By saying it was "Athena" who "bore" the child, it may be that Apollonius was really talking about one of the priestesses who had ritually assumed the goddess's identity, as was a common practice of the female priest in Greece (again, see Connelly 2007, 83, 104–15). Given that both Aglaurus and Pandrosos were equated with the goddess herself, the one as Athena Aglaurus and the other as Athena Pandrosos, perhaps one of them, in particular, was believed to have conceived and borne the Athenian king.

Whoever the mother of Erichthonius may have been, these stories indeed allude to the theme of divine birth. The implication in the legend that Erichthonius was "born" from Ge/Gaia also recalls the oldest symbol of Neith, the click beetle, an insect that appears to emerge spontaneously from the earth. Thus, embedded in the story is the condition of "pure" parthenogenesis, to refer to my taxonomy. Yet in the legend of Atthis's birth of Erichthonius, and in the stories of the unions of the daughters of Cecrops with gods, a *hieros gamos* union also lurks.

I propose that the motif of Athena's "disgust" over Hephaestus's attempted rape may point to a situation in which one of her priestesses, either Atthis or, more likely, one of the daughters of Cecrops, was believed to betray the practice of pure parthenogenesis, to which she was originally dedicated, and capitulate to *hieros gamos* divine birth. We see this most clearly suggested in Ovid's story, in which Herse was "wooed" by the god Hermes and money was exchanged for her body. Is this an element of poetic fiction, or might it reflect an authentic legend—and, thus, possibly, a historical episode—in which one or more of the daughters of Cecrops was "bought" for her parthenogenetic services by the patriarchal religious establishment? The maidens' "peeking" at the child Erichthonius and spying the "snake" in his chest may well refer to a "peeking into" the mysteries of divine conception with a god, given that, as we saw in Chapter 2 in relation to the cult of Asclepius, miraculous conception was sometimes symbolized as union between an earthbound female and a snake.

This idea finds further support in a related series of motifs connecting the snake with the daughters of Cecrops. A fragment of Sophocles (in Kerenyi 1978, 42 and n187) gives the three daughters, or one of them, the epithet *drakaulos*, "serpent." The explanations for this are varied: either it was (1) because Athena allowed the serpent to live with her; (2) because the goddess lived with the double-formed (half-snake) Cecrops; or (3) because one of the sisters used to spend nights with the serpent who dwelt in the Acropolis, and days with Athena (*Etymologicum Magnum* and Suda, s.v. *drakaulos*, in Kerenyi, 42n188). The motif of the "cohabitation" of the snake and the priestesses, and the implication that Athena's "permission" was needed to sanction the presence of the snake in her precincts, may suggest a coexistence yet tension between the (pure parthenogenetic?) Athena cult and the (*hieros gamos?*) "serpent" cults associated with male gods. The symbolism of one of the daughters of Cecrops "spending nights" with the serpent, but "days" with Athena, is particularly suggestive in this regard, and calls to mind the other instances of priestesses who were reportedly shut up to have intercourse with gods at night, reported by Herodotus, which I discussed in Chapter 2.

Further, Kerenyi (1978, 39, 43) notes the similarities in the names *Aglaurus,* daughter of Cecrops, and *Agraulus,* the wife of Cecrops and the mother of all three daughters. Sometimes the names are used interchangeably, as in Euripides (*Ion* 496) and Apollodorus (3.14.2), in which the mother of the girls herself is called *Aglaurus.* The occasional transposition of letters in the name, Kerenyi suggests, was a deliberate attempt simultaneously to *reveal* and *conceal* a mystery. In this case, he contends, the letter play points to the idea that Aglaurus and Agraulus were one and the same. This "simultaneity" of motherhood and daughterhood, he proposes, was a motif referring to an instance of incest with Cecrops. I suggest, instead, that the mythologem of Aglaurus's being, as Kerenyi (1978, 46) expresses it, "the double of her mother" once again points to the mystery of "replicating" or "twinning" inherent in the condition of pure daughter-bearing parthenogenesis. The name play thus suggests that

Agraulus's conception of her *daughter* Aglaurus was thought to have been accomplished without Cecrops; that is, it was parthenogenetic. Her three daughters nevertheless coming to be named "daughters" of Cecrops could well mirror the mythologem of Athena coming to be named "daughter" of Zeus. Such possibilities allow for the conjecture that a pre-Cecropian, female-governed, parthenogenetic cult to Athena/Neith existed in the days prior to the official establishment of Athens and the absorption of the cult into the patriarchal city-state.

This idea that the cult to Athena/Neith originally may have been controlled by women finds support in legends about Cecrops indicating that prior to his rule, matriarchal conditions prevailed in Greece: monogamous marriage did not exist, fatherhood was deemed unimportant, and kinship was reckoned through the motherline. Moreover, women participated in voting and civic affairs and were counted as legitimate Athenian citizens. These conditions are all attested by Varro and Clearchus (the pupil of Aristotle) by way of their reports that all such social structures were *overturned* under Cecrops's reign. According to Varro (in St. Augustine *City of God* 18.9), when the women of Athens voted in favor of Athena over Poseidon as the tutelary deity, the men retaliated swiftly and severely. Claiming that they needed to appease the wrath of Poseidon, the men stripped women of the right to vote, forbade them from giving their own surnames to their children, and rescinded their citizenship as Athenians. According to Clearchus, Cecrops "was the first man to join one woman to one man; before his time unions had been loose and promiscuity was general . . . [E]arlier men did not know who was their own father, there were so many" (in Athenaeus 13.555d, 1950, 6:5, trans. Gulick).

These accounts indicate that under Cecrops, women lost previously held status in the political and domestic spheres. They could no longer participate in civic affairs or even be counted as legitimate citizens, a strike that served to "erase" them from public life. By being forced into marrying monogamously and reckoning their kin through the fatherline, they were also "erased" in the private realm, as well, their bodies now controlled so that men could be sure who their own sons were. By reversing the matriarchal condition (expressed, as we have seen, by the Libyan Auses), in which fatherhood was accorded little importance, the Greeks created a situation in which inheritance could flow through the patriline. In short, as Harrison ([1903] 1957, 262) affirms, these stories likely indicate that Cecrops "introduced the social conditions of patriarchy" in Attica. Kerenyi (1978, 44) says of this period, "The masculine appear[ed] not *graciously* and paternally, but *aggressively*" (see also Tyrrell 1984, 28–39). That women were apparently much more autonomous and empowered in all spheres prior to Cecrops's kingship supports my conjecture that they could have had a position of primacy in the Athena cult, as well. Even during the patriarchal period, the most prestigious religious position at Athens was the priesthood of Athena Polias, which was held for life by its incumbent and which afforded her high status and many perquisites (see, e.g., Dillon 2001, 84–9, and Connelly 2007, 59–64). I contend this was a vestige of the old matriarchal condition.

The *Aglaurus/Agraulus* name play, then, may both "reveal and conceal," to refer back to Kerenyi's concept, the mystery of pure daughter-bearing parthenogenesis in association with the earliest stratum of Athena's cult at Athens. But the stories of the conception of Erichthonius and the punishments of the daughters of Cecrops point to some sort of change in the priesthood. Perhaps the maidens' "peeking" into the infant's chest and seeing the serpent represents their peering into the *hieros gamos* mystery, marking a grave betrayal of the Amazonian mysteries of Neith/Athena. The various stories of their deaths and punishments inflicted on them may refer to their breaking of this taboo. The "anger" of Athena recorded in myth may represent the conflict that ensued between the virgin priesthood associated with the goddess and the *hieros gamos* priesthood associated with male gods. It also may represent conflict that occurred within the very ranks of the parthenogenetic priesthood itself, as it grappled with new pressures and demands.

It is significant that the transgression of the daughters occurred, according to legend, at the moment when Athena was establishing the "rock" on which the Acropolis—that is, Athens itself—was to stand. These events point to the possibility that as the Neith/Athena cult was being made the religion of the state, its associated priesthood was being "yoked in marriage" to male gods by male sacerdotal officials. Just as women's bodies were now being controlled so as to allow for inheritance and power to flow through the male line, so priestesses' bodies were being used to engender what was believed to be heroic male lineages that would do the bidding of "most high" Zeus and stand in service to patriarchy.

That the story of the transgression of Cecrops's daughters was a tremendously important one in the Athena cult at Athens can be seen in a detail revealed by Pausanias (1.27.1–3) of a little-known ritual in his day (second century C.E.). According to the chronicler, the night before the Skira festival in honor of Athena, two of the *arrephoroi,* the "Bearers of the Sacred/Secret Offerings," carried something on their heads, presumably in baskets, that was given to them by the priestess of Athena.[17] Pausanias reports the belief that neither this priestess nor the virgins had any knowledge of what was being carried. The virgins descended by the natural underground passage that crossed adjacent precincts within the city of "Aphrodite of the Garden." There they deposited their items, and took up something else, also presumably enclosed in baskets, which they brought back up. After completing these duties, the virgins were released from service and two others were chosen in their place. The night before the Panathenaia, another mysterious—and probably related—basket carrying also occurred. This ritual was known as the Hersephoria, which connects it specifically to Cecrops's daughter Herse (Kerenyi 1978, 56).

Immediately before his description of this ritual, Pausanias notes that adjoining the temple of Athena Polias was a temple dedicated to Pandrosos, whom he calls "the only one of the sisters to be faithful to the trust" (Pausanias 1931–5, 1:139, trans. Jones). The placing of this allusion here suggests that he is implying a connection between the mysterious basket-carrying ritual and the "faithful" sister Pandrosos. Moreover, the rite itself recalls the enclosing of Erichthonius in the chest, and Athena's orders that the chest not be opened. Thus it seems clear that the meaning of the ritual relates to the ancient story of the daughters of Cecrops and the conception and rearing of the legendary Athenian king, as numerous scholars have concurred, among them Burkert (1966), Kerenyi (1978, 55–7), and Goff (2004, 98–100).

According to the scholiast on Lucian,[18] the contents of the baskets of the *arrephoroi* were serpents and male phalli made of dough, and the rite here is explained as fertility magic, a reckoning accepted by most modern scholars. Burkert (1966), for example, interprets the maidens' nocturnal descent with phallic snakes to symbolize the act of sexual intercourse, and posits that what they retrieved was the representation of a swaddled baby (i.e., Erichthonius). Goff (2004, 100) writes, "The *arrephoroi* thus enact the process of human reproduction." I agree, but would add, according to the argument I have been making thus far, that what they enacted symbolized no ordinary kind of human reproduction.

I propose, specifically, that the rite carried out by the *arrephoroi* symbolized the mystery of *hieros gamos* divine birth contained in the story of Erichthonius. Given that this practice was considered transgressive from the viewpoint of the old guard of the Athena cult, however, I suggest the ritual served as a marker by the priestesshood of (1) the original centrality of daughter-bearing parthenogenesis in the pre-patriarchal cult to Athena/Neith, and (2) the need for her priestesses to resist the constant temptation to "go over to the other side," that is, to capitulate to what must have been the seductive lure of sexual union with gods. The ritual furthermore served as a kind of eternal "penance" that the priestesshood of Athena was constrained to enact in order to "make amends" to the goddess for what was seen as the violation by one (or more) of the daughters of Cecrops of her vow to practice "pure" parthenogenesis only. On the occult level, the rite therefore allowed for an uneasy but stable coexistence of the "old" and "new" aspects of the Athena cult at Athens in a time of social/spiritual transition and upheaval.

A closer examination of the specific elements of the ritual helps give this conjecture life. The secret "phalli" carried by the *arrephoroi*, I contend, were symbols of the *priapus/herm* possibly used in the *hieros gamos* ritual by one (or more) of the daughters of Cecrops to simulate the fecundating phallus of the god, a concept I discussed in Chapter 1. The young priestesses' "not peeking" at these very sexual objects thus served symbolically to supply the element of "restraint" that the daughter(s) of Cecrops had been unsuccessful in maintaining when supposedly faced with the opportunity to have intercourse with a god. I propose that the girls' path by a grotto sanctuary of Aphrodite and Eros served as a further test, in that it forced them to confront visually stone phalluses and representations of the child Eros, the god of love and eroticism (Kerenyi 1978, 56–7), yet still remain focused on their task.

That the ritual exchange of baskets took place in this specific spot has further symbolic significance: the basket of Athena's (parthenogenetic?) secrets would always be left in the very garden of sexual temptation, underscoring the idea that the lure of *hieros gamos* was ever present for the virgin priestess. The taking up of the "swaddled child" perhaps symbolized Athena's/the priestesshood's willingness to care for the progeny of a *hieros gamos* union, despite her/their displeasure with the situation—and, at the same time, to keep the entire situation "under wraps." The "obedience" of the priestesses in staying the path and not looking at the objects they were carrying at any phase of the ritual, I propose, served as an apology and offering to the goddess— one that was thought critical to restore and maintain her favor.

That the meaning of this journey would not have been directly expressed indicates that these principles were thought to be mysteries that required the utmost secrecy. As Kerenyi (1978, 39) notes, Greek devices expressing the mysteries "at once hint[ed] at the inexpressible and veil[ed] it." Indeed, the very term *arrephoros*, "Bearer of the Sacred/Secret Things," suggests a veiled reference to the parthenogenetic priestess herself as ultimately "bearer"—that is, vessel—of the divine child. This is further suggested by Herse's name, which, in Greek, connotes "child" (Kerenyi 1978, 40, 56, and n253). As Goff (2004, 101) notes, Pausanias's claim that not even the senior priestesses had any knowledge of the contents of the baskets may reflect not ignorance on the part of the priestesshood regarding the rite, but a refusal to discuss it. Perhaps even if divine birth were no longer attempted by Pausanias's time, the senior priestess (presumably the priestess of Athena Polias) may have known the original significance of the basket-carrying ritual and understood that it was not to be talked about.

It is worth noting here that the famous *karyatids,* or maidens, who serve as columns upholding the roof of the special structure known as the Erechtheion on the Athenian Acropolis (named for Erichthonius) hold elaborate baskets on their heads (see, e.g., Dillon 2001, 50–2). This suggests their identification either with the *arrephoroi* or with another group of young virgin priestesses who carried baskets during the Panathenaia, the *kanephoroi* (Connelly 2007, 125). Given the associations I am making here, it may be that the *karyatids* represented holy *parthenoi* of the Cecropian era's parthenogenetic cult.

One final detail related to the daughters of Cecrops regards the Plynteria, or "Washing Day," festival, which commemorated the death of Aglaurus. During the annual festival, the statue of Athena was taken to the sea to be bathed, and her *peplos* was washed.[19] Some have suggested (e.g., Guthrie 1967, 103) that this rite echoes the myth of Hera's virginity being "renewed" by her bath in the Canathus Spring at Nauplia, which also may have had its ritual analogs in the cult to Hera, which I discuss in Chapter 5. Thus, the Plynteria may have served as yet another ritual related to Cecrops's daughters in which the populace was forced to focus its attention on the "virgin/parthenogenetic" aspect of Athena as represented by her *peplos,* originally the symbol, as I have shown, of her virgin motherhood. That this rite required dedication year after year also may have rendered it a form of propitiation for the large-scale theological diminishment of the goddess's powers as Holy *Parthenos,* the great creatrix, under orthodox religion.

A further hint that young *parthenoi* priestesses in the cult of Athena at Athens indeed at one point may have been aspirants in the divine birth processes can be found in the myth of Oreithyia. Oreithyia was said to have been abducted and raped by the Boreas, that is, the North Wind, and to have had several children by him.[20] As the daughter of the legendary Athenian king Erechtheus, the grandson of King Erichthonius, it is likely that she, like the daughters of Cecrops, was a priestess of Athena by virtue of her ties to the royal house. That she indeed held a priestly role is affirmed by a fragment of Acusilaus (frag. 30, in Dillon 2001, 38), which says her abduction occurred while she was participating as a *kanephoros*, or "basket carrier," in the procession to Athena at the Acropolis. As I discussed in Chapter 2, the North Wind, in particular, was credited with having the powers to induce spontaneous parthenogenetic conception in animals; thus this mythologem likely references Oreithyia as a holy *parthenos*. That Oreithyia's impregnating agent was the "wind" and not one of the Olympian gods may further be a veiled reference to the practice of pure parthenogenesis in association with the cult of Athena. Her position as a great-granddaughter of Erichthonius suggests that attempts at pure parthenogenesis continued alongside the practice of *hieros gamos* parthenogenesis for a number of generations after the daughters of Cecrops, and her position in the lineage suggests that such practices were handed down the female line.

Other Myths of Parthenogenetic Transgressions

I now turn to other stories depicting Athena's wrath, an analysis of which may support the hypothesis that her priestesshood experienced a contentious transition from pure parthenogenesis to *hieros gamos* divine birth.

Medusa

One such story involved Medusa. Hesiod (*Theogony* 270–80) writes that Medusa was one of three mythological "Gorgon" sisters who dwelt in Libya. Diodorus Siculus (3.54.3), however, euhemeristically names her queen of the Gorgons, whom he identifies as one of the historical tribes of female Amazon warriors in North Africa. Pausanias (2.21.5–7) offers a similar rationalized account in which Medusa was a Libyan huntress and warrior queen who reigned over those living around Lake Tritonis. According to the chronicler, she was slain one night by Perseus while she was encamped in North Africa with an army. The Greek hero cut off her head and buried it under a mound of earth in the marketplace in Argos.

Legends indicate that Medusa was apparently involved in a grave transgression vis-à-vis Athena: Apollodorus (2.4.2–3) states she dared to compare herself in beauty to Athena, while Ovid (*Metamorphoses* 4.773–803) writes that she inflamed the goddess's rage by being violated in Athena's shrine by Poseidon. In the former case, Athena punished Medusa by turning her hair into snakes; in the latter, she did so by guiding Perseus's hand in beheading her. Upon her death, it was revealed that Medusa had conceived by the god two beings: a human son, Chrysaor, and a "winged horse," Pegasus (Apollodorus 2.4.2–3).

I put forth here a somewhat different perspective on her myth than that offered by a number of feminist scholars. Although several studies have made important contributions to our understanding of the Medusa figure and archetype, none has seriously considered Medusa's possible historicity, and few have taken into account her probable Libyan provenance.[21] My analysis here, in contrast, proceeds on the euhemeristic assumption that Medusa was a historical Amazon of North Africa.

As I argued in the previous chapter, Neith/Athena was most likely the primary goddess of the Amazons of Libya. I suggest, then, that, as an African Amazon queen, Medusa was probably a priestess of this goddess, in particular, which we see in the aforementioned myths of her close association with Athena. This argument is strengthened by the legend that Asclepius received his healing powers from the "blood" that flowed from Medusa's decapitated neck, a gift granted him by Athena (Apollodorus 2.10.3). The motif can be interpreted to mean that Asclepius somehow acquired healing knowledge that was originally "in Medusa's blood," that is, possessed by her as a priestess of this goddess.[22] As a priestess of Neith/Athena, Medusa may well have been involved in parthenogenetic practices, as well, given Neith's mythological and cultic associations in this regard. I propose the possibility that Medusa may even have been a "true" *parthenos,* a divine birth priestess, who had risen to her rank as queen by defeating other "false virgins" in the ancient tradition that the Libyan Auses of Lake Tritonis preserved.

Medusa's encounter with Poseidon is typically interpreted as a rape. Read euhemeristically, the event might even be seen as the rape of a priestess of Athena/Neith by a priest of Poseidon. However, that the primary rival to the cult of Neith/Athena in ancient Libya was the cult of Poseidon, and that Poseidon was one of the major gods by whom earthly females were thought to have given birth to divine children and heroes (see Theoi Project 2000–7, s.v. *Poseidon: Poseidon family; Poseidon loves 1 and 2*), may allow for a different interpretation of this episode. I propose that the violation of Medusa "in Athena's temple" can be read as Medusa's having engaged in a ritual *hieros gamos* with Poseidon—perhaps under duress or pressure. The telling detail in this regard is Athena's anger toward, and punishment of,

Medusa. This motif has been interpreted from a feminist perspective as a patriarchal trope to symbolize the ultimate (and patriarchally desired) female capitulation to the male power system, expressed through female-on-female violence (see, e.g., Marler 2002, 22, and Valentis and Devane 1994, 142–63). But I suggest that Athena's "wrath" may point to an ancient belief that Medusa's engagement with Poseidon was ultimately a willing one.

Lefkowitz (1993) has already opened the door to such an idea with her argument that females in Greek myths were not *raped* by gods, but rather seduced or abducted, and, at least initially, gave their consent to the encounter. She discerns that while such episodes were often violent and lacked mutuality, they generally included an element of temptation and pleasure to which these female figures responded. Visual depictions of erotic pursuit similarly include possible allusions to attraction on the part of females (Deacy 1997, 45–52). I am not suggesting here a return to the misguided Freudian notion that "all women want to be raped," which Brownmiller (1975) has cogently critiqued. Rather, I offer the hypothesis that a number of "rape" situations between gods and mortals in mythology specifically describe scenarios in which priestesses may have been considered irresistibly drawn into the realm of *hieros gamos* in the ritual trance state.[23] In Medusa's case, for example, the detail that the encounter with Poseidon took place "in Athena's temple" may suggest she was specifically engaged in ritual trance—perhaps literally in a temple of the goddess—at the time. As I proposed in Chapter 1, it is likely that if divine conception of any type were indeed attempted by priestesses, it was done in a deliberately induced non-ordinary state of consciousness. It may be that priestesses were thought to have unwittingly found themselves in the terrain of *hieros gamos* by virtue of the sudden and unbidden "entrance" into their non-ordinary state of what was considered to be a masculine deity. We will recall here from Chapter 1 the excerpt from the *Testament of Reuben* (5:5–6) attesting to an ancient belief that male beings could indeed intrude into women's trance space with the predatory intent to impregnate them:

> As [the Watchers] continued looking at the women, they were filled with desire for them and perpetrated the act in their minds. Then they were transformed into human males, and while the women were cohabiting with their husbands they appeared to them. Since the women's minds were filled with lust for these apparitions, they gave birth to giants. For the Watchers were disclosed to them as being as high as the heavens.
>
> (Collins 2008, 266)

I propose that in such situations involving priestesses dedicated to Virgin Mother goddesses and pure parthenogenesis, a power struggle was believed to have ensued, of which we see suggestions in the stories of various "nymphs" in Chapter 4 who attempted to "metamorphose" into other beings in order to evade the god. It is possible, as well, that certain priestesses were thought to have dared to solicit such a visitation. This was possibly done with the intention of having a non-ordinary sexual experience.[24] It also may have been done out of a sense of curiosity, supported by a belief that they possessed the discipline to "look" without going further. Such priestesses, however, may have been thought to become disoriented and forgetful of their virgin vows (a state generated by the male deity), and/or overpowered by the intense erotic pull of the moment such that they finally "leapt" over the precipice. In that sense, their fitful encounters may have been seen simultaneously as rapes (the god overpowering them) and seductions (their ultimately agreeing to the intercourse). The story of Cecrops's daughters, with its themes of "temptation," "peering," and "leaping," is particularly suggestive of this phenomenon.

Perhaps Queen Medusa's story thus reflects an instance of a priestess who similarly was believed to have been tempted, lured, or pressured into "peeking" into *hieros gamos* with Poseidon. It may be that she underestimated the degree to which she would be challenged to break her virgin vow to Neith/Athena by entering into such otherworldly territory. Her historical murder may have been viewed as a cosmic punishment for her betrayal of the Amazonian daughter-bearing parthenogenetic practice dedicated to Neith/Athena. The turning of her hair into "snakes" may also refer to both her dreadlocks as an African queen, as well as the motif of "taboo" regarding *hieros gamos* divine birth, one we also saw in operation in the stories of the transgressive viewing of Erichthonius, who was surrounded by a snake or was serpentine himself. These provocative ideas may ultimately be unprovable, but the analysis of similar such stories of goddesses' wrath in this and subsequent chapters will, I hope, render them more than just outlandish speculations.

Arachne
Another dramatic story depicting Athena's upset over transgressions related to divine birth involves Arachne. According to Ovid (*Metamorphoses* 6.1–150), Arachne was a Lydian "maiden" (again, indicating she was a virgin/*parthenos*) distinguished by her skill as a weaver. When she refused to acknowledge that her gift was granted by the grace of Athena, the goddess challenged her to a weaving contest.

On her tapestry, Athena depicted events such as her victory in claiming Athens over Poseidon, as well as instances in which mortals had been punished for blaspheming by trying to equate themselves with, or challenge, deities. Arachne, however, chose to weave numerous scenes of mortal women (and a few female deities) being impregnated by gods who had transformed themselves into animals, humans, and other phenomena—that is, she audaciously chose to depict *hieros gamos* divine birth, the bane of Athena's existence! Her scenes were of Zeus's unions with Europa, Asterie, Leda, Antiope, Mnemosyne, Persephone, and an unnamed daughter of Asopus; Poseidon's dalliances with Bisaltis, Demeter, Melantho, Medusa, and Aeolus's wife and daughter; Apollo's encounter with Isse; Dionysus's moment with Erigone; and Cronos's tryst with Philyra, the mother of Cheiron. Athena tore up Arachne's tapestry, struck her several times on the forehead with a shuttle, and ultimately transformed her into a spider who would eternally spin her thread and weave her web.

As a weaver gifted by Athena, Arachne could be read as a priestess of Athena, perhaps one who was also involved in attempting divine birth herself. For, as I showed in the previous chapter, weaving was a symbol of the incarnation of souls and was connected with Neith, thus rendering it a metaphor for parthenogenesis. The motif of Athena striking Arachne with the shuttle further calls to mind a mysterious symbol depicted over anthropomorphic images of Neith that some have conjectured may be a weaving shuttle (see, e.g., Budge [1904] 1969, 1:451). It may be that, as a priestess, Arachne hubristically believed herself destined to be greater and ultimately more glorified than the goddess herself in her parthenogenetic abilities. It also may be that she challenged the utility of pure parthenogenesis, finding value in the concept of *hieros gamos* unions with gods, as depicted in her tapestry. Surely such hubris and sacrilege would have been seen as worthy of punishment from the standpoint of a pure parthenogenesis cult dedicated to Athena. That the spider also spontaneously spins thread out of its own body renders it symbolic of parthenogenesis, thus making Arachne's metamorphosis into this creature a particularly fitting fate for one who may have challenged the goddess's parthenogenetic authority.

Aethra

Yet another story suggesting a transgressive *hieros gamos* union on the part of a priestess of Athena is that of the legendary princess Aethra. Pausanias (2.33.1) relates that in obedience to a dream in which Athena appeared to her, Aethra waded across the channel from

Troizen in Argolis to the island of Sphaeria, carrying libations for the dead hero Sphaerus. After she crossed, however, she had intercourse with Poseidon on the island. Because of this supposedly unexpected encounter, Aethra established on the island a temple of Athena Apaturia (Deceitful), and renamed the island Hiera (Sacred Island). She also established a custom for the Troizenian maidens of dedicating their maidenhood belts before wedlock to Athena Apaturia.

Given Aethra's role in establishing a temple to Athena, it is likely that she was a priestess of the goddess. What is particularly interesting is that both Apollodorus (3.15.7, 3.16.2) and Hyginus (*Fabulae* 37) relate that her intercourse with Poseidon occurred *on the same night* as her intercourse with Aegeus, king of Athens. Apollodorus relates that Aegeus, fearing that he would not have an heir, had consulted the oracle at Delphi about the problem, and was advised, essentially, not to have intercourse before returning to Athens—and his wife. He traveled to Troizen, where he shared the oracle with King Pittheus. The king privately discerned the oracle's meaning: Aegeus would have a son by whomever he consorted with next. Pittheus thus shrewdly put the king in bed with Aethra, his daughter, and conception did indeed follow. The child of the union was the legendary hero Theseus, whose warfaring exploits in Greek mythical history are legion.

As Plutarch (*Greek and Roman Parallel Stories* 34) remarks, it was understood that *Poseidon* was the child's father, not Aegeus. I propose this episode thus describes an instance of the second type of *hieros gamos* divine birth outlined in my taxonomy in Chapter 1, *hieros gamos* by surrogate, whereby the god was thought to come through the body of the human male during the sex act. In Aethra's case, then, it seems human seed was used, but the soul of the child was thought to come from the god himself. It is thus likely that the encounter between Aethra and Aegeus was not a chance one, but a ritual act conducted with specific purpose: to engender what was believed to be a heroic/divine heir for the previously sonless (and hence anxious) king of Athens. As a priestess of Athena knowledgeable about such mysteries, Aethra may have been conscripted for the task. The setting of the encounter may also have been the island of Sphaeria, where her union with Poseidon was said to have occurred.

Like Athens, Troizen was also a location that Athena and Poseidon both contended for (Pausanias 2.30.6), suggesting a power struggle between the cults dedicated to the two gods there. Thus, one may conjecture that Aethra was pressured by the Poseidon cult (perhaps her father was a follower?) to turn her services toward *hieros gamos* activity with the god. Given that, as we have seen, Athena was thought to be completely opposed to her priestesses cavorting with Poseidon, it is likely that the "deception" in Aethra's case may be some deception rendered on the part of the Poseidon cult to engage her services. Perhaps such a "deception" was thought to have occurred, again, in the trance state. It also may be that Aethra's dream was thought to have been sent not by Athena, but by Poseidon himself, and that this may have been understood as the "deception." I suggest that Aethra's changing the name of the island to "Sacred," her setting up a temple to Athena, and her establishing the custom of girls offering their "belts," that is, their "virginity" itself, to the goddess may have been a form of propitiation to circumvent or lessen the wrath she may have fully expected to experience on the part of the Holy *Parthenos* she served. As we saw in the case of the Athenian maidens required to carry in ritual fashion the sacred objects of the goddess without looking at them, and as we will see later in the case of the Locrian maidens sent to minister Athena's sanctuary in Ilion (Troy) in recompense for the rape of an Athena priestess, having virgin girls conduct ongoing rites in Athena's honor seems to have served to appease the goddess in cases when the purity of her pure parthenogenetic priestesshood had been violated.

Auge

Yet another female who incurred the wrath of Athena was Auge, the daughter of King Aleus of Tegea. According to the tradition told by various writers, Auge was impregnated by the hero Heracles while he was still a mortal roaming the earth.[25] After Auge gave birth to Telephus, she left the child in the precincts of the sanctuary of Athena for protection and rearing (Apollodorus 2.7.4). In displeasure, the goddess sent a pestilence on the land, and Auge's father tracked down the cause to the infant left in the sanctuary. He subsequently set the infant out to be exposed for death on Mt. Parthenion and sent Auge away to be sold into slavery. She was subsequently given to the prince of Teuthrania, who made her his wife.

Although this appears to be a story of mere earthly union, there are several clues that it may represent a *hieros gamos* encounter. One is Heracles' ambiguous ontological status as both human and divine, with his full apotheosis occurring after his death (Apollodorus 2.7.7). It may be that by uniting with Heracles, Auge was understood to be uniting with a "god."

Furthermore, it seems clear that Auge was a priestess of Athena. This is suggested first of all by the fact that she was a princess. As we saw in the cases of the daughters of Cecrops and Erechtheus, royal daughters were frequently priestesses, possibly because their role automatically provisioned it. Indeed, one story specifically says that Aleus appointed his daughter priestess of Athena to guard against an oracle that her son would kill Aleus's male children (see, e.g., Frazer's commentary in Apollodorus 1967, 2:252–54n2).

The possibility that Auge's conception of Telephus was thought to be a divine one is further strengthened by the motif of her leaving her child in a temple to Athena. For this recalls Athena's having "taken in" the parthenogenetically conceived child Erichthonius despite the fact that she was unhappy with the manner of his conception. The reference in Auge's myth to Mt. Parthenion, "Mountain of the Virgin," located on the border between Argolis and Arcadia, also has parthenogenetic associations, not the least of which is its very name. I propose the name was an indicator that the mountain was the location of a divine birth priestesshood. This possibility is indeed intimated by Callimachus (*Hymn 4 to Delos* 70–1), who identifies Mt. Parthenion as a "holy hill" associated with Auge and mentions it as second in a list of places in Greece that Leto solicited to provide sanctuary while she gave birth to her son by Zeus, Apollo. As I argue in Chapter 4, Leto was a holy *parthenos;* thus, her soliciting of the "mountain" for her confinement lends support to the idea that it was a place where such priestesses were thought to find a holy sisterhood. Mt. Parthenion also appears in the story of Atalante, who was herself exposed on the mountain, only to be raised by a "she-bear" and to become dedicated to the priestesshood of Artemis. Atalante gave birth to a child significantly named Parthenopaeus by the god Ares (Apollodorus 3.9.2; Hyginus *Fabulae* 99). As I discuss in Chapter 4, the bear was a symbol of Artemis, another parthenogenetic goddess, and thus the story of Atalante's being "raised" by the bear may well allude to her being raised by a divine birth priestesshood on Mt. Parthenion that was dedicated to Artemis. The fact that Auge was honored as a heroine with a special mound tomb that featured a bronze statue of a naked woman, still seen in Pausanias's day (8.4.9–10), is the final piece of information indicating that she was believed to merit the status of a holy *parthenos.*

These many details, then, suggest that the myth of Auge's union with Heracles was considered a form of *hieros gamos,* again perhaps one conducted under duress or subterfuge—or perhaps one ambivalently entered into by a priestess caught between her loyalty to her vows and her desire to experience intercourse of a particularly intense nature. Indeed, Apollodorus (2.7.4) refers to Heracles as having "debauched" (*ephtheiren*) Auge, a situation that recalls

Medusa's so-called rape by Poseidon. Moreover, as I argued earlier in the chapter, the pomegranate symbol found at the earliest level of Athena's cult in Tegea suggests that the goddess there retained perhaps more fully than in other locations her identity as a Virgin Mother. That her virgin priestesses correspondingly should have been bound to pure parthenogenesis would have made Auge's transgression a severe one, indeed.

Iodama

Another story that may allude to this dynamic is that of Iodama. As Pausanias (9.34.1) relates, legend held that when this priestess entered Athena's sacred precinct in Coroneia in Phocis one night, she suddenly encountered the goddess herself. Looking upon the head of Medusa that Athena wore on her tunic, however, Iodama was turned to stone. Pausanias reports that a specially designated woman of his own day (probably another priestess of Athena) was still wont to light a fire daily on an altar dedicated to Iodoma, simultaneously repeating three times aloud that Iodama "was living and asking for fire."

We again may discern in this the possible history of a priestess who took a trance journey to encounter the realm of the divine, perhaps even to attempt parthenogenetic conception. But in Iodama's case, something evidently went wrong: she looked at the face of Medusa, the high priestess who had already transgressed against pure parthenogenesis in her (perhaps unwitting) union with Poseidon in the temple of the goddess. Might this refer to the temptation on Iodama's part to go the way of the unfortunate high Libyan priestess and consort with a god? Iodama's being "turned to stone" may be read as her not surviving her trance journey as a result of her having broken a taboo, and her being found dead and in a state of rigor mortis. As in the case of holy *parthenoi* who were thought to have been successful in their pursuit of divine conception, however, Iodama seems to have achieved divine honors nonetheless, as evidenced by the altar that was kept to her. Perhaps the altar and corresponding ritual were allusions to a story of a parthenogenetic priestess's believed near miss in fulfilling her ultimate goal, an attempt that was deemed still worthy of honor.

Cassandra and the Taboo of the Palladium

The myths suggest that Athena was clear about when she considered a rape of one of her virgin priestesses to be a rape and when she considered it not to be. In contrast to the above-mentioned episodes, in the case of Ajax's assault of the priestess Cassandra, Athena apparently discerned a bona fide rape worthy of punishment. Apollodorus (E6.20–22) relates that during the sack of Troy, the Locrian hero Ajax raped Cassandra as she clung to the wooden statue of Athena; it is likely that this was the very Palladium itself, which was the most holy statue to Athena at Troy. In retaliation, the goddess sent a plague upon the Locrians three years after they regained their own country. The Delphic oracle told them that to appease Athena they would need to maintain the presence of two maidens as suppliants at the goddess's sanctuary in Ilion (Troy) over a 1000-year period, and they did so. The maidens lived in an ascetic manner, tending to and never leaving the sanctuary, and were replaced when they died.[26] Because the Ilians stoned to death any new priestesses whom they caught outside the protected precinct of the sanctuary, the Locrians began sending replacements by night, eventually smuggling them in as infants with their nurses.[27]

The rape by Ajax of Cassandra at Athena's most holy statue was a particularly grave transgression given that, according to one tradition, males were not even supposed to look at the Palladium. Plutarch (*Greek and Roman Parallel Stories* 17) relates, on the authority of Aristeides the Milesian in his *Italian History,* that the nobleman Antylus was blinded for breaking this taboo when he rescued the statue from the burning shrine of Vesta in Rome. This Palladium was purportedly the same statue that had stood in Athena's temple at Troy, and was supposedly the very image the goddess herself had fashioned to commemorate her fallen comrade Pallas.[28] The detail that males were not to look at the statue, a taboo we assume also functioned in the earlier days in Troy, supports the conjecture that the early Athena cult was largely the province of women, and that certainly its most central mysteries, which I propose were parthenogenetic, were not for men's eyes.

Triteia

One final female figure worth mentioning in relation to Athena is Triteia. According to Pausanias (7.22.8), Triteia was, like Pallas, the daughter of Triton, the "river" in North Africa, and was considered to be a priestess of Athena. One legend held that Triteia mated with Ares and gave birth to Melanippus, who founded an Achaian city that he named after his mother. In the sanctuary of Athena in that city was a replica of the Palladium, by which Athena was worshipped. The local people gave divine honors to Triteia, venerating her in tandem with Ares.

Here we have the apotheosis, or divinization, of the priestess of Athena thought to have given birth to a god's child, which is perfectly in line with the argument I have made that parthenogenetic mothers were raised to the level of divinity. This legend also brings us full circle back to ancient Libya and the river Triton, pointing to the enduring connection between Athena and North Africa in her Greek cult. As a "daughter of the river Triton," Triteia, whose name also recalls Athena's surnames *Tritogeneia* and *Tritonis,* was also classified as one of numerous "nymphs" who populated Greek legend in connection with Artemis, in particular. I further explore the topic of the nymphs as virgin priestesses in the next chapter devoted to Artemis.

CHAPTER 4

ARTEMIS'S DIVINE BIRTH
PRIESTESSHOOD

Artemis was another Greek goddess who possessed the title *Parthenos*. There are many clues that she, like Athena, was originally considered a Virgin Mother. Numerous myths also suggest that a divine birth priestesshood was similarly dedicated to this goddess in early Greek cult. One of the key indicators in this regard is Artemis's important relationship with the so-called nymphs. Such stories include many instances of broken virgin vows and seductions or "rapes" by male gods, resulting in retaliatory wrath on the part of the goddess. I propose this suggests that, like Athena's divine birth priestesshood, the Artemisian priestesshood was believed to undergo a transition from pure parthenogenesis to *hieros gamos* practice.

ARTEMIS AS VIRGIN MOTHER

As she was known in Greece, Artemis seems to have had four distinct and overlapping identities that may reflect how she was seen and adopted during different time periods and in various regions. In one aspect, she was the twin of Apollo and daughter of Leto (e.g., *Hymns to Artemis* 9.2 and 27.3). In another, she was the goddess of the nymphs of Arcadia, the mountainous, forested center of the Peloponnesus. In a third, she was centered in Tauris and Bauronia, where at one time human sacrifices may have been offered to her.[1] In a fourth, she was the Asiatic fructifying and all-nourishing nature goddess of Ephesus in Anatolia.

Classics scholars generally agree that Artemis originated in the pre-Greek era.[2] Her name does not appear to be Greek, and, according to Guthrie (1967, 99), in her early form she was "one of the greatest, if not the greatest, of the deities worshipped by the inhabitants of pre-Hellenic Greece, of Western Asia Minor, and of Minoan Crete." He thus contends (101) that the patriarchal invaders who established what was ancient Greece found this goddess already in place when they came to occupy these regions and that they incorporated her into what became the Olympian pantheon. Artemis's identification with the Phrygian Cybele, who yoked lions to her chariot,[3] and with the Cappadocian Ma has prompted suggestions of her possible Asiatic origin; she also may have derived from the Minoan Mistress of the Animals or from an Arcadian cult (Guthrie 1967, 99, 106). On Crete, she was identified with the mother goddesses Britomartis, Dictynna, and Eileithyia.[4]

Artemis's probable pre-Greek aspect as goddess of nature may be reflected in her Homeric title *Potnia Theron*, Mistress of the Wild Animals (Homer *Iliad* 21.470). In Greek mythology, her realms were always the mountains, where she was said to have dwelt (Callimachus *Hymn 3 to Artemis* 19–20). Numerous animals were sacred to her or depicted by her side in text and iconography, including deer, leopards, lions, bears, fish, buzzards, and snakes.[5] Pausanias (8.22.4–8) further relates that in Stymphalus in Arcadia, where a great festival was held to her, her sanctuary contained carvings of the Stymphalian birds. These were deadly creatures that Heracles slew as one of his 12 labors, and were considered sacred to her. Behind the temple stood marble statues of maidens with the legs of birds, underscoring her ornithological associations. Such imagery suggests a connection between Artemis and what appears to have been a bird goddess of the Neolithic period in Old Europe, confirming Artemis's great antiquity (Gimbutas 1999, 155–7).

In Ephesus, where a monumental temple famous throughout the ancient world stood in her honor, Artemis's statue reflected her attributes as a goddess of animals, fertility, and nurture. Numerous large protrusions suggestive of breasts emanated from her chest, while a variety of animals and insects were depicted in relief covering her entire body and crown (Baring and Cashford 1991, 329). Such imagery leads Farnell ([1896–1909] 1977, 2:455–6) to conclude that Artemis was in the earliest Greek religion an earth goddess, associated chiefly with wildlife, growth of the fields, and human birth. At Ephesus, she was worshipped in this "old way" right through classical times (Guthrie 1967, 103). Given that the other primal Greek goddess who was similarly characterized, Ge/Gaia, was the parthenogenetic "creatrix" of all of nature's animal manifestations,[6] I propose that in her original form, Artemis, too, was a parthenogenetic goddess. Like Athena, Artemis held the title *Parthenos*, Virgin. In the Homeric *Hymn 9 to Artemis* (2), she is named *parthenos iocheaira*, "Virgin of Profuse Arrows"; in *Hymn* 27 (2) she is called *parthenon aidoiên*, "Revered Virgin." Apollodorus (1.4.1) affirms that Artemis remained a stalwart virgin, and Diodorus Siculus (5.3.4) specifically says that "she made the same choice of maidenhood" as had Kore [Persephone] and Athena. On the Black Sea and in Thrace, the archaic Artemis as war goddess also appeared under the name *Parthenos*. That she was an archaic goddess indicates that her virginal aspect was "not the product of a relatively late and exclusively Greek development" (Kerenyi 1978, 20).

Much has been made of the seemingly contradictory fact of Artemis's having been a virgin, yet, originally, an "All-mother" (Guthrie 1967, 101); a fierce guardian of her followers' chasteness, yet protector of those who gave birth. But, as Guthrie (1967, 103) notes, the "childlessness" of Artemis that was characteristic of her in classical times and later was not "original." Her identification with Eileithyia, the goddess of childbirth, he says, "is a strong indication that she was once . . . a patron of women's life in all its phases and was therefore supposed to have experienced them all herself." All, I suggest, except for sexual union. As with Athena, who was similarly a virgin and preferred the virginity of her followers, the paradoxical aspects of Artemis's own sexual status are resolved if we consider the possibility that Artemis was originally a parthenogenetic goddess, at once virgin and generative.

ARTEMIS AS GODDESS OF THE AMAZONS

Artemis's principle attributes were the bow, quiver, and arrows or a spear.[7] She was the paragon of the huntress; ancient legends recount her love for slaying wild beasts and episodes of her engaging in, or resting from, hunting expeditions.[8] Guthrie (1967, 102) confirms that Artemis's huntress aspect was indeed pre-Greek, suggesting it was one of her most archaic characteristics. Farnell ([1896–1909] 1977, 2:427) further posits that Artemis probably reflected quite ancient totemistic ideas of hunting and fishing tribes in which women held particular status.

Since Amazonian imagery figures large among the "nymph" priestesses of Artemis, as I discuss throughout this chapter, it is important to note that, like Neith, Artemis was a patron goddess of Amazons.

Greek writings identified two sets of legendary Amazons, one, as discussed in Chapter 3, located in ancient North Africa and another whose homeland was variously posited as western Anatolia (contemporary Turkey) or northeastern Anatolia along the Black Sea (Bennett 1967, 12). The latter, in particular, was the location of the legendary Thermadon River and the Amazon-founded city of Themiscyra. Hence, this group of warrior women is frequently referred to as the Thermadon Amazons. Legend and iconography record this group as having unsuccessfully marched on Athens and been vanquished by the Greeks.[9] Callimachus (*Hymn 3 to Artemis* 237–47) relates that in Ephesus, Amazons set up a statue to Artemis under a large oak tree.[10]

Just as Diodorus treated the Libyan Amazons as historical women, so various writers describe actual locations where the legendary Thermadon Amazons were said to have had a presence.[11] Writing about the places of interest of his time, Pausanias (2.22.9) relates that Celenderis, for example, was the location of Theseus's defeat of the Amazons. In 2.21.4, he mentions that in Troezen, *Lyceia,* or "Wolfish," was a surname of Artemis among the Amazons, and that a temple to Artemis Lycea stood there. Elsewhere (3.25.3), he reports that in Pyrrichos, a village in Lacedaemonia, a sanctuary was dedicated to Artemis Astrateia, so named because the Amazons were said to have stayed their advance (*strateia*) here. These "women of Thermadon," he says, dedicated a wooden image of the goddess in the shrine, and another to Apollo Amazonius. On the island of Patmos, southwest of Samos, was a place called the Amazonium, suggesting an Amazon presence there, as well (Bennett 1967, 9). Herodotus (4.105–19) relates that when the Thermadon Amazons were defeated in their war against the Greeks (an event dated to after the Trojan War), they eventually settled at the foot of the Caucasus Mountains between the Black and Caspian seas. There they interbred with the Scythians and became the Sauromatians, a people of his day whose women were warriors and hunters, whom he describes at length. Recent archaeological evidence by Davis-Kimball (2002) has confirmed the presence of warrior women in this part of the world in the Iron Age, lending weight to the possibility that the accounts such as Herodotus's attesting to Amazon-like tribes in the region were indeed historical in nature.

NYMPHS IN ANCIENT LITERATURE

It is important in constructing the argument that "nymph" was in many cases a marker for a divine birth priestess, a holy *parthenos,* to first outline the nature and classification of "nymphs" as they were traditionally represented in Greek thought. In legend and cult, nymphs were frequently portrayed as minor divinities of the wild places. They fell into many (sometimes overlapping) classes, according to the areas of nature they inhabited. The Oceanids, daughters of the great river Oceanus thought to encircle the earth, were the oldest and presided over the fresh waters.[12] Among their ranks were the *Naiades* (nymphs of springs, rivers, streams, wells, and fountains), *Nephelai* (nymphs of rainclouds), and *Aurai* (nymphs of moist, cool breezes). A partial list of other nymph classes includes the *Dryades* and *Hamadryades* (nymphs of trees, forests, and groves), *Meliai* and *Melissai* (nymphs of the mountain ash tree and/or honeybees), *Epimelides* (nymphs of pastures), *Leimonides* (nymphs of flowery meadows), *Oreiades* (nymphs of the mountains and caves), *Anthoussai* (nymphs of flowers), *Nereides* and *Haliai* (nymphs of the sea), *Lampades* (torch-bearing nymphs of the underworld), *Asteriai* (nymphs of the stars), and *Mainades* and *Thyiades* (orgiastic nymphs of Dionysus) (Theoi Project 2000–7, s.v. *Nymphai*). In certain cases, nymphs were further grouped according to names derived from the towns and cities with which they were associated, such as the *Nysiades* (nymphs of Nysa), *Dodonides* (nymphs of Dodona), *Lemniai* (nymphs of Lemnos), and so forth.[13] The multiple-figured maidens known as the Muses, the Charities, and the Graces were also closely related to the nymphs (Harrison [1903] 1957, 289).

Each Greek island had its own *Naias* nymph who represented the primary water source of the island, generally a well or spring. These nymphs were often considered the daughters of the nearest mainland river, whose streams were thought to supply their spring with fresh water. In Greek mainland towns and cities, also, *Naias* nymphs were associated with the primary sources of fresh water, and were similarly thought to be daughters of the local river god. Greek colonies also sometimes gave their local nymph the name of a nymph daughter of a river in Greece, as in the case of the Sicilian nymph Arethusa (Ovid *Metamorphoses* 5.578–641). Various other springs and fountains outside Greek mainland or colonial towns had their own nymph or nymphs.

Nymphs were venerated and honored with sanctuaries in many parts of Greece, especially near springs, groves, and caves.[14] They often had cults, particularly at springs that were thought to possess special properties, such as healing or the granting of special inspiration (Theoi Project 2000–7, s.v. *Naiades*). Testimonies to the cult of the nymphs in Homer (*Odyssey* 13.102–12) indicate that such female figures were worshipped at least as far back as the eighth century B.C.E., and probably earlier. The Homeric descriptions had counterparts in archaeologically established cult practice in the early archaic period, as at the Corycian cave of Mt. Parnassus (Larson 2001, 123–4), which I discuss more fully in Chapter 7.

ARTEMISIAN NYMPHS AS A SPECIAL CASE

As a whole, nymphs were considered particularly identified with Artemis. In Greek mythology, these female figures were Artemis's favorite companions. In Callimachus (*Hymn 3 to Artemis* 13–6), the goddess asks Zeus to grant her a choir of 60 Oceanid nymphs, all nine-year-old maidens. She also asks for 20 nymphs of the Amnisus River in Crete as handmaids to tend her buskins and hounds. Artemis was generally associated with nymphs of all classes, however. Homer (*Odyssey* 6.107–8) describes her as the tallest and most lovely among her nymph companions. At least two of her favorite hunting partners, Britomartis and Cyrene, were identified as nymphs (Callimachus 189–91, 206–7). Elsewhere, nymphs accompanied Artemis in the hunt or in her travels, assisted her with her hunting tasks, or joined her in her bath out in the wild. Nymphs in her company were also depicted as relishing the foot race.[15]

In various mythological scenes, Artemis performed dances with nymphs, typically in circle formation.[16] During their dances, nymphs sometimes also sang to the goddess in praise. Thus not only did nymphs accompany Artemis, they also actively venerated her. Apollonius Rhodius (*Argonautica* 1.1222–5), for example, writes of nymphs of Pegae in Mysia singing the praises of Artemis by night. Callimachus (*Hymn 3 to Artemis* 170) describes them circling her in dance. The Homeric *Hymn 3 to Apollo* (157–61) similarly refers to the maidens of Delos singing praises to Artemis and to honored ancestors. Virgil (*Aeneid* 1.498–500) says that 1,000 mountain nymphs typically wove their dances around Artemis by the banks of the Eurotas River or over the Cynthian slopes of Delos.

Nymphs, particularly those associated with Artemis, frequently occupied an ambiguous ontological status, somewhere between human and divine. While some legends grant a nymph supernatural status, others render the very same figure human, underscoring the flexibility and ambiguity with which they were viewed. We see this, for example, in the case of a number of Artemisian nymphs. Herodotus (4.35.1) relates that two virgins named Arge and Opis, for example, who came from the land of the "Hyperboreans," were the first to bring the worship of Artemis and Apollo to the island of Delos. After their death, they were

buried behind the temple of Artemis and given divine honors, which
included having hymns sung to them by the Delians and Ionians.
Yet Callimachus (*Hymn 4 to Delos* 292–3), who names these original
Delian maidens Opis, Loxo, and Hecaerge,[17] calls them "daughters of
Boreas," that is, of the North Wind. This latter genealogy renders them
nymphs, making it uncertain as to whether they should be classified as
"nymphs" or historical priestesses. Callisto is another female companion of Artemis with murky ontological status, a fact noted by Apollodorus himself (3.8.2). The mythographer reports that while Hesiod
describes Callisto as a nymph, other writers identify her as the daughter
of either Lycaon, Nycteus, or Ceteus, making her a mortal.

The existence of these and many other "nymph/woman hybrids"
throughout mythology is, I believe, a clue to what I propose was likely
the true meaning of the "nymph" epithet in many cases. First, it is
important to note that nymphs enjoyed a very ancient genealogy that
in some cases rendered them as "predating" any of the Olympian gods.
Moreover, this ancient lineage connected them with parthenogenesis.
Hesiod (*Theogony* 129–30) and Apollonius Rhodius (*Argonautica*
1.498), for example, state that nymphs, particularly the Oreides of
the mountains, were the offspring of Ge/Gaia, who brought them
forth parthenogentically in the early stages of creation before she
began producing offspring sexually with Uranus. Thus the earliest
nymphs themselves, the mountain nymphs, in particular, were considered the parthenogenetic progeny of the Earth Mother. Later, when
Ge/Gaia's son/lover Uranus was castrated by Cronus, the *Meliai*, the
fruit tree or honey nymphs, were born spontaneously from the bloody
drops she received (Hesiod *Theogony* 180–7). Here we have another
parthenogenetic story in the birthing of nymphs. Yet a third legend
regarding the parthenogenetic emergence of nymphs can be found in
Pausanias (10.32.9), who relates that ancient poets depicted nymphs
as being spontaneously born of trees, especially oaks. This is relevant
to the discussion in Chapter 6 of Dodona as a possible location of a
divine birth priesthood, as the oak tree was the central symbol of
that oracular center. Thus these older stories render "nymphs" in their
status as goddess-like figures in their own right as originally associated
with what I have labeled pure parthenogenesis.

Upon further analysis, one finds that the vast majority of nymphs
were virgin maidens.[18] As I discuss in the rest of this chapter, as well
as in Chapters 6 and 7 on Dodona and Delphi, numerous such virgin nymphs specifically were said to have given birth to the children
of gods such as Zeus, Poseidon, Dionysus, Apollo, and Hermes.
When the child of such a union was a male (the great majority of cases),

he was generally honored as the founder of a lineage. The town, city, colony, or landform (e.g., mountain) he was associated with was also frequently named after him. When the child was a female, she was sometimes considered a "nymph," as well, and either also had children via unions with gods or became the wife of the local hero/leader/king. Sometimes she was gifted with other special powers. As a mother of a divine child, the "nymph" herself frequently was rendered the eponym of a town, city, island, or lake.[19]

Thus, as mothers of heroes and heroines through unions with gods, nymphs served the very functions I have been ascribing to divine birth priestesses. The final element that characterizes what I have identified as holy *parthenoi*—apotheosis—can be seen in the case of the nymphs, as well. Certainly the establishment of cults in their honor demonstrates that many of them were divinized. I propose that the honoring of them through eponymous place names was also part of this "divinizing" process, as it served as a way of "immortalizing" them. Moreover, I suggest that the very granting of the epithet *nymph* itself, which connoted a divine being, was a mark of the divine status they were seen to achieve precisely in recognition of what was believed to have been their divine birthing of a god's child.

That nymphs were in many cases originally mortal humans before their apotheosis is indicated most strongly in the cases of "nymph/human hybrids," mentioned earlier. One can read such legends depicting female figures as both "nymphs" and "mortals" as indicative of situations in which human women were later (probably after their death) granted divine status as nymphs. Thus I propose that the "nymph" title was in many cases the posthumous marker for a historical virgin priestess who had been part of a divine birth cult in her lifetime. I posit that the ancient genealogy pointing to certain nymphs as parthenogenetic offspring of Ge/Gaia suggests that originally such priestesses may have been involved in attempts at pure parthenogenesis in consonance with their dedication to the Earth Mother. Such priestesses may have become affiliated with Artemis as her cult came to prominence. The emphasis on virginity in the myths about Artemisian "nymphs" suggests that these priestesses continued to engage in parthenogenetic practices until, like Athena's early priestesses, they experienced the intrusion of patriarchal religion. At that point, as the myths to be explored attest, they encountered forces attempting to lure them into *hieros gamos* practices.

I wish to make it clear that in suggesting that certain so-called nymphs may represent historical priestesses, I do not mean to suggest that *all* nymphs who can be identified in the primary sources should be thought of in this way. The category of "nymph" is complex and multivalent, and in many instances no doubt designated what were believed to be non-corporeal spirit beings associated with nature.[20] I merely wish to tease out a category of female figures generally identified in the ancient literature as "nymphs" whose ontological status is in fact hazy.

Reading various legends of nymphs as possible histories of priestesses in remote antiquity provides a great deal of suggestive evidence about the functioning—and fate—of the early Artemisian divine birth priestesshood. The idea that such myths indeed reflected very ancient cult practices finds at least some support in the fact that ethnographic commentators of the Hellenistic period frequently describe similar activities associated with mythological nymphs indeed enacted in the cults of their day. Pausanias (3.10.7, 4.16.9), for example, writes of maidens of Caryae holding "chorus dances" every year to Artemis that resemble the mythological accounts of song and dance, mentioned earlier, conducted by "nymphs" in honor of the goddess.[21]

Looking back from this perspective at legends discussed a bit earlier, Herodotus's account of the maidens Opis and Arge becomes a history of the foundation of the cult of Artemis on Delos. Moreover, the mythologem that they were the "children of the Boreas/North Wind" can be read as an allusion to their own parthenogenetic capacity, given, as I discussed in Chapter 3, that the Boreas was associated with parthenogenetic impregnation. Seen in this light, the numerous descriptions in the ancient texts of Artemis's "nymphs" as athletes and hunters, moreover, can be interpreted as accounts of Amazon priestesses. As such, these accounts correspond perfectly with those describing what I argued earlier were probably historical Amazon women who venerated Artemis. Callisto, who is identified as a "tree nymph" belonging to Artemis's sacred circle, was one such figure who may have had a real history. Ovid (*Metamorphoses* 2.410–6) describes her in clear Amazonian terms as

> not one who spent her time in spinning soft fibres of wool, or in arranging her hair in different styles. She was one of Diana's [Artemis's] warriors, wearing her tunic pinned together with a brooch, her tresses carelessly caught back by a white ribbon, and carrying in her hand a light javelin or her bow.
>
> (Ovid 1955, 61, trans. Innes)

Artemis's favored "nymph" Britomartis, described as "delighting in running and in the chase" (Pausanias 2.30.3), likewise may have been a real priestess who worshipped Artemis on Crete.

The legends about nymphs affirm that virginity was a requirement for entering and remaining in the Artemisian retinue, which was indeed an important aspect of the historical Artemisian priesshood, particularly at Ephesus (Strabo 14.1.23). Callisto is portrayed on one occasion, for example, as touching Artemis's bow and pledging eternal virginity to the goddess, a vow Artemis rewarded by making her the leader of her troupe (Ovid *Fasti* 2.155–60). But the stories also indicate that the nymphs' virginity was constantly under attack. Apollodorus (1.4.5), for example, relates a legend that Artemis shot the hunter Orion as he attempted to rape Opis. That Herodotus names Opis as one of the first historical priestesses of Artemis at Delos suggests that the Orion mythologem reflects an actual male intrusion into the Delian precinct.[22] I thus posit that the various legendary instances of nymphs fending off male gods and mortals represent the effort of the Artemisian priesthood to fight the mounting pressure under patriarchy to join the ranks of *hieros gamos* cults or to disperse their energies altogether by engaging in conventional sexual relations.

Legendary Nymph/Priestesses in Artemis's Retinue

I now turn my attention to specific legends about Artemisian nymph/priestesses.[23] These stories suggest that, in many cases, Artemisian priestesses may have been considered fiercer in their resolve to remain true to their vows than their counterparts in Athena's cult, whose extant stories, examined in Chapter 3, overwhelmingly reveal capitulation to the lure of sexual intercourse with gods.

Syrinx

Syrinx was one Artemisian nymph/priestess who was reportedly successful in avoiding predation by a god. A huntress, she lived in the mountains of Arcadia as a virgin dedicated to her goddess. The woodlands god Pan is said to have pursued her through the wilderness until she came to the river Ladon, where she begged the "sisters of the water" for help. These female figures transformed her into the river reed (*syrinx,* from where her name derives), which subsequently issued forth a witching kind of music that inspired Pan to wax together reeds of different lengths and create what came to be known as "pan pipes" (Ovid *Metamorphoses* 1.688–710).

With Syrinx we have a case of a female changing her form to escape the sexual advances of a male god. The magical nature of what is described in this and numerous other stories of "metamorphosis" may suggest, as I posited in the cases of Athena's priestesses Medusa and Iodama, that the realm of the pursuit being described is in fact the landscape of trance. Such a possibility is lent particular support in cases of "metamorphosis," as the phenomenon may well reference what is known in studies of indigenous shamans as *transmorphing*, or *shape shifting*.[24] This is the process of mentally and/or physically assuming the psychological and physical aspects of an animal, insect, plant, or earth form to access what is believed to be its strength and perceptions, in order to achieve wisdom and spiritual power, heal others, transmit prophecy, and so forth.[25] Shape shifting was considered in the ancient Graeco-Roman world to be a standard power of holy persons and magicians.[26] The legendary herbalist and magician (*pharmakos*) Mestra, for example, was said to possess the capacity to transform herself into any animal (Hesiod *Catalogue of Women* frag. 70, 2007, ed. Most). Proteus, the legendary seer, similarly was considered to be a shape shifter. Virgil (*Georgics* 4.440–5) says of him, "[He] changes himself into flame and hideous beast and flowing river. But when no strategem wins escape, vanquished he returns to himself, and at last speaks with human voice" (Virgil 1947, 1:227, trans. Fairclough). As I proposed in Chapter 1, it is likely that any kind of attempt at divine conception, whether of the pure parthenogenetic or *hieros gamos* variety, to refer to my taxonomy, would have been conducted in the deepest level of trance possible. Again, this may mean that a priestess believed to be in such a state was thought vulnerable to many kinds of intrusions from the spirit world—including a visitation by a lustful male god. We will again recall here the discussion of Medusa from Chapter 3, and the excerpt from the *Testament of Reuben* (5:5–6) attesting to a belief in antiquity that incorporeal male entities could indeed invade women's trance state with predatory sexual intent.

The story of Syrinx suggests that the attempt to "change shape" during such an episode into the likeness of plants, animals, and other objects may have been a means whereby a priestess was thought to be able to escape the unbidden visitor's clutches. Syrinx's myth therefore may describe a priestess who was particularly determined to stay on the pure parthenogenetic path devoted to Artemis and evade her spirit-world pursuer by any means necessary. The myth hints that another of her coping mechanisms may have been to call mentally upon the "female spirits of the waters." This may reference what was believed to be her prayerful communication to attempt to access the subtle awareness and assistance of other nymphs/priestesses in her hour of need. Syrinx's transformation into reeds may reference the fact that the attempt of this priestess to escape the predations of Pan resulted in her ultimate death in the trance state, and was therefore a form of self-sacrifice in loyal service to her goddess and her virgin vow.

Pholoe
Another nymph/priestess, Pholoe, is said to have escaped the god Pan partly through her own efforts and partly through the intervention of Artemis herself. Legend relates that after fleeing from the god in the woods of central Italy, Pholoe lay exhausted. Artemis roused the maiden by flicking her with one of her short arrows, which allowed her to outwit the approaching god by plunging herself deep into a nearby lake. Statius, in whose *Silvae* (2.3.1–61) this story appears, portrays the goddess on this occasion as disgustedly uttering to her nymph comrades, "Must my chaste band of followers ever grow fewer?" (Statius 1928, 1:109).

Such a sentiment may well reflect what plagued Artemis's pure parthenogenetic priestesses as they saw more and more of their number preyed upon by male gods and mortals. That Pholoe was also the name of a mountain in Arcadia is important here. Pausanias (8.27.17) relates that on this very mountain, Artemis shot to death the hero Buphagus because "he attempted an unholy sin against her godhead" (Pausanias 1931–5, 4:43, trans. Jones). Given that the name *Pholoe* appears in both Statius and Pausanias, the two stories may be related, although they are set in different geographical locations. Taken together, they may indicate that a divine birth priestesshood to which Pholoe belonged was located on the Arcadian mountain and that the attempted transgression against Artemis's godhead was in fact an attempted "rape" of Pholoe, whether by the human Bouphagos or the divine Pan while she was in trance. That she served as the eponym of the mountain indicates that she was considered to have been an important figure in the Artemisian cult. Again, I would argue that such "immortalization" reflected her status as a holy *parthenos*, even though no child is attributed to her in the extant legend.

The ambiguity expressed in the combined stories of Pausanias and Statius as to whether it was Artemis (on Mt. Pholoe) or one of her priestesses (Pholoe) who suffered an attempted violation against her is repeated in the story of Orion, mentioned earlier. In Callimachus (*Hymn 3 to Artemis* 265) and Hyginus (*Fabulae* 195; *Poetic Astronomy* 2.34) we hear that Artemis shot Orion for attempting to violate *her*, while Apollodorus (1.4.5) relates a tradition that she shot the hunter as he attempted to rape *Opis*, the priestess of Delos. Such stories, taken together, emphasize the idea that nymph/priestesses were considered hypostases (doubles) of goddesses they served (Opis being the cultic "equivalent" of Artemis). We also see this phenomenon in other cases, such as that of Eucleia, a virgin whom Plutarch (*Aristides* 20.6) says was "regarded by most as Artemis." I propose these legends with mortal male figures therefore refer to rape attempts made by human males against these (human) females. At the same time, a transgression against one of her priestesses was seen as a violation of the goddess herself.

It may well be, then, that the stories of "Artemis" slaying or outwitting various sexual predators reference priestesses who killed or foiled those who tried to tamper with the Artemisian cult.[27] This may be implied, for example, in the legend of Actaeon, son of Autonoe and Aristaeus, who was reared as a hunter on Mt. Cithaeron in Boeotia. One day while on a hunting excursion, Actaeon spied Artemis bathing. In punishment, the goddess angrily transformed him into a stag and drove his own hunting dogs to tear him to pieces.[28]

Ovid (*Metamorphoses* 3.178) adds that the nymphs were with Artemis at the time, and that all were naked. Hyginus (*Fabulae* 181) notes that the name of the stream in which they bathed was called *Parthenius*, "of the Maiden." These latter two details suggest that the transgression being described was in fact the male peering into female-only mysteries in association with Artemis. The name of the stream, *Parthenius*, which also emphasizes the importance of the virgin aspect, may indicate that these mysteries had to do with parthenogenesis. A detail offered by Diodorus Siculus (4.81.4–5) that Actaeon in fact sought to *seduce* Artemis may reference an attempted rape of one of her divine birth priestesses. This may find confirmation in Pausanias (9.2.3), who relates another story that Artemis drove Actaeon's hounds to kill him so as to prevent him from taking Semele as his wife. Semele was also likely a holy *parthenos* by virtue of the fact that she gave birth to Dionysus via her union with Zeus (Hesiod *Theogony* 940). Thus it may have been Semele-as-Artemis, specifically, who was Actaeon's intended victim in these related legends.

Arethusa

A similar case of male intent to disrupt the female mystery rituals through sexual predation can be found in the story of the river god Alpheius, who planned to rape Artemis at her all-night revels. The goddess tricked him by smearing her face and those of her "nymphs" with mud so that the river god could not distinguish her from the rest. In another tradition, the "nymph" Arethusa is named as the specific object of Alpheius's pursuit.[29] Again, this suggests that, as in the case of Pholoe, the two variants should be read together as a case of an Artemisian priestess who was pursued by a god. As in the story of Syrinx, Arethusa's experience involves shape shifting, suggesting the episode took place in the landscape of trance. In this case, to escape the god, Arethusa was transformed into a spring (some say by Artemis) and reemerged on the island of Ortygia off the coast of Sicily.[30] Again, as in the case of Syrinx, this could be a reference to her suicide or death.

Britomartis
Some stories of "nymphs" more explicitly refer to suicide as a means of protecting one's virginity. One such story is that of Britomartis, the "most loved" of Artemis's hunting companions (Callimachus *Hymn 3 to Artemis* 190–1). Myths relating that Britomartis was from Gortyn (Callimachus 190–1) or Caeno (Diodorus Siculus 5.76.3) suggest she was a nymph/priestess of Cretan origin. One tradition relates that to flee from King Minos of Crete, who had fallen in love with her on sight, she threw herself from the top of a cliff into fishing nets cast upon the water. According to the legend, Artemis subsequently turned Britomartis into a goddess. Indeed, in historical times, Britomartis was worshipped in Crete and Aegina (Callimachus *Hymn 3 to Artemis* 190–205; Pausanias 2.30.3). Another tradition says that to evade the lustful king, Britomartis jumped off a boat and fled into a grove, where a temple dedicated to her as Aphaea, "The One Who Disappeared," was allegedly erected (Antoninus Liberalis *Metamorphoses* 40). Her name, according to the ancient lexicographers, means "sweet virgin," which again emphasizes the virginal aspect in association with Artemis (Farnell [1896–1909] 1977, 2:476).

The story first suggests that nymph/priestesses of Artemis in some cases had connections with royal houses, as did several of Athena's priestesses mentioned in Chapter 3. We see this phenomenon in legends about Iphigeneia, daughter of the legendary king Agamemnon, who was a priestess of the goddess.[31] The story also suggests that Britomartis, as Artemis's "favorite," was a particularly respected and renowned priestess. This may be because of her particular talents. Diodorus Siculus 5.76.3) says Britomartis was known as *Dictynna,* "She of the Nets," because she invented the nets used in hunting.[32] Such an invention clearly would have rendered her an elevated personage along the lines of other famous legendary individuals who had brought significant inventions to humankind, such as Asclepius in the area of medicine. Britomartis's plunging into nets from a cliff, or her "disappearance" into the woods, ultimately suggests that she sacrificed herself in service to her goddess. Given that she is not credited with having birthed divine children, it may be this factor—self-sacrifice—that afforded her not only the title "nymph," but also full apotheosis into a goddess of high standing in her own right.

The Virgin of Tegea

Although she was not specifically called a nymph, an unnamed Tegean virgin similarly is said to have committed suicide to preserve her virginity. Pausanias (8.47.6) relates a story that this maiden, on the command of the lustful despot Aristomelidas of Orchomenus, was taken into captivity by a certain Chronius. Before she was delivered up to the despot, she killed herself for fear and shame. Accordingly, in a vision, Artemis stirred up Chronius against Aristomelidas, whereafter he slew the despot, fled to Tegea, and set up a sanctuary to the goddess. The insertion of Artemis into the story again suggests that here we have a history of a probable priestess of Artemis who wished to preserve her solemn vow to Artemisian (parthenogenetic) virginity.

Nicaea

It appears that not all Artemisian nymph/priestesses successfully avoided union with gods or mortals. One such individual was Nicaea. Although her story appears late, mainly in Nonnus's fifth-century C.E. work *Dionysiaca* (15.151–385, 16.1–405), I include it here as a possible survival of much older mythological material.[33] According to the poet, Nicaea was a virgin huntress dedicated to Artemis. She shot through the heart the shepherd Hymnus when he would not desist from pursuing her. The god Eros, angered by her cruelty, inspired Dionysus to fall in love with the maiden. Dionysus was finally able to succeed in ravaging her by tricking her into drinking the waters of a Naiad fountain that he temporarily turned to wine, thereby sending her into a stupor. After a half-hearted attempt to commit suicide by hanging, Nicaea gave birth to a daughter, Telete. Telete became a *mainad,* one who joined in the all-night revels associated with Dionysus.

In the detail of the "drunken sleep" we have what I propose is the most direct reference thus far to a non-ordinary state of consciousness on the part of an Artemisian priestess. It is highly likely that the "wine" motif in the story references the special wine mixture associated with the Dionysian revels, which, I submit, was entheogenic, as follows. Plutarch relates (*Table-Talk* 3.2.1–2/648B, 649A–B) that wine, when mixed with the berries of the ivy plant, created in the

imbiber "a disorder and a derangement like that induced by hen-
bane and many similar things which excite the intellect to madness"
(Plutarch 1969, 8:221–3, trans. Clement and Hoffleit). In other
words, it engendered a psychotropic, non-ordinary state of consciousness. The "ivy" reference here affirms that the "wine" being
described is a Dionysian sacrament, as ivy was an important element
in Dionysian rituals. Elsewhere (*Roman Questions* 112/291A–B),
for example, Plutarch says that ivy leaves themselves had the capacity
to "bring on a wineless drunkenness" and a "distracting breath of
madness," that is, again a psychotropic state. He adds that "women
possessed by Bacchic [i.e., Dionysian] frenzies rush straightway for
ivy and tear it to pieces, clutching it with their hands and biting it
with their teeth" (Plutarch 1927–69, 4:169, trans. Babbitt). This
was likely done, I propose, to allow them to maintain or intensify
their ecstatic trance state. Another possible piece of evidence supporting the argument that the "wine" mentioned in ancient accounts
frequently referred to an enthogenic substance can be found in the
legend of Aristaeus, who was said to have invented the mixing of
honey and wine (Pliny *Natural History* 14.6). That Aristaeus was
said to possess knowledge of the future (Cook 1895, 10) suggests
that his "mixing" involved creating psychoactive substances, given,
as Iamblichus attests (*Mysteries of Egypt* 1.3/Letter of Porphyry), the
ability to prophesy was thought to be generated through the drinking
of certain philters.

The story of Nicaea thus suggests either that she may have willingly
imbibed intoxicating wine, not quite anticipating the consequences,
or that she was "drugged." The result, I posit, was that she entered
into a non-ordinary state of consciousness in which it was thought
that she was unable to resist the amorous presence of the god. In
short, I contend that she experienced, unwittingly or not, what the
mainadic revelers attempted to achieve regularly in their nocturnal
ecstasies with the god.[34] For we will remember from Chapter 2 that
Dionysus was known for purportedly uniting sexually with women, as
attested in the well-documented case of the *basilinna,* who engaged
in a *hieros gamos* with the god in Athens. That Nicaea's condition may
have been aided and abetted by *mainades* is specifically suggested by
the motif that her daughter, Telete, became an ecstatic reveler in the
train of the wine god. It is also suggested by the choice of the girl's
name, *Telete,* or "Mystic Initiate," another likely reference to her
status as a *mainad.* Pausanias (9.30.1–4) attests to the presence of a
statue of Telete at the sanctuary of the Muses in Boeotia, where it was
placed next to that of the god Orpheus. This indicates that she was

moreover given divine honors that would have befitted her status as the supposed child of a god.

Telete is one of the few *females* mentioned in mythology said to have been born of a *hieros gamos* union, which makes the story of Nicaea particularly noteworthy. Nicaea's mother was said to have been the goddess Cybele/Artemis herself (Smith 1870, s.v. *Cybele*). This, again, could mean that her mother was in fact a holy *parthenos* dedicated to Artemis. The "father" of Nicaea is identified as the river god Sangarius (s.v. *Nicaea*). I suggest, however, that impregnation by the "waters," like impregnation by the "wind" (Boreas), in fact may have been considered a veil for pure parthenogenetic conception. Thus I suggest that Nicaea's mother was a priestess of Cybele/Artemis who was thought to have conceived her in *pure* parthenogenetic fashion, and that she belonged to the pre–*hieros gamos* generation. The story may well reference, then, a lineage of divine birth priestesses of Anatolian Artemis. As the eponym of what became the most important town in Bithynia (located in Anatolia), Nicaea enjoyed the kind of "immortalized" status I have argued was befitting a holy *parthenos* thought to have given birth to a god's child. In the reign of Constantine (325 C.E.), the Bithynian Nicaea was the location of the celebrated Council of Nicaea, out of which emerged the Nicaean Creed, the uniform statement of Christian doctrine. It is interesting to note that this doctrine, which established a belief in "one God, the father Almighty," bears the name of an Amazonian *parthenos* dedicated to Artemis (see Smith 1854, s.v. *Nicaea;* Stillwell et al. 1976, s.v. *Nicaea*).

Aura

Another nymph whose legend also appears only in Nonnus (*Dionysiaca* 48.238–978) was Aura. A nymph/priestess of the hunt and another "daughter" of Cybele (1.28), Aura, too, was seduced by Dionysus's turning a stream into wine. This situation was apparently arranged, however, by Artemis herself in retaliation for Aura's having insulted the goddess for having too "feminine" a body. Driven mad, Aura ate one of the progeny of the union; the other, Iacchus, was taken by Artemis and raised by the nymph/priestess Nicaea.[35]

The story is so similar to that of Nicaea that it may well represent a variant of the latter. In it, however, we have the additional motif of a sacrilege being committed against Artemis, and a resulting punishment. The story of Aura's hubris recalls legends associated with Arachne and Medusa in relation to Athena, which recount what I argued were parthenogenetically related transgressions against the goddess. Thus it is likely that Aura's real sacrilege was in fact her having broken her virgin vow with a god. The detail of her being driven "mad" may well refer to the original "madness" of Dionysian ecstasy that the wine had induced in her, in which state she committed her transgression. The "eating" of her child suggests a possible attempt to euthanize the purported children of her union. The rescuing of the other child by "Artemis" may reflect an attempt by the Artemisian priesteshood to save what was thought to be the product of a *hieros gamos* union, in the manner of Athena's rescue of Erichthonius.

Phylonome

Another nymph who did not escape a god's pursuit was Phylonome. A brief mention of her story appears only in Plutarch (*Greek and Roman Parallel Stories* 36), who attributes the legend to Zopyros of Byzantium in the third book of his *Histories*. The daughter of Nyctimus and Arcadia, Phylonome was a huntress in the company of Artemis who was impregnated by Ares in the guise of a shepherd. No description of her subsequent fate is offered, but one can imagine it would not have been favorable, as numerous other stories tell of Artemis punishing errant virgins with death.

Callisto, Polyphonte, and the Arktoi

One such instance of Artemisian wrath involved Callisto, who, as mentioned earlier, valiantly pledged eternal virginity to the goddess. Callisto eventually fell prey to Zeus's seduction. The nymph/priestess continued in Artemis's retinue until she became advanced enough in her pregnancy to be detected at her bath. According to legends, Callisto was turned into a bear as the result of her sexual union, some say by Artemis,[36] and as such gave birth to a son named Arcas. Artemis subsequently slew Callisto for not having protected her virginity (Apollodorus 3.8.2), and Zeus placed her among the stars as Arctus (Ursa Major), the Great Bear constellation (Pseudo-Eratosthenes *Constellations* 1).

Apollodorus further reports that Zeus gave Arcas over to the care of the "nymph" Maia to rear in Arcadia.[37] That Callisto's son became the eponym of Arcadia and, correspondingly, the ancestor of the Arcadian people (Pausanias 8.4.1) indicates his importance in the genealogy of Greeks. It was even said that as king, he introduced to his land agriculture, bread making, and weaving. His role as "hero" once again corresponds with the idea that *parthenioi,* or sons of virgins, were special souls destined for greatness and leadership.

Like some of the nymph/priestesses mentioned previously, Callisto was fairly robustly apotheosized, as evidenced by the fact that she was honored at her grave in Arcadia. Upon it, in fact, was a sanctuary of Artemis Calliste, that is, Callisto-as-Artemis (Pausanias 8.35.8). Arcas's grave was said to be located near the altar of Hera at Mantineia in Arcadia, which further supports the idea that he and his mother may have been historical personages (Pausanias 8.9.3).[38]

It is important to reiterate here, as mentioned in Chapter 1, that, according to one tradition, Zeus seduced Callisto by transforming himself into Artemis herself (Apollodorus 3.8.2; Hyginus *Poetic Astronomy* 2.1). Again, this hints that some Artemisian priestesses may have been associated with lesbian love, and that Artemis's divine birth priesthood, in particular, tended naturally to be populated in large part by maidens who preferred, or cultivated erotic love for, the female sex. In this Amazonian lesbian context, the capitulation or conscription of pure parthenogenetic divine birth priestesses dedicated to Artemis into *hieros gamos* divine birth practices may have been experienced as a particularly egregious violation by the venerable elder priestesses of this tradition. This would explain the particularly virulent "wrath" of Artemis, which, as mentioned, appears to have resulted in the murder of a number of her legendary priestesses, Callisto among them. As in the case of the murders of various male transgressors into the parthenogenetic mysteries, it may be that murders of nymph/priestesses that were attributed to "Artemis" were in fact carried out by senior sacerdotal leaders who were desperately attempting to preserve the original code.

The motif of Callisto's transformation into a bear becomes particularly important as we explore other Artemisian legends and cultic activities involving this animal. The bear also appears, for example, in the legend of Polyphonte of Thrace, who is said to have rejected the activities of Aphrodite (i.e., sexual relations) and headed to the mountains as a companion and sharer of sports with Artemis. While her choice may have pleased Artemis, it angered Aphrodite, who made Polyphonte go mad, fall in love with a bear, and couple with it. In disgust, Artemis turned the beasts of the wilds against the maiden (Antoninus Liberalis *Metamorphoses* 21).

The bear was an important aspect of the historically documented cult of Artemis in Brauron, where one of the goddess's most celebrated shrines was located in antiquity, and where the yearly Arkteia festival was celebrated in her honor (Herodotus 6.138). The foundational myth for this festival was that a tamed she-bear once scratched a virgin girl when roughly handled by her. The girl's brothers speared and killed the animal, an event that was followed by a plague upon the Athenians. The oracle told the Athenians that in order to be released from their suffering, their young virgins would thereafter have to "play the bear" (Suda, s.v. *Arktos ê Braurôniois*). Accordingly, the Arkteia was instituted in which young girls aged five to ten were required to don saffron robes and "dance the bear," that is, mimic bear movements, perhaps in a ritual dance.[39] The girls were called *arktoi*, "little bears," and seem to have been housed for a period of time—possibly as long as a year—in special "parthenons" associated with the temple (Zaidman 1992, 344; Blundell 1995, 30).

Putting the legends of Callisto and Polyphonte together with the legend of the Bra800nians, one may read the "bear" as a symbol that represented both virginity and punishment for transgressions against the goddess. Both Callisto and the Bra800nian maiden had displeased Artemis, the former by copulating with a god and the latter by treating the goddess/the bear badly. In both cases, the punishment was that virgins were made to "play the bear" (i.e., become the virgin Artemis herself): Callisto by literally being transformed into the animal, and young virgins of Brauron by symbolically doing so. That the punishment was the same in both cases may suggest that the transgression was the same, as well: the violation of parthenogenetic vows. Polyphonte's being made to have sexual relations with the bear thus represented a double transgression against Artemis. The Suda (s.v. *Arkteusai*) confirms that the bear was a symbol of virginity, noting "for the virgins are called 'being bears,'" as Euripides and Aristophanes show." Moreover, he says, the verb *arkteusai*, "to be a bear," was used specifically to mean "to consecrate a virgin to Artemis before marriage."

I thus suggest that the legendary Bra800nian maiden was in fact a trainee in Artemis's ancient retinue of divine birth priestesses, and that the cultural memory of her "treating the bear roughly" was a veil for the fact that she had been careless about her role. It may also have referenced a possible injunction by her male line to do away with the practice of pure parthenogenesis entirely ("killing" the bear). Thus I see the ritual that was established in Brauron in historical times of prepubescent virgin girls being required to "play the bear"—that is, "play" Artemis in her role as *Parthenos*—as akin to the ritual of propitiation (not peeking) that the young virgin priestesses had to carry out on the Acropolis in association with Athena, discussed in Chapter 3. According to the Suda (s.v. *Arktos ê Braurôniois*), the Athenians decreed that no virgin might be given to a man in marriage if she had not "played the bear" for the goddess, indicating that the propitiation was something that eventually was extended to virgins more broadly. Related to this was a widespread Greek custom whereby girls who were about to have sexual relations were also expected to dedicate their virginal lingerie to Artemis (Suda, s.v. *Lusizônos gunê*). Callimachus (*Hymn 4 to Delos* 296–9) refers to another rite on Delos whereby before marriage maidens brought to the priestesses of Artemis offerings of their maidenhair. Such rites echo that of the brides of Troizen, who were required to dedicate their maidenhood belts to Athena as a result of the priestess Aethra's having succumbed to Poseidon (Pausanias 2.33.1), as I discussed in the previous chapter.

Most scholars have interpreted the Arkteia as a puberty ritual, or period of preparation thereof (e.g., Farnell [1896–1909] 1977, 2:437; Sourvinou-Inwood 1988, 25–30), but the literary accounts and scenes on ritual kraters found at the site from the late archaic age[40] depict the girls as between five and ten years old, much too young to begin menstruating. Moreover, if one interprets the Arkteia and the dedication rituals described above as normal "rite of passage" celebrations, then one continually bumps up against the paradox of a goddess who was completely hostile to sexuality itself being solicited for her blessings on human sexuality. One text on the Artemisian ritual even declares that the virgin girls must serve as *kanephoroi*, basket carriers, before marrying in order to satisfy the goddess. Otherwise, Artemis *would have been offended by the loss of their virginity* (scholiast on Theocritus 2.66, in Sissa 1990, 77). Again, I propose that the paradox is resolved if we consider these rites instead as a form of "eternal" propitiation to Artemis for the ultimate disempowerment of her pure parthenogenetic priestesshood.[41] By forever after "satisfying" the goddess in these ways, the citizens of Brauron and Athens were able to maintain an uneasy accord with her. The particular elements involved in the Arkteia may even hint at the structure of the original divine birth priestesshood itself as an institution that (1) took in initiates for training beginning as early as five years of age; (2) required them to wear saffron robes as a sign of their role; (3) required them to live in seclusion in special precincts (parthenons) associated with the temple; and (4) taught them how to "mimic" the bear, that is, become like Artemis in her virgin/parthenogenetic aspect.

Atalanta

Yet a third legend associated with Artemis involves the bear as well as the suggestion of a parthenogenetic transgression. Although the maiden in this case is not specifically identified as a "nymph," her attributes so closely resemble those of the many nymph followers of Artemis that her nymph status is implied. The figure in question is Atalanta, about whom nearly identical Boeotian and Arcadian variants of her story are told.[42] In the Boeotian legend, Atalanta's father, having wished for a son, exposed her on Mt. Parthenion. In her infancy, Atalanta was suckled by a she-bear, and after she grew up she lived in a state of virginity, participating in the hunt, slaying centaurs who pursued her, and earning a reputation as the swiftest of mortals in foot races. Emphasizing her might, Pausanias (3.24.2) speaks of a spring that Atalanta was believed to have called forth from a rock by striking it with her spear.

When Atalanta's father later saw the girl and recognized her as his daughter, he insisted she marry. The maiden, however, having been told by the Delphic oracle to avoid marriage, made it a condition that she would agree to wed only the young man who could beat her in a foot race. One suitor, Hippomenes (Melanion in the Arcadian story), was able to conquer her by throwing in her path three golden apples given to him by Aphrodite, apples whose beauty distracted Atalanta from her race. Later, at the instigation of Aphrodite, who was angered over not having been properly thanked for her gift, the newly married couple had intercourse in the temple of Cybele. The goddess turned them into lions and yoked them to her chariot for having profaned her sacred precinct.[43] In some renditions of the tale, Atalanta was the mother of Parthenopaeus by the god Ares (Apollodorus 3.9.2).

Here again we have a story replete with parthenogenetic references. We have, for example, the exposing of Atalanta on Mt. Parthenion, "Virgin Mountain." As we may recall, a priestess of Athena mentioned in Chapter 3, Auge, also exposed an infant on this hill: her own son conceived through her *hieros gamos* union with Heracles. Atalanta's being reared on the mountain by a "bear," the animal into which girls had to "transform" in the Arkteia ritual, and her becoming a dedicated virgin who loved hunting and racing (i.e., an Amazon/nymph/priestess) indicate that she was likely raised and trained by a pure parthenogenetic priestesshood dedicated to Artemis that was located there. The stories of Atalanta and Auge thus suggest that Mt. Parthenion was a popular place for exposing unwanted infants in antiquity precisely because parents ambivalent about leaving their children to die knew there was a chance their progeny would be found and raised by the priestesses who lived there.

The detail that Atalanta was distracted from the race by the "golden apples" is also significant. Although in this story these apples are attributed to Aphrodite and are portrayed as symbols of sexuality, the golden apples originally belonged to Ge/Gaia, and, I argue in Chapter 5, were originally symbols of parthenogenesis.[44] Thus it seems that once again what is being referenced here is the distraction of a priestess in her attempt to engage in pure parthenogenetic conception, and her seduction into the realm of *hieros gamos* union. The god involved here, Ares, is mentioned in one version of the story. The name of Atalanta's son by this god, *Parthenopaeus,* which recalls *parthenos,* thus likely serves as a reference to her transgression against the goddess and the priesthood to whom she owed her very life.[45]

Chione

Another story of sacrilege regards Chione, also a probable nymph/priestess. Chione dared to criticize Artemis for being "fair of face," and otherwise to speak haughtily to her. The goddess is said to have shot the maiden in the mouth and killed her (Hyginus *Fabulae* 200; Ovid *Metamorphoses* 11.301–45). The telling detail in this legend is that Chione is said to have slept with both Apollo and Hermes in the same night. By Apollo, she bore Philammon, and by Hermes, Autoclyus. I propose that this exceptionally bold priestessly feat was what was considered Chione's real folly—as well as the reason for the goddess's disgust with her.

Melanippa

The nymph/priestess Melanippa also encountered Artemis's wrath. Melanippa was herself the daughter of another nymph named Chariclo and the immortal centaur Cheiron. The latter was renowned for his skills in hunting, medicine, and prophecy. According to one version of her legend, Melanippa had two sons by Poseidon (Neptune): Boeotus, the eponym of Boeotia, and Aeolus, the eponym of Aeolia (Hyginus *Fabulae* 186). According to another tradition, in which she was known as *Hippe,* she conceived a child by Aeolus, a grandson of Zeus. For having ceased hunting and worshipping Artemis, she was transformed into a horse by the goddess (Hyginus *Poetic Astronomy* 2.18). Another legend relates that Melanippa was "tricked and molested" by Aeolus and fled to the mountains to give birth. As her father came angrily searching for her, she prayed she might assume another shape so as not to be recognized, and was changed into a horse. For her piety, Artemis placed her among the stars as the constellation of the horse (Pseudo-Eratosthenes *Constellations* 18).

The insertion of Artemis into the story suggests that Melanippa was a priestess of this goddess. Thus, we can read the legend as relating a case of yet another priestess who violated her virginal vows by consorting with a god (or another god's progeny), but probably under conditions of confusion or duress. As the daughter of a "nymph" and an immortal centaur (i.e., a divine being), Melanippa also represents another rare instance of a female child of a divine union. According to the argument I have been developing, she thus would have possessed special attributes of some kind. And that indeed seems to have been the case: both Hyginus (*Poetic Astronomy* 2.18) and Ovid (*Metamorphoses* 2.635–75) state Melanippa was a prophetess. Ovid, in particular, indicates that her powers approached those of the gods themselves. Calling her by the name of Ocyrhoe, the poet details the prediction she made to the young Asclepius. She prophesied that the boy eventually would become the "healer of the world," would possess the power to bring the dead back to life, would be killed by Zeus for doing so, and would become divinized.[46] She also predicted the death of her father and the subsequent loss of his immortal status.[47] Ovid relates that it was in fact Melanippa/Ocyrhoe's breaking of the taboo against "knowing too much" that resulted in her animal transformation. That Melanippa's mother was a "nymph" hints that she, too, may have been a holy *parthenos*. Again, this may point to the existence of family lineages of priestesses engaged in divine birth practice.[48]

Coronis

The story of Asclepius's mother Coronis also reveals hints of a possible transgression by an Artemisian priestess. Coronis became pregnant with Asclepius as a result of engaging in union with Apollo. Spurning the god, she took another (mortal) lover while with child. According to Pindar (*Pythian Ode* 3.8–46) and Pausanias (2.26.6–7), Artemis shot Coronis dead while she was giving birth in order to avenge the insult to her brother. Hyginus (*Poetic Astronomy* 2.34), on the other hand, says she did so out of spite toward the god for a nasty trick he had played on her. Given, again, that Artemis's association with Apollo was probably a late development in her mythology, I suggest that the underlying reason for Artemis's wrath was the fact that her priestess had been lured into *hieros gamos* with a god. Coronis's having died in childbirth was likely seen as a punishment on the part of the goddess for her not having more vigilantly kept her virgin vows. The child, Asclepius, said to have been rescued from Coronis's funeral pyre by the god Hermes (Pausanias 2.26.6–7), went on to become a healer of great fame. Stories associated with Asclepius strongly suggest he was an actual historical Greek personage.[49] This emphasizes the likelihood of Coronis's historicity, as well.

LETO AND THE DIVINE BIRTH CULT ON DELOS

A discussion of Artemis would not be complete without an analysis of Leto, the goddess's mother in the Hesiodic tradition. The stories involving Leto and Artemis point to an older mythological and cultic substratum in which both figures were most likely parthenogenetic. In the Hesiodic genealogy (*Theogony* 404–8), Leto (Latin: Latona) was the granddaughter of Ge/Gaia. Her parents were the Titans Phoebe and Coius, and her siblings were Asteria and Hekate.[50] Hesiod (*Theogony* 918) and Homer (*Iliad* 1.9; *Odyssey* 11.317) refer to her as the mother of the twins Artemis and Apollo by Zeus, to whom she was married before Hera was. Later writers make her merely Zeus's concubine, persecuted during her pregnancy by Hera.[51]

A variety of attributes, symbols, and stories associated with Leto suggest that in her pre-Greek form she was understood to be parthenogenetic. One of the most striking in this regard is her connection with weaving, a symbol of parthenogenesis associated, as I have shown, with both Neith and Athena. Pindar (*Nemean Ode* 6.35b; Threnoi/Dirges 3, Race 1997, 361) calls Leto "goddess of the golden spindle" and "goddess of the golden distaff." This recalls, in particular, the Palladium statue, in which Pallas Athena, that representation of Amazonian virginity, was portrayed with a spindle and distaff in one hand. Another parthenogenetic symbol associated with Leto was the *ichneumon,* or tracker, an Egyptian weasel-like animal that hunted crocodile eggs. According to Aelian (*On Animals* 10.47) the *ichneumon* was thought to be "both male and female in the same individual, partaking of both sexes, and nature [had] enabled each single same animal both to procreate and to give birth" (Aelian 1959, 2:343, trans. Scholfield). He reports that in Heraclepolis, this creature was sacred both to Leto and Eileithyia. The perceived hermaphroditic element of this animal in association with Leto and Eileithyia (who, again, was identified with Artemis) suggests an ancient conception that these two goddesses themselves possessed the attributes of this animal—that is, they were parthenogenetic in nature.

Some Greek legends separate Leto's birth of Artemis in both time and place from that of Apollo. This supports the argument that the Apollonian element was a later insertion into what was originally a pre-Greek story depicting matriarchal consciousness. According to the Homeric *Hymn 3 to Apollo* (15–6) and the Orphic *Hymn 34 to Leto,* Leto gave birth to Artemis on the island of Ortygia,[52] located along the coast of Ephesus in ancient Anatolia, while she gave birth to Apollo on Delos.[53] The Ortygia locale first of all emphasizes Artemis's

Ephesian aspect. Athenaeus (1.31d) points to a tradition that attributed an Eastern origin to Leto, as well, noting that a mountain village
near Ephesus was formerly called *Letous,* "Leto's Village," but was
renamed *Latoreia* after "an Amazon of that name." This not only
points to ancient worship of Leto in Anatolia, but also connects Leto
with both Artemis and the Amazons, suggesting that the Amazons
honored Leto as well. Aristophanes (*Themophoriazusai* 120) similarly
hints at an Eastern connection for Leto when he has his character
Agathon utter in the same breath praises to Artemis, Leto, and "the
tones of the Asiatic lyre, which wed so well with the dances of the
Phrygian Graces" (Oates and O'Neill 1938, 2:873, trans. anon.).
This eastern geographical setting also points to Artemis's Ephesian
aspect, which represented the goddess in her oldest form as creatrix,
and which, as I argued earlier, was most likely parthenogenetic. Thus,
if their stories should be connected in mother/daughter fashion at
all,[54] Leto, as mother of the parthenogenetic Artemis, would, by logic,
herself have to have been parthenogenetic. The story of Artemis's
"birth" from Leto therefore seems to reference a condition of pure
parthenogenesis, and thus I would argue that the story of Zeus's
impregnation of Leto was a patriarchal intrusion into this mythology.

The more popular legend in later times held that Artemis was born
on Delos along with Apollo. Even in this case, however, Apollodorus
(1.4.1) relates that Leto was said to have given birth first to Artemis,
who thereupon helped her mother deliver Apollo. Again, this detail
points to both Artemis and Leto as "older" goddesses in relation
to Apollo. It also emphasizes the closeness of their mother/daughter
bond, which is suggestive of the matriarchal condition. Indeed,
Artemis is rendered as having been quite fierce, even risking death,
in defending her mother. One ancient legend, for example, says that
she shot Tityus dead for attempting to rape Leto.[55] Leto is depicted
as reciprocating her daughter's affection. Homer (*Iliad* 21.502–4)
describes her as lovingly collecting Artemis's scattered arrows once
when the latter was assaulted by Hera.

Moreover, in Callimachus (*Hymn 3 to Artemis* 21–2), we hear
Artemis declare that because her own mother gave birth to her without pain, she was forever after rendered by the Moirae, or Fates, a
helper to women in childbirth. Thus Artemis's loyalty to her motherline extended more widely to womankind, in general, which again
is suggestive of her roots in matriarchal tradition. In the Orphic
Hymn to Prothyraea, Artemis is identified with Eileithyia, the one
who allayed labor pangs, eased pain as the child came through the
mother's vagina, cared for infants, and guarded the race of humans.

In the Orphic *Hymn to Diana* (Artemis), she is identified as one who similarly assisted with births, despite what the hymn pointedly refers to as the goddess's own virginity. Again, Artemis's aspect as helper to women in childbirth is not at odds with her virginal aspect if we consider her as originally having been a Virgin Mother herself. The Homeric *Hymn 3 to Apollo* (92–5) relates a tradition that the goddesses Dione, Rhea, Ichnaea, Themis, and Amphitrite and other immortals assisted Leto in her travail on Delos. The list is significant in that all of these goddesses were themselves from the "older" generation of Hesiodic deities, again pointing to Leto's cult as originally predating that of Zeus—and thus possibly having been one associated with pure parthenogenesis rather than *hieros gamos*. Dione was a daughter of Oceanus and Tethys, or, according to others, of Uranus and Ge, or of Aether and Ge.[56] She also was the primary female deity worshipped at the oracular site of Dodona, and is important to the discussion in Chapter 6, in which I argue that Dodona was possibly the site of a divine birth priestesshood. Rhea was a daughter of Uranus and Ge, and, accordingly, a Titan sister of Themis. The mother of Zeus, Rhea was also connected with the Thracian Cybele, who was a form of Artemis herself (Hesiod *Theogony* 135; Strabo 10.3.15). Themis had similar parentage to Rhea and also married Zeus. She was said to have possessed the Delphic oracle as the successor of Ge/Gaia prior to the usurping of the site by Apollo.[57] This is also important to my discussion in Chapter 6 of Delphi as the possible site of another divine birth priestesshood. Ichnaea, whose name also appeared as a surname of Themis, was worshipped as a goddess in Ichnae (Strabo 9.5.14; Stephanus Byzantius, s.v. *Ichnai*). Amphitrite was either an Oceanid or a Nereid. She was a goddess and sea consort of the god Poseidon, but preferred her virginity.[58] According to the Homeric *Hymn 3 to Apollo*, these goddesses subsequently sent for Eileithyia to assist Leto. Given, once again, that Artemis was identified with Eileithyia, this detail returns us to the mythologem of Artemis herself having been the one who assisted her mother in the birth of Apollo.

Several legends suggest that the true "midwife" in Leto's birth process was the tree that she clasped or leaned against as she brought her children forth. In this motif we also see a possible symbol of pure parthenogenesis. Strabo (14.1.20) and Hyginus (*Fabulae* 53) identify the tree as an olive. That the olive tree was said to have been invented by Athena (Pausanias 1.24.3), and therefore was sacred to her, renders it, I suggest, a parthenogenetic symbol in connection with her origins as a pure parthenogenetic/autogenetic goddess. I mention the olive again in Chapter 6 in connection with virgin birth when I discuss Porphyry's analysis of Homer's "cave of the nymphs." There, the olive tree appears strikingly juxtaposed with nymph/priestesses and that other symbol of parthenogenesis, the loom. Most of the other stories of Leto's travail say she rested on the *palm* tree, not the olive (e.g., Homeric *Hymn 3 to Apollo* 117; Callimachus *Hymn 4 to Delos* 209–10), but even in this apparently the connection to Athena could not be shaken: Ovid (*Metamorphoses* 6. 335) says the palm was "Pallas's [Athena's] tree" *(Pallidas arbore palmae)*. A further detail pointing to the parthenogenetic associations between Athena and Leto is the legend that Pallas Athena conducted Leto from Cape Sounion to Delos in preparation for her birth of Apollo (Hypereides Delian frag. 70, in Kerenyi 1975, 145n124). Athena's presence again emphasizes the idea of a pre–*hieros gamos* element in the story.

The palm tree mentioned in the myth may well be the *date* palm, which was also a parthenogenetic reference. For as Neumann (1963, 241) notes, the date palm was one of the central figures of Egyptian art as a symbol of the "goddess as the tree that confers nourishment on souls." He emphasizes that "the motherhood of the tree consists not only in nourishing; it also comprises generation, and the tree goddess gives birth to the sun." The palm tree was a reference, then, to the parthenogenetic birth of the god—and the king as proxy—as a manifestation of the solar principle. Thus this motif once again puts Leto in association with the great tradition of the parthenogenetic birth of the sun god—in this case, the Greek Apollo.

A CASE OF TWO LETOS?

I must now more fully address the fundamental problem that exists in Leto's mythology: the ambiguity as to her ontological status. The mythologems I have related thus far hint at her being an older, primal, parthenogenetic goddess who gave birth to a "daughter" goddess. Even her Hesiodic genealogy, which depicts her as the daughter of Titans, suggests as much. Yet, at the same time, in her stories she appears to resemble more closely the nymphs and mortals who engaged in *hieros gamos* unions with Zeus. In this aspect, she is more like a divine birth *priestess* who was later apotheosized for her role in bringing a god to birth. I thus propose that Leto's story is a conflation of two myths: that of an older Titanic goddess named Leto (Leto I) who parthenogenetically gave birth to Artemis and that of a mortal woman named Leto (Leto II) who was thought to have given birth to Zeus's holy son Apollo as part of a divine birth priestesshood on Delos. It may even be that this "second" Leto was originally a pure parthenogenetic priestess of Artemis who was believed to have been seduced into *hieros gamos* union, as I have argued was the case with so many other female figures.

Our hypothetical Leto II as an alleged holy *parthenos*—a mortal mother of a god—is more in line with the mothers of Zeus's three other favored sons: Hermes, Dionysus, and Heracles. As mentioned earlier, the mothers of these three gods were, respectively, Maia, Semele, and Alcmene. Semele and Alcmene were clearly mortal women in Greek legend. In Chapter 7, I provide evidence that Maia and her six sisters, collectively known as the Pleiades, were, originally, also mortal. Moreover, that Apollo's ontological status is also in accord with that of the holy *parthenioi* born to these women further strengthens the argument that Leto should be considered one of their earthly number. As I mentioned in Chapter 2, various traditions treat Hermes, Dionysus, and Heracles euhemeristically as individuals who walked the earth and were apotheosized upon their death. Apollo is also portrayed in this way, which becomes particularly clear in one legend, related by Pausanias (10.6.1), that the Delphians called upon him to kill a violent man who had pillaged their oracular sanctuary.

A mortal status for Leto II is also more consistent with that of the numerous female personages who provoked Hera's wrath by coupling with Zeus. In only one other instance is Hera depicted as jealously responding to a dalliance on the part of Zeus with a goddess: the case of Aphrodite (Suda, s.v. *Priapos*). In all other instances, her jealousy is directed toward "nymphs" (Callisto, Aegina, Othreis, Iynx) or mortal women/heroines (Side, Io, Elare, Semele).[59] This is significant, given that Zeus was supposedly married to six other goddesses before Hera, ordered as follows in Hesiod's *Theogony* (886–921): (1) Metis, (2) Themis, (3) Eurynome, (4) Demeter, (5) Mnemosyne, and (6) Leto. Moreover, legends record his successful or attempted sexual liaisons with the goddesses Asteria, Dione, Gaia, Hybris, Nemesis, Persephone, Selene, Styx, and Thetis.[60] Yet we hear nothing of Hera's complaints regarding these divine pursuits. Hera's legendary jealousy of Leto's union with Zeus, which caused Leto to roam the known world in search of a place to give birth (e.g., Callimachus *Hymn 4 to Delos* 55–204), was fitting of her behavior toward "nymphs" and mortals almost exclusively. This supports the argument that Leto II should be categorized as one of them. Moreover, that Sappho identified Leto as "the most devoted of friends" with Niobe before the two became mothers (Sappho 1958, frag. 85, trans. Barnard) further suggests a mortal status for her, given that Niobe was mortal.

Another clue to the existence of an earthly Leto II is the appearance of Mt. Parthenion in her myth. Callimachus (*Hymn 4 to Delos* 71), who calls this Arcadian mountain "holy," mentions it as first in a list of places in Greece that Leto sought for her travail with Apollo. In speaking about Athena's priestess Auge in Chapter 3 and Artemis's priestess Atalanta earlier in this chapter, I established Mt. Parthenion, "Mountain of the Virgin," as not only a place where infants were frequently left to die in the ancient world, but also a probable location of a divine birth priestesshood dedicated to Artemis. Thus that Leto solicited this location early in her search lends support to the idea that she was a human holy *parthenos* seeking out a particular precinct where her extraordinary event could be properly supported. Not just any location would do; a special place was required where women were present who understood the nature of virgin birth and would handle it in proper ritual fashion. Moreover, a priestesshood dedicated to Artemis may have been her first choice, given that her numerous associations to this goddess suggest Leto II was likely in service to her. Several of the other places and individuals we hear of in Callimachus (*Hymn 4 to Delos* 55–204) that she approached were also related to divine birth: the "nymphs" of Thessaly; King Asopus, whose many daughters all were said to have given birth via gods (Larson 2004, 138–45); and the "nymph" Melia, who herself was said to have been parthenogenetically born of Ge/Gaia, as I mentioned earlier. Leto is said also to have refrained from petitioning the cities of Aegialos and Argos, governed by Inachus, given that this king himself venerated Hera. Yet embedded in this detail, too, is a reference to divine birth: Inachus's own daughter Io, a priestess of Hera, had given birth to the son of Zeus, a topic I discuss at length in Chapter 5.

DELOS AS LOCATION OF A DIVINE BIRTH PRIESTESSHOOD

The place that eventually admitted Leto was the island of Delos. Clues that Delos was the location of a divine birth priestesshood are plentiful. The first is the fact that the original name of the island, *Asteria,* was also the name of one of Leto's sisters, who herself had been sexually approached by Zeus. Asteria, however, had evaded the god's clutches by throwing herself into the sea (Callimachus *Hymn 4 to Delos* 34–6; Apollodorus 1.4.1).[61] That "Asteria as woman" and "Asteria as island" were equated is indicated by the detail in Callimachus that Hera decided not to punish the "island," despite its having welcomed Leto, because of the sacrifice "she," that is, Asteria, had made in avoiding Zeus's embraces. Legends relate that Asteria-as-landmass wandered about the sea until Leto set foot on it, whereby it became moored to the earth.[62]

I propose the mythologem of Asteria as a "moorless" island references the fact that it was the home of a divine birth "sisterhood" of a particular nature, perhaps one to which Asteria-as-woman had belonged. This priesthood, I propose, may have been known specifically for taking in holy *parthenoi* who had run into trouble in one way or another during the patriarchal age, when their practice was becoming more subject to male intrusion, ever more hidden from public view, and ever more misunderstood.

This idea finds support in another legend, that of Rhoio, daughter of Staphylus and Chrysothemis. As Diodorus Siculus (5.62.1–5) relates, Rhoio was made pregnant by Apollo. Her father, believing the situation to have been caused by a man, angrily shut her up in a chest and cast her into the sea. The chest washed up on none other than the island of Delos, where Rhoio gave birth to Anius. Rhoio's story further resonates with divine birth references in that the maiden had two virgin sisters, one of whom was named *Parthenos*. That this sister's name, as we have seen, was a surname for Athena and Artemis (as well as Hera, as I discuss in Chapter 5) in their virginal aspect suggests that Parthenos was a holy *parthenos* of one of these goddesses. To evade their father's wrath (supposedly for a mishap in which his supply of wine was destroyed), Parthenos and a third sister, Molpadia, committed suicide by hurling themselves off a cliff into the sea. Apollo subsequently rescued the maidens and established them in the cities of the Cherronesos. Parthenos was worshipped with divine honors in Bubastus, while Molpadia was venerated in Castabus. The latter was given the name *Hemithea*, "Half Goddess," we are told, because Apollo "had appeared to humans."

The names and details of this story suggest that Rhoio, Parthenos, and Molpadia were in fact holy *parthenoi* sisters. Although the latter two are not specifically named in association with birth, their connection with Apollo and their subsequent divinization suggest that they, like Rhoio, were indeed involved in the practice and engaged in *hieros gamos* with the god. Again, I earlier pointed out other cases, such as that of Nicaea and Melanippa, in which divine birth seems to have been a family affair, with a priesthood either passing from mother to daughter, or being adopted simultaneously by all female siblings in a household. Hyginus (*Poetic Astronomy* 2.25) relates a legend that Parthenos was in fact the daughter of Chrysothemis by Apollo, hinting that the mother of the girls was also a holy *parthenos*. As we will recall from Chapter 3, the story of Cecrops's daughters, too, was replete with details suggestive of the maidens' unions with gods and their hurling themselves into the sea, possibly in response to their having broken the taboo regarding *hieros gamos* divine birth. Self-sacrifice by jumping into the sea was also a method used by priestesses to avoid union with male gods, as we saw in the cases of Britomartis and Asteria. Thus Parthenos and Molpadia's action in this regard may well similarly reference either their having broken their commitment to pure parthenogenesis under one of the goddesses, or their having killed themselves to avoid a god, in this case, presumably Apollo, the god who "appeared" to humans. That the reason for their suicide in the myth is the depletion of their father's "wine" may affirm that it was in a trance state under the effect of entheogenic wine that the transgression with Apollo took place. Hyginus (*Astronomica* 2.25) notes the tradition that Parthenos was turned into the constellation Virgo, the "Virgin," by Apollo, which emphasizes her status as a holy *parthenos*.

Thus clearly Leto II would not have been the only priestess impregnated by a god to have turned to Delos in a time of desperation. That a preexisting divine birth priestesshood was indeed present to receive Leto on the island is suggested by Callimachus (*Hymn 4 to Delos* 226–7), who mentions the presence of "nymphs" of Delos singing at the birth of Apollo the "holy chant" of Eileithyia. Again, I have argued that nymphs were in fact priestesses. This argument is strengthened in this case by a further reference to the nymph/maidens' singing on Delos that appears in the Homeric *Hymn 3 to Apollo* (155). Here the poet notes that the singing of the maidens was made particularly famous by the fact that it "mimicked all people's voices and their babble" such that "anyone might think it was he himself speaking" (trans. West 2003, 83). As Burkert (1985, 110) notes, such singing has been compared "to the Pentecostal miracle and the speaking of tongues in the New Testament." In short, the singing was a kind of oracular utterance that reveals the inspiration and presence of the deity: it was a magico-religious act. Thus those who engaged in it, I suggest, were of a special sacerdotal class.

Returning to Callimachus's detail that the chant of the "nymphs" was addressed to Eileithyia, we should note that this goddess was identified with Artemis, as I have shown. This further indicates that the original priestesshood on the island may well have been dedicated to this latter goddess. Given, too, that priestesses in general were identified with the goddesses they served, the mythologem mentioned earlier of "Artemis" having assisted her mother "Leto" in the birth of Apollo may reference the fact that it was this goddess's priestesshood that came to Leto II's aid.

Legends held that as a result of Delos having offered hospitality to his mother, Apollo rendered the island particularly blessed (Homeric *Hymn to Apollo* 88). Historical and archaeological records attest to Delos as an important cult location in the historical period. Strabo (10.5.2) reports that the neighboring islands, the Cyclades, made it famous by sending sacred envoys, sacrifices, and choruses composed of virgins, and celebrating a great festival there to Artemis, Leto, and Apollo. A sanctuary older than those of either Leto or Apollo, dated c. 700 B.C.E., was dedicated to Leto's nemesis, Hera (O'Brien 1993, 227), which also points to its possible early connections with divine birth given, as I argue in Chapter 5, Hera was also probably originally a parthenogenetic Great Mother. Late writings attest to Delos as having been the location of an oracle, as well,[63] and a brief allusion to this effect in the Homeric *Hymn to Apollo* (79–81) suggests the oracle was of some antiquity. The presence of an oracle on Delos would also support my hypothesis, mentioned in Chapter 2, that divine birth priestesshoods were also by nature oracular, an idea I develop more fully in Chapters 6 and 7 when I describe the oracles at Dodona and Delphi, respectively.

One final point is worth exploring regarding Delos as the location of Apollo's miraculous birth. This concerns the names of the island: *Asteria* and *Delos*. *Asteria* derives from *aster*, "star." Pindar says that the island was known as the "far-shining star of the dark-blue earth" (Hymns frag. 33b, 1997, 233, trans. Race). Callimachus (*Hymn 4 to Delos* 53) also points to the origins of the name *Delos* as meaning "clear, visible, manifest" in his statement that once the island planted its roots, it no longer floated as an "unseen, unknown, obscure" (*adêlos*) landmass upon the water. The later name *Delos* thus connoted the coming into being, or manifestation into form, of the "light of the star" (*Asteria*) itself. I suggest that this connotation, combined with the island's association with the "stars," also possibly points to an esoteric belief that Apollo, the manifestation of "light" as the sun, hailed from the starry realms. I return to this idea in Chapter 6 when I discuss the belief held by some Greeks that the gods originated from the Milky Way. I argue there that an esoteric strain in early Greek religion may have even held that the divine children born of virgins hailed from the constellation known as the Pleiades, in particular. Thus the very names of the island of Apollo's birth may confirm the idea that the conception and birth of this god involved what was thought to be a kind of "drawing down" of his spirit from the astral realms, a process that, to the ancient Greek mind, could only have been accomplished by a holy *parthenos*.

Apollo's supposed birth on Delos may well have been a significant marker in the history of the divine birth priestesshood on the island. Diodorus Siculus reports (12.58.6–7) that in the fifth century B.C.E., a decree was established making it unlawful for any human being to be born or die on the island. Every pregnant woman thus had to be conveyed to the neighboring island of Rheneia in order not to pollute Delos.[64] Perhaps, then, Apollo's supposed birth on the island marked what was understood to have been the end of the divine birth priestesshood there.

CHAPTER 5

HERA'S DIVINE BIRTH PRIESTESSHOOD

Hera is the third Greek goddess to have borne the title *Parthenos*. Legends and cultic activities concerning this Olympian queen of the gods indicate that in her earliest form she, like Athena/Neith and Artemis, was considered a great virgin creatrix. In her case, this quality was retained even in the era of Olympic religion, with myths relating that she gave birth to Ares, Hephaestus, and Typhon parthenogenetically. One particularly strong indicator that a priestesshood devoted to divine birth may have been dedicated to Hera at an early period is the story of Io, who, records indicate, may have been a historical figure, and whose story includes the dramatic themes of *hieros gamos* and Heraian wrath. Hera's sanctuary at Olympia similarly was imbued with parthenogenetic themes, all of which point to the possibility that the famed Olympic Games may have originated in her cult of divine birth. These themes will be elaborated upon throughout this chapter.

HERA AS VIRGIN MOTHER

In the Hesiodic genealogy, Hera was the eldest daughter of the Titans Cronus and Rhea. Like her siblings Hestia, Demeter, Hades, and Poseidon, she was initially swallowed by her father Cronus before her youngest brother, Zeus, solicited Metis for advice on how the children could be disgorged (*Theogony* 453–500; Apollodorus 1.2.1).

In the Homeric and Hesiodic traditions, Hera was not only the older sister but also the wife of Zeus. The marriage of Hera and Zeus itself was referred to as the *hieros gamos,* "sacred marriage."[1] As a result of being the only truly betrothed goddess in the Olympian pantheon, Hera came to be known as the "goddess of marriage."[2] The consensus among classics scholars, however, is that Hera's "marriage" with Zeus was the mythical representation of the (probably forced) merging of the pre-Olympian Hera cult with that of the Olympian pantheon.[3] Hera's legends, iconography, and cult clearly indicate that she was a goddess of pre-Greek antiquity. Indeed, as I show in Chapter 6, at the primitive oracle of Dodona it was the goddess Dione who was Zeus's consort, not Hera. This points to a period of theological flux before Hera's position became fixed in the Olympian cult (Harrison [1903] 1957, 316).

Hera's various aspects suggest that she was in fact originally an earth goddess, a "Mistress of the Animals," and a queen of heaven, indicating that she was once a Great Goddess of the sky, earth, and underworld. Vestiges of her earlier, enlarged identity can be seen, for example, in her Homeric title "Queen of the Gods," and her command over the seasons, earthquakes, atmosphere, rain, wind, moon, and stars (rendering her a queen of heaven).[4] That she was connected with the abundance of the earth and nature more broadly, as well, can be seen in her association with various trees, plants, and fruits including the willow (*lygos*), asterion, lily, pomegranate, and wheat.[5]

Hera was also, like the more archaic form of Artemis, a "Mistress of the Animals." Birds were sacred to her, including the peacock, the hawk, and the dove.[6] That one of Hera's most sacred animals was the cow is indicated by a number of literary and cultic references. One of her primary epithets, for example, was "cow-eyed mistress," *boôpis potnia* (Homer *Iliad* 1.551, 568; 14.159). As Cook (1914–40, 1:444) notes, Hera's epithet *boôpis,* "cow-eyed, cow-faced, of cowlike aspect," must have come down to Homer "from a distant past . . . and presupposed the primitive conception of Hera as a cow."

Strong indicators that Hera was originally conceived as a parthenogenetic goddess can be found on the island of Samos, located off the coast of ancient Anatolia (Turkey). There, one of the primary and earliest seats of her worship, she was known as *Hera Parthenia,* "Hera the Virgin."[7] Pindar (*Olympian Ode* 6.88) also refers to her with this epithet. According to some writers, the ancient name for Samos itself was *Parthenia.*[8] Some say this derived from the name of the river Parthenios because the goddess Hera had been brought up there as a virgin.[9] That the name of the goddess and the entire island sacred to her was known as "Virgin" indicates that Hera's earliest primary characterization when she first emerged in Greek cult was that of *Parthenos.*

From mythological and cultic evidence, it is clear that Hera at Samos was also at the same time a creatrix; thus I propose she was considered a Virgin Mother. Lore and archaeological finds associated with the island, including votives in the shape of sphinxes, griffins, lions, and other animals confirm that Hera was a generative "Mistress of the Animals" not originally linked with Zeus or other Olympian deities (O'Brien 1993, 45–54). The idea of Hera's virgin mother-hood is contained in a title at Lesbos that has been attributed to her: "female origin of all things" (*genethlê pantôn*) (Alcaeus frag. 129, in O'Brien 106 and n52). In examining cultic evidence on the island, O'Brien (6, 71–74) concludes that Hera came to be viewed as the wife of Zeus in the Samian cult only with the imposition of Olympian mythology, perhaps as late as the late seventh century B.C.E. Even then, the evidence suggests that Zeus's influence on her cult at Samos was minimal.

The Samians held that Hera was born on their island by the side of the river Parthenios/Imbrasos under a willow hedge. Hera's temple, the Heraion, was built around the willow, which was reportedly still standing in the second century C.E. and was considered the oldest extant tree in Greece (Pausanias 7.4.4, 8.23.5). I contend that the presence of the willow supports the argument that Hera was a Virgin Mother whose priestesses may have attempted divine birth. For, in Greek, the willow was known as the *lygos,* and, in Latin, the *agnus castus,* or "chaste lamb," so named because it had an important repu-tation as a hedge whose leaves quelled sexual desire, according to the ancient writers.[10] That Hera is said to have been "born" under this "chaste" hedge emphasizes the goddess's virginal aspect as core to her earliest identity. Moreover, at Samos the *lygos* had a central role in rituals associated with her, as I will discuss shortly. The importance of the *lygos* to the Heraian cult, and the fact that it was an anaphro-disiac, brings up the question as to whether it may have been used by priestesses of Hera to help them maintain the virginity thought necessary for the task of pure parthenogenetic conception. Given that the ancient sources mentioned above say it was also used to regulate menstruation, one may conjecture that it could have been used to time the reproductive cycle to assist attempts at divine conception through *hieros gamos,* as well.

The foundational myth of the tenth-century B.C.E. Heraion at Samos centered on Admete, daughter of the Mycenaean hero Eurys-theus. According to this legend, Admete, a priestess of Hera, fled from Argos to Samos (for an unspecified reason), saw Hera in a vision, and undertook care of the goddess's temple there. The Argolids convinced pirates to steal Hera's sacred icon so that the Samians would punish Admete for negligence. But when the thieves could not launch their ship from its place on the beach, they superstitiously abandoned the image there and offered it sacrificial cakes instead. The Samians found the statue the next day, set it by the *lygos* hedge, and bound it there with branches so that it would not stray. Admete freed the goddess, bathed her, and put her back on her pedestal in the temple (Menodotus, in Athenaeus 15.672a–e).

That Hera's priestess in the myth was named *Admete,* literally, "Untamed," suggests that she was unmarried, a virgin of the pre-Zeus cult. As O'Brien (1993, 59) notes, her name is thus suggestive of a pre-Greek epoch, before marriage came to be understood as the domestication and yoking of young women. Perhaps Admete "fled" Argos as a result of her rebellion over restrictions imposed on her priestess-hood there. It may be that those restrictions specifically related to the attempted infiltration of the older Heraian cult by the Zeusian cult.

That the myth of Admete and the binding of Hera was tremendously important to the Samians is reflected in the fact that it was annually reenacted in the Tonaia, or "Tight Pulling," festival conducted in honor of the goddess. This involved the annual procession of the goddess's cult statue to the sea and its purification and "feeding" with barley cake offerings (Athenaeus 15.672–3). O'Brien believes it was only during a later stage that the rite came to represent the marriage of Hera and Zeus,[11] with the goddess now confined by the "subordinating bonds of Greek wedlock." I propose that at that later stage, as in the associated myth, Hera's being ritually "purified" and returned to the *lygos* symbolized a yearly return to her own origins as a Virgin Mother. Such an act served as a reminder of Hera's parthenogenetic capacity even in the Zeusian epoch.

At Hera's other main cult center of Argos, the goddess also had roots in the pre-Olympian Bronze Age, and retained vestiges of her original parthenogenetic identity. Kerenyi (1975, 132) assigns the beginnings of the cult to 2000 B.C.E., which indicates that Argos may in fact have been Hera's oldest cult site in Greece. O'Brien (124) affirms that remains found in Mycenaean-era tombs there are suggestive of Heraian iconography. Zeus had few ties to the early Argolid; as on Samos the existence of his cult there was initially separate from and secondary to that of Hera. Moreover, Homeric references to him as "spouse of Hera" (*posis Hêrês*) (*Iliad* 10.5) indicate the goddess's preeminence and suggest the existence of pre-Olympian myths in which Hera, and not Zeus, was the region's dominant deity (O'Brien 1993, 3–4, 121–2).

What is particularly noteworthy about the Argive cult to Hera was its myth that the goddess annually bathed to restore her virginity in the Canathus spring at Nauplia.[12] Pausanias (2.38.3) adds that the story was told as a "holy secret" at the mysteries celebrated in the goddess's honor. This myth once again underscores the importance of virginity in relationship to Hera, and implies that *partheneia*, virginity, represented her original state. Given that the myth of Hera's virginity was also part of a "holy secret" in relation to her mystery rites, I propose that such *partheneia* was understood specifically to have been an indicator of her parthenogenetic powers. I further propose that the "restoration" of her virginity represented, as did the "binding to the *lygos*" motif in Samos, a felt need for Hera to be returned regularly to her original state as Holy *Parthenos*, her condition under the oldest stratum of the cult.[13] At Argos, as at Samos, this was perceived as necessary, I suggest, precisely because of the imposition of the Zeus cult over hers, and her forced "marriage" with the god, a relationship that was on some level understood to be unnatural for her.

HERA'S PARTHENOGENETIC BIRTH OF ARES, HEPHAESTUS, AND TYPHON

Hera's parthenogenetic ability was retained even in Olympian myth. The first indication in this regard is the pure daughter-bearing parthenogenetic condition hinted at in her relationship with her daughter, Hebe. Hesiod (*Theogony* 922) reports that Hebe was Hera's daughter by Zeus. However, that the names *Hera* and *Hebe* are probably semantically related, both being derived from two different extensions of the same Indo-European root (Adams 1987, 176), suggests that the two goddesses can be seen as "doubles" of one another. Moroever, that *Hebe* means "Youth" emphasizes the idea that Hebe was the "younger version" of Hera. Thus Hera and Hebe were possibly early Argolic mother/daughter deities of the earth's cyclical renewal, as were Demeter and Persephone elsewhere (O'Brien 1993, 118). In such a matriarchal schema, the daughter is the parthenogenetic offspring of the mother, an idea I explored in the case of Leto and Artemis in Chapter 4.

The more direct and striking evidence for Hera as a pure parthenogenetic goddess, specifically of the son-bearing variety, lies in the miraculous birth stories of Ares, Typhon, and Hephaestus. We find the myth of her parthenogenetic birth of Ares, the war god, in Ovid (*Fasti* 193–260). According to this story, Hera conceived a child with the help of Flora/Chloris, a "nymph" who had received a special flower that would make women pregnant. The "nymph" touched Hera's bosom with the plant, and immediately the goddess conceived Ares.

The motif of the "magical flower" affirms that plants and herbs were thought in antiquity to have the power to facilitate conception without the need of a male, probably through their chemical absorption into the body. I return to a related topic in Chapter 7, when I discuss women's practice of vaginal fumigation and the role of "vapors" in the trance/impregnation of the Delphic priestess. The myth further indicates that the possession of knowledge for inducing birth miraculously was specifically thought to be the province of "nymphs." This supports the argument I have been developing thus far that "nymphs" were in fact priestesses of divine birth.

Another legend relates that Hera parthenogenetically bore Hephaestus, the heavenly smithy.[14] In yet another story, she miraculously produced Typhon, a serpentine and winged monster (Homeric *Hymn to Apollo* 300–64). On Hera's request, the female serpent Python, who guarded the oracle of Ge/Gaia at Delphi, took in Typhon and raised him (West 2003, 99). As I argue in Chapter 7, the oracle of Delphi was also likely a location of a divine birth priestesshood. We thus begin to see in the story of Hera and Typhon the emergence of a network of relationships in service to the protection of female parthenogenetic power, which was considered to have been an attribute of both divine and mortal women. This is further emphasized by the fact that Python was also known as *hêrôis*, or "mistress/heroine," which is but another form of the name *Hera* (Fontenrose 1959, 119, 377–8). These terms thus suggest an identification between Hera and Python. Moreover, as we will recall from Chapter 2, *hêrôis*, or "heroine," is also found in Pindar (*Pythian Ode* 11.7). This connects Hera and Python with the concept of the human heroine more broadly, which supports the argument I made in Chapter 2 that *heroine*, like *nymph*, was a marker for the divine birth priestess.

HERA, THE HESPERIDES, AND THE APPLES OF PARTHENOGENESIS

An important legend that also alludes to Hera's parthenogenetic capabilities is that of the golden apples of the Hesperides. In one version, Ge/Gaia gave to Hera as a "wedding" present an orchard of golden apple trees that were guarded by an immortal serpent and "nymphs" known as the Hesperides (Apollodorus 2.5.11). In another version, Hera had Ge/Gaia's apples cultivated in her own gardens "near distant Mt. Atlas." When the Hesperides, Atlas's daughters, kept picking the apples from the trees, Hera installed the serpent there as a guardian (Hyginus *Poetic Astronomy* 2.3).

Both versions of the myth redound with parthenogenetic references. First is the mythologem of Ge/Gaia's gift of the golden apples. As I noted in Chapter 3, Ge/Gaia was, at her deepest level, a parthenogenetic goddess.[15] Her "passing on" the apple to Hera therefore suggests an interchangeability between the two goddesses, pointing to their identification, which I propose was based specifically on their mutual parthenogenetic nature. I thus argue that the tree of the golden apples was ultimately a symbol of parthenogenetic ability.

This is further supported by the fact that the other inhabitants of this paradisiacal garden were similarly associated with parthenogenesis. The Hesperides themselves were, in Hesiodic theogony, parthenogenetically born daughters of the goddess Nyx (*Theogony* 270). That Hesiod (*Theogony* 214–5) calls them "nymphs" and that Diodorus Siculus (4.27.1–2) identifies them as historical women further suggests that they were in fact ancient holy *parthenoi*, according to my argument in Chapter 3 about the meaning of the "nymph" title. Moreover, various legends place the garden of the Hesperides in Africa,[16] and Hesiod (*Theogony* 270) makes a point of locating them near the Gorgons and Medusa. As I argued in Chapter 3, the Gorgons were probably historical Libyan Amazons whose queen, Medusa, was likely a holy *parthenos* in service to Athena/Neith. Such tribes were moreover most likely ancestors of the Libyan Auses, who I similarly argued also may have attempted divine birth. Thus it appears that what is being described in the myth of the Hesperides is a North African precinct that was part of a larger cult of divine birth.

The guardian serpent, too, has parthenogenetic associations. The Greeks believed Ge/Gaia gave birth spontaneously to snakes,[17] and to Python, the great serpent who guarded Delphi, in particular (Ovid *Metamorphoses* 1.438–40). Apollonius Rhodius (*Argonautica* 4.1396) specifically calls the serpent of the garden of the Hesperides, whom he names Ladon, a "son of Ge/Gaia," which also implies a parthenogenetic status for him. Elsewhere, Ladon is named the offspring of none other than Hera's parthenogenetically born son Typhon (Apollodorus 2.5.11; Hyginus *Fabulae* 151). Moreover, with the garden of the Hesperides we have a replication of the situation at Delphi: (1) a precinct originally sacred to Ge/Gaia, (2) guarded by her parthenogenetically born serpent progeny, (3) associated with Hera's son Typhon, and (4) administered by nymph/priestesses. Again, as I discuss more fully in Chapter 7, Delphi, the site of an oracular priesthood, was also likely the location of a divine birth cult. That the Hesperides are said to have possessed the power of "sweet song" (Hesiod *Theogony* 518; Apollonius Rhodius 4.1399) further indicates that, like the Delphic priestesses, they possessed powers of inspiration and prophecy. This motif also connects them with the "nymphs" of Delos, who, as I noted in Chapter 4, were credited with the ability to make supernatural utterances and may have been part of a divine birth cult. Thus I contend that the myth of the Hesperides' garden references a divine birth/oracular precinct associated with Ge/Gaia and Hera.

I suggest that although the motif of Ge/Gaia's gift of the golden apples was a reminder of Hera's own parthenogenetic nature, this meaning was lost under patriarchy. Over time, the apple came to be misinterpreted as a symbol of heterosexual eroticism and fertility. Henceforth, it came to be associated in both myth and ritual with weddings.[18]

As Faraone (1990, 219) notes, in ancient Greek the word for apple, *mêlon*, also was used for pomegranates and other fruit. Thus I suggest that the apple and pomegranate were analogs for one another from the religious perspective. That means, by extension, the pomegranate was also a symbol of parthenogenesis. It is for this reason, I submit, that the pomegranate abounded as a votive to Hera, and that its presence in the hand of her statue at Argos was considered "something of a holy mystery" (Pausanias 2.17.3). That the pomegranate originally was not a symbol of marriage, or of fertility arising from sexual union, is further suggested by the fact that after around 600 B.C.E., the rich supply of pomegranates at Hera's cult center at Samos suddenly stopped. O'Brien (1993, 63–6) contends this corresponds with the time period in which Hera probably came to be viewed as Zeus's wife. As she explains, the pomegranate was dropped as a votive during this time probably because, as "the earth's votive *par excellence*," it was no longer seen as an appropriate symbol for a goddess who was not an Earth Mother. I would argue that, specifically, it was no longer seen as appropriate for a goddess whose Virgin Mother status had been disrupted.

HERA AS (VIRGIN) MOTHER OF HEROES

Hera's name is etymologically linked not only to "hero" (*hêrôs*), but also to "season" (*hôrâ*); thus "hero" would have meant "he who belonged to the goddess of the season/Hera," (O'Brien 1993, 3–5, 116–7). Hera was considered the protector of citadels and heroes more generally, particularly those of Argos (*Iliad* 1.208–9; *Odyssey* 4.513, 12.72). As we will recall from Chapter 2, heroes were frequently sons of gods by either heroines or "nymphs." That is, they were understood to be *parthenioi*, children of holy virgins. Thus Hera's "protectorship" over heroes underscores the idea that a close relationship must have existed between this goddess and the institution of the divine birth priestesshood thought to have bred such children. Even Homer (*Iliad* 18.59) has Zeus declare that "from [Hera] were born the long-haired Achaeans" (*seio ex autês egenonto karê komonôntes Achaioi*). This seems to reference an earlier mythological stratum in which it was "Hera" who was considered to have been the mother of Achaean heroes who fought at Troy (O'Brien 1993, 164).

The inference here, I suggest, is that the goddess produced these heroes parthenogenetically, an idea that is strengthened if we consider that Ge/Gaia was also credited with having parthenogenetically spawned human beings.[19] Thus Homer's oblique reference seems to allude to a time when Hera was indeed considered the parthenogenetic creatrix of heroes. I propose this is a hint that she once was thought to supersede even Zeus in his role as father of such "divine" humans. That the Dorian Argives built their sanctuary to Hera near Mycenaean hero tombs on the hill called Prosymna also suggests that the Argives understood Hera as the goddess who regulated the hero's short lifespan by returning him to the earth (O'Brien 1993, 168). If we consider that priestesses served as doubles/proxies for their goddesses, we could read this complex of cultic and mythical material as indicating that it was in fact Hera's *priestesses* who were credited with bringing forth the heroes of Mycenae and Argos.

In the condition of *hieros gamos* divine birth, divine honors for what was thought to be a child of a holy *parthenos* were all the more elevated for those who underwent a premature death, with full apotheosis reserved for those figures who agreed to a full-blown ritualized self-sacrifice (i.e., Asclepius, Dionysus, and Heracles). Nowhere was premature death made easier than on the battlefield. This is why, I propose, the great theater of Bronze Age warfare served as a particularly prolific source of heroes for cultic worship.[20] With Zeus assuming "fatherhood" of many of Greece's finest sons, the worship of local heroes became an extension of the worship of Zeus. Hero worship thus became a means of keeping in place the new Olympian order (O'Brien 1993, 118).

Yet the cult of the hero—and Olympian religion itself—was originally dependent on the goddess and her priestesses for its very existence. For one primary way in which a hero was thought to come onto the earthly plane was through his mother's sexual liaison with a god.[21] Correspondingly, as we will see with Hera's priestess Io below, and as we saw with legendary priestesses and "nymphs" associated with Athena and Artemis, it is likely that the Heraian priestesshood was conscripted into what was believed to have been the birthing of heroes via gods, those leaders necessary to fuel the patriarchy. I again also suggest that while priestesses may have derived power from such a role, they may not have been entirely happy with this new male-dominant state of affairs.

Nowhere do we see the distortions resulting from this situation more vividly than in the story of Hera's relationship with Heracles, Zeus's son, and arguably Greece's most famous hero. His mother was Alcmene, a granddaughter of the legendary Mycenaean king Perseus. As such, she was a descendant of Io.[22] Given her genealogical rela-tionship to Io, who I argue shortly was herself a priestess of Hera, and given the fact that Hera's "wrath" toward Alcmene was particularly virulent, I suggest Alcmene was originally a priestess of Hera.

According to Hesiod (*Shield of Hercles* 1–26), Zeus visited Alcmene's bed and impregnated her with Heracles. That same night, her husband, Amphitryon, returned and made love to her, also impregnating her with another child. In another tradition recorded by Apollodorus (2.4.3–5), Zeus engaged with Alcmene "in the like-ness" of her husband.[23] Taken together, these stories suggest an instance of *hieros gamos* by surrogate, to return to my taxonomy. They also recall the episode referred to in Chapter 3 in which Athena's priestess Aethra was said to have been visited by Poseidon and King Aegeus "on the same night," indicating that the god was understood to have come to her through the body of the king. Thus I propose that the legend of Alcmene refers to a ritual intercourse enacted with Zeus through Amphitryon to engender a hero.

Pseudo-Eratosthenes (*Constellations* 44) reports that it was not possible for the sons of Zeus to achieve divinity before one of them had been nursed by Hera. Thus, Hermes brought Heracles shortly after his birth to the breast of Hera, without revealing the child's identity. The goddess unknowingly nursed the future hero, some say while she slept. When, however, she realized what was happening, she pushed the baby away and the milk that was spilled produced the Milky Way.[24] The degree to which Hera wished to do away with Heracles can be seen in the legends of her relentless pursuit of the hero throughout his life.[25] If we consider the possibility that Hera-cles may have been a historical person, Hera's attitude can be read euhemeristically as a murderous mission that was actually attempted by the leaders of the older matriarchal order to do away with this problematic *parthenios*. For Heracles, more than any other hero, is legendarily credited with having introduced patriarchal Olympian ways to Greece.[26]

EVIDENCE FOR DIVINE BIRTH PRIESTESSES OF HERA AT SAMOS

Having reviewed the mythic evidence linking Hera with parthenogenesis, we now turn to additional lore and cultic practices suggesting that her priestesses at some period were holy *parthenoi*. The first indicators in this regard are the toponymic legends at Samos, which have distinct associations with miraculous birth. According to Pausanias (7.4.1–3), *Samia* was the name of a "nymph" whose father was the "river" Maeander and whose husband was Ancaeus, the first king of the island and ruler over the people known as the *Leleges*. Her "nymph" moniker, as I have posited in the last several chapters, is a likely indicator that she was a divine birth priestess. Moreover, her husband, Ancaeus, a hero of Jason's Argonautic expedition, was a supposed son of the god Poseidon, indicating that he himself was considered a divinely born individual.

The Samian historian Menodotus (in Athenaeus 15.671) attests that a sanctuary to Hera was established by "Leleges and nymphs." The "Leleges" are thought to have been the ancient Carians, historically the aboriginal inhabitants of the island (Kerenyi 1975, 157). The remark that "nymphs" were involved in the founding of the sanctuary probably refers, again, to priestesses of divine birth. Indeed, an ancient designation identifying Samos as the "city of nymphs" (Hesychius s.v. *astu numpheôn*) further suggests that the entire island was dominated by a divine birth priestesshood, as I suggested Delos may have been. It is likely, then, that the "nymph" Samia was in the lineage of such native Lelegian/Carian priestesses.

A further clue to this is the fact that one of her children, Samos, was the eponym of the island. As I discussed in Chapter 3, such eponymous naming was largely reserved for ancestors believed to be the children of "nymphs" and gods. Another possible indicator of Samia's status as a holy *parthenos* is the name of her daughter, *Parthenope*, which directly references the Holy Virgin aspect of Hera. The idea that Samia was part of a hereditary lineage of divine birth priestesses is strengthened by the fact that Parthenope herself is said to have given birth to a son, Lycomedes, via the god Apollo (Pausanias 7.4.1–2).

It is also significant that Samia's son Samos, who eventually became king of the island, married a woman named *Parthenia*, who became the island's queen. Some say that the ancient name of the island, *Parthenia*, in fact derived from hers.[27] Given the identification of the name *Parthenia* with Hera in her Virgin Mother aspect, these associations suggest that Queen Parthenia was a priestess of Hera, and also possibly a holy *parthenos*.

Although, according to Pausanias (7.4.1–3), Samia's husband was considered to be King Ancaeus, her son's becoming the eponym of the island suggests that Samia was thought to have engendered her children through unions with a god. It may be that such unions involved a *hieros gamos* by surrogate relationship with Ancaeus, a purported divine son of Poseidon himself. That Poseidon and Apollo began appearing in such stories associated with the island suggests that these legends reflect a time period in which the male cult had already intruded into the sphere of the goddess, and in which *hieros gamos* divine birth had taken hold. That Parthenia and Samia were *married* priestesses may suggest a further imposition of *hieros gamos* by surrogate. Thus their ritual unions by this stage may have resembled that of Athena's priestess Aethra, who was believed to have conceived the hero Theseus with King Aegeus as surrogate for Poseidon (Chapter 2).

EVIDENCE FOR DIVINE BIRTH PRIESTESSES OF HERA AT ARGOS

The stories of the priestess Admete and the "nymph" Samia suggest that priestesses held high status in the cult of Hera at Samos. The pre-eminence of female priests was also emphasized at the goddess's cult at Argos: In a tradition extending back to the Bronze Age, the calendar of that city was reckoned according to names of priestesses who had held office during particular time periods. The list of successive women, averaging two or three per century, is preserved in the fifth-century writings of Hellanicus of Lesbos (O'Brien 1993, 121, 133). Statues of priestesses, presumably the very leaders commemorated in the calendar, stood before the entrance to the Heraion, again emphasizing the pre-eminent role women held in the cult (Pausanias 2.17.3).

Pausanias (2.17.1–7) provides a description of the environs of the Argive Heraion and its cult practices that further points to priestesses' intimate involvement with the mysteries associated with the goddess. He reports that near the sanctuary, for example, was a brook called "Water of Freedom." Priestesses used the waters for purifications and "secret" sacrifices. They also obviously were involved with what

Pausanias calls the "holy mystery" related to the pomegranate that Hera's enthroned statue held. As I discussed earlier, the pomegranate was likely a symbol of parthenogenesis.

Pausanias continues that above the Argive Heraion flowed the river Asterion, on whose banks grew the asterion plant. The vines and leaves were woven into garlands for the statue of Hera, and the plant was made as an offering to her. *Asterion* was one of the ancient names for cannabis, according to the first-century C.E. Greek physician Dioscordes.[28] Hesychius adds *phalis* as another equivalent, which may have been a title of a priestess of Hera at Argos.[29] Writings at least as early as the fifth century B.C.E. indicate that the Greeks knew cannabis to be a substance capable of engendering a non-ordinary state of consciousness.[30] The plant's use as an offering to the goddess suggests it was considered particularly sacred; I contend this was precisely due to its psychotropic properties. That the ancient term *phalis* was also possibly a female sacerdotal title suggests that Hera's priestesses used asterion/cannabis as a means of conjoining with their goddess in a state of *entheos*. I propose they may have used it as a means by which they induced the trance thought necessary to achieve divine conception. The plant's name, *asterion*, "little star," suggests that it was thought to bring users in contact with the astral realms, in particular, which would correspond with Hera's aspect as a goddess of the heavens. I speak more about the use of entheogens in association with divine birth priestesses in Chapter 7, when I discuss Delphi.

The idea that the priestesses of Hera may have used asterion to assist their attempts to achieve divine conception may find support in the identification between the plant name *asterion* and the original name of Delos, *Asteria*. For in Chapter 3, in which I discussed Delos/Asteria as the possible site of a divine birth priesthood, I noted that *Asteria* may have been a reference to the star realms from which the priestesses were believed to incarnate divine children. I also present the case in Chapter 6 that the divine birth priestesses of Dodona, called the *peleiades*, or "doves," similarly thought themselves to be in communication with the stars, particularly the asterism that anciently bore their name: the Pleiades. I argue, as well, that the dove itself was a symbol of parthenogenetic birth. Thus it is significant that the dove was one of Hera's sacred birds. Doves were found in association with her temples at Argos and Delos, and one related statue even depicts Hera with wings (O'Brien 1993, 73; 178, fig. 22; 227–31). This iconography and Homer's characterization of her in the *Iliad* (5.778–9) as one who moved "like a quivering dove" suggest that one of Hera's early epiphanies may have been as a dove.

As I mentioned earlier in relation to the Samian priestesses Parthenia and Samia, if Hera's priestesses indeed attempted to engage in parthenogenesis, it is likely that they sought to achieve the pure form in the earliest period of the cult, and the *hieros gamos* and surrogate forms in the later. Such practices, I propose, would have been patterned after Hera's own trajectory as initially a Holy *Parthenos,* and later a consort of Zeus. However, that the main god with whom Hera's priestesses were thought to unite with sexually was also Zeus, as exemplified by the myth of Hera's priestess Io, to be discussed shortly, means that Hera's holy women would have found themselves ontological rivals of the very goddess they served. Although she does not make the case that female figures who consorted with Zeus may have been priestesses of Hera, Lyons (1997, 97) similarly observes the strange ontological position of Zeus's legendary human consorts vis-à-vis the goddess: "These heroines, by sleeping with Zeus and bearing him sons, act out the role of 'wife of Zeus,' which by rights belongs to Hera. Thus assimilated to her, they invade her sphere of action as wife and in some sense threaten her sovereignty." This bizarre predicament seems to have found expression in the mythological motif of Hera's vindictive jealousy toward mortals and "nymphs" who engaged in *hieros gamos* with the head of the Olympian pantheon. As I noted in Chapter 4, it was not so much Zeus's liaisons with other goddesses that bothered Hera. Rather, what provoked her particular wrath were his unions with those I am arguing were her priestesses. Thus if the argument that Hera's priestesses indeed were holy *parthenoi* has any merit at all, the situation they encountered with the intrusion of patriarchy into their cult must have seemed to them especially uncomfortable.

Io as a Divine Birth Priestess of Hera

Io is one mytho-historical figure with a particularly detailed story supporting the idea that priestesses of Hera at Argos at one point were involved in a divine birth cult. According to legend, Io was forced into a *hieros gamos* union with Zeus and subsequently gave birth to the divine king Epaphus.

With Io, as with numerous other female figures discussed so far, we have a situation of ambiguous ontological status attributed not only to Io herself, but also to her parents and her child. By several accounts, she was the daughter of Inachus, about whom Pausanias (2.15.4, 2.22.4) reports two simultaneous legends. According to the older tradition, Inachus was a king who named the Argive River after himself and set up sacrifices to Hera—that is, he himself was a priest of the goddess. In the later tradition, Inachus was not a man but the god of the river itself. The more popular tradition affirmed that Inachus, in whatever form, was Io's father (see also Herodotus 1.1), while Hesiod (*Catalogue of Women* frag. 72, ed. Most 2007, 145) says her father was Peiren and Apollodorus (2.1.3) says it was Iasus. Io herself is also depicted as a mortal in the earliest stories about her. Hesiod identifies her as a priestess of Hera whom Zeus raped. Herodotus (1.1) similarly refers to her as a human woman. In later accounts, however, she is rendered a "nymph" daughter of the "river god" Inachus (Bacchylides 19.18; Aeschylus *Prometheus Bound* 590, 663). The scholiast on Pindar's *Nemean Ode* 10.8 makes her the daughter of a nymph, and Apollodorus (2.1.3) says she was the granddaughter of a nymph named Ismene.

I propose that Io's transformation from king's daughter to "nymph" underscores her role as a holy *parthenos* of Hera and is a marker of her divinization as a result of having given birth to what was believed to have been the son of a god. Moreover, that Io served as an actual historical human priestess of Hera at Argos is confirmed by chronological tables of the priestesses of Hera at this city, which place Io at the head of the list under the name *Kallirhoë* or *Kallithyia*.[31] Her father, Inachus's status as "river god" thus may have been simply an indicator of the degree to which Inachus was regarded as a holy priest in his own right. The legends that Io's mother and grandmother were "nymphs" also suggest that Io may have been yet another woman who was part of a hereditary lineage of divine birth priestesses of the *hieros gamos* or surrogate variety.[32]

According to the ancient stories, Zeus had his way with the maiden and impregnated her, much to Hera's displeasure. In one version, Zeus changed Io into a cow to attempt to shield her from detection, but Hera set Io under perpetual surveillance. When this failed, the goddess sent a gadfly to infest her, thereby forcing Io to wander over much of the known world. In another version, it was Hera herself who turned Io into a cow (Aeschylus *Suppliants* 299). The goddess subsequently instructed the eponymous Argive hero Argus to tie Io to an olive tree and guard her. In this story, Zeus sent Hermes to steal the maiden, which he did by slaying Argus. Hermes subsequently set Io to wander about the world. The stories converge in Io's at last coming to rest by the banks of the Nile, where she was returned to her human form, gave birth to a son, Epaphus, and was subsequently worshipped by the Egyptians as the goddess Isis.[33]

Greeks, too, not only identified Io with Isis in her cow epiphany, but also equated her son Epaphus with the Egyptian Apis of Memphis (Herodotus 2.38, 3.28.1). Considered to be the reincarnation of the god Osiris (Plutarch *On Isis and Osiris* 20/359B),[34] Apis was believed to appear periodically on earth in the form of a miraculously born "sacred calf" that was distinguished by special bodily markings. Herodotus (3.28.1) writes,

> Apis—or Epaphus—is the calf of a cow that is never afterwards able to have another. The Egyptian belief is that a flash of light descends upon the cow from heaven, and this causes her to receive Apis.
> (Herodotus 1972, 214–5, trans. Sélincourt)

Aelian (*On Animals* 11.10) similarly relates that the holy cow's conception of Apis was achieved through a "flash of light from the heavens." Other sources refer to the conception being generated by the light of the moon, in particular (e.g., Plutarch *On Isis and Osiris* 43; Suda, s.v. *Apides*). Once identified, the sacred Apis bull was ritually housed and honored. After its death and ritual burial, the nationwide search for another incarnated Apis commenced (see Mysliwiec 1998, 76–80). The royal woman who gave birth to the pharaoh was assimilated to the holy cow who birthed the literal Apis calf. Her son, the pharaoh, bearing the title "mighty bull," was identified with Apis and, like Apis, was regarded as the guarantor of fertility and abundant harvests (76).

Thus Io was considered a human incarnation of the holy cow who gave birth to Apis as Epaphus. Taken together with the story of Io's conception via Zeus, the legends of the "cow's" miraculous conception thus suggest that the mechanism of conception for Io—and, by extension, perhaps other divine birth priestesses—was thought to involve the stimulation of the woman's egg through a kind of supernatural light connected with the heavens or, more specifically, the "moon."[35] The fact that Io herself was equated with the moon and that *Io* was a mystic name by which the Argives knew the moon (John Malalas *Chronicle* 2.7) even points to a possible deeper substratum of legend recalling women's perceived ability to conceive in pure parthenogenetic form (from a "ray of the moon") rather than through *hieros gamos*.[36] The Roman poet Propertius (*Elegies* 2.33.1–22) provides hints suggesting that down through the ages rites pertaining to Io may have preserved a memory of what was indeed her original role as "virgin" in service to Hera. Referring to ten-day rituals dutifully performed in her honor by Italian Roman women, Propertius angrily calls

Io a goddess who "often separates lovers," and asks her in rhetorical frustration, "What good it is to you that the girls sleep alone?" In her identification with Isis, we have the divinization of Io not just as a "nymph," as was the case with numerous other consorts of gods, but as a full-blown goddess. As Cook (1914–40, 1:454) notes, she was "at once a priestess and a goddess, human yet divine." Again, I would argue that her apotheosis was a consequence of her purported success in having given birth to a holy one. The fact that the Ionian Sea was said to have been named after her (Apollodorus 2.1.3; Aeschylus *Prometheus Bound* 839–40) is no doubt also indicative of Io's great antiquity and ancestral importance.

Epaphus, like his mother and various sets of his legendary grandparents, was, as a *parthenios,* similarly considered both human and divine. As the "living Apis," he became the legendary ruler of Egypt, and from his line, according to Plutarch (*On the Malice of Herodotus* 11/856E), sprang "the most notable royal families" headed by the kings of Egypt and Argos. Ephaphus's apotheosis also corresponds with the hypothesis I have put forth that *parthenioi,* children of virgin priestesses, were considered supernatural beings themselves. It also suggests he may have undergone a ritual death.

All of these connections furthermore suggest that Io was profoundly tied to Egypt and Africa.[37] While the Greek legends claim her migration was from Argos to Egypt, I propose that the degree of her intertwining with Africa suggests that in fact Io, and, by extension, her father Inachus, had African origins. Indeed, the ancients themselves sometimes regarded Inachus as an immigrant who had come across the sea as the leader of an Egyptian or Libyan colony and had united the Pelasgians, whom he found scattered on the banks of the Inachus (Smith 1870, s.v. *Inachus*). Moreover, Herodotus (6.52–3) establishes Io's lineage as purely Egyptian, something he could not have done if he had assumed her to have been originally Greek.[38] In short, it seems the story of Io's migration from Argos to Egypt could have been a modification of actual events either through generations of distortions in the oral tradition, or through a deliberate theological intervention to "claim" the holy priestess for Greece.

DIVINE BIRTH MOTIFS IN HERA'S CULT AT PLATAEA

The ritual bathing of Hera's statue that took place at Hera's cult on Samos, and possibly at Argos (see Avagianou 2008, 160–1), also may have been enacted in the Daidala festival in Plataea, a town in Boeotia.

According to Pausanias (9.3.1–9), the ritual commemorated Hera's reconciliation with Zeus on an occasion when she was angry with the god. To help Zeus out of his predicament, the clever despot of Plataea told Zeus to make a wooden image, dress it, carry it in a wagon, and claim he was celebrating his marriage with the nymph Plataea, daughter of Asopus. Hera heard the news and appeared on the scene. When she tore off the dress only to find wood and not a bride, she laughed at the joke and made up with Zeus.

The Plataeans held the festival of the Daidala every 6 years or less, and the Great Daidala every 59. The festival involved creating, dressing, and processing to the Asopos River a *daidala*, a wooden image made from the oaks of the nearby grove, setting it on a wagon next to a bridesmaid, and carrying it from the river to a wooden altar on the summit of Cithaeron. There it was burned in a great conflagration along with a cow and a bull sacrificed to Zeus and Hera, as well as animals offered by local participants.

Given that Hera was associated with iconic and aniconic wooden images elsewhere (see, e.g., O'Brien 1993, 17–41), it is probable that originally the *daidala* did not represent a "false" wife of Zeus as in the myth, but rather Hera herself. The primitiveness of the aniconic image furthermore suggests that the Daidala was a rite of great antiquity that celebrated Hera in her pre-Olympian, pre-Zeusian form. It is significant that *Plataea* was the Indo-European name of the Earth Goddess (Burkert 1985, 135), which hints at a cultic embrace of Hera's early role in this capacity, in particular. Once again, I would argue that this connection with Earth, a parthenogenetic creatrix, indicates the celebration initially honored Hera's own parthenogenetic capacity. Like the rites at Samos and Argos, the Daidala at Plataea can be read as a festival that not only maintained a vestige of Hera's earlier preeminent role as Holy *Parthenos,* but also attempted to reconcile the imposition of the Zeus cult there. The mythological motif of Hera and Zeus "making up" over a quarrel suggests as much. The detail in the ritual of the "bridesmaid" riding in the cart alongside the wooden image was probably a later insertion to commemorate the "marriage" of Zeus and Hera, as well.

The myth also supports the idea I discussed earlier that the imposition of the Zeus cult corresponded with the transition of the Heraian priestesshood from a practice of pure parthenogenesis to one of *hieros gamos* divine birth with Zeus. In this myth, we have the motif of the "nymph" Plataea, that is, a priestess, who was likely devoted to Hera as the original female venerated at this location. Although Zeus's threat to couple with this nymph/priestess was not carried out in the myth, it may point to the existence of a ritual practice involving priestesses and this god.

DIVINE BIRTH MOTIFS IN HERA'S CULT AT OLYMPIA

In her temple at Olympia, as elsewhere, Hera clearly predated Zeus (Parke 1967, 181). Every fourth year at the temple, 16 married women wove a *peplos* for the goddess. These women also administered games named after the goddess called the *Heraia*, which consisted of special foot races for maidens—*parthenoi*—that, in the Hellenistic period, were run on shortened courses in the Olympic Stadium. The girls wore tunics to just above the knee, bared the right shoulder as far as the breast, and let their hair hang freely. Winners were awarded crowns of olive leaves and a portion of a cow sacrificed to Hera, and were allowed to dedicate statues of themselves to the goddess (Pausanias 5.16.2–8).

I propose that these games had their roots in the cult of divine birth dedicated to Hera. The first clue in this regard is the fact that the administrators of the maidens' games wove the *peplos* for the goddess. This calls to mind the *peplos* woven and dedicated to Athena at the Panathenaia in Athens. I suggest the *peplos* at Olympia fulfilled the same function as it did for the Athena cult: it was a reminder of weaving, the symbol of parthenogenesis, and thus a marker of Hera's own parthenogenetic capacity.

Moreover, the lore surrounding the establishment of the 16 *peplos* weavers and the maidens' games is redolent with divine birth associations. Pausanias (5.16.2–8) states that both institutions were founded in ancient times by Hippodameia, in thanks to the goddess for her marriage with Pelops. A tracing of the genealogy reveals that Hippodameia was the daughter of King Oenomaus of Pisa. Oenomaus was the legendary son of the god Ares and the mortal Sterope, one of the Pleiads, or Seven Sisters, as I discuss in Chapter 7.[39] That Hippodameia held such a prominent place in the cultic lore of Olympia suggests she was not only a princess, but a priestess of Hera at her sanctuary in Olympia, which originally belonged to the Pisans. Moreover, her position in the lineage of Sterope, a Pleiad and divine birth priestess, suggests that she herself was a holy *parthenos*, in particular. Indeed, Cook, Frazer, and Cornford all independently discern that the "marriage" of Hippodameia and Pelops represented a *hieros gamos* (see Cornford, in Harrison [1912] 1963, 226). That Hippodameia's father, Oenomaus, required Pelops to beat him in a chariot race before he could marry her suggests the story references a moment of transference of kinghood from the elder to the younger. Indeed, the motif that an oracle told Oenomaus he would die if his daughter should marry, and the fact that he did indeed dispatch himself after losing the race, supports this reading.[40] Furthermore, I propose that the motif appearing in the legendary stories that Oenomaus was "in love with" his daughter[41] suggests that, prior to the installation of Pelops as the male partner in the *hieros gamos*, it was the king himself who conducted the ritual with his daughter.

Such stories thus indicate that Hippodameia was holy *parthenos* of Hera during a time of *hieros gamos* by surrogate. Royal incest may have served at this period as a means of attempting to retain the divine birth lineage clearly in the paternal line. The motif of the "transfer" of kingship through marriage with the priestess of Hera also may indicate a time in which *hieros gamos* was increasingly used as a means of legitimizing kingship through the male's spousal association with the holy *parthenos*. In short, it was a time in which the male consort was becoming more important than the priestess of divine birth herself.

The stories also indicate, however, the presence of an older cultic substratum at Olympia. Clues to this reside in a legend related by Pausanias (5.16.2–8) about the establishment of the "sixteen women" who wove Hera's *peplos* and administered the Heraian games. The geographer relates that some time after the Eleans invaded the region held by the Pisans, the Eleans chose a woman from each of the 16 cities of Elis to broker peace between the two groups. Those selected were the oldest, most noble, and most esteemed women of their districts. After succeeding in their peacemaking efforts, the women were entrusted with the management of the Heraian games and with the weaving of the goddess's *peplos*. In Pausanias's day, the Eleans still adhered to ancient customs by choosing the 16 women in twos from each of the eight tribes into which they had divided.

I suggest that the institution of women's political leadership at Olympia did not spring up suddenly in the later period, but is a remnant of an earlier matriarchal time when women were likely an integral part of tribal governance. One particularly telling clue to what I propose was the true nature of the female Elean governing body is the fact that the 16 women took responsibility for arranging two choral dances named after holy *parthenoi*. One was called the "Hippodameia" in honor of the divine birth priestess described earlier. The other, the "Physcoa," commemorated an eponymous maiden from the Elean region who was said to have borne a son by Dionysus. The fact that both female figures whom the 16 Elean women honored were holy *parthenoi* suggests these women were guardians of a priest-esshood of divine birth.

Pausanias's report that, even in his day, the women considered their various duties "sacred" and purified themselves in the Piera spring before performing any of their rituals, underscores their religious function. Here we will call to mind the *gerarai*, those 14 historically attested guardians of the *basilinna* who engaged in a *hieros gamos* with Dionysus in Athens, as discussed in Chapter 2. The ancient characterization of the *gerarai* as "venerable" is quite similar to the description of the 16 Eleans as the "most noble and esteemed" women of their region. The seriousness with which both groups took their sacred duties—we recall that the *gerarai* swore an oath that they were chaste and would conduct rites of Dionysus according to ances-tral practice—is another point of convergence. These resemblances, and the fact that both groups honored holy *parthenoi* who engaged in union with Dionysus (Physcoa in the case of the Eleans), support my supposition that the 16 Elean women were part of a much older priestesshood dedicated to divine birth that was located at the sanctu-ary of Olympia. Moreover, we will recall my argument that the older term *basile* may have served as a clue to the origins of the *gerarai* and the *basilinna* in a pre–*hieros gamos,* matriarchal time. I similarly sug-gest that the 16 Elean women having been "*peplos* weavers" hints at their origins in a much older practice of pure parthenogenesis, given the associations between weaving and parthenogenesis that I have presented.

This brings us to the detail that the 16 Elean women, under the direction of the holy *parthenos* Hippodameia, established the games called the *Heraia*. In these games, which were exclusively the domain of *parthenoi*, we have a tie with the legendary Amazonian virgin nymph/priestesses of Artemis, who relished athletic contests. As we recall from Chapter 4, foot races enacted by virgin girls are also attested historically in association with Artemis's Arkteia rite. The women's choral dances at Olympia in honor of Hera echo those of the nymph/priestesses and historical cults in honor of Artemis. We thus see in the cultic complex of Olympia activities typically associated with goddesses who were originally parthenogenetic: athletic games enacted by virgin girls, the weaving of the *peplos,* choral dancing and singing, matriarchal political leadership, and foundational legends centering on priestesses of divine birth. Thus, at Olympia, as at Argos, Plataea, and Samos, rituals in honor of Hera seem to have recalled a time of matriarchal social order when the goddess and her priestesses alike were honored as virgin mothers.

This argument is supported by the fact that the name of the month in the Greek calendar at Olympia known as *Parthenios* (our late August–September) probably derived from the "*parthenoi* games" held during that period (Cornford, in Harrison [1912] 1963, 230). Once again, the name *Parthenios* recalls the Virgin Mother aspect of Hera, and, I would argue, of her maiden priestesses. Moreover, its permanence in the calendar suggests that the Heraia enjoyed a certain fixity and gravity, which, as Cornford (229–238) argues, is one indication that the maiden foot races were probably older than the male-only Olympic Games that were founded on the same soil, but whose calendar was somewhat variable.[42] The fact that, as we have seen, at Olympia the cult to Hera preceded that of Zeus, the god to whom the Olympic games were ultimately dedicated, further supports the idea that female-exclusive activities would have predated male-exclusive activities there. We end this chapter, then, with the intriguing possibility that one of the most beloved traditions in the world, the Olympic Games, may have originated not only in an Amazonian female custom, but in nothing less than the Greek cult of divine birth. The memory of this may well be preserved in the ritual of the opening of the games. For Greek women, now "playing" the role of the Elean priestesses, still light the sacred torch at the altar to Hera at Olympia in front of her temple during this event. It is thus none other than the burning flame of Hera *Parthenos* and her holy *parthenoi* that is carried around the world and guides the games until their safe conclusion.

CHAPTER 6

THE DIVINE BIRTH
PRIESTESSHOOD AT DODONA

Thus far, I have considered several specific cult locations where I proposed a divine birth priesthood may have existed at some point in ancient Greece, among them Athens, Delos, Mt. Parthenion, Samos, and Argos. I now turn my attention to one of the two other major locations where myth and cult suggest such a priesthood similarly may have dwelt: the oracular site of Dodona.

The oracle of Dodona, located in a stormy area of northwestern Greece at the foot of Mt. Tomarus, was known as the oldest oracular center in Greece.[1] Herodotus (2.52–7) provides two legends attesting that Egyptians founded the oracle. According to one, recounted by the priests of Theban Zeus in Egypt, the oracle at Dodona was established by a priestess of Theban Zeus who had been carried off from Egypt by Phoenicians. Another priestess, who was simultaneously abducted, founded the oracle of Ammon (also identified with Zeus) in the Oasis of Siwah in ancient Libya.[2]

According to the other foundational legend, told to Herodotus by three Dodonian priestesses of his day named Promeneia, Timarete, and Nicandra, the oracle was established by a "black dove" that flew away from Egyptian Thebes. The bird alighted on the famous oak tree at Dodona, spoke in a human voice, and declared that an oracle to Zeus be established on the spot. Parallel with the first version of the legend, a second black dove was said to have flown to Libya and instructed the Libyans to found the oracle of Ammon/Zeus there, as well.[3]

The two legends may not be incompatible, as the prophetesses at Dodona came to be known as *peleiades,* that is, "doves."[4] The second story thus may be a symbolic iteration of the first, the "black" motif simply reinforcing the fact that the founding priestess was Egyptian, as Herodotus (2.57.1) himself suggests. It also may be that this priestess brought her particular form of cult to a site already established. This could reconcile Herodotus's account with that of Strabo (7.7.10), who reports an early claim that Dodona was founded by the Pelasgians, the oldest settlers of Greece.[5] The oldest finds at the site date from the Bronze Age (2500–1100 B.C.E.), and worship there is estimated to have commenced at the end of the third or beginning of the second millennium B.C.E. (Dakaris 1971, 14, 16).[6]

Dakaris (1971, 17, 83), an overseer of antiquities at Epirus, notes evidence for two different cultures that had provenance over the site. The earlier culture worshipped what he proposes was "the Earth goddess," while a later culture, which arrived c. 1900–1400 B.C.E., worshipped Zeus. An indication that Ge/Gaia indeed may have been the first goddess venerated at the site can be found in verses Pausanias (10.12.5) reports were first chanted by the Dodonian priestesses:

Zeus was, Zeus is, Zeus shall be; O mighty Zeus.
Earth sends up the harvest, therefore sing the praise of Earth as Mother.

Dakaris (1971, 85) asserts,

Ancient tradition, cult symbols unrelated with the worship of Zeus in Greece (doves, boars, double-bladed axes, tripods), the prophetic powers of the oak, the chthonian form of the temple of Zeus, confirm beyond doubt the preexistence of a chthonian cult to the Great Goddess, who was worshipped in Greece at least from the beginning of the third millennium B.C., if not from the Neolithic Age. The sacred oak at Dodona is part of the cult of Mother Earth.

The idea of the Earth Mother being a foundational figure at Dodona—perhaps the original source of the oracle before the "arrival" of Zeus—is consistent with the history of all the other ancient oracles of Greece, such as Delphi, Olympia, and Corinth, where the cult of Zeus or Apollo was preceded by the cult of the Earth goddess (Ge/Gaia) or Themis (Dakaris 1971, 84).

The earliest formal goddess name that appears in association with Dodona is *Dione*. In Hesiod's genealogy (*Theogony* 353), Dione was a female Titan, a daughter of Oceanus and Tethys.[7] Thus she was, in fact, an "older" deity than Zeus, although at Dodona, she was characterized as his "wife." As in the case of Hera, it was probably only with the establishment of the worship of Zeus that the original pre-Hellenic Earth goddess at Dodona became his spouse, and, accordingly, took his "name" (Dakaris 1971, 87). For it is generally agreed that *Dione*, like *Zeus*, derived from the general term for "deity" (*Dis/dios*), whose root has the meaning "shine."[8] Dakaris further posits that when Zeus worship was adopted at Dodona, the prophetic powers of the goddess were transferred to the male god, as was the iconography of the oak tree.

Thus it is likely that at some later date, Zeus "arrived" at what was already a functioning oracular site dedicated to a goddess at Dodona. It is reasonable to assume, following on the reports of Herodotus about the "founding" of the site by the Egyptian priestess, that the nature of the Zeusian cult that was laid over the earlier cult was, in some sense, Egyptian. Herodotus (2.52) indeed further emphasizes the influence of Egypt on Greek religion more generally. He states that the Dodonians of his day fully believed that the Egyptians had brought to the early people of Greece, the Pelasgians, the names of all deities, and that it was in fact the oracle at Dodona that had sanctioned the use of these names. Prior to that, in remote antiquity, the Pelasgians were thought to have prayed to deities for whom they had no names or titles, merely calling them *theoi* (gods). Parke (1967, 57, 59) notes that Herodotus implies it was through the Egyptian priestess who arrived at Dodona that the knowledge of the names of the deities—and perhaps even their identities, characteristics, and cults altogether—was first established at Dodona and then spread throughout Greece.[9]

It is likely, then, that the god the Egyptian priestess of Thebes brought with her to Dodona was none other than "Theban Zeus," whom Herodotus (1.182, 2.42, 4.181) confirms was identified with Amun-Re. Cook (1914–40, 3.1:882) reports that Zeus was identified with Amun of Thebes at least as far back as 900 B.C.E.[10] The cult of Amun-Re at Thebes was associated with the practice of divine birth of the pharaoh throughout much of the Bronze Age (see Rigoglioso 2007, 74–94; Rikala 2008, 116–25). Moreover, as I discussed in Chapter 2, Herodotus (1.181–2) attests that, in his day (fifth century B.C.E), *hieros gamos* rites were still taking place between virgin priestesses and Theban Zeus/Amun-Re at the oracular temple at Thebes. I thus propose that the black, prophetic "dove" priestess who arrived at Dodona from Thebes most likely was a holy *parthenos* herself who established a *hieros gamos* cult at Dodona in service to Theban Zeus. Following on the pattern I have discerned with the priestesshoods of Athena, Artemis, and Hera, it may have been that she laid this cult over what was already a priestesshood dedicated to a parthenogenetic goddess (Ge/Gaia or an early form of Dione), and, correspondingly, to pure parthenogenesis. I provide further evidence for the existence of a divine birth priesthood at Dodona later in the chapter.

GENERAL CHARACTERISTICS
OF THE DODONIAN PRIESTLY CASTE

Ancient accounts vary as to the gender of the prophets who served at Delphi. Homer (*Iliad* 16.235) calls the prophets of the archaic period *Selloi*, and describes them as men with unwashed feet who slept upon the ground (i.e., ascetics). Pausanias (1.36.4) mentions a legendary male seer from Dodona named Scirus, said to have lived at the time when the Eleusinians were at war with Athens. Strabo (7.7.12), writing in the late first century B.C.E. when the sanctuary was in a period of ruin, reports a later shift in the gender of the sacerdotal personnel: at some point in the life of the oracle, three old women (*graiai*) were designated as prophetesses.[11]

There are various indicators that priestesses served at the site much earlier, however. As mentioned, Dakaris (1971, 16, 92) posits that the goddess-venerating pre-Hellenes founded the oracle prior to 1900 B.C.E. This predates the arrival of the Hellenic tribe of the Selloi, from whom the name of Homer's priests was most likely taken. Given that the site was first dedicated to a goddess, and that the gender of the sacerdotal personnel in Greece generally corresponded with that of the deity, Dakaris presumes the conjoined presence of a priesthood there from its earliest period. Herodotus's report of the oracle's "founding" by an Egyptian priestess carried over by the Phoenicians further suggests priestesses could have been present at the site anywhere from the early to late Bronze Age.

Justin (17.3.4) affirms the presence of prophetesses at Dodona in the late Bronze Age. He relates that when the Trojan War hero Neoptolemus/Phyrrus consulted the oracle of Zeus there, he "abducted" from the temple a woman named Lanassa, a granddaughter of Heracles, by whom he had eight children. Lanassa's presence at the temple indicates that she probably was a priestess there. Correlating the episode to around the time of the Trojan War gives us a date in the mid-thirteenth century B.C.E. The presence of priestesses at the oracle in this period is also attested by Ephorus (in Strabo 9.2.4), who writes that in the era of migrations,[12] two generations after the Trojan War, the Boeotians consulted the prophetess at Dodona about returning to their native land. A fragment from a lost play of Euripides alludes to priestesses being present at Dodona even prior to the Trojan War (Parke 1967, 72–3).

These last few references indicate that female priests were present at the site from early times. The account of Lanassa's abduction also speaks of a time when priestesses at Dodona apparently suffered disempowerment at the hands of men during the period of patriarchal incursions into the region. That power conflicts between priestesses and men may have ensued at the sanctuary in the late Bronze Age is further suggested by an episode recounted by Ephorus (in Strabo 9.2.4). According to this story, on one occasion some Boeotian emissaries became displeased over the prophetess's oracular response, casting her on a burning pile and killing her.[13] The temple authorities (presumably men) called the Boeotians to trial before the priestesses. When the accused argued it was not customary for women to be judges, an equal number of men were chosen to hear the testimony conjointly. The priestesses voted for condemnation, while the men voted for acquittal; the men's vote prevailed. Despite such episodes, it is well documented that in the classical and Hellenistic periods, women were the exclusive mantics at Dodona,[14] although most likely the temple authority structure of the late Bronze Age, mentioned by Ephorus, persisted as a male institution.

The duties of the Dodonian prophetesses included "feeding" Zeus and Dione with offerings of food, and soliciting their answers to petitioners' questions (Philostrates *Imagines* 2.33). Over the history of the oracle, a number of methods of divination were used. Early on, the oracular inquiries and responses were oral. By the Hellenistic period, inquiries were written on small, flat lead tablets that were folded.[15] Such inquiries frequently could be answered in "yes or no" fashion, and responses were most commonly given orally. Questions were submitted by individuals (mostly men), as well as by representatives of certain groups, cities, and tribes (Dakaris 1971, 88). The majority of the inquiries preserved on the tablets center around themes of marriage, children, home, property, business, and health, and questions regarding which deities to invoke for aid. Petitioners also sought the blessings of Zeus and Dione for specific projects or endeavors. Occasionally envoys from Greek states made petitions on official matters.

The earliest divinatory practices at Dodona may have involved the interpretation of various types of sounds: the rustling of the leaves of the site's sacred oak tree (Homer *Odyssey* 14.327–8, 19.296–7), the murmuring of a fountain at the foot of the oak (Pliny *Natural History* 2.228; Servius on Virgil's *Aeneid* 3.466), and the ringing of bronze wind chimes or the sounding of a bronze bowl struck by means of bones hung on chains suspended from a nearby statue that

were activated by the wind (Strabo 7.3 frag.). Other possible methods
of divination included dream incubation (Lycophron, in Eustathius
on Homer's *Iliad* 16.233),[16] divine frenzy (Plato *Phaedrus* 244b),
casting lots (Cicero *On Divination* 1.34.76), or observing the flight
of a flock of doves (Dionysius of Halicarnassus 1.14.5).

EVIDENCE FOR A DIVINE BIRTH
PRIESTESSHOOD AT DODONA

Numerous legends associate "nymphs" with the ancient oracle of Zeus
at Dodona. According to the argument I developed in Chapter 4,
this likely indicates the presence of a divine birth priestesshood there.
Pherecydes (3 F 90) specifically calls the nymphs of this oracular site
"Dodonides," and names them Ambrosia, Coronis, Eudore, Dione,
Phaisyle, Phaeo, and Polyxo. That he identifies them as "nurses" of
Zeus affirms the possibility that an older, pre-Zeusian cultic substratum was associated with Dodona.[17] Furthermore, that the name *Dione*
is included in the list also affirms that the goddess who was later cast
as Zeus's "wife" at the site originally belonged to the older layer of
the cult. The appearance of the name *Dione* in association with one of
the Dodonian "nymphs" also may reference yet another possible case
of a priestess who served as a proxy for this goddess.

Again, it may be that, as with Hera and Ge/Gaia, the goddess
Dione (perhaps known by a pre-Zeusian name originally) was initially
considered a Holy *Parthenos*. Correspondingly, her priestesshood at
first may have been associated with pure parthenogenesis rather
than *hieros gamos* divine birth. Dione is listed by Hesiod (*Theogony* 353)
as one of the *Kourai*, who, as I discussed in Chapter 2, were a
"holy race" of *parthenoi* tasked with "rearing" the children of gods.
Although Hesiod describes this group of holy females in patriarchal
terms as being at the bidding of male gods, it may be that originally
they had a pure parthenogenetic function. Dione's inclusion in this
group at the very least affirms that she had some kind of connection
with miraculous birth. Moreover, as we saw in Chapter 4, her presence at Leto's birth of Apollo and Artemis on Delos further points to
her association with the cult of divine birth. As in the case of all the
other cults discussed thus far, with the imposition of "Zeus" religion
at Dodona, a transition from a practice of pure parthenogenesis to
hieros gamos may have taken place.

An interesting detail in Hyginus (*Astronomica* 2.21) may strengthen
the idea that the Dodonian nymphs were priestesses of divine birth. On
the authority of Pherecydes, the mythographer says Zeus transformed

these nymphs into the asterism known as the Hyades, located in the constellation of Taurus. In their identification with the Hyades, who were known as virgin daughters of Atlas, the Dodonian nymphs thus would have been the half sisters of the Pleiades. Given that, as I discuss later, the Pleiades were strongly associated with Dodona and *hieros gamos* divine birth, their close genealogical relationship with the "nymph" Hyades suggests the latter's own connection with such a practice. We therefore have an equation among the Dodonian "nymphs," Hyades, Pleiades, and divine birth.

The association of "nymphs" with Dodona may explain why at this particular location Zeus bore the uncharacteristic surname *Naïos,* "of flowing springs." The term *naiad* (*naïs*), similarly related to the Greek verb *naô,* "flow," was used from the time of Homer onward as a substitute or qualifier for *nymph* (Larson 2001, 8). Moreover, the words for tree nymphs, *dryad* or *hamadryad,* share the root *dru,* meaning "tree" or "oak," indicating an affinity between nymphs and oaks. As mentioned earlier, one of the central features of Dodona was its sacred oak tree. I thus propose that the god name exclusive to Dodona, *Zeus Naïos,* could have meant "Zeus of the Nymphs"—that is, "Zeus of the Holy *Parthenoi.*"

The important role "nymphs" had at this oracular site is attested by two eponym-related legends. Several sources (e.g., Epaphroditus, in Stephanus Byzantius, s.v. *Dôdônê*) claim that the name *Dodona* derived from *Dodone,* the name of a "nymph"—again, a moniker indicating that she was probably a divine birth priestess.[18] Another legend relates that it derived from *Dodon* (Stephanus Byzantius, s.v. *Dôdônê*), the name of a male with a divine birth story. Dodon's mother was Europa, a Phoenician princess (priestess) impregnated by Zeus, who took the form of a bull and abducted her from Phoenicia to Crete.[19] This story indicates that Europa was understood to be a holy *parthenos.* Indeed, Europa's role in relationship to divine birth is emphasized by Hesiod (*Theogony* 357), who lists her as one of the "holy race of Kourai" along with Dione. This is further supported by the fact that in Crete, she was honored with her own festival known as the *Hellotia,* a name that, according to the *Etymologicum Magnum* (s.v. *Hellôtia,* in Larson 1995, 139), was the Phoenician equivalent of *parthenos.* Thus the very name of the festival, according to my definition of *parthenos,* referenced the priestess who was thought to conceive in divine fashion. Moreover, during this festival, a garland of myrtle, 20 cubits in circumference and said to enclose Europa's bones, was carried in procession (Athenaeus 678a–b). Such veneration indicates that Europa was considered to be a historical ancestor who was thought to merit divine honors because she had successfully borne what was believed to be the son of a god.[20]

Europa's importance is underscored by Herodotus (4.45.1), who speculates that the entire continent of Europe may have been named after her. It is likely that his conjecture is true, as many important cities and landforms were named after other holy *parthenoi,* among them, as we have seen, the Ionian Sea (after Io), the city of Nicaea, and other locales. I furthermore suggest that the "fertilizing horn" of Zeus-as-bull, to which Europa clings in innumerable representations (e.g., Cook 1914–40, 1:526), may reference a herm or phallus that she was thought to have used in her *hieros gamos* ritual with the god.

That Dodona may have been named after either a divine birth priestess (Dodone) or the son of Zeus (Dodon) by a holy *parthenos* supports the thesis that Dodona was associated with a divine birth cult. Moreover, that Europa's "abduction" may have occurred not only on what was believed to be the level of sacred trance,[21] but literally, is suggested by Herodotus. In several places (e.g., 1.21, 1.173, 4.45, 4.147), he portrays the abduction of this priestess from western Asia as a historical event. We will recall that the founding Egyptian prophetess of Dodona was similarly abducted to her new location, as was Hera's priestess Io, about whom legends of a historical abduction from Greece to Egypt also circulated (see, e.g., Herodotus 1.1, 1.7). These stories hint that divine birth priesthoods may have been present throughout the known world in antiquity, and that trafficking in such women became a lucrative business in the patriarchal Bronze Age or earlier.[22]

The idea that a divine birth cult dedicated to Zeus may have existed at Dodona is also strengthened by the fact that a sacred virgin priesthood devoted to this god was documented elsewhere, where it had particular resonances with Dodona. According to Parke (1967, 24–5), at Tralles in Caria (West Asia) in 200 C.E. or later, the local cult to Zeus Larisius included priestesses who were officially designated "concubines" to the god. It is significant that one of them describes herself in a dedication as having descended from ancestors who were "concubines and with unwashed feet," given that, as mentioned earlier, the very phrase "unwashed feet" was used by Strabo to describe the Selloi, the priests of Zeus at Dodona. The reference to "ancestors" also indicates that, although the dedication is of late date, the custom had roots deeper in antiquity. These pieces of information may indicate a link or affinity between the sacerdotal practices of Tralles and Dodona as they related to "concubines of Zeus."

As to when the priestesshood of Dodona may have become involved in attempts at *hieros gamos*, again, Herodotus's legend of the arrival of the Theban priestess via Phoenicians could put the event anywhere from the early to late Bronze Age. The length of time such a priestesshood may have functioned is similarly indeterminable. By the time of Strabo's writing (first centuries B.C.E.–C.E.), the prophetesses are described (7.7.12) as being old (*graiai*), thereby indicating they were past childbearing age. It is most likely that a divine birth priestesshood would have functioned earlier in the oracle's history, when literary evidence suggests the priestesses were younger. Herodotus (2.56), for example, writing in the fifth century B.C.E., lists the three prophetesses of Dodona, with whom he reportedly personally spoke, as ranging in age from oldest to youngest, and does not imply an "elderly" status for them. Justin's (17.3.4) statement that Lanassa was abducted from Dodona and bore eight children indicates that certainly around the thirteenth century B.C.E. the Dodonian priestesses were of childbearing age.

As to who the supposed progeny of such unions might have been, the legends mentioned thus far provide one hint: Dodon, the miraculously born son of Europa. As I discuss in the rest of the chapter, other myths of divine birth are also associated with Dodona, among them, those of the legendary seven maidens known as the Pleiades. I argue that, given the strong linguistic/symbolic connections among Dodonian doves/*peleiades*, Dodonian priestesses/*peleiades*, and the mythological Seven Sisters known as the *Pleiades/Peleiades* (also conceived as doves, as I show), it may be that these legendary maidens served as mythological templates for the divine birth priestesses of Dodona.

THE DOVE AS A PARTHENOGENETIC SYMBOL

To consider the possibility that a divine birth priestesshood may have existed at Dodona, it is necessary to look at the presence and meaning of the dove at the site. As mentioned earlier, prophetesses of Dodona were named *peleiades*/doves.[23] Hesiod (*Catalogue of Women* frag. 181, ed. Most 2007, 259) and the scholiast on Sophocles' *Trachiniae* 1167 mention that doves dwelt in the hollow of the site's oracular oak tree. In other legends associated with Dodona, these birds are said to have dissuaded individuals from cutting down the oak on two separate instances.[24] Philostrates (*Imagines* 2.33) describes a visual depiction of Dodona in which a golden dove was perched on a tree tied with wreaths, explaining that the bird gave prophecy. A bronze coin from Dodona confirms these connections: on it, three doves (the same as the number of priestesses thought to have served the oracle at a time) surround the oak (Dakaris 1971, plate 38.3). Moreover, as mentioned earlier, observing the flight of doves was a method of divination at Dodona. The Aetolians and their Acarnanean and Epirot neighbors around Dodona, in fact, believed doing so was one of the most accurate ways of deriving oracular messages, the other being interpreting the rustling of oak leaves (Pausanias 7.21.2–3). Thus, the dove, in conjunction with the oak, was the primary religious symbol at Dodona, and was seen as an oracular being in and of itself.

The main goddess of Dodona, Dione, also had associations with the dove, suggesting that the original goddess of the site had a dove epiphany. That the name *Diônê* resembles the Hebrew term for dove, *ϒVNH/ionah/ione*, may be suggestive in this regard.[25] The identification of Dione with the dove persisted throughout time. Dione's daughter by Zeus, Aphrodite,[26] possessed the dove as one of her sacred totems.[27] Statues of Aphrodite holding a dove were found at Dodona.[28] Interesting in this regard is the fact that during the "Festival of the Embarcation" at ancient Eryx in Sicily, where an important temple to Aphrodite stood, Aphrodite in the form of an immense multitude of doves/pigeons was sent off to North Africa. It was said that nine days later, the birds returned in the wake of a particularly beautiful dove/pigeon whose rose color was taken to be a sign of the goddess (Aelian *On Animals* 4.2). Here, again, we see the pathway of the sacred dove between Africa and Europe in connection with ancient oracular centers, which calls to mind the advent of the "dove/priestess" at Dodona as discussed by Herodotus.

It is highly significant to the argument that Dodona was the site of a divine birth priestesshood that a myth retained by Hyginus (*Fabulae* 197) makes a connection among doves, Aphrodite, and parthenogenetic birth. According to this story, an egg of wondrous size fell from the sky into the waters and was rolled to the shores by fish. After doves sat on it, out hatched Venus (i.e., Aphrodite), who was later called "the Syrian Goddess." Since she excelled over the rest in justice and uprightness, Zeus put the fish that had discovered her egg among the stars as a constellation, and because of this, Syrians did not eat fish or doves, considering them as gods.

What is particularly noteworthy is that the story relates an episode of pure parthenogenesis in which no male was involved. That the dove here is rendered "divine" for its role in this process further underscores the relationship between this bird and female (parthenogenetic) deity. The myth thus may be a vestige of a more ancient story in which Dione-as-dove gave birth to Aphrodite in pure parthenogenetic fashion, and it may describe what I identified in Chapter 1 as the pure daughter-bearing phase of the divine birth cult, in particular. With this in mind, we may revisit the chant of the priestesses at Dodona referred to earlier:

> Zeus was, Zeus is, Zeus shall be; O mighty Zeus.
> Earth sends up the harvest, therefore sing the praise of Earth as Mother.
>
> (Pausanias 10.12.5)

The second line of the chant refers to the parthenogenetic nature of the goddess Ge/Gaia, while the first closely resembles the formula attributed to Neith at the temple of Saïs, which, as I discussed in Chapter 3, speaks of the mystery of Neith's autogenetic/parthenogenetic nature:

> I am everything that has been, and that is, and that shall be, and no one has ever lifted my garment (*peplos*).
>
> (Plutarch *On Isis and Osiris* 9)

Thus the Dodonian chant may be a vestigial allusion to what I am suggesting may have been an earlier pure parthenogenetic cult at the site. The myth of the doves that hatched Aphrodite out of the great egg may then explain the ancient connection between the dove and Aphrodite. Significantly, it indicates that the dove was ultimately a symbol of parthenogenetic fertility, not heterosexually generated fertility, a point I return to later in the chapter.[29] For now, it is important to emphasize that this story describes an intimate relationship between a schema of symbols all associated with Dodona: the dove, Aphrodite/Dione, and pure (daughter-bearing) parthenogenesis.

It is thus tremendously significant that, as mentioned earlier, the Dodonian prophetesses themselves were known as *peleiades*, "doves." Herodotus (2.57) attempts to explain away the use of this term with the conjecture that it may have arisen because the language of the Egyptian priestess who founded the oracle sounded to the native Pelasgians "like the twittering of doves." Strabo (7.1a frag.), writing in a later time when the priestesses of Dodona were elderly women, guesses that the title emerged out of the linguistic confluence between the words for *dove* and *old women* (*peliai*) in the neighboring Molossian language. However, I propose a different origin of this term for the Dodonian priestesses, one, again, that may have linked them with a divine birth cult.

In considering this argument, it is important to look at the religious meaning of the dove. For the Greeks, as for numerous cultures throughout the ancient world, the dove was an extremely important bird, both in practical and spiritual terms.[30] Doves were bred in antiquity to carry messages back and forth between distant cities and even across continents, and, as mentioned, their behavior was observed as a means of divination (Hansell 1998, 70, 128–34; Aelian *On Animals* 8.5). Thus doves were seen as "messengers" not just on the terrestrial plane, but between the celestial and earthly realms, rendering them transmitters of divine wisdom and divine will. Doves were also thought to be bringers of the "ambrosia" that conferred divinity, as well. They are said to have carried "ambrosia" to Zeus, a substance he apparently needed to reinforce his immortality (Homer *Odyssey* 12.62–6). A later version of the story represents doves as feeding the infant Zeus with ambrosia when Rhea concealed him from his father Cronos in the Dictaean cave in Crete (Athenaeus 11.491a–b). In these motifs, the doves serve a similar role to Hera, who completed the divinization of the miraculously born child through her "milk," which I discussed in Chapter 5.

Moreover, the dove in the Hellenistic world symbolized the soul. Roman iconography shows the human soul as a dove held in the hand of the deceased (Strong 1969, 136). The dove/pigeon's practical characteristic of following its human owner in flight and always returning to the place it was bred, no matter what the distance (Hansell 1998, 132, 134), rendered it a metaphor for the soul that returned to its place of celestial origin after death, as well. This can be seen in images of the dove flying out of the mouths of dead Roman emperors (77). This idea persisted in the Roman term for catacombs, *columbaria*, literally, "dovecotes," the term for the dwelling places of doves (Bachofen 1973, 21). In Egyptian tomb paintings, a dove sometimes hovers above the dead person as an image of the soul that was poised to go back to its eternal home in the stars (Baring and Cashford 1991, 596; Drewermann 1994, 124). Christian iconography continued the tradition by depicting the dove as the Holy Spirit flying either to or from the mouths of dead saints and martyrs (Hansell 1998, 78).

The dove was perceived not just as the soul of the human being, but as the essence of divinity itself—often in its feminine aspect. In ancient Greek texts and/or iconography, the dove appears as a sacred totem associated with several goddesses in addition to Aphrodite, including Rhea, Demeter, and Persephone.[31] In cultures preceding or near Greece, the dove was similarly considered one of the sacred animals of numerous goddesses: in Babylonia, of Ishtar; in Persia, of Anahita; in Anatolia, of Cybele; in Phoenicia, of Ashtoreth; and in Rome and at Ephesus, of Artemis/Diana.[32] In fact, the etymology of another ancient Greek word for dove, *peristera*, may come from a Semitic phrase meaning "bird of Ishtar" (Griffiths 1970, 543n5). A flock of doves resided at the temple to Aphrodite at Paphos. So important was the dove in the cult there that the name *Paphos* was also but a variant of the word for dove.[33] Doves also appear in profusion in the sacred iconography of Cyprus, ancient Hierapolis in western Anatolia, and the palace of Cnossos at Crete (Hansell 1998, 25–8, 30–1, 39–40). Christians subsequently adopted the dove as the symbol of the "Holy Spirit."

We saw earlier that the dove appears as a major figure in at least one creation story in which generative power is depicted in parthenogenetic terms. The dove's ability occasionally to lay barren eggs without copulating, creating what the Greeks called a "wind egg" (Pliny *Natural History* 10.79–80) may have strengthened its reputation as a symbol of virgin birth. It is significant that the dove was simultaneously seen as a *source of divine wisdom* and the *agent of conception* of divinity into human form. This is perhaps indicated most clearly in the Christian tradition, in which the dove is depicted as both the herald/agent of Mary's virginal conception of Jesus[34] and the "Holy Spirit" that descended on Jesus at his baptism (Matthew 3:16; Luke 3:22). The dove persisted as a symbol of Mary as Holy Virgin Mother (e.g., Hawkins [1633] 1950, 199–210). The ancient connection of the dove with oracular virgins is retained by the Rosicrucians, who claim to be inheritors of the Greek esoteric tradition. They consider the Colombe, the dove, to be a symbol for "conscience," and they conceive her as a "vestal virgin" who is a prophetic priestess (McDavid 2005, 26).

Interestingly, Horapollo (*Hieroglyphics* 2.32) notes that in Egyptian antiquity the symbol of the *black* dove, in particular, denoted a widow who remained faithful to her spouse after death, for the bird was believed to remain solitary after the death of her mate. As we will recall, it was a *black dove,* specifically, that served as the foundational symbol of Dodona, demonstrating the oracular center's connection with Egypt. The black dove of Herodotus therefore may have been a multivalent symbol that denoted not only the dark-skinned priestess from Africa who founded Dodona, but the woman who served as a virgin spouse of Zeus and made the choice to be bound to him all of her life like a widow whose husband was no longer on the earthly plane.[35] Thus, again, because of these many associations I contend that the dove originally was a symbol of virgin birth.

THE DOVE AND THE PLEIADES

Another piece of information that is significant to the argument that the dove priestesses/*peleiades* of Dodona may have attempted divine birth is the fact that the Greeks associated the dove with the Pleiades,[36] a star cluster that was, like the dove, considered to have tremendous religious and agricultural importance. Lamprocles (in Athenaeus 11.491c) expressly refers to the Pleiades as "you who are set in the sky, bearing the same name as the winged doves (*peleiades*)," affirming the connection between the asterism and these birds. According to Athenaeus (1.489–91), the same idea was held by numerous other writers. We have already seen that the Greeks held doves/*peleiades* and Dodonian priestesses/*peleiades* to be equivalent. Thus, I maintain that, for the Greeks, doves, the dove priestesses of Dodona, and the stars known as the Pleiades were analogs for one another.

Mythologically, the Greeks further identified the Pleiades specifically with the "Seven Sisters"—the seven daughters of Atlas and the ocean nymph Pleione who were born on the Arcadian mountain Cyllene (Apollodorus 3.10.1).[37] According to one tradition, these mythological sisters were virgin hunting companions of Artemis who, with their mother Pleione, were pursued in amorous (and unwelcome) fashion for many years by the giant hunter Orion. Out of pity, Zeus metamorphosed them into doves and placed them among the stars.[38] These women were understood to be the very "doves" who brought "ambrosia" to the infant Zeus in the mythologem mentioned earlier (Athenaeus 11.489–91), indicating their perceived role as bestowers of divinity.[39]

Astronomically, the Pleiades were familiar to the ancient Greeks as the seven stars located at the "nape of the bull's neck" in the constellation of Taurus.[40] They are mentioned by Homer (*Iliad* 18.486; *Odyssey* 5.272), Hesiod (*Works and Days* 383; 615–20), Pliny (*Natural History* 18.60, 66.1, 74), and nearly all of the classical poets and writers, who make numerous astronomical and poetic references to them.[41] Their name may have been derived from that of their mythological mother, *Pleione,* or from *pleiōn,* "more, larger, many."[42] Aratus (*Phaenomena* 263–7), the Greek poet and naturalist, says that although they were small and dim, they were widely famed, and their presence marked the beginning of summer and winter. Significantly, Hyginus (*Astronomica* 2.21) notes that no other constellation held this honor, underscoring their great astronomical importance. Specifically, the Pleiades' helical (dawn) rising on the eastern horizon in the middle of May at the approach of harvest, and their cosmical (dawn) setting on the western horizon at the beginning of November at sowing time, were closely observed events, tied as they were to the agricultural calendar.[43] The Pleiades thereby were connected with the seasonal cycles, notions of time, agriculture, food, and human survival. That the Greeks identified these stars with doves, the symbol throughout the ancient Mediterranean world for both the human and divine spirit, and that they linked them to important religious festivals, indicates that they attached great astrological/mystical importance to the Pleiades. Indeed, the Greeks connected the astral/mythological Seven Sisters with the very concepts of "life" and "death" by virtue of the fact that these "star women" served as harbingers of summer harvest and winter sowing. Such seasonal events in association with this star cluster thus had great religious import. Plutarch (*On Isis and Osiris* 69/378D–E) underscores this conception in his comment on what he calls the "gloomy, mirthless, and sorrowful offering-festivals" of winter:

> The women at Athens fast in the Thesmophoria, sitting on the ground . . . calling that festival one of grief because Demeter bewails the descent of Kore to the underworld. This month is indeed, at the time of the (setting of the) Pleiades, the season of sowing.
> (Plutarch 1970, 227, trans. Griffiths)

This observation points to the Greeks' deeply felt association between the "disappearance" of the Pleiades beneath the earth's horizon at dawn in winter (and their corresponding "reign" over the night sky 12 hours later) and the cyclical disappearance of Persephone into the underworld and her "reign" over the realm of death. This suggests a perceived occult equivalence between these stars and the two (parthenogenetic) goddesses.[44] In the spring/summer, correspondingly, Demeter, Persephone, and the Pleiades were seen as the source of birth, life, and abundance; Demeter was the primary deity connected with the harvest.[45] Given these theological connections and the fact that the Greeks credited Demeter with bringing the gift of agriculture to humanity, it may be that the Greeks also anciently believed the Pleiades to be the esoteric "source" of crop wisdom, as have some indigenous peoples around the world (Allen [1899] 1963, 401).

The spiritual import attributed to the Pleiades can be seen further in Pythagoras's referring to this star cluster as the "lyre of the Muses" (Porphyry *Life of Pythagoras* 41). His metaphor points to a probable ancient understanding of this star group as a source of divine inspiration and knowledge related to esoteric/philosophical/mathematical concepts of music and harmony. The connection between the Pleiades and music is further attested in legends that Hermes, the son of the Pleiad Maia, was the first to observe the harmony of musical sounds and their nature, and that he invented the lyre (*Homeric Hymn to Hermes* 51; Diodorus Siculus 1.16). According to one tradition, he even gave the instrument seven strings to correspond to the number of Pleiades (Ovid *Fasti* 5.105).

Pliny the Elder (*Natural History* 37.28) affirms the Pleiades' spiritual significance to the Greeks in his comment that the "sandastros" stone was seen to have religious associations and uses by virtue of the fact that its star-like particles resembled the arrangement of this star cluster. He elsewhere notes (7.57) that the Pelasgians, whom we recall were likely among the early founders of the oracle of Dodona, possessed tremendous knowledge of the stars astronomically and astrologically, as they reportedly had obtained these arts from the Babylonians and introduced them into ancient Latium in Italy. He also records a legend (7.57) that the "founder" of astrology—the method of divination that relies on the interpretation of the positions and relationships among the various heavenly bodies—was none other than Atlas, the mythological father of the Pleiades themselves. This reference suggests that the legendary Atlas was an important observer of the starry realms and one of the first to give an account of them (Pliny 1855, 7.57n74, ed. Bostock). Indeed, Diodorus Siculus (3.60.3, 4.27.5) says the myth that Atlas "held the sky upon his shoulders"[46] was an allusion to his having discovered the spherical nature of the stars. Pliny's reference also contains a euhemeristic implication that Atlas may have been a historical North African king. Thus, in Atlas we have a possible historical personage who possessed important esoteric astrological knowledge.[47] That astrology was a concern of the Pelasgians, and that this divinatory art was linked with the Pleiades through Atlas, supports the conjecture that Dodona was a sacred locale where great mystical importance was accorded to the stars in general—and the Pleiades in particular. The idea that Atlas may have had an African provenance is emphasized by his ancient identification with the great eponymous mountain of northwestern Africa (Herodotus 4.184; Cook 1914–40, 1:156). This would correspond in general with what I have argued was strong African influence at Dodona.

THE PLEIADES AS THE SEAT OF IMMORTALITY

It is significant to this argument that the constellation of Taurus the Bull, in which the Pleiades are located, was anciently considered to be a source of divinity. This is suggested as far back as ancient Sumer, where the bull Gugalanna, husband to Erishkegal, Queen of the Underworld, and brother-in-law of Inanna, Queen of Heaven, was referred to as the "bull of heaven" (Sandars 1972, 87–8; Wolkstein and Kramer 1983, 55). The "heavenly" placement of Gugalanna suggests that he was conceived as Taurus itself, and therefore connected theologically to the Pleiades, who reside in that constellation. An ancient astronomical engraving from Mesopotamia (c. 301–164 B.C.E.) has been identified as depicting a mythological connection between Taurus and the seven stars of the Pleiades, confirming that the Mesopotamians indeed saw these two asterisms as religiously significant and related (Krupp 1991, 243). As mentioned in Chapter 5, the Egyptians conceived the gods Apis and Osiris in bovine form, as well (Plutarch *On Isis and Osiris* 20/359B, 35/364E–F, 37/365 E–F, 73/380E). That Osiris was related to Taurus and was similarly connected religiously with the Pleiades is possibly suggested in the Egyptian Book of the Dead, in which the "the Seven Cows and their Bull" appear as a key motif in the soul's journey to the afterlife. Budge affirms ([1895] 1960, 327–8, 644) that the celestial bull refers to Osiris; I thus propose that what is being referenced in this instance is the constellation of Taurus. The "seven" cows, correspondingly, must refer to the Pleiades.

Perhaps most significant to this discussion of the Pleiades in relation to Dodona is the fact that Taurus the Bull was seen by the Greeks as none other than Zeus himself, the primary male god associated with this ancient oracular center.[48] As I discussed earlier, as celestial bull, Zeus carried off and impregnated Europa with the namesake of Dodona. Where the bull constellation is, so are the Pleiades, "riding" his back, which is where Europa is placed on many scenes depicting her abduction by Zeus in his epiphany as bull (see, e.g., Cook 1914–40, 1:531–46). The astral location of the Pleiades in the constellation of Taurus may further explain why the *peleiades* as doves/stars were associated with Zeus at Dodona. Silver coins of Crete struck by Nero show Zeus with a thunderbolt in one hand and scepter in the other, surrounded by seven stars. On another copper struck by Trajan, the infant Zeus is seated with the stars above (Cook 1914–40, 1:547 and fig. 415). Although such images are late, I suggest they hark back to an early association of Zeus with the Pleiades.[49] Of further significance is the fact that in antiquity, as now, the sign of Taurus was considered to "belong" to Venus/Aphrodite (Porphyry *On the Cave of the Nymphs* 22), who, we will recall, by one account was the daughter of Zeus and Dione. These mythological connections do indeed point to a complex occult relationship among these deities, Taurus, the Pleiades, and the locale of Dodona in the Greek conception.

Taurus also was in some Greek traditions seen as not a bull but a female cow, which may speak of an older matriarchal substratum of myth. In particular, the constellation was identified with Io, the divine birth priestess of Hera discussed in Chapter 5, who was transformed into a cow for her transgression with Zeus.[50] This would further render the constellation the domain of the parthenogenetic female associated with "cow-eyed" Virgin Mother Hera, as well as of the parthenogenetic Egyptian cow goddess Hathor (later, Isis). Indeed, the Egyptians called the Pleiades *Athur-ai,* Stars of Athyr, that is, Hathor (Allen [1899] 1963, 399). Plutarch (*On Isis and Osiris* 69/378E) notes that the Egyptians even gave the name *Athyr* (Hathor) to the entire month marking the Pleiades' dawn setting (i.e., November). Hathor was sometimes conceived in septenary form as the "Seven Hathors" (Budge [1895] 1960, 185–6), a possible further confirmation of the identification of this bovine goddess with the Seven Pleiadian Sisters. Such associations suggest that Taurus and the Pleiades originally may have been considered the exclusive realm of the female in general, and of parthenogenesis in particular.[51] This idea is further supported, again, by the fact that the stars that form the head of the celestial bovine, the Hyades, were considered "nymphs," as were the Pleiades themselves, whose divine birth stories I discuss later.

Of particular importance is the reference in the Egyptian Book of the Dead, mentioned earlier, to the "the Seven Cows and their Bull" as a motif the deceased soul encounters in its journey in the afterlife. Budge indicates ([1895] 1960, 327–8, 644) not only that the bull refers to Osiris, but also that the cows refer to Hathor.[52] Again, the Pleiades and their location in Taurus certainly must be implied here, since the journey being described is a celestial/otherworldly one. In the ritual addressed to the Seven Cows and their Bull, the deceased must present the cows and bull with offerings and recite their names in the hope that he will be "allowed into their train, and . . . be born on their thighs." "Thighs" most likely refers to the vagina/vulva; the reference is clearly a female birth image that would be applicable to the cows only. This motif therefore suggests that the "train" the departed human soul enters, and from which it is (re)birthed, is that of the cows/Hathor/the Pleiades. Budge (328) emphasizes the centrality of this part of the journey, stating that the chapter in which this information appears

> is one of the most important in the Book of the Dead, for it was written with the object of providing the deceased with animal food and milk in the Other World. The god addressed is Osiris, or one of

his forms, and Osiris was himself the Bull of Amenti; the food therefore that Osiris is asked to give is himself. Now the seven kine are only
incarnations of Isis, Hathor, and other goddesses, and the milk with
which the kine supply the deceased is the milk of these goddesses; he
therefore drinks the divine milk whereon the gods themselves live . . .
In the Turin Paypyrus . . . the Chapter is said to be "a very great and
real mystery."

We thus also have in this reference Hathor/the seven Pleiades as the
source of "divine milk" or ambrosia for the ascending/descending
soul, which once again calls to mind the ambrosia that the Pleiades
(as doves) fed Zeus in Greek mythology. It also calls to mind the
"divine milk" that Hera provided to complete fully the king/hero's
divinization, which Hathor was similarly thought to bestow upon
the Egyptian pharaoh (Rigoglioso 2007, 79). One may discern from
this cross-cultural motif that for both the Greeks and the Egyptians,
the Pleiades themselves were seen to confer divinity and immortality. That is, they (1) were understood to be the source of divinity,
(2) were believed to grant full empowerment to the divinely born
child, and (3) were understood to assure the continued existence of
the soul after death. It is not far-fetched therefore to suggest that the
Pleiades also may have been thought to "send" divine or semidivine
souls into human incarnation via virgin priestesses, which is what I am
proposing may well have been an activity believed to have taken place
at Dodona in remote times.

The Greeks themselves posited several celestial locations with Pleiadian associations as the source and destination of human and divine
souls. One was the mythical "Alcyonian Lake," which Dionysus
traversed to reach the spirit world and rescue his deceased mother
Semele, who had conceived him via Zeus (Pausanias 2.37.5–6). The
name of the lake probably derives from Alcyone, one of the Pleiades,
and the mother, by Poseidon, of several Greek heroes (Apollodorus
3.10.1). The association of the realm of the deceased with Alcyone
again points to the idea that the Pleiades were thought of as the seat
of souls in the afterlife/otherworld.

The Pleiades also may be implied in ancient beliefs regarding the
role of the Milky Way in the life of the human soul. For the Pleiades,
located on the fringes of the Milky Way, are scientifically considered
to be a part of this luminous beltway of light composed of tens of
billions of stars. Greek writers identify the Milky Way variously as
(1) the path and destination of souls in their journey in the afterlife, (2) the place from which souls, in the form of light and stars,

reincarnated, (3) the abode of deities and demigods (*daimones*), and (4) a road leading to the palace of Zeus. A belief in the Milky Way as the destination of human souls is expressed, for example, by Heracleides, and referred to by Iamblichus, Philoponus (on Aristotle's *Meteorology* A.8), and Stobaeus (*Anthology* 1.906; see Gottschalk 1980, 100–5). Porphyry (*On the Cave of the Nymphs* 28) also reports that Pythagoras believed souls were "assembled in the Milky Way." A belief in the Milky Way as the home of deities and *daimones,* as a road to the palace of Zeus, or as the road of the deities can be found, for example, in Pindar (*Hymns* frag. 30.2, ed. Race 1997, 231) and Ovid (*Metamorphoses* 1.168–76). Plato (*Phaedrus* 249a–b) holds that the souls of those who lived three lives as philosophers returned to the company of the deities in the "place above heaven," while those who had lived moral, albeit not philosophical, lives resided "some place in heaven." He also puts forth the idea (*Timaeus* 41d–42e) that each newly created soul was implanted in a single star, and that the soul who had lived well on earth returned to its star after death.

Certainly, these attributes of the Milky Way correspond with the very characteristics I am suggesting may have been ascribed to the Pleiades at Dodona and elsewhere. The idea of the Pleiades as a home of souls may be obliquely referenced throughout Porphyry's *On the Cave of the Nymphs.* We see numerous allusions in this mystical work suggestive of the asterism, as well as of divine birth. For example, Porphyry (10–2, 18) identifies incarnating human souls as both "nymphs" and "bees." Nymphs, as I have argued, were associated with divine birth, as were bees, the ancient symbol of the parthenogenetic goddess Neith. To explain the equation of souls with bees, Porphyry references the widely held ancient belief, to which I referred in Chapter 3, that bees were spontaneously generated (i.e., parthenogenetically born) from the rotting carcasses of cattle. By analogy, Porphyry says, souls coming into *genesis* (incarnation) were understood to be "likewise 'born from cattle.'" The heavenly bovine from which souls emerged, he notes, was none other than the celestial constellation of Taurus the bull. Given the closely allied Egyptian belief, mentioned earlier, that it was the seven cows/Hathor/the Pleiades who were the actual generative source of reincarnated souls, one could argue that Porphyry is referencing Pleiades, in particular, as the perceived incubator for souls emerging from Taurus. Porphyry (19) stresses that the ancients did not simply call *all* souls entering into incarnation "bees," but specifically those "who were to live just lives and return after performing acts pleasing to the gods." Thus, he is referencing the incarnation of the "special" soul—a description that somewhat resembles that of the child of the holy *parthenos* as an exalted (if not always moral) figure. I analyze the bee's association with parthenogenesis more fully in Chapter 7. Again, these accounts support the idea that the Dodonian dove priestesses/*peleiades* could have been seen as special women who miraculously incarnated holy beings from the Pleiades.

Another idea Porphyry (28) discusses that may allude to the Pleiades is one he attributes to Pythagoras: "[Souls] are assembled in the Milky Way [*galaxia*] which derives its name from 'milk' [*gala*] because they are nourished with milk when they first fall into *genesis*" (Porphyry 1983, 36, trans. Lamberton). I suggest that Porphyry is referencing here not simply human breast milk, but also the cosmic "ambrosia of immortality" that I have demonstrated was associated with Hera and Hathor as parthenogenetic mothers. This idea is strengthened by the fact, as we will recall here from Chapter 5, that the "milk" of the Milky Way was specifically believed to have issued from Hera's breast. Again, as mentioned earlier, this celestial "milk" was also likely the divine nectar the Pleiades brought to Zeus.

The Pleiades' connection with the Milky Way is further suggested by the extended genealogy of the seven mythical maidens who bore the name of this asterism. While the grandfather of these seven Pleiadian sisters, Oceanus, is generally portrayed as a terrestrial river forming the circumference of the earth, in fact, he was celestial in nature. This is demonstrated by Homer (*Iliad* 14.201, 302), who calls Oceanus the place "whence the gods have risen"—that is, the "source" or "abode" of the gods. Thus, as Cook (1914–40, 3.1:482) asserts, the river Oceanus simply meant the Galaxy, or the Milky Way. This mythologically affirms the Pleiadian maidens' connection with this body of stars. It is also interesting that the Milky Way was sometimes compared with "a tree whose trunk traversed the night sky" (1:482). The image of the "tree" calls to mind the Dodonean oak. Thus I propose that the Dodonean oak was seen as the terrestrial counterpart of the Milky Way and was understood as providing an esoteric "link" to it, and to the Pleiades who formed a part of that beltway.[53] Such a link involved, I suggest, both communication with such realms in the form of prophecy, as well as what was believed to be the incarnation of beings from this region.[54]

Considering what I have discussed about the Pleiades and Greek beliefs in souls and divinities issuing from the Milky Way and Taurus, it is not unreasonable to suggest that the Pleiades, a specific constellation located within these starry bodies, may have been considered a location of ancient deities and demigods whom the dove priestesses/*peleiades* at one point were thought to have conceived. Such an idea may be depicted on an ancient Aupulian amphora found in a rock-cut grave at Canosa. The amphora shows Zeus as a bull kneeling at the feet of Europa. As Cook (1914–40, 3.1:620) writes, "A dove brings up a wreath as an omen of successful love, and four stars indicate the sky, which is the true home of the metamorphosed god." The schema depicted here of a holy *parthenos* who bore the namesake of Dodona, a bull/god, stars, and doves seems to provide a visual analog for what I am arguing was a probable divine birth priestesshood—which became yoked to *hieros gamos* practice—at this oracular center.

The astral aspect associated with Europa and Zeus is further supported by an examination of their extended genealogy. After Zeus consorted with Europa, he bestowed her in marriage upon the Cretan king Asterion (or Asterios, or Asteros), whose name means "starry."[55] Tzetzes (*Historiarum Variarum Chiliades* 1.473, in Cook 1914–40, 1:546–47) states that three of Europa's children—Minos, Rhadamanthys, and Sarpedon—were sons of Zeus *Asterios,* in particular, which further points to an association with Taurus (Zeus as "starry" bull). The duplication of the names of the king and the god further suggests that Europa's husband (Asterion) was considered the earthly "double" of Zeus (Asterios), which may once again refer to a situation of *hieros gamos* by surrogate. As I noted in Chapter 4, the former name of Delos was *Asteria,* where, as I have posited, a divine birth priestesshood was also possibly located. I also presented evidence in Chapter 5 that the *asterion* plant sacred to Hera at Argos, where Io was the famous "cow" priestess believed to have mated with Zeus, was the entheogen cannabis, which may have facilitated priestesses' "astral" trance journeys related to miraculous conception. Thus, the stars indeed seem to have loomed large in what I am proposing were divine birth cults. The theme is echoed at Delphi, where Apollo's "home," known as the Hyperborea, also may have been considered an astral location (see Chapter 7).

There is, moreover, ample cross-cultural evidence to demonstrate that the Pleiades have far and wide been considered the creator of the universe, the center of heaven, the locus of divinity, and the origin place of humanity (see Rigoglioso, 2007, 418–23). This suggests that Hyginus's brief remark (*Poetic Astronomy* 2.21) that the Pleiades were "believed to lead the circular motion of the stars" may indicate that at some stage the Greeks themselves held this asterism to be the focal point of the entire cosmos. Later in the chapter, I include a statement by Diodorus Siculus that lore the Greeks held about the Pleiades was tremendously old, and originated in Africa. This may suggest its arrival on Greek soil was the product of cultural diffusion, thereby rendering the Greek story a direct relative of many of the cross-cultural references found worldwide to the Pleiades as the seat of immortality and the central point of the universe.

The Seven Sisters as Holy *Parthenoi*

Significant to the argument that the Dodonian priesshood may at some period have involved a virgin birth component is the fact that the Pythagoreans considered the number commonly associated with the Pleiades, seven, to be the number of "virginity." As Iamblichus (1988, 71) explains, this is because "seven" has no factors other than one and itself. The fifteenth/sixteenth-century occultist Agrippa ([1651] 2004, 269) elaborates that the "virginal" status of the number seven owes to the fact that among the numbers from one to ten (the decad), it is the only number that *both* (1) when multiplied by another number creates none of the numbers of the decad (unlike five) *and* (2) is not produced by the multiplication of any number. Philo of Alexandria (*On the Contemplative Life* 65) notes that other mystical groups of antiquity, among them the Therapeutae of Egypt and elsewhere, also knew seven to be the number of virginity. Iamblichus (1988, 71) further notes the particularly parthenogenetic nature of the number seven in his observation that the Pythagoreans associated it with Athena by virtue of the fact that she was born of neither a mother nor a father.[56]

The parthenogenetic nature of this number corresponds perfectly with the nature of the seven Pleiades themselves as both virgins and mothers in Greek myth. In the Hindu conception, the Pleiades are known as the "Seven Mothers of the World." Andrews (2004, 23) notes the striking similarity between this concept of the "seven world mothers" and the theory of Oxford professor Bryan Sykes, based on studies of mitochondrial DNA, that almost everyone of European descent on the planet can trace an unbroken genetic link back to one of only seven women (Sykes 2001, 8, 54, 195–6). This Hindu characterization of the Pleiades as "mothers of the world" is in complete alignment with Greek myths naming the Pleiades ancestral mothers who created entire lineages. Diodorus Siculus (3.60.4) specifically emphasizes that the Greeks themselves held this belief:

> [The Pleiades] lay with the most renowned heroes and gods and thus became the first ancestors of the larger part of the race of human beings,

giving birth to those who, because of their high achievements, came to
be called gods and heroes; Maia the eldest, for instance, lay with Zeus
and bore Hermes, who was the discoverer of many things for the use
of mankind; similarly the other Atlantides [i.e., Pleiades, daughters of
Atlas] also gave birth to renowned children, who became the founders
in some instances of nations and in other cases of cities. Consequently,
not only among certain barbarians but among the Greeks as well, the
great majority of the most ancient heroes trace their descent back to
the Atlantides. These daughters were also distinguished for their chastity and after their death attained to immortal honor among men, by
whom they were both enthroned in the heavens and endowed with the
appellation of Pleiades.

(Diodorus Siculus 1935, 281, trans. Oldfather)

Significantly, Diodorus also says that the tradition about the
Pleiades was foreign to Greek soil. The story, he reports, originally
belonged to the "Atlantians" (3.60.1), whom he identifies elsewhere
(3.54) as a civilized historical people of North Africa once invaded
by the Libyan Amazons (3.54). The idea for an African origin for
the Pleiadian myth is consonant with the various other stories connecting the Pleiades—and Dodona—to Africa. These include the
myth that the Seven Sisters' father was possibly the North African
king Atlas, and the legend of the "founding" of Dodona by a holy
parthenos from Egypt. The detail that the Pleiades' mother may have
been an "Amazon queen" (scholiast on Theocritus 13.25) could also
place their story in ancient Libya, where, as I discussed in Chapter 3,
legends and ethnographic accounts attested to the presence of historical Amazon women.

Thus, the myth that eventually made its way into Greek religion,
and that seems to have left signs of its presence at Dodona through
the multivalent term *peleiades,* was, according to Diodorus, a very
ancient African story about "the first ancestors of the larger part
of the race of human beings." That is, it was a story about the dawn
of the human race itself as it emerged from these "seven mothers." In
the light of theories proposing that *homo sapiens sapiens* originated in
Africa and spread to all other continents by land and by sea (see, e.g.,
Birnbaum 2001), the story of the Pleiades thus could be interpreted
as a kind of ur-myth that was carried with human migrations out of
Africa to all continents. This hypothesis may explain why so many
peoples around the world have similar stories concerning this asterism. The various cross-cultural Pleiadian legends point to a possible
ur-myth that expressed the theme of women's reproductive mysteries
in consonance with the star realms, set in a context of matriarchy

(see Rigoglioso 2007, 418–23). That theme takes a divine birth turn in the Greek legends, in particular, as I have already mentioned, and as I now discuss in more detail.

A bit later in his treatment of the Pleiadian religious story, Diodorus mentions that the native Atlantians called the Pleiades "nymphs." Larson (2001, 11), drawing on the scholiast on Pindar's *Nemean Ode* 2.17 and the Homeric *Hymn 4 to Hermes* (4–6, 244), corroborates this classification, distinguishing the Pleiades as nymphs of a "heavenly" sort in contrast to the more general "earthly" nymphs usually associated with springs, lakes, or streams. As I have argued, the "nymph" classification is a clue to a female's identification as a holy *parthenos,* and we see this borne out in the stories of the Pleiades' sexual relationships with gods, as expressed both in the works of Diodorus and in the extended mythology of the Seven Sisters.

As indicated, of the seven Pleiades—Maia, Electra, Taygete, Alcyone, Celaeno, Sterope, and Merope (Apollodorus 3.10.1)[57]—all but one, Merope, are considered to have given birth via a major Greek god: Zeus, Poseidon, or Ares. As I detail below, many of their resulting progeny indeed were significant heroes in Greek legend (and in one case, a god), which corresponds with my theory that the purported purpose of virgin conception was to generate divine children/heroes. Diodorus states outright that these seven women were considered human ancestors who were immortalized simultaneously on account of (1) their "chastity," and (2) their birthing of gods' children. Thus he affirms my hypothesis that the Pleiades were legendary holy *parthenoi* who were apotheosized historical priestesses.[58] I propose that the *peleiades,* or "dove/Pleiad" priestesses of Dodona, patterned themselves after these legendary Pleiades, taking on even their name and animal totem to identify themselves.

Maia, the Recluse

The eldest Pleiad, Maia, is said to have become the mother, by Zeus, of the god Hermes (Apollodorus 3.10.1). That Maia's name means "nurse" (Liddell and Scott, 7th ed., s.v.) calls to mind the Pleiades' "nursing" of the infant Zeus, and Hera's nursing of Heracles. Further, it underscores what I have proposed was the perceived role of the Pleiades as the source/conveyer of immortality. In the Homeric *Hymn 4 to Hermes* (4–6), Maia is described as a mountain "nymph" who was "modest" and "shunned the company of the blessed gods, dwelling within a cave's shadow" on Mt. Cyllene (trans. West, 2003b). I propose these details indicate Maia was a cave-dwelling holy *parthenos* who lived in solitude. That she "avoided" the gods suggests that she did not actively seek out a *hieros gamos* relationship but favored her celibate status. This perhaps is a clue to her originally having served as a priestess of pure parthenogenesis. Such an idea is lent support by the excerpt from the first-century *Revelation of Adam,* noted in Chapter 1, in which a similar image—the "muse/nymph" who spends time on the mountain in solitude— is specifically connected with self-generative activity:

> From the nine muses one separated. She came to a high mountain and spent some time seated there, so that she desired her own body in order to become androgynous. She fulfilled her desire and became pregnant from her desire. He [the illuminator] was born. The angels who were over the desire nourished him. And he received glory there and power.
>
> (Barnstone and Meyer 2003, 186–7)

Maia's son Hermes achieved full apotheosis and was regarded as the psychopomp, or spirit, who transported souls between the worlds. He also was thought to be the inventor of the alphabet, numbers, astronomy, music, the art of lightning, gymnastics, the lyre, measures, weights, and many other things.[59] As such, he was identified with the Egyptian god Thoth,[60] which further corresponds with Diodorus's location of the origin of the Pleiadian myth in North Africa. As Hermes Trismegistus ("thrice-great" Hermes), he was considered in antiquity to be the author of many books thought to contain the sum total of human and divine knowledge (see, e.g., Iamblichus *On the Mysteries* 1, 2; Plutarch *On Isis and Osiris* 61/375F). Extant tractates from the first through third centuries C.E. attributed to him concern alchemy, astrology, magic, and spiritual teachings.[61] Hermes, then, like Apollo and Dionysus, was one of the higher-level beings said to have been born of a holy *parthenos*.[62]

Electra, Priestess of Athena
According to Apollodorus (3.12.1–3), by Zeus the Pleiad Electra bore Dardanus, whose legendary lineage founded Troy.[63] Apollodorus's account also may indicate that Electra was a priestess of Athena, specifically, as the mythographer relates that she took refuge at the Palladium, the sacred statue of Pallas Athena, at the time of her *phthora,* literally "destruction, ruin, or perdition." That *phthora* also has the connotation of "seduction" (Liddell and Scott, 7th ed., s.v.) implies the situation involved a sexual encounter. Zeus subsequently threw the Palladium into the territory of Ilios (Troy), where it became the foundational religious image. I propose this episode references the

THE DIVINE BIRTH PRIESTESSHOOD AT DODONA   165

hieros gamos encounter between Electra and Zeus thought to have resulted in the conception of Dardanus. The implication that Electra did not welcome the union yet at the same time was "seduced" suggests, as I posited with Medusa in Chapter 3, that she may have been a pure parthenogenetic priestess of Athena who was thought to have ultimately capitulated to the lure of the god. That Zeus roughly disposed of the Palladium also implies the god was angered by her initial resistance. Perhaps this episode alludes to a historical power struggle at the time of the founding of Troy in which priests of the Zeus cult pressured priestesses of the Athena cult into practicing *hieros gamos* divine birth in order to produce what they believed would be the "divine" founding fathers of the new *polis*.

It is worth noting that other legends regarding Electra also connect the Pleiades with Troy. Electra, who, by Apollodorus's account, was essentially the founding ancestress of Troy by virtue of her being Dardanus's mother, was said to have loosed her hair in grief when she saw the city of her son perishing in flames. She was subsequently placed among the stars as a comet and called *Cometes,* "Long-Haired."[64] In another story, she was said to be the seventh and least visible star on account of her grief at the destruction of Troy.[65] According to others, all of the Pleiades lost their brilliance on seeing the destruction of this city (Servius on Virgil's *Georgics* 1.138). These details hint at a possible ancient belief that Troy was founded by divine heroes from the Pleiades, and suggest that the city had connections to Libya (home of the Seven Sisters' father, Atlas) and the Libyan Amazons (given the ancient reference mentioned earlier to the Pleiades possibly being born of an Amazon queen). Such legends are certainly striking in light of my argument in Chapter 3 that the Libyan Auses were most likely Amazons who may have attempted divine birth.

Taygete and the Artemisian Connection in Sparta
Another Pleiad who unsuccessfully resisted the advances of Zeus was Taygete. By her union with this god, she bore Lacedaemon, legendary founder of the country he named after himself, whose capital was Sparta (Pausanias 3.1.2; Apollodorus 3.10.2). Taygete was the eponym of Mt. Taygeton (Pausanias 3.1.2), located in the range that divides Messenia from Laconia in the Peloponnesus.

According to the argument I have put forth throughout this book, her serving as an eponym is likely a sign of her immortalization in recognition for her having miraculously borne a hero. Taygete's intense devotion to Artemis is an indicator that she was probably a priestess of this goddess. In one tradition, Taygete resisted Zeus's embraces by being turned into a deer or cow by Artemis. In thanks, Taygete dedicated the Ceryneian hind to her (Pindar *Olympian Ode* 3.29–30; scholiast on *Olympian Ode* 3.53). I propose this signifies Taygete's original commitment to pure parthenogenesis. The possibility that Taygete was a priestess of Artemis is strengthened by the fact that Mt. Taygetus was considered particularly sacred to this goddess (Callimachus *Hymn 3 to Artemis* 188). In historical times, a temple to Artemis was located in the vicinity of this mountain in the village of Limnae.[66] Taygete's son Lacedaemon is himself said to have married a "nymph" named Sparta, after whom he named the city (Pausanias 3.1.2–3). By Sparta he had a son, Amyclas, from whose lineage emerged the Spartan king Tyndareus and the famous Helen (Apollodorus 3.10.3–4; Pausanias 3.1.1–3).

Given the strong associations between the Pleiad Taygete, Artemis, virgin maidens, and Sparta, it is particularly interesting that the name *Pleiades* appears in association with the choruses of virgin girls for which Sparta was famous.[67] The Pleiades are specifically mentioned in one of the *parthenia*, or "maiden songs," written by the poet Alcman in the late seventh or early sixth century B.C.E. In the largest extant fragment of one of his songs, which was performed at dawn by *parthenoi*, probably in honor of Artemis of the Dawn (Artemis Orthria), the maidens speak of carrying some kind of offering item to the goddess. As they carry this item, the girls sing:

> A Pleiades of doves [the maidens Hagesichora and Agido] are
> Contending at dawn before the altar of Artemis
> For the honor of offering the sacred *pharos* [plow or *peplos*]
> Which we have brought to the goddess.
> They are the white star Sirius rising
> In the honey and spice of a summer night.
> (Archilochos et al. 1980, 139, trans. Davenport)[68]

That Sirius was another star famed in antiquity for its practical and mystical resonances indicates that the song is indeed referencing the Pleiades-as-asterim. What is being described here is a summertime dawn ritual in which maidens apparently competed for the honor of offering a sacred item to Artemis Orthria. The item in question was the *pharos*, which has been variously translated as *peplos*, that is, a "sacred cloak or mantle," or *arotron*, "plow." Garzya (in Alcman 1954, 56–7) discusses scholarly arguments in favor of both interpretations, and notes that in terms of actual cult practices, both types of objects were presented in Greek rites. Each translation offers interesting possibilities about the meaning of this ritual that, I contend, are congruent with the idea that it refers to holy *parthenoi* as priestesses of divine birth in association with the Pleiades.[69]

I propose that the translation of *pharos* as *aratron*, "plow," lends to the interpretation that this particular hymn, sung at dawn, was conducted on the day of the heliacal (dawn) rise of the Pleiades in mid-May. As we will recall, this was the time that commemorated the beginning of summer and the harvest season. That the girls may have been presenting the goddess of dawn, a version of Artemis, with an agricultural implement would be somewhat in concordance with this interpretation, even though a plow may have been more appropriate to the winter season, the time of sowing.

I contend the song would have been an allusion to much more than just the physical commencement of the harvest, however. The maidens spoken about, Hagesichora and Agido, are here identified as "Pleiades" in their aspect as doves, which indicates that we are also in the realm of divine birth. For it was in their aspect as holy *parthenoi* that the Seven Sisters were transformed to doves in myth. Additionally, the dove, as I argued earlier, was a reference both to the bird that parthenogenetically bore Aphrodite, and to the incarnating "divine" soul.

During this ritual, the maidens were identified with Pleiades-as-doves not only in text, but also by virtue of the fact that, as Davenport (in Archilochos et al. 1980, 137) reports, the entire chorus of girls was dressed to resemble doves. I propose this indicates that *all* girls present were understood to have assumed the identity of the Pleiades as both mystical asterism and parthenogenetic Seven Sisters. The primary characteristic of the chorus is that it was composed of *parthenoi,* virgin maidens. Thus, I propose that if we understand *pharos* as "plow," the song reveals that the girls were understood to reference the starry Pleiades not just as the harbinger of the summer harvest, but as the source of their founding ancestors, the Pleiadian son Lacedaemon among them. It also suggests that the chorus girls were "representatives" of the holy *parthenoi* believed to have borne such divine children. The chorus *parthenoi* themselves, then, stood as representatives of the original (and possibly, by Alcman's time, no longer functioning) divine birth priestesshood. At a deeper level, the ritual, which honors the goddess Artemis, in particular, the Virgin Mother herself, may well have held an earlier memory of pure parthenogenesis, rather than *hieros gamos* divine birth.

If we interpret *pharos* as "robe," or *peplos,* we are now in a context akin to that of the Panathenaia, at which virgins presented the sacred *peplos* to Athena. I argued in Chapter 3 that the *peplos* was a symbol of

Athena's original capacity as virginal creatrix, in connection with her association with the "great weaver" Neith. As we will recall, women also presented the *peplos* to Hera at Olympia in what I proposed was also a reference to Hera's original virgin motherhood. I suggest that, by analogy, the robe in the case of the dawn ritual at Sparta was also a symbol of parthenogenesis, understood as a capacity of Artemis Ortheia.

The allusions to doves and Pleiades in both the text of the song and the ritual itself moreover suggest, again, an understanding of the role of both the Pleiades and *parthenoi* in divine birth. The only element we miss in the interpretation of *pharos* as *peplos* is the specifically agrarian reference (plow), which renders the hypothesis that the ritual took place in May at the heliacal rise of the Pleiades a bit more conjectural. Nevertheless, given that the moment of dawn was so critical in identifying when the Pleiades were about to rise over the horizon to commemorate the commencement of summer, and given that the song implies the ritual was conducted precisely at dawn, I believe the interpretation I have offered for the timing of the rite still holds.

Alcyone, Celaeno, Sterope, and Merope
Three other Pleiades bore by gods progeny who are somewhat lesser known, although all of these individuals founded city-states. One was Alcyone, who, by Poseidon, had a daughter Aethusa and four sons, Hyrieus, Hyperenor, Hyperes, and Anthas (Apollodorus 3.10.1; Ovid *Heroides* 19.133). Pausanias (2.30.8) lists the latter two as kings of Troezenia. Hyrieus was the eponym of the town Hyria, near Aulis (Larson 2001, 142), affirming his likely role in the town's founding. Alcyone's daughter Aethusa conceived a son by Apollo named Eleuther (Pausanias 9.20.1), the founder and eponym of Eleutherae in Boeotia (Stephanus Byzantius, s.v. *Eleutherai*). That Aethusa herself engaged in sexual union with the god indicates that she followed in her mother's footsteps as a holy *parthenos*. Likewise, Hyperes' daughter Arethusa was impregnated by Poseidon and gave birth to the hero Abas, eponym of the Abantes (a synonym for Euboians). Hera thereafter turned Arethusa into a spring.[70]

The Pleiad Celaeno, also by Poseidon, conceived Lycos, whom the watery god transferred to the legendary Islands of the Blessed, the abode of happy departed spirits thought to be at the extremities of the earth (Apollodorus 3.10.1). By this god Celaeno also conceived Euphemus and Nictaeus (Hyginus *Poetic Astronomy* 2.21; *Fabulae* 157). Finally, by Ares, the Pleiad Sterope (sometimes called Asterope, or "starry eyed") bore Oenomaus, who, as we will recall from Chapter 5, became the king of Pisa.[71] Sterope also may have borne Euenus (Plutarch *Greek and Roman Parallel Stories* 40). As discussed in Chapter 5, Sterope's granddaughter Hippodameia founded the foot races in honor of Hera (later turned into the Olympic Games) as well as the council of "sixteen women," who, I argued, probably served the cult of *hieros gamos* divine birth at Olympia.

The only Pleiad who supposedly gave birth to a child as a result of intercourse with a mortal was Merope, wife of Sisyphus of Corinth (Apollodorus 1.9.3, 3.10.1). Merope is said to have been ashamed of this fact, and one legend states that her star was the least visible because of it.[72] I contend this story refers to a priestess of divine birth who broke her vow to abstain from sexual relations with human men in nonritual encounters.

These Seven Sisters, I conclude, served as a model for the holy prophetesses of Dodona at some point during the history of the oracle. I propose that such later *peleiades* took their name, ornithological iconography, and sacred function from their septenary forebears, becoming women who attempted to bring divine children from the astral Pleiades to earth. Whether the adoption of such motifs happened before or with the arrival of the priestess of Zeus/Ammon from Egypt cannot be determined from the extant mythology and history. But these numerous combined legends at the very least suggest that Dodona was indeed a site with esoteric roots in ancient Africa, one focused on the theme of miraculous birth.

CHAPTER 7

THE DIVINE BIRTH
PRIESTESSHOOD AT DELPHI

Delphi is the second of two major oracular sites in Greece at which
priestesses prophesied. As I show in this chapter, these priestesses
were considered "wives" of Apollo. Moreover, Delphic lore is replete
with stories of oracular "nymphs" who gave birth to the children of
gods. Several of these nymphs and their children were the eponyms
of towns and natural formations associated with Delphi, which is a
sign of their heroic immortalization. In light of the argument I have
been making throughout this book, these clues suggest that Delphi
was also the site of a divine birth priestesshood.

DELPHI'S ORIGINS

Located on Mt. Parnassus, north of the Gulf of Corinth in central
Greece, the ancient oracle at Delphi was characterized by the rocky
wall of Phaedriades overhanging the town, the fountain of Castalia
issuing from a cleft in this wall, and the Corycian cave on the heights
above leading to the summit of Parnassus.[1] The oracle's origins
are thought to date back at least to Mycenaean times, if not earlier
(Dempsey [1918] 1972, 35). Although it was generally assumed in
antiquity that the oracle at Dodona was the older of the two, Delphi
became the more politically prestigious site during the period of
recorded history.

According to Diodorus Siculus (16.26), Pausanias (10.5.7),
and Plutarch (*Obsolescence of Oracles* 42/433C, 45/435D), the
Delphians said their oracle was founded when local people noticed

that breathing vapors from a particular chasm granted anyone the ability to prophesy freely. Diodorus reports that to cope with repeated instances of people in a state of ecstasy leaping into the chasm, the local residents chose a single woman to serve as prophetess. So that she could sit safely while in ecstatic trance without succumbing to the hole, they devised for her a special cauldron-like seat with three legs, known as a tripod.

The enduring belief that Delphi's prophecy-inducing fumes issued from the earth in part may have been what led to an original identification of the site with Ge/Gaia, the Earth goddess (Pausanias 10.5.5).[2] In the oracle's earliest days, the priestess who delivered divine prophecy, known as the *Pythia,* is recorded as having been in service to this goddess, who was considered the oracular authority there.[3] The establishing of Ge/Gaia as the source of divine information also may have derived partly from the belief that earth was the abode of the dead, who were endowed with prophetic powers, as demonstrated in the Greek practice of hero worship (Dempsey [1918] 1972, 6).

Legends relate that at some later stage the deity of the oracle was Ge/Gaia's daughter Themis, a Titan and goddess of law or right order.[4] That Aeschylus (*Prometheus Bound* 210) identifies Themis with Ge/Gaia suggests she may, in fact, have been understood as merely another manifestation of the same deity. The playwright also mentions a belief (*Eumenides* 1.1–10) that Themis subsequently granted her seat at Delphi to her sister Phoebe, who was the mother of Leto and Asteria. Yet another tradition names the goddess Nyx/ Night as having taken the place of Ge/Gaia (Plutarch *Divine Vengeance* 28/566C).

According to the ancient stories, eventually the oracle was taken over by the god Apollo, who, as we will recall, was the son of Leto by Zeus. As such, he was also the grandson of Phoebe and the great-grandson of Ge/Gaia. Aeschylus (*Eumenides* 1.1–10) says the transition occurred peacefully when Phoebe gave the oracle as a birthday gift to Apollo, who thence took the name *Phoebus* from her. The more prevalent form of the legend in the Greek world, however, was that Apollo took possession of Delphi by slaying Python, the serpent that Ge/Gaia had posted to guard the oracle.[5] The *Homeric Hymn 3 to Apollo* (300) indicates this creature was a *drakaina* or "she-dragon," thus clearly a female being.[6] Hyginus (*Fabulae* 140) and the scholiast on Pindar's *Pythian Odes* (in Dempsey [1918] 1972, 186n3) state that before the days of Apollo, it was Python herself who gave oracles on Mt. Parnassus.[7] In fact, according to Homer

(*Odyssey* 8.80; *Iliad* 9.405), a more ancient name of Delphi seems to have been *Pytho*. As Parke (1939, 10) notes, because the Greeks believed snakes were born from the ground,[8] it is likely that Python was considered to be but a manifestation of Ge/Gaia. Indeed, Ovid (*Metamorphoses* 1.438–40) writes that Ge/Gaia spontaneously produced Python after the time of the legendary flood. Given Python's identification with, and parthenogenetic birth from, Ge/Gaia, Apollo's slaying of Python could be read as an act of violence toward the pure parthenogenetic priestesshood.[9] I return to this theme later in the chapter.

THE GENERAL FUNCTIONS OF THE PYTHIA AT DELPHI

Plutarch writes (*Greek Questions* 9/292F–293A) that originally the Pythia delivered prophecy only one day a year, the seventh of the spring month Bysios (approximately our March), which was considered the birthday of Apollo. In early times, he reports, there was but one Pythia, and only people who lived in the region near the oracle consulted it (Strabo 9.3.7). As its reputation grew over the centuries, individuals and solemn embassies from throughout Greece and surrounding nations sought the counsel of the god. As Delphi came to be thronged with petitioners, eventually two priestesses were appointed, with a third who acted as an assistant.[10] Prophecy was then given on the seventh of every month—that is, the seventh day after each new moon (Connelly 2007, 74)—with the exception of the winter months.[11] According to Plutarch (*E at Delphi* 9/389A–C), the three winter months at Delphi belonged to Dionysus, while the summer months belonged to Apollo.

Three days before she delivered prophecy, the Pythia is said to have prepared by fasting and bathing in the Castalian spring. Her preparatory process was intended to free her from distractions and upset so that she could deliver the god's messages as accurately as possible and not cause herself harm in the process. The male officials of Delphi also were required to bathe in the Castalian spring before participating in the solemnities, as were inquirers. In contrast to Dodona, it seems that women as well as men could petition the Pythia.[12]

The order of petitioners was chosen by lot, except in the case of certain prestigious individuals or states, and an omen was taken before a question could be posed, usually based on the behavior of an animal about to be sacrificed (Euripides *Ion* 229). The shivering and bleating of a sacrificial goat over which a libation was poured, for example, was considered one important sign as to whether the divination should proceed (Plutarch *Obsolescence of Oracles* 45/435B–C). The degree to which omens were taken seriously is attested by an anecdote related by Plutarch (51/438A–B). In one instance, he writes, a negative omen was thought to have resulted in the Pythia leaping from her tripod, falling into convulsions, and dying a few days later. Under normal circumstances, the petitioner was required to make an offering of a sacred cake purchased at the site, as well as of a sacrificial animal (Euripides *Ion* 229, *Andromache* 1140; Plutarch *Lycurgus* 5.3). Then, the petitioner entered the sanctuary, a small structure about eight by ten feet.

Prior to meeting the petitioner in the temple, the Pythia chewed the leaves of the sacred laurel and drank from the Cassotis spring (Lucian *Double Indictment* 1; Tzetzes on Lycophron 6). Thereafter, she "descended" into the small sanctuary (Plutarch *Oracles at Delphi* 6/397A, 22/405C, 28/408D; *Obsolescence of Oracles* 51/438B). In this location a golden statue of Apollo stood (Pausanias 10.24.4), along with the sacred "navel" stone or *omphalos,* and the tomb of Dionysus. On the eternal flame on the altar she burned laurel leaves and barley, and perhaps myrrh (Plutarch *Oracles at Delphi* 6/397A; Aeschylus *Libation Bearers* 1035–7). At some point during these ministrations, she prayed (in historical times) to Pallas Athena, the Corycian Nymphs, the streams of Pleistus, and the gods Bromius, Poseidon, and Zeus (Aeschylus *Eumenides* 1.19–29). Next, she mounted a high tripod positioned over or near the entrance of a chasm, in order to receive the vapors emanating from the earth (Strabo 9.3.5).

The inquirer was seated on one side of the sanctuary, while the priest delivered to the Pythia the individual's question (Euripides *Andromache* 1102). It was believed that the deity (Apollo in historical times) responded through the body of the Pythia, speaking his words through her own voice.[13] Her state was generally referred to as "mania," "divine madness," "frenzy," "ecstasy," or "enthusiasm."[14] In some cases, the Pythia was known to deliver an oracle even before the petitioner put forth his question (Herodotus 1.47; Plutarch *Concerning Talkativeness* 20/512E). The priest translated the response, which was rendered in varying states of coherence, into understandable form (Euripides *Ion* 100). In early days, the Pythia is said to have delivered some of the god's spoken responses in improvisationally produced hexameters. Later, however, as the prestige of the oracle declined, the priestess delivered almost all oracles in prose (Plutarch *Oracles at Delphi* 23/405E, 7/397D, 17/402B, 24/406B–F).

The Pythia's state of possession is thought to have been induced in a variety of ways. One claim by the ancients is that it was stimulated by the priestess's exposure to vapors from the cave in, near, or over which her tripod was placed.[15] Pausanias (10.24.7) states that the water the Pythia drank from the Cassotis spring, which was connected with an aqueduct plunging under the oracular cave, made her prophetic. Aelian (*On Animals* 11.10) affirms that the state was aroused by the drinking of a "sanctified draught." In short, it appears that the Pythia's oracular ability was provoked by her ingesting or absorbing some kind of psychotropic substance, be it fumes from the earth, chemicals in the water, a special entheogenic brew, or a combination thereof. Elderkin (1940, 49–52) makes the case that a myth Pausanias relates (10.5.9–14) of the temple at Delphi having been reconstructed five times of five different materials indicates that the precise substances the Pythia used to induce intoxication changed over time. He suggests that the first temple, reportedly made of "laurel," represents a time when the priestess achieved her trance by chewing laurel leaves and drinking water of the sacred spring. Further examination of this idea reveals that at least from the fifth century B.C.E., if not earlier, chewing laurel leaves was indeed thought by the Greeks to bring a person into direct communication with the deities (i.e., it was an entheogen), and was used by prophets and poets to provoke divine inspiration (Theophrastus *Characters* 16.4; Parke 1939, 26n1).

The second temple, said to have been made by "bees" from beeswax and feathers, Elderkin posits, represents a phase in which the priestesses imbibed the intoxicating drink called "mead," made of fermented honey and water, and, later, wine. That the Greeks explicitly understood "honey" to be an intoxicant can be seen, for example, in the Orphic myth in which Zeus circumvented his father Cronus by means of such a substance, which put the elder god into a torpor (Porphyry 16). Moreover, the connection between prophecy/supernatural knowledge, entheogens, and honey is suggested by the common claim that special poets and sages, including Hesiod, Pindar, Sophocles, Plato, Virgil, Lucan, and Ambrose, were said to have been "fed by bees" during infancy in order to have bred in them wisdom and eloquence (Cook 1895, 7–8). The legendary Aristaeus, who was similarly fed in his infancy on "nectar and ambrosia," purportedly invented the mixing of honey and wine (Pliny *Natural History* 14.6). That this likely refers to his having developed a form of entheogen is strengthened by the fact that he was said to possess knowledge of the future (Cook 1895, 10), thought to be a common power granted through the use of psychotropic substances (Iamblichus

On the Mysteries 1.3/Letter of Porphyry). Thus, evidence suggests that the Pythia entered a profound non-ordinary state of consciousness brought about by entheogens in order to carry out her prophetic work. Given my argument that holy *parthenoi* also carried out their attempts at divine conception in non-ordinary states activated by special substances, this is significant.

The founding of almost all Greek colonies, and numerous decisions regarding kingships, the beginning of wars, and the healing of disease and plagues, were made based on the advice of Apollo at Delphi. Through the Pythia, the god was also thought to give counsel on establishing cults, honoring and propitiating deities, punishing various crimes, and improving moral conduct. Individuals consulted him/the Pythia on personal matters, as well, regarding love, marriage, children, vocation, travel, health, finances, and so forth.[16] Among those who had the highest respect for the oracle at Delphi were Pythagoras (who was the disciple of the Pythia Themistoclea), Pindar, Socrates, Plato, Cicero, and Plutarch.[17] Plutarch himself held the priesthood at Delphi from 105–26 C.E., was a member of the oracle's governing institution known as the Amphictyonic League in the reign of Hadrian, and spent his old age at the sanctuary (Dempsey [1918] 1972, 63n3).

By the sixth century B.C.E., Delphi was at the height of its power as the great pan-Hellenic center of religion. Throughout the centuries, it received substantial monetary income and gifts of treasures and artwork (Plutarch *Oracles at Delphi* 29/409A) totaling what would in today's currency be worth tens of millions of dollars (Smith 1854, s.v. *Delphi*). In 548 B.C.E., at the height of its influence, the temple was destroyed by fire, only to be rebuilt, with the maxims of the seven wise men inscribed inside (Pausanias 10.5.12–3).[18] The sanctuary was successively taken over or plundered several times from 357 B.C.E. on. The Pythia continued to utter prophecy throughout such transitions, however, until the emperor Theodosius closed the oracular center in 381 C.E. (Smith 1854, s.v. *Delphi*).

THE HISTORY AND NATURE
OF THE PRIESTESSHOOD AT DELPHI

At Delphi, the prophetic priests were almost exclusively female. Pausanias (10.5.8–9) names the first priestess Daphne, one of the "nymphs" of the mountain, who prophesied when Ge/Gaia was the site's oracular authority. Another priestess he mentions is Pyrcon, a woman who prophesied on behalf of Poseidon during the period when that god is said to have shared the oracle with Ge/Gaia. Yet another was Phemonoë, whom Pausanias lists as the first prophetess of the god Apollo at the site. Although the geographer notes that a male prophet, Olen, is recorded as having given prophecy there, he says "tradition . . . reports no other man as prophet, but makes mention of prophetesses only."

From Pausanias's account, it appears that women priests functioned as prophetesses at the site from the time Ge/Gaia was considered the oracular authority. Thus, it may be that the entire sacerdotal cadre at Delphi, comprising prophetesses and other personnel, was once exclusively female. As Dempsey ([1918] 1972, 21) further observes, the story of Apollo's takeover of the site doubtless illustrates a conflict of different cults. The fact that at nearly all other Apollonian temples, such as those in Didyma and Claros, males delivered prophecy (Parke 1939, 13–4) indicates the strength and enduring nature of the women's tradition at Delphi. The priestess title *Pythia*, presumably taken from the name *Python*, also served as a persistent reminder of the pre-Apollonian cult in which oracular wisdom was seen as the provenance of the feminine—the female serpent of Ge/Gaia.

At a certain point in the oracle's history, the sanctuary came to be superintended by the Amphictyonic League, which consisted of male representatives from numerous cities (Strabo 9.3.7). That the league was named after Amphictyon, its founder, suggests that male leadership took over Delphi in the mid-second millennium B.C.E., for Amphictyon is supposed to have lived c. 1500 B.C.E. (Bostock, in Pliny 1855, 7.57n73). Direct evidence for the imposition of a male clergy over what was once exclusively the province of prophetesses can be seen in the eventual appearance of a priesthood whose role was to send a single member to stand by the Pythia and write down her utterances in ordered form for the inquirer (Herodotus 8.36; Plutarch *Obsolescence of Oracles* 51). Two to five priests were chosen by lot for this role from among the noble families of Delphi (Euripides *Ion* 416). Possibly a separate group[19] of five sacred male functionaries, known as the *Hosioi*, or Holy Ones, also operated at Delphi. These were chosen from the most ancient families, who claimed descendancy from Deucalion, the Greek "Noah" (Plutarch *Greek Questions* 9/292D–E).

Lycoreia, a town situated on one of the heights of Parnassus above the sanctuary, was supposedly founded by the legendary Deucalion. By historical times, its inhabitants populated the town of Delphi surrounding the sanctuary (Strabo 9.3.2). The Lycoreians may have been Dorians (Smith 1854, s.v. *Delphi*), who, around the eleventh century

B.C.E., probably seized the oracle, perhaps bringing the worship of Apollo with them (Dempsey [1918] 1972, 34–6). The *Homeric Hymn 3 to Apollo* (390–5) hints that male clergy in association with Apollo may have arrived earlier, however, from Crete and the palace of Cnossus. This suggests the transition from a female-exclusive, Ge-serving priesthood to a male-controlled, Apollo-serving clergy may have taken place during the Mycenaean period of the Bronze Age, c. 1600–1100 B.C.E., which corresponds roughly with the establishment of the Amphictyonic League, mentioned earlier. Archaeological finds confirm the presence of a Cretan ritual pouring vessel at Delphi dating to c. 1500 B.C.E. (Parke 1939, 8). That the sanctuary experienced other appropriations and invasions throughout its early history is suggested by Strabo (9.3.8), who briefly mentions a plundering of the temple in the time following Homer.

Precisely how the Pythia was selected throughout the various periods of the history of the oracle at Delphi is not mentioned. Parke (1939, 33) conjectures that in historical times she may have been recruited from among the older and chaste female attendants of the temple who Plutarch (*Numa* 9.5–6) indicates were charged with keeping the sacred flame eternally lit on the hearth (a group that again calls to mind the *gerarai* of the Basilinna and the "sixteen women" of Hera's Olympia). Plutarch (*Obsolescence of Oracles* 51/438C) claims that in his day, the first century, the Pythia was an uneducated peasant who did not engage in social relations outside of a very limited circle within the cult precinct. He describes her (*Oracles at Delphi* 22/405D) as "inexperienced and uninformed about everything," a woman of the peasant class who "brings nothing with her as the result of technical skill or of any other expertness or faculty as she goes down in the shrine [to prophecy]" (Plutarch 1927–69, 5:405, trans. Babbitt).

I submit, however, that by Plutarch's time, the Pythias may have been purposely chosen for their ignorance precisely because their "simplicity" rendered them less interested in and ambitious for divine knowledge themselves, and thus more easily controllable and malleable for the purposes of the patriarchal priesthood and state. I base my assertion on the fact that several Pythias of an earlier era were evidently quite learned and spiritually advanced. One was known as Themistoclea, whose name recalls the older cult at Delphi dedicated to Themis. It is from her that the famous philosopher and mathemetician Pythagoras admitted he took many of his doctrines (Diogenes Laertius *Pythagoras* 8.8, 8.21; Suda s.v. *Puthagoras*). This indicates that the Pythias of the pre-Hellenistic period indeed must have possessed impressive knowledge. I conjecture that such women entered the priestesshood at Delphi with a good deal of spiritual understanding. I also propose that their knowledge was further enhanced by their regularly engaging in a state of *entheos,* "at-one-ment," with the Delphic god himself as a part of their work, a process that no doubt was thought to result in the priestess's own acquiring of divine knowledge.

The Pythia Phemonoë also must have been a talented and accomplished intellect, given that Pausanias (10.5.7) says she was credited with having first used hexameter verse in delivering oracles. The geographer additionally describes (10.12.2) the literary and musical sophistication of Herophile, the itinerant prophetess of the pre–Trojan War era. Herophile wrote poetically rendered oracles in a state of possession induced by the god Apollo and sang them while standing on a cliff of Delphi during her periodic visits to the sanctuary. Diodorus Siculus (16.26.6) also hints at an elevated status for the Pythia in remote antiquity. He writes,

> It is said that in ancient times oracles were delivered by virgins because of their physical purity and their resemblance to Artemis. They were in effect well-suited to keep the secret of the oracles they rendered.
>
> (trans. Sissa 1990, 35)

Here, we see the Pythia of a more ancient period described as a woman with enough spiritual maturity to possess esoteric secrets—and to keep silent about them. She was, Diodorus tells us, also similar to Artemis. Given that Artemis was a powerful, self-sufficient virgin goddess who defended female figures against male predation, this allusion may indicate that the original Pythias were hardly subservient and submissive in character.

Even in later times, the priestesses must have possessed a special constitution in order to be successful in their position. As Goff (2004, 282) notes, various accounts of possession in Greek literature "indicate that far from offering a simple primal 'release,' the experience . . . [was] usually structured and learned; and . . . [could] provide a demanding intellectual engagement that require[d] poise and self-control from the participant." It is likely that the Delphic Pythias of all ages had to be capable of undergoing an extensive training, as well, for, as Goff further observes (223), "it is difficult to see how the institution would function without such an apprenticeship." Indeed, the idea implied in Plutarch's writings that an ignorant woman could be plucked from the countryside, plied with entheogenic substances, placed in front of a petitioner without preparation for her role, and be expected to prophesy adequately and keep up the reputation of the oracle seems highly suspect, particularly given that such activity apparently involved tremendous mental and physical challenges. Plutarch himself (*Obsolescence of Oracles* 51/438B, 386B), as well as Lucan (*Civil War* 5.115–236), for example, describe the threat of psycho-physical danger under which Pythias operated, resulting in some cases in their mad raging and eventual death.

The dramatic contrast between the erudition of priestesses associated with Delphi prior to the fifth century B.C.E., such as Phemonoë, Herophile, and Themistoclea, and the supposed "simplicity" of the Pythias of Plutarch's first century C.E. points to a probable erosion of the power of the Delphic priestesshood over time. That one of the maxims inscribed in the walls of the later Delphian sanctuary was "Keep women under rule"[20] indicates the degree to which the Apollonian regime must have imposed patriarchal order over the original female-centered cult.

THE PYTHIA AS "WIFE" OF APOLLO

Although precisely how the Pythia was selected for office is not known, it is clear that in classical times and later she was expected to be chaste and was not allowed to marry during her term of office.[21] According to Diodorus Siculus (16.26.6), all Pythias were *young* virgins until the third century B.C.E., when one was raped by a Thessalian named Echecrates. Thereafter, the citizens of Delphi required that the women chosen for the role be at least 50 years old, presumably on the assumption that women of that age would not invite male attention. What is interesting to the argument of this book is that despite the fact that in later times the Pythia was an older woman, the memory of the original Delphic prophetess as young virgin was retained in the priestess's attire: she always prophesied wearing the dress of a maiden (Diodorus Siculus 16.26.6). I propose this served as a memory of the virgin Delphic prophetess who was also a holy *parthenos*. I argue later in the chapter that the type of divine conception attempted by the maiden Pythias originally was probably of the pure variety, corresponding with the pure parthenogenetic nature of Ge/Gaia. For now, I turn my attention to evidence that during the Apollonian period of the oracle, *hieros gamos* divine birth was attempted.

I will first explore numerous indicators that the Pythia's "possession" by Apollo for oracular purposes was considered to be a form of sexual intercourse with the god. Plutarch (*The Oracles at Delphi* 22/405C–D), for example, describes the Pythia of his day as a chaste woman who submitted herself to the will of Apollo as a bride submitted to her husband. Much earlier, the legendary prophetess Herophile, just mentioned, claimed outright to be "the wedded wife of Apollo" (Pausanias 10.12.2). That Pausanias notes she also referred to herself as the god's "sister," as well as his "daughter," calls to mind the schema in Egypt in which the parthenogenetic mother of the pharaoh was simultaneously conceived as the "wife," "sister," and "daughter" of Amun-Re. (Rigoglioso 2007, 70–9; Troy 1986, 53–5). We thus see in this description of Herophile a strong suggestion that the oracular Apollonian priestesses mimicked the practices of priestesses in ancient Egypt. And indeed, we will recall from Chapter 2 that Herodotus (1.182), in listing various instances of priestesses engaging sexually with gods, specifically names the prophetess at Patara in Lycia as customarily engaging in *hieros gamos* with Apollo. Thus, *hieros gamos* was known to be an aspect of the Apollonian priestesshood.

The explicitly sexual nature of the Pythia's engagement with Apollo is depicted in several writings, some of which stop just short of describing the event as culminating in a literal physical conception. In *Divine Vengeance* (29/566D), for example, Plutarch describes an underworldly journey in which a character named Thespesius encounters a curious Delphic image: an invisible ray of light coming from a tripod, passing through the bosom (*kolpos*) of "Themis," and resting on Mt. Parnassus. In passing by this tableau, Thespesius hears the disembodied, high-pitched voice of the prophetess foretelling events, including the time of his own death. As Cook (1914–40, 2.1:206) notes, in fifth century Greek art, Themis represented "the prototype of the *Pythia*." Thus what is being depicted in this excerpt of Plutarch, he suggests (2.2:1216–17, note to 2:208f), is the Pythia "on the Delphic tripod impregnated by the central pillar of light," that is, impregnated by the metaphorical phallus of Apollo himself. Indeed, Plutarch elsewhere (*Obsolescence of Oracles* 42/433D–E) identifies Apollo with light, noting that the ancient equation of this god with the sun was but an esoteric analogy indicating that it was by the power of light that Apollo kindled prophecy in the Pythia. Plutarch also specifically notes that many individuals in generations prior to his own even went so far as to consider the sun to be Apollo's "offspring and progeny" (*ekgonos kai tokos*). Here again, we see a blatant birth reference in association with the luminary aspect of the Delphic deity.

The ray of light as an impregnating motif in parthenogenetic situations is also seen in the legend, discussed in Chapter 5, of the Egyptian bull god Apis/Osiris. Again, according to that legend, a cow (mythologically, Isis or, in the Greek tradition, Io) was thought to conceive Apis by means of a flash of light from either "heaven" or the moon.[22] As we will recall, this miraculous, parthenogenetic incarnation of Apis/Osiris was thought to result periodically in the literal birth of a bull with special marks on its body—the living Apis. Interestingly, this earthly bull was nursed with milk by several cows that remained enclosed especially for this purpose (Aelian *On Animals* 11.10). This custom calls to mind the "sacred kine" associated with Osiris that the Egyptians believed nourished the soul in the afterlife, which I suggested in Chapter 6 represented the Pleiades. The Greeks identified the divinely impregnated cow with Io (Aelian *On Animals* 11.10), who I argued in Chapter 5 was a divine birth priestess of Hera. The implication of all this is that Io, too, was thought to conceive Epaphus through the action of a ray of light.

The Pythia is frequently depicted in Greek literary references and artistic representations as demurely seated in the bowl of the tripod when giving prophecy.[23] But Christian apologists writing about the phenomenon describe her posture as being markedly sexual, echoing in explicit fashion what Plutarch merely imples. Origen (*Contra Celsum* 7.3), for example, declares,

> While the prophetess of Apollo is sitting at the mouth of the Castalian cave *she receives a spirit through her womb*; after being filled with this she utters oracular sayings, supposed to be sacred and divine . . . [T]hat spirit . . . enters the soul of the prophetess, not by open and invisible pores which are far purer than the womb, but through the latter part . . . And this happens not just once or twice . . . but every time she is believed to have prophesied under the inspiration of Apollo. (italics mine)

And elsewhere (3.25), he writes,

> Worst of all the oracular spirit, Apollo, free from any earthly body, passes into the so-called prophetess seated at the Pythian cave through her genitals.

Origen (7.5) further chastises the god Apollo for experiencing his "sole source of delight . . . in the private parts of a woman,"[24] implying that the union between god and priestess was indeed understood to be one of sexual intercourse.

John Chrysostom (*Homily 29 on First Corinthians* 2) echoes these sentiments, stating

> I am compelled now to bring forward and expose another disgraceful custom of [the Greeks], which it were well to pass by, because it is unseemly for us to mention such things; but that you may more clearly know their shame it is necessary to mention it, that hence at least ye may come to know the madness and exceeding mockery of those that make use of the soothsayers. . . . [T]his same Pythoness then is said, being a female, to sit at times upon the tripod of Apollo astride, and thus the evil spirit ascending from beneath and entering the lower part of her body, fills the woman with madness, and she with disheveled hair begins to play the bacchanal and to foam at the mouth, and thus being in a frenzy to utter the words of her madness.
> (Chrysostom 1975, 170, trans. Chambers)

Longinus (*On the Sublime* 13.2) takes the sexual metaphor one step further, suggesting that the priestess on her tripod was "made pregnant" (*enkumôn*) by the divine power. Thus, that the Pythia's physical posture when prophesying was similar to that assumed by Greek women in childbirth is significant.[25] Sissa (1990, 40) suggests that the Pythia "perched upon a high tripod evoked a [literal] scene of birth." Indeed, I suggest this was precisely because originally the Pythia was believed literally to give birth not only to the god's thoughts, but to his progeny as well.

This idea is further supported by other allusions to birth in association with Delphi. The original day devoted to consultation with the Pythia each year, the seventh of Byzios (February–March), was the anniversary of an important birth indeed—that of Apollo (Plutarch *Greek Questions* 9/292E). Leto's birthing of Apollo was also commemorated at Delphi by the presence of a bronze statue of a wolf, the animal into which Leto was said to have transformed herself before delivering Apollo at Delos (Aelian *On Animals* 10.26). As I suggested in Chapter 4, it is likely that Leto II (Leto as mortal) was herself part of a divine birth priestesshood. That her birthing of Apollo was remembered at Delphi lends strength to the idea of a link between Delos and Delphi as divine birth "sisterhoods."

The birth metaphor was also present in Delphi's being famously considered the *omphalos,* the "navel of the earth," a motif familiar to Pindar (*Pythian Ode* 4.74), Bacchylides, the tragedians, and other Greek writers (Cook 1914–40, 2.1:187n5). The earliest authority referring to Delphi as "navel [*omphalos*] of the Earth" is Epimenides (in Plutarch *Obsolescence of Oracles* 1/409F). Euripides (*Ion* 5) similarly calls Delphi "earth's mid-navel" (see also Strabo 9.3.6). Such a motif, I propose, rendered this oracular location the symbolic "womb" of the earth itself, the central point from which creation was thought to have emerged. I suggest that, at Delphi, this belly symbolism had its visual analog in the sacred stone, considered to be an *omphalos* or navel, which stood draped in fillets in the Delphic temple where the Pythia prophesied (Strabo 9.3.6). An egg-shaped stone thought to be a representation of this *omphalos* was indeed unearthed by excavators in the innermost sanctuary of the temple. On it, the "fillets" are rendered carved into the stone as a bas-relief that covers it in a net-like pattern. Scratched on one side of the *omphalos* is the Greek name for the earth goddess (see Parke 1939, plate 2, 9). I suggest the stone represents an extremely pregnant belly, or perhaps an egg (the parthenogenetic World Egg?).

According to legend, Delphi was established as the central point of the earth when two eagles or crows that Zeus sent out from East and West met there (Strabo 9.3.6). Parke (1939, 10), however, believes that the association with Zeus was late, and that the legend in fact may predate even the cult to Apollo at the site. Harrison ([1903] 1957, 320) similarly proposes that the *omphalos* of Delphi was "the very seat of the Earth-Mother," affirming that the womb symbolism at Delphi belonged to the cult of Ge/Gaia and her daughters Themis and Phoebe. A phrase of Clement of Alexandria (*Exhortation to the Greeks* 2.19P) speaks of "mystic symbols" of Themis that included a symbol of the female womb/vulva, indicating that there were indeed "mysteries" associated with the worship of this goddess that focused on the female generative organ. That *Delphi* may be linguistically related to *delphys*, "womb" (Gimbutas 1989, 263), further underscores the possible connection between the ancient oracular center and female reproduction. Again, such symbolism is in alignment with the proposition that Delphi was a site of both prophecy and divine birth, which in its earliest days may have been of the pure parthenogenetic form associated with Ge/Gaia. Sissa (1990) provides an image of the Delphic prophetess that conjures beautifully what I argue may have been the Pythia's original dual role. The Pythia was, she says, "an inspired pregnant woman in a temple—a woman who simultaneously open[ed] her mouth and her vagina" (52).

In this light, it is worth exploring briefly the correspondence between the Pythia's intake of the earth's vapors "through her womb" and the ancient practice of vaginal fumigation. Fumigation of the vagina with dry or moist, warm vapors was a common practice in Greece to cure a host of reproductive and bodily ills. Fumigations were prepared by pounding, mixing, and heating a wide range of ingredients, including *cassia castoreum,* myrtle leaves, and powdered animal horns, to name a few. To produce the requisite vapors, these substances were either heated in bronze or earthenware pots or applied directly to hot coals. Women positioned themselves with legs spread over the vessel or over the coals to permit the entry of the fumes into their vaginas. Another common treatment was to insert into the vagina preparations made from herbal and animal medicines, as well as refined products such as honey and wine. Fumigations and vaginal insertions were used to induce girls' first periods, assist in difficult labors, soothe the womb after childbirth, remedy infertility, cause abortion, reposition a displaced uterus, and so forth (Sissa 1990, 45–8).

Sissa (1990, 49) comments that "the practice of exposure to vapors implies a conception of the body as a sponge, a soft, porous tissue that vapors could *impregnate* as they would impregnate a fabric. In this was the Greek view of the texture of the female body" (italics mine). Perhaps Sissa's choice of the word "impregnate" is more apt than she realizes. As I discuss in Chapter 8, in recent decades scientists have found that meiosis of human ova can be spontaneously induced through chemical means. Might the ancient use of chemicals through vapors to "remedy infertility" sometimes have resulted in the activation of the parthenogenetic process, or at the very least have been part of the preparations holy *parthenoi* engaged in to help them in their attempted reproductive work? Perhaps the Pythia's absorption of the "vapors" of Mother Earth through her vagina was seen as a necessary physical component of a ritual by which she was believed, under the right conditions, to become impregnated—in later times by the god Apollo.

DIVINE BIRTH MYTHS, LEGENDS, AND TOPONYMS AT DELPHI

The idea that the spiritual possession of the Pythia by Apollo in some cases was believed to result in a literal conception of a child is lent strength by the fact that numerous myths associated with Delphi have themes of miraculous birth. I now explore such stories to argue for the original centrality of divine birth at this important oracular center.

One of the most well-known female figures associated with Delphi was Daphne, who, as mentioned, Pausanias (10.5.5) relates was the site's first priestess. That she was reportedly "appointed" to her role by Ge/Gaia indicates she belonged to the pre-Apollonian cult. Pausanias refers to her as a "nymph," which once again points to the fluidity between the "priestess" and "nymph" identities, supporting my argument that in many cases the two were in fact one. Two other Daphnes named in myth are probably identical with the Daphne of Delphi. Diodorus (4.66.5–6) calls one of them the daughter of the prophetic priest Tiresias. According to the tradition recounted by Diodorus, Daphne (also known as Manto [Pausanias 7.3.1]) was a prophetess who was made prisoner in the war of the Epigoni and was given as a "present" to Apollo. Daphne is also named elsewhere as the "nymph" daughter of the river god Ladon and Ge/Gaia in Arcadia, or of the river god Peneius in Thessaly. Phylarchus (in Cook 1914–40, 1:522) and Parthenius (*Love Romances* 15) give her a human father—the legendary Spartan king Amyclas—thereby alluding, again, to her historicity. As the daughter of either of the river gods, Daphne was said to have been chased by a lusty Apollo but changed into a bay (laurel) tree after praying to Ge/Gaia for protection as she fled. As the daughter of either Ladon or Amyclas, she was said to have been a huntress.[26] Another story relates that she and her hunting companions stabbed Leucippus to death when they discovered he had posed as a woman in order to infiltrate their bath (Pausanias 8.20.2).

We see in this composite that Daphne was a prophetess who was initially dedicated to Ge/Gaia. She probably also had affinities with Artemis, as her hunting aspect suggests, and as Parthenius states directly in his story (*Love Romances* 15), which was taken from the lost elegiac poems of Diodorus of Elaena and the twenty-fifth book of the historian Phylarchus (Thornley and Gaselee 1935, 305). Daphne's love of hunting and Artemis suggest she even may have been an Amazon. That she was considered a "nymph" indicates, I submit, that she was a holy *parthenos*. The stories of Apollo's predation of her, as well as her being given as a "war prize" to this god suggest that she was present at Delphi at the time of the arrival of the Apollonian cult, and that she was pressured into turning her skills toward *hieros gamos* divine birth. Her resistance to Apollo further indicates that she did not go willingly. Her being transformed into a "laurel" likely references an episode in which she was thought to engage in shape shifting when "visited" by the god in a trance state, as I suggested in Chapter 4 Artemis's priestess Syrinx did. The legend may imply that Daphne's choice to shape shift rather than succumb to the god sexually was believed to have resulted in her death.

Another prophetess associated with Delphi, whom I mentioned earlier, was Herophile. Although Pausanias (10.12.5) depicts her as an itenerant rather than resident priestess at Delphi, her story is still worth exploring here for its divine birth themes. I previously discussed Herophile's self-identification as the "wife, sister, and daughter" of Apollo, which suggests, by analogy with the Egyptian schema, that she was in a *hieros gamos* relationship with the god. The fact that, according to Pausanias, Herophile "passed the greater part of her life in Samos," one of the primary locations of Hera's cult, and that her name means "beloved of Hera," indicates she was also probably a priestess of Hera. She called herself "Artemis," as well (10.12.2).

That Herophile was a virgin prophetess who strongly identified with what I have argued were two Virgin Mother goddesses suggests she may have been part of a priestesshood that was devoted to pure parthenogenesis before it became associated with *hieros gamos* divine birth. The feasibility of this idea is strengthened by the fact that she claimed her mother was an "immortal nymph" of Trojan Ida (10.12.3). The "nymph" designator, once again, may be a sign that Herophile's mother also was a holy *parthenos*. The fact that Herophile was one of the rare *female* children of such a woman points to the possibility that she was considered the product of pure or daughter-bearing parthenogenesis.[27] Certainly, Herophile's reputation as a particularly gifted prophetess and poet—Pausanias (10.12.5–6) notes that she sang her oracles in verse—is in harmony with my argument that the *parthenios* was seen as a particularly unique or holy child. In this, she resembles Melanippa, who was similarly an especially talented prophetess and daughter of another "nymph," Chariclo, as I discussed in Chapter 4. Herophile's extraordinarily holy nature is stressed by a legend, recorded by Plutarch (*The Oracles at Delphi* 9/398C–D), that in her inspired verses, she claimed that she would not cease prophesying even after death, but that she would orbit the moon and become one with its face. Moreover, she asserted that her spirit would forever be borne onward "in voices of presage and portent." Her association with the moon here is particularly interesting, given, as I discussed in the case of Io in Chapter 5, and as I discuss again later, the moon was credited with instigating parthenogenetic conception (e.g., Plutarch *On Isis and Osiris* 43; Suda, s.v. *Apides*).

One legend pointing to the possible existence of a pure parthenogenetic cult at Delphi prior to the advent of the Apollonian cult is that of Deucalion, who landed his ark on Mt. Parnassus after the great flood. When he and his wife Pyrrha consulted the oracle there on how to repopulate the earth, the goddess Themis, Ge/Gaia's daughter, told them to throw over their shoulders "the bones of their mother." Realizing that by "bones of their mother" Themis meant the stones of the earth, the couple began scattering rocks behind them, as instructed, from which sprang up new men and women (Apollodorus 1.7.2; Ovid *Metamorphoses* 1.368–410). In this story, we see Ge/Gaia in her pure parthenogenetic capacity, her daughter Themis (possibly a reference to a historical Pythia?) as possessing knowledge of this female mystery, and the information being revealed at the oracle of Delphi, in particular—a trinity involving parthenogenesis, the prophetess, and the site of Delphi.

Another piece of evidence in favor of the argument that Delphi may have been the site of a divine birth priestesshood is the fact that many of the eponyms of towns, mountains, caves, and streams in and around Delphi were either holy *parthenoi* or their progeny. *Pytho,* the original name of Delphi, likely derived from *Python,*[28] the name of the she-dragon who inhabited the site. In her role as a female serpent, guardian of Ge's oracle, and prophetess in her own right, Python was deeply connected to parthenogenesis in three ways. First, as mentioned, the Greeks believed snakes were born whole and fully formed from the earth (Plutarch *Table-Talk* 2.3.3/637B), and we hear in Ovid (*Metamorphoses* 1.438–40) that Python, in particular, was spontaneously produced by Ge/Gaia after the legendary flood. Python was thus a daughter-born *parthenios,* a parthenogenetic offspring/manifestation of Ge herself. This reference could therefore be read as an allusion to the existence of a pure parthenogenetic priestesshood at Delphi in association with the Ge/Gaia cult. Second, we will remember from Chapter 2 that snakes were seen as instigators of miraculous birth at the temples to Asclepius.

Third, in Chapter 5, we learned that Python was the foster mother of Hera's parthenogenetically produced son Typhon. Moreover, Apollodorus (1.6.3), who calls Python *Delphyne,* specifically refers to her as a *kore,* which implies her "maidenhood," that is, her "virginity." The picture of Python/Delphyne rendered from this composite is of a virgin "snake" prophetess who cared for another's parthenogenetic progeny. This speaks of a divine birth cult at Delphi that was thought not only to birth such individuals, but also to raise them communally, as I suggested in Chapter 4 may have been the case on Mt. Parthenion and Delos.

A miraculous birth theme also undergirds the name *Parnassus,* the mountain on which the oracle of Delphi was located. The mountain was named after the child of a "nymph" named Cleodora and the god Poseidon. This hero, Parnassus, is said to have founded the earliest town on the mountain, which was swept away in the flood of Deucalion's time (Pausanias 10.6.1). Thus, here we have a mountain named after the child of a virgin's (nymph) conception via a god. According to Pausanias, the boy Parnassus also was said to have had an earthly father named Cleopompus. In this we again see the motif of a *parthenios* with two identified fathers, one divine, one terrestrial. This could point to another possible situation of *hieros gamos* by surrogate, or it could be simply an indication that in some cases males stepped in as parental caretakers of children believed to be holy *parthenioi*. In accordance with other such purported offspring of gods, Parnassus had special gifts, as well. Not only was he a heroic founder of a town, he was also said to have discovered the important practice of augury from observing birds' flying behavior (Pausanias 10.6.1). I propose, then, that Cleodora was a holy *parthenos* associated with Delphi in remote times. From this legend, we can discern not only that a divine birth priestesshood emerged after the flood, as suggested by the story of Deucalion, but that it also existed prior to this (possibly historical) catastrophic event.

The idea that Parnassus was the site of a divine birth cult is further bolstered by the legend that it was the place where Leto first brought her miraculously born son Apollo (Euripides *Iphigenia in Tauris* 1240–5). According to the Homeric *Hymn 4 to Hermes* (552–63), Leto left Apollo on Mt. Parnassus to be raised by the Thriai, three virgin priestess sisters whom I discuss further shortly. As in the case of Python's foster motherhood of Typhon, here we have another instance of "virgins" rearing the divinely born child of another woman in the vicinity of Delphi. Like Python, the Thriai possessed the art of prophecy, which the *Hymn* in fact states they taught to Apollo. These details again point to the possibility of Delphi as the location of an oracular divine birth priestesshood that also served as a sanctuary and spiritual training ground for other children thought to be *parthenioi*.

The name of the cave on the great plateau above the oracular precinct of Delphi, *Corycia,* derived from the "nymph" of the same name. Corycia is said to have had via Apollo a son, Lycorus, who in turn became the eponym of the towering summit of Lycoreia as well as of the ancient nearby city of that name (Pausanias 10.6.3; Dempsey [1918] 1972, 46n5). What is of special relevance to the argument that Delphi was the site of a divine birth priestesshood is the fact that the Corycian cave was "sacred to the nymphs" (Aeschylus *Eumenides* 1.20–5 Smyth 1926, n2). It was, in fact, the most popular cave of the nymphs in antiquity, the subject of more references in ancient literature than any other cave.[29] The Corycian cave was used in Neolithic and Mycenaean times, although it is unclear whether its cult use dates back that far, as clear evidence of cult activity is not found until the sixth century B.C.E. The number of votives found there far exceeds those of any other excavated cave. Among them were terracotta figures, 80 to 90 percent of which were seated or standing women, often wearing *polos* crowns, a likely sign of their priestly association. Some 23,000 *astragaloi*, or knucklebones of sheep or goats used like dice for divination, were found there, confirming the oracular use of the cave in antiquity. Also discovered was the earliest representation of the nymphs' circle dance, a clay spoked wheel around the perimeter of which nymphs stand with their hands joined (Larson 2001, 234–8).

Thus, the Corycian cave, located just above Delphi, appears to have possessed an oracle of its own in connection with the "nymphs." The Corycian "nymphs" may have been one and the same with the Thriai, given that *thriai* means "pebbles," which were also used for divination (Larson 2001, 12). Again, what emerges here is an entire female oracular tradition located on Mt. Parnassus in which women were believed to birth the children of gods and/or nurse the divine progeny of others. Cleodora, the mother of Parnassus, was also likely a part of this tradition. That Corycia was said to have given birth to the child of *Apollo*, in particular, indicates she may have been one of the Pythias of the Apollonian cult.

The possibility that the Corycian "nymphs" of Parnassus were historical women is strengthened by another legend. According to Callimachus (*Aetia* 75.56–8), who cites the fifth-century chronicler Xenomedes, the Corycian "nymphs" were the earliest inhabitants of Ceus. They came to the island after having been driven from Parnassus by a "great lion." As Larson (2001, 183–4) notes, this claim indicates some connection with Delphi, perhaps a colonization. Aristotle (*Constitution of the Ceians* no. 26, in Larson 184) similarly describes Ceus as once frequented by "nymphs"; Ovid (*Heroides* 20.221–2) agrees with Xenomedes in identifying these nymphs as Corycian.

The motif of such "nymphs" being driven out of Parnassus by a "lion" is particularly interesting here. As Larson (2001, 184) observes, the "lion" could refer to the zodiacal sign of Leo. The Greeks considered the planetary "ruler" of the sign of Leo to be the sun (Porphyry *On the Cave of the Nymphs* 22), which was identified with Apollo.[30] Thus, Leo the "lion" was the astrological house of Apollo. Perhaps this motif references an exodus of many of the holy *parthenoi* of Parnassus to Ceus when the cult of Apollo invaded the mountain.

Like the Corycian cave, the Delphic spring Cassotis was similarly named after a "nymph" of Parnassus. As we will recall, according to Pausanias (10.24.7), the water of this spring had the power to make the Pythias prophetic. Another spring, known as Castalia, located at the foot of Mt. Parnassus, was also named after a "nymph" who was a daughter of the river god Achelous. According to the scholiast on Statius's *Thebais* 1.697 (in Smith 1870, s.v. *Castalia*), Castalia was a maiden who threw herself into the spring in order to escape Apollo's pursuit. Here, we have another instance of what I suggest was a holy *parthenos* who, like Daphne, resisted the lure of *hieros gamos* divine birth in association with this god's cult at Delphi.

Other traditions also associate the Castalian spring with divine birth stories. A scholiast on the Homeric *Hymn 3 to Apollo* (in Smith 1870, s.v. *Castalia*) says the spring's name derived from Castalius, the son of Apollo (by whom, he does not state). The scholiast further names Castalius as the father of Delphus, while Pausanias (10.6.2–4) says that Castalius was the *son* of Delphus. Delphus, the geographer relates, was the founder and namesake of the city of Delphi itself. Pausanias reports two different traditions making Delphus the son of Apollo and either Celaeno, daughter of Hyamus, or Thyia, the daughter of an indigenous resident of the region. According to Pliny (*Natural History* 7.57), like Parnassus, Delphus also possessed special and magically related skills, which would befit a *parthenios*: he taught humans the art of divining by inspecting entrails. Thus, again, we have here the major toponyms of Delphi—Cassotis, Castalia, and Delphi itself—commemorating/ immortalizing holy *parthenoi* or their heroic children, all of whom seem to have been involved in a hereditary practice of both prophecy and miraculous birth. That the god Apollo is specifically mentioned as the father of both Castalius and Delphus again suggests that their respective mothers (Celaeno or Thyia, in the case of the latter) were Pythias who were both prophetesses of the god and holy *parthenoi*.

The Delphian Thyia was also said to have been the first priestess to celebrate ecstatic rites in honor of Dionysus (Pausanias 10.6.4). At Delphi, the priestesses of Dionysus were subsequently called "Thyiads" in her honor. As mentioned in Chapter 2, at Delphi, the Thyiads conducted the festival known as the *Heroïs*, most of whose rites were kept secret. According to Plutarch (*Greek Questions* 12c–d/293), however, judging by the portions of the festival performed in public, it is likely that the secret aspect of the rite had to do with an honoring of Semele. Again, as the mother of Dionysus by Zeus, Semele would have been a holy *parthenos*. As we will recall, the name of the festival was taken from one form of *heroine, hêrôis*, a term I also argued was a marker for the divine birth priestess. That this rite thus apparently had an occult miraculous birth theme (in that it was related to Semele), and that its name referred specifically to the holy *parthenos* would correspond with the general nature of the prophetic/virgin cult on Mt. Parnassus as I have been characterizing it.

THE BEE AS A SYMBOL OF DIVINE BIRTH AT DELPHI

One of the most suggestive pieces of evidence supporting the argument that a divine birth priestesshood may have existed at Delphi is ancient title of the Pythia at Delphi: *Melissas Delphidos,* or "Delphic Bee" (Pindar *Pythian Odes* 4.60–1). In Chapters 3, 4, and 6, in my discussions of Neith, Artemis (of Ephesus), and Dodona, respectively, I briefly discussed the bee's connection with parthenogenesis in the ancient world. I will now fully explore the bee as a symbol of both prophecy and parthenogenesis to explain why this creature was a particularly apt totem for Virgin Mother goddesses. I also provide evidence for the assertion that the Pythia was given the title "Bee" to designate what was once considered her own capacity for miraculous birth.

The bee was first of all an apt symbol for the Pythia because bees were associated with prophecy. They were seen to have the "power of foreknowing," as being able to predict the wind, rain, frost, and sun so as to know whether to leave or stay close to their hives on a given day (Aristotle *History of Animals* 9.40, 627b.10; Pliny *Natural History* 11.10). In fact, ancient beekeepers used bee behavior to inform neighboring farmers of stormy weather (Aelian *On Animals* 1.11). The behavior of a swarm in settling upon houses and temples was also seen to presage important public and private events. One legend recounts that bees settled upon the lips of Plato when still an infant, thereby announcing that he would be characterized by "sweet" speech—that is, special knowledge (Pliny *Natural History* 11.18; Cicero *On Divination* 1.36.79). Virgil (*Georgics* 4.220) goes so far as to maintain that bees possessed a portion of "divine reason." Bees were also seen as exemplars of spiritual values for their industry; their cleanliness; their "abhorrence of luxury and delicate living"; their vegetarian diet; their "love of song" as expressed by their humming and their attraction to clapping and the tinkling and clashing of cymbals; and their instinctive knowledge of the sacred discipline of geometry, as evinced by their building of six-sided honeycombs.[31] Certainly, all of these characteristics correspond with those of the virgin Pythia, a prophetess who was privy to divine knowledge and who conducted her office with purity and dedication.

What is perhaps most significant in the naming of the Delphic prophetesses as "Bee," I propose, is the fact that *the honeybee itself reproduces parthenogenetically,* at least in part. The queen bee produces males—drones—spontaneously out of her own body without the need for fertilization by sperm.[32] Now, it is true that ancient naturalists were unaware of the role of the queen bee in the generation of the hive. They incorrectly identified the queen as "king,"[33] and some wrongly assumed that all the other bees—both worker bees and drones—were female.[34] Nevertheless, bees were traditionally connected with parthenogenesis in the ancient mind in a number of other ways. According to Pliny (*Natural History* 11.16), no one in antiquity had ever witnessed sexual intercourse among bees. This lent them a reputation as being "chaste"—that is, virgins—and led to a variety of suppositions as to how bees were produced.[35] Although Pliny confirms that bees were observed to hatch in their cells, other writers speak of their spontaneous generation—that is, their parthenogenetic birth—from flowers (Virgil *Georgics* 4.197–203; Pliny *Natural History* 11.16). Still others believed that dead bees, preserved in the house through winter, could be brought to life again under the spring sun by being kept hot all day in the ashes of fig-tree wood (Pliny *Natural History* 11.22).

An even more widely held belief, mentioned in previous chapters, was that bees could be generated from the carcasses of oxen and bulls.[36] Antigonus of Carystus (*Historiarum Mirabilium* 19, in Cook 1914–45, 1:514), writing about 250 B.C.E., reports

In Egypt if you bury the ox in certain places, so that only his horns project above the ground and then saw them off, they say that bees fly out; for the ox putrefies and is resolved into bees.

Virgil (*Georgics* 4.281–5, 315ff.) and Ovid (*Fasti* 1.376–80) relate a similar belief in their accounts of Aristaeus, the son of Apollo and the "nymph" Cyrene. When Aristaeus's swarms died because he had offended the nymphs, the magician Proteus told him to kill a heifer and bury its carcass in the earth. When he did so, swarms of bees issued out of the decaying animal.

Similar methods for procuring bees from bulls were believed by the ancients to have come from Egypt or Libya (Cook 1914–40, 1:515). Herodotus (2.38–41) describes, for example, an Egyptian custom in which male bulls were buried with their horns poking out of the ground, and were allowed to decay before their bones were collected. Ransome ([1937] 2004, 117–8) suggests this process may have resulted in the breeding of bees and other insects and may have led to the belief in "bull-born" bees.

THE THRIAI AS EARLY DELPHIC BEE PRIESTESSES

The great antiquity of the bee's association with the priestesses of Delphi is indicated in the reference to the legendary Thriai, the three prophetesses who dwelt on Mt. Parnassus and served as nurses of Apollo. In the Homeric *Hymn 4 to Hermes* (553–64), Apollo vividly depicts them as bees:[37]

> There are certain holy ones, sisters born—three virgins gifted with wings: their heads are besprinkled with white meal, and they dwell under a ridge of Parnassus.
>
> These are teachers of divination apart from me [Apollo], the art of which I practiced while yet a boy following herds, though my father [i.e., Zeus] paid no heed to it. From their home they fly now here, now there, feeding on honey-combs and bringing all things to pass. And when they are inspired through eating yellow honey, they are willing to speak truth; but if they be deprived of the gods' sweet food, then they speak falsely, as they swarm in and out together.
>
> (Hesiod 1943, trans. Evelyn-White, 404–5)

The identification of the Thriai with bees is indicated by their winged adornment and their habits of "flying," "swarming," and "feeding on honeycombs." In this account, their ability to prophesize is made possible by their "eating yellow honey," which, as Elderkin (1940, 51) proposes, was a probable reference to entheogenic mead used at Delphi as a method of trance induction at some point during the history of the sanctuary. The excerpt serves to connect bees, female prophecy, entheogenic substances, and virginity at Delphi. Thus, the Thriai can be seen as precursors of the Pythias themselves, "bee" priestesses who were both virgins and trance prophetesses. That the Thriai are depicted as "older" than Apollo strengthens the idea that the institution of the Pythia and its association with the bee predated the Apollonian cult, and probably belonged to the Ge/Gaia cult there.[38]

Further, the motif of the Thriai's heads being "besprinkled with white meal" may be an indicator of their status as holy *parthenoi*, in particular. For in the fifth century B.C.E., Athenian poet Hermippos (frag. 25, in Dillon 2001, 38) mentions the "white-powdered" *kanephoroi*, or virgin basket carriers of Athena at Athens. In the *Ecclesiazousae* (730–4), Aristophanes'character Chremes humorously treats his sieve, clotted with flour, as a mock *kanephoros,* presumably referring to the basket bearer whose head is sprinkled with flour. That the *kanephoros* originally may have been a divine birth priestess of Athena in the earliest days of the goddess's cult at Athens is suggested by the legend, mentioned in Chapter 3, that the *kanephoros* Oreithyia was abducted and raped by the Boreas, the North Wind, while she was participating in the procession to Athena at the Acropolis. Thus, the story of Oreithyia may reference a memory of the *kanephoros* as holy *parthenos* who was thought to bear divine children. The whitening of the face/head of the priestess, then, may have been a widespread custom to denote a woman's role as holy *parthenos.*

THE BEE AND THE CAVE OF THE NYMPHS

In arguing for the possible existence of a divine birth priestesshood at Delphi, it is also necessary to return to *On the Cave of the Nymphs,* Porphyry's commentary on a particular excerpt of Homer's *Odyssey,* in which the bee figures as an important metaphor. As we will recall from Chapter 6, in this work (15), the neo-Pythagorean philosopher reports the ancient belief not only that bees were born from cattle, but that incarnating human souls themselves were seen as bees. Again, he describes human souls as "bees" emanating from *cosmic* bulls, the latter of which are precisely the moon and the constellation of Taurus (18). What is particularly interesting is that in this discussion he reveals that the bee was known as a symbol of priestesshood not just at Delphi, but more broadly in connection with what I have argued were goddesses originally considered to be parthenogenetic. He writes (18),

> The ancients used to call the priestesses of Demeter "bees" [*melissai*] as initiates of the chthonic goddess, and to call Kore [Persephone] herself "Melitodes" or "honey-like" and the moon [Artemis/Selene],[39] which presides over *genesis* [that is, incarnation of human souls], they also called "the bee," among other reasons because the moon is also called a bull and Taurus is its exaltation, and bees are born of cattle. Souls coming into *genesis,* are likewise "born from cattle."
>
> (Porphyry 1983, 31, trans. Lamberton)

That priestesses of Demeter were known as *Melissai,* or "Bees," is echoed by the scholiast on Pindar's *Pythian Ode* 4.106 (in Cook 1914–40, 1:443) and Callimachus (*Hymn 2 to Apollo* 110). In a fragment of Apollodorus of Athens (244 F 89), the women who performed the ritual of the Thesmophoria in honor of Demeter and Persephone were also known as *Melissai*. Hesychius (s.v. *Melissai*) echoes that women initiated into Demeter's mysteries were known as *Melissai*. Lactantius (1.22) adds to the list of priestesses with the title of *Melissa* those who served the Great Mother cult.[40]

We can discern from Porphyry's passage, as well, that the "virgin" Artemis/Selene/moon, herself, also possessed the title "Bee" and was specifically considered the goddess who presided over the incarnation of human souls, who descended from the heavens in the form of bees.[41] As mentioned in Chapter 6, Porphyry (19) stresses that the ancients did not simply call *all* souls entering into incarnation "bees," but specifically those "who were to live just lives and return after performing acts pleasing to the gods." Thus, Artemis was seen as the regulator of the incarnation of the special, exalted soul—the soul of what I would suggest was in some cases thought to be the child of a holy *parthenos*.[42]

Porphyry's reference to Taurus as the "exaltation" *(hupsoma)* of the moon/Artemis may also be an allusion to the Pleiades. I interpret his statement to mean that, even beyond Artemis/the moon, the ultimate governor of *genesis*—that is, the ultimate source of souls—was considered to be the constellation of the bull/cow. As I discussed in Chapter 6, Taurus and the Pleiades are associated by virtue of the fact that the Pleiades reside in and form part of this constellation. The most appropriate time for generating bees from bulls (again, a perceived parthenogenetic process) was thought to be when the sun entered the sign of Taurus (springtime) (Ransome [1937] 2004, 113). This underscores the connection in the Greek mind between parthenogenetic generation of souls and the celestial abode of Taurus/the Pleiades. Moreover, bees were known to collect honey twice a year at two critical times: the heliacal rising and cosmical setting of the Pleiades (Virgil *Georgics* 4.231–5), which further indicates the perceived association in the ancient world between bees and the asterism of the Seven Sisters, in particular. Thus, the "bee" reference in relation to Delphi may also point to an occult connection between the Pythias and the Pleiades, as I have argued was the case for the prophetesses of Dodona.

Porphyry's work as a whole is an exegesis of lines 13.102–12 of Homer's *Odyssey*, which contain not only a reference to bees, but, in light of the arguments I have been developing throughout this book, an entire program of divine birth symbols. Given that Porphyry himself stresses (36) that Homer, in his capacity as theologian, "has hinted at images of more divine things in molding his little story," it is worth examining these references in some detail. The lines in question read:

> At the head of the harbor is a slender-leaved olive tree,
> and nearby it a lovely and murky cave
> sacred to the nymphs called Naiads.
> Within are kraters and amphoras
> of stone, where bees lay up stores of honey.
> Inside, too, are massive stone looms and there the nymphs
> weave sea-purple cloth, a wonder to see.
> The water flows unceasingly. The cave has two gates,
> the one from the north, a path for men to descend,
> while the other, toward the south, is divine. Men do not
> enter by this one, but rather it is a path for immortals.
> (*Odyssey* 13.102–8, in Porphyry 1983, 21, trans. Lamberton)

The various motifs in this excerpt could be read as references to female prophecy and divine birth, particularly the olive tree, "nymphs," bees, and looms. The "nymph" epithet, as I argued in Chapter 4 and elsewhere, was likely a marker of a holy *parthenos*. The loom was symbolic of parthenogenesis by virtue of its association with Neith/Athena, as I discussed in Chapter 3. Porphyry himself affirms (14) that the loom symbolizes the process of incarnation, and equates Homer's "sea-purple cloth" with "the flesh, woven of blood" of the incarnating human. I argue that he specifically connects weaving with parthenogenesis in his observation (14) that Kore/Persephone, "the overseer of all things sown in the earth," was also depicted as a weaver, as well as in his comment (7) that Demeter raised Kore/Persephone in a cave among "nymphs." Again, an extended argument could be made that their mother/daughter aspect was representative of pure, daughter-bearing parthenogenesis, to refer to my taxonomy in Chapter 1.[43] The olive was a symbol of parthenogenesis by virtue of its association with Athena (32), as well as its appearance as the sacred tree to which Leto clung to give birth to her miraculously conceived son, as we saw in Chapter 4. Porphyry suggests that the placement of the olive tree at the "head" of the harbor near the cave is significant, and I argue that its presence there announces that the visitor has come to the lair of the *Parthenos* in her manifestation as both goddess and priestess.

That in this cave bees deposit their honey "in stone amphoras" is also significant to this argument, for Porphyry says (14) that the "stone" of the amphoras represents "human bones." This calls to mind the ancient story mentioned earlier that Deucalion and his wife were able to assist in the repopulation of the human race after the Great Flood by throwing "the bones of their mother," that is, the stones of Mother Earth, over their shoulders. This, too, was a parthenogenetic story, as Ge/Earth spontaneously produced humans from such stones.

Finally, the reference to water flowing unceasingly in this "murky" and "lovely" place may indicate that the cave is symbolic of the "watery" womb itself. Indeed, Porphyry notes (6) that the ancients made the cave "a symbol of the generated and perceptible cosmos," "a symbol of all the unseen powers," and "a symbol . . . of all those [powers] participating in matter" (10)—that is, the powers of manifestation and incarnation. The cave, he emphasizes, is a sacred temple and symbol of a cosmos that is "both holy and pleasing, though by nature . . . shadowy and 'murky'" (12). Such a description could also be applied to the human womb, particularly as it may be experienced by the fetus.

Porphyry's interpretation of the cave as the "image of the cosmos in which souls dwell" (12), and his idea that the advanced "bee" soul enters material existence when it enters the "pleasant grotto"/cave of the cosmos, also lends to the idea that holy *parthenoi* literally may have been thought to conceive their divine progeny—and perhaps also give birth to them—in caves. Indeed, as we saw in Chapter 6, the Pleiad Maia was said to have conceived Hermes through union with Zeus in a cave. Creusa, the daughter of the legendary Athenian king Erechtheus (grandson of the miraculously born Erichthonius), was impregnated by Apollo and gave birth to her child in a cave, where she left him to die. Interestingly, it was a Delphic Pythia who found and raised the infant (Euripides *Ion* 12–28, 1334–69), which suggests an intimate connection among Creusa, Apollo, the cave, virgin birth, and the priesshood of Delphi.[44] Caves were nymphs' most common cult site, and it is partly because caves were used in antiquity as homes for bees that nymphs and bees tended to be identified (Larson 2001, 9). As we have seen, the Corycian cave, located just above Delphi and named for the "nymph" Corycia, figured prominently in Delphian myth and cult as an oracular precinct in its own right and had a divine birth legend associated with it. Thus, the cave in general may have been the place where the priestess attempted her conception ritual, and the Corycian cave, in particular, may have been the location of the Pythian bee/nymphs' efforts in this regard.

Homer's reference to the mythical cave of the nymphs having "two gates" is especially fitting in this context. As Porphyry (31) explains, "The cave in question is endowed not with one entrance but two . . . the one is appropriate to the gods and to the good, the other to mortals and to the less good" (1983, 38, trans. Lamberton). These gates, he suggests (20), refer to the constellations of Cancer and Capricorn, or the northern and southern "summer and winter tropics." They represent, he says, celestial portals through which human or immortal souls incarnate. We may be able to discern another Pleiadian reference here, given that, as I discussed in Chapter 6, summer and winter were also heralded, above all, by the positioning of the Pleiades, the star cluster from where, I suggested, the Dodonian priestesses may have been thought to incarnate divine children. The reference to the cave of the nymphs, bees, honey, and loom having "two celestial portals" for two different kinds of souls—human and divine—thus completes the miraculous birth schema perfectly.[45] The entire symbolic complex of the "cave of the nymphs" can be read as a reference to both the womb (murky chamber) and ritual location (cave) of the holy *parthenos* (nymph) who, under the influence of entheogenic substances (bee honey/mead), incarnated (wove into existence/gave flesh and bone to) divine souls (who passed through the "southern gate"). The motif of the "two portals" can also be read in multivalent fashion as symbolizing the two entry points by which the god was thought to enter the oracular holy *parthenos:* through her "third eye" (for the conception of the god's wisdom) and through her womb (for conception of the god's child).

Returning to my argument about Delphi, I posit that all of these associations may help explain the deeper meaning of Diodorus Siculus's statement, mentioned earlier, that the Pythias of old were revered because of their "resemblance to Artemis." I suggest that the Pythia's title *Bee,* and her "resemblance" to Artemis, were indicators that she was considered the earthly counterpart of this goddess as conductor of special, parthenogenetically produced "bee" souls in their path to incarnation. It may well be that while the Greek men of science did not grasp the fact that the queen bee produced some of her progeny parthenogenetically, the Pythias understood this mechanism, given that they were believed to be privy to non-ordinary knowledge through their *entheos* with Apollo.

As mentioned earlier, bee parthenogenesis always results in the formation of male offspring. Thus, it may be that under the pre-Apollonian Ge/Gaia cult at Delphi, the bee served as a metaphor for *pure parthenogenesis* of the *son-bearing* kind, to refer to my taxonomy outlined in Chapter 1. Later, it would have referenced *hieros gamos* divine birth. In fact, even if the Pythia had embraced the erroneous ancient belief that all bees but the "king" were female, and that mating took place through female bees' intercourse with the "king," the metaphor still would have been an apt one: the "king" in this case would have been perceived as Apollo, and the Pythia would have been rendered the female bee who "mated" with her king.

THE "BIRDS AND THE BEES" AT DELPHI AND DODONA

Another motif that also makes an appearance at Delphi is the dove, which I argued in Chapter 6 was a parthenogenetic symbol. Elderkin (1940, 49) notes that sacred doves were indeed present at Delphi, as attested by Diodorus Siculus (16.27.2). Their presence is also implied in a scene in Euripides' play *Ion* (1189ff), in which doves that dwelt in the halls of Apollo flew into a banquet tent at Delphi and imbibed poisoned wine. Elderkin affirms (52) that the dove of Delphi, for which Euripides specifically uses the term *peleia,* further references the *peleiades,* the priestesses of Dodona, thereby suggesting a cultic connection between the two oracular centers. Given the mythological connections between doves and the star cluster of the Pleiades, the presence of the dove at Delphi may thus also reference this asterism. In support of this is the fact that the Pleiades were sometimes iconographically depicted as a cluster of grapes, whence they were also called *botrus* ("bunch of grapes") (Smith 1870, s.v. *Pleiades*). Elderkin posits that certain Cretan coins depicting doves with bodies in the form of a bunch of grapes thus connect doves with the sacred "wine" that may at a certain period have been used at Delphi as an intoxicant for the Pythia. The presence of sacred *peleiades/*doves at Delphi (who imbibe wine) seems to provide a cultic link between Delphi and Dodona, doves, the Pleiades. Furthermore, it also provides a link to entheogens, as the "poison" in the wine the doves drink in *Ion* is no doubt a psychotropic substance, given that, in antiquity, poisons were almost always entheogens when taken in smaller doses (see Hillman 2008, *passim*).

Another point of convergence between Delphi and Dodona is suggested by Varro's remark (3.16.7) that bees were called the "Birds of the Muses." This calls to mind Pythagoras's reference, mentioned in the previous chapter, to the Pleiades as the "lyre of the Muses" (Porphyry *Life of Pythagoras* 41). As I suggested, this metaphor likely demonstrated an ancient understanding of this star group as a source of divine inspiration, one that also linked it to the esoteric aspects of music and harmony. Varro's metaphor regarding bees as transmitters of the divine music of the Muses may, I propose, reference the drone of the hive, in particular. That this sound was associated with trance induction is suggested by the passage discussed earlier in which the bee priestesses known as the Thriai "swarmed" and delivered prophecy.

The connection between the drone of bees and trance may also be suggested by a curious koan about Delphi put forth by the Pythagoreans: "What is the oracle at Delphi? The tetraktys, which is the harmony in which the Sirens are" (Iamblichus *Life of Pythagoras* 82).

The tetraktys was a sacred geometrical/mathematical figure that to the Pythagoreans symbolized the sum of the cosmos and, when properly studied, served as the key to unlocking its depths and mysteries. The Sirens were the legendary sea "nymphs" who lured listeners with their bewitching song/sound (e.g. Homer *Odyssey* 12.39ff). In light of the present discussion about the bee and prophecy, the meaning of this koan may well be that the oracle at Delphi provided an entry point to the knowledge of the cosmos by means of a specific sound frequency accessed on the subtle realms by the Pythia in trance. That sound frequency was that of the "Sirens," an intense vibratory emanation likely akin to the piercing buzz/drone of the beehive. Thus, the concept of the bee as the "bird" of the "Muses"—those inspirers of divine knowledge—may be yet another reference to the bees' connection with non-ordinary states of consciousness and prophecy. Taken together, these two statements about bees and the Pleiades serving as "instruments" of the Muses seem to underscore a sacred equation among bees, birds/doves, music, divine inspiration, the stars of the Pleiades, Delphi, and Dodona.

Just as (Dodonian) doves were present at Delphi, (Delphian) bees also likely were present at Dodona. For before bees were domesticated, they constructed their combs in the hollows of oak trees, as they still did on occasion afterward (scholiast on Nicander, in Cook 1895, 18). We can expect, then, that the oak of Dodona housed these creatures as well as the sacred *peleiades*. That doves and bees, both anciently considered symbols for the divine soul, were probably present at both Dodona and Delphi emphasizes, I propose, the sisterhood between these two oracular sites. It also casts new light on the folkloric expression, "the birds and the bees." It suggests that rather than being a euphemistic allusion to sexual intercourse between humans, the expression may be a hidden reference to a much greater mystery: parthenogenetic birth.

The sisterhood between the oracles of Delphi and Dodona is further suggested by the genealogy reported by Apollodorus (1.1.3), in which Themis and Phoebe, goddesses who originally served as the oracular deities at Delphi, were the Titan sisters of Dione, the oracular deity of Dodona.[46] This renders the two primary oracular shrines in ancient Greece governed by the same female lineage—a sisterhood in the most literal sense. Moreover, Phoebe's daughters, as we will recall, were Leto and Asteria (Apollodorus 1.2.2), one the virgin mother of Apollo, the other a stalwart virgin who became the namesake of the "third D"—Delos—another possible oracular site of divine birth. And, ultimately, both Delphi and Dodona, as I have discussed, were originally the province of the parthenogenetic Ge/Gaia.

Throughout the last two chapters I have discussed numerous correspondences suggesting a strong link between Delphi and Dodona—the existence at both places of the female prophetic tradition, of *hieros gamos* relationships between the priestesses and their resident god, of the presence of birds and bees as representatives of the divine soul, of stories of the "nymphs" bearing holy children, and of common roots in Ge/Gaia and the Titan sisters. These phenomena suggest that both Dodona and Delphi were locations of virgin cults dedicated to attempting first pure parthenogenesis and, later, *hieros gamos* divine birth at some point during their respective histories.

REVISITING THE MEANING
OF THE TERM *PARTHENOS*

Having explored a wide array of evidence attesting to the possible existence of priestesses of divine birth in ancient Greece, we may take another look at that problematic term, *parthenos*. Bernal (1987–2006, 3:577–8) provides an analysis of its possible origin that is intriguingly relevant to this discussion. Noting similar conjectures by other scholars, among them Henri Gauthier and Arno Egberts, he suggests that *parthenos* may have been borrowed from the Egyptian *Pr tḥn*. *Tḥn* may be related to *Tḥnw*, the name of the ancient Libyan people known to the Egyptians who produced both olive oil and faience. In Egyptian, faience, a type of earthenware made of natron (sodium nitrate) and decorated with opaque colored glazes, was called *tḥnw*. This has led Gauthier (1925–31, 2:139) to translate the term *Pr tḥn* as "house of faience/crystal." Bernal, however, observing that the adjectival form *tḥnt* is defined as "brilliant, flashing, jewels, blue green," interprets *Pr tḥn* to mean something closer to "house of the brilliant." Hagan (2000, 64, 82, 95) notes that in the Egyptian Book of the Dead, *tḥnt* (which she interprets as "crystal") is treated as something sacred in nature and is referred to ceremonially as "heaven and earth, the eyes of *Her* [that is, Hathor]," in particular. Bernal affirms that *ṯḥnt* was used for "bright eyes of divinities."

Thus, the Greek *parthenos* may have been borrowed from a word that meant "house of the brilliant/heavenly eyes of Hathor." Significantly, as Hagan points out (2000, 27, 31, 90), the Egyptian Book of the Dead specifically refers to the gods as "the Shining Ones." Moreover, the word *Her*, which formed a part of Hathor's name, itself meant "shiny faced." The names of Greek gods also frequently had the connotation of "bright" and "shining," particularly those associated with the major (divine birth) oracular centers of Dodona and Delphi: *Zeus, Dione,* and *Phoebe/Phoebus* (i.e., Apollo) (Cook 1914–1940, 1:1, 3.1:500). The "sparkling" Milky Way itself was said to be made of Hera's milk. Similarly, the names of various *parthenoi* had astral connotations as well, such as those of two of Athena's (divine birth) priestesses, *Aglauros* (3.1:241, 499) and the Pleiad *Electra* (Smith 1870, s.v. *Electra*), as well as *Asteria* (likely a priestess of Artemis) and the Pleiad *Sterope* or *Asterope*. Moreover, we have seen *parthenoi* associated in various instances with the place and/or entheogenic plant name *Asterion,* "starry." Ultimately, all of these names are stellar references. It is likely, then, that "house of the sacred/brilliant" referred to the astral realms that were considered the home of the deities. As the "house of the brilliant/heavenly eyes of Her/Hathor," the celestial cow goddess (who in Greece was Hera), those realms were likely, again, located in the constellation of the bull/cow, Taurus. Here, we will recall my argument that holy *parthenoi* were believed to incarnate holy beings from the stars, possibly the Taurian Pleiades in particular. It is also important to note that Neith was associated with both the *Ṯḥnw* people and with the product of their land, *ṯḥn* (Bernal 1987–2006, 3:578). From the Saitic period, there are direct references to Nt *ṯḥn,* Nt being the transliteration of Neith's name from hieroglyphics.

These associations both strengthen the idea that *parthenos* (and *Parthenon*) were borrowed from the Egyptian *Pr ṯḥn,* and possibly more fully illuminate the meaning of the term. For, according to the argument presented throughout this book, the *parthenos* herself was indeed none other than the "house" of the "sacred/brilliant"; she was the very "dwelling" understood to serve as the temporary home of the incarnated astral being. Thus, I propose that the term *parthenos,* as borrowed from the Egyptian, may itself have meant something akin to "holy vessel for the divine star being who has descended from the heavenly cow/Hathor/Neith."[47] We will recall that Neith was firmly identified with Athena. We will also remember that Hera had resonances with Hathor/Neith in her epiphany as heavenly cow. Therefore, we may well have in the Greek term *parthenos* a linguistic reference to the stellar abode of the Graeco-Egyptian autogenetic creatrix in her manifold forms, which would have rendered it a beautiful and fitting honorific title for her priestesses of divine birth.

CHAPTER 8

IS VIRGIN BIRTH POSSIBLE? AND
OTHER OUTRAGEOUS QUESTIONS

As I indicated at the beginning of this book this analysis has ignored
the question of whether or not miraculous conception may be possible. Yet the tremendous amount of evidence explored in the previous
chapters suggesting that divine birth may well have been a bona fide
religious practice attempted in ancient Greece naturally leads one to
wonder: Is there any scientific possibility that women ever could have
produced children without the participation of human males?

Parthenogenesis is indeed a natural reproductive mode for a variety
of living creatures. In addition to the honeybee, which we explored
in Chapter 7, organisms that can reproduce asexually include certain
species of aphids, fleas, ants, earthworms, cockroaches, wasps, scorpions, grasshoppers, snails, frogs, shrimp, fish, lizards, snakes, and,
occasionally, sharks.[1] In mammals, parthenogenetic egg cleavage has
been reported in mares (van Niekerk and Gerneke 1966), ferrets
(Chang 1957), mice, rats, hamsters, Guinea pigs, rabbits, and sheep
(Beatty 1967).

Scientists generally assume that spontaneous parthenogenesis rarely
occurs in mammals (deGrouchy 1980, 6) and that, when it takes
place, it does not produce live births. However, researchers have been
conducting experiments to stimulate parthenogenetic activity in mammals and other living creatures for more than a century. Mouse eggs
have been stimulated to divide in test tubes with chemicals, enzymes,
temperature shifts, or electric shock (Cohen 1998–9, 36, 38). Eggs
of certain animals in whom meiosis (division of the egg) has been
artificially stimulated have even been brought to term, such as those

of sea urchins and turkeys.[2] Pincus (1939) claimed to have produced three live rabbit births by inducing meiosis in rabbits using hormone injections, treating the expelled eggs with chemical agents, and transplanting parthenogenetically activated eggs back into the rabbits.[3]

Human eggs have been observed to divide spontaneously in the laboratory up to the pre-embryo stage known as a blastula (Shettles 1956, 1957). They also have been chemically induced to divide parthenogenetically through vacuum pressure (Muechler et al. 1989) as well as through exposure to calcium ionophore (Winston et al. 1991), acid Tyrode's solution (Johnson et al. 1990), and puromycin (De Sutter 1992). Such procedures, however, have reportedly not resulted in live births.

In 1996, Jerry L. Hall, PhD, director of ViaGene Fertility in Los Angeles, began experimenting with activating parthenogenetic development in mice eggs by exposing them to a combination of ethanol (alcohol) and cytochalasin, and reported a remarkably successful activation rate of between 50 percent and 70 percent of the eggs. With Yan-Ling Feng (Feng and Hall 2001), he successfully stimulated mouse embryos to reproduce parthenogenetically through similar means all the way to the trophoblast stage—the point at which a placenta begins to grow. After they transplanted embryos to the uteri of foster mouse mothers, however, the National Institutes of Health, at whose facilities they were conducting some of the work, told the research team to destroy the animals, presumably because of the potential ethical implications of the study. The fact that some of the sacrificed fetuses had completed half of the gestation period suggests they could have resulted in viable births (personal communication, August 17, 2004).

Consistent with the work of other researchers, Hall has also achieved parthenogenetic division with human eggs by exposing them, as he did with mice eggs, to ethanol (alcohol) and cytochalasin. In May 2003, researchers from Gaithersburg, MD–based Stemron Corp. reported that they had grown the human embryos through parthenogenesis to the point where stem cells appeared. The team managed to obtain stem cells from one of the eggs, but the cells died after a few days (Associated Press 2003). According to Hall, no one has yet implanted parthenogenetically conceived human embryos into human wombs.

This brief foray into the history of parthenogenesis indicates that human and mammalian eggs can be made to divide artificially through chemical, electrical, and other means. This brings to mind the herbal fertility remedies of the ancient world, such as vaginal fumigation and pessaries—as well as the mysterious "flash of light" associated with divine conception, discussed in several chapters of this book. Although no parthenogenetically activated human ovum has been brought to term, the fact that no such eggs have been implanted in a woman's womb leaves the question open as to whether such eggs could, in fact, grow into viable fetuses. Thus, strictly on the scientific level, the door may be slightly ajar to human parthenogenesis as an artificial reproductive option for humans.

Such a possibility may be relevant to the thesis of this book—or it may not. For this study has considered non-ordinary conception not as a scientific event, but rather as a spiritual one, one occurring in a realm beyond the laws of nature. The idea that humans possess the capacity to defy the workings of the body in miraculous ways has persisted throughout time. We find it in reports, for example, of the "superhuman abilities" supposedly developed by certain holy men and women in the East. In Tibetan Buddhism, such abilities are termed *siddhis*, and are thought to be attainable by adepts at particular stages in the training of their consciousness.[4] Allione (1984, 190n17) writes that *siddhis*

> include the power to pass through walls, to transform stones into gold, to walk on water without sinking, to enter fire without being burned, to melt snow with one's body heat in extreme cold, to travel to a far-distant cosmos in a few seconds, to fly in the sky and walk through rocks and mountains, extraordinary abilities to read minds and know the future, and the development of all the senses far beyond their ordinary capacities. One can also radiate beams of light from the body and stand in sunlight without casting a shadow, make one's body vanish and other so-called miracles.

Magical capacities have also been attributed to shamans cross-culturally, as well, including the ability to change into animal forms (Eliade 1964, 477–82). Whether one contends such capabilities are achievable or not, it is reasonable to assume that the theoretical "final frontier" regarding magico-spiritual practices—the ability to reproduce life from one's body in non-ordinary ways—also would be an area that spiritual adepts would be keen to explore. Indeed, would not the ultimate accomplishment of mind/spirit over matter be to generate life within oneself through magical means? Would that not, in fact, render the practitioner something of a divine creator himself or herself?

The topic of whether miraculous conception may have been associated with any sort of *siddhic* practice has hardly been given consideration in literature about supernormal abilities.[5] Yet such stories *do* appear—as the foundational legends of many of the world's religions. In the Buddhist tradition, Maya is said to have given birth miraculously to the Buddha (Rhys 1922, 123). In Taoism, the virgin Lao is said to have conceived Lao-Tzu by the sight of a falling star (141). A legend asserts that Zarathustra's (Zoroaster) mother conceived him by drinking a cup of "Homa," the sacred drink (and probable entheogen) that so often figures in Persian and ancient Hindu legends (as Soma) (Hartland 1909–10, 1:12–3). The Manichaeans related that Terebinthus, said to have been the writer of the books from which Mani, their founder, derived his doctrines, was born of a virgin (142). Various Native North American nations claim virgins have given birth to individuals who have served as miracle workers. For the Tsalagi (Cherokee) and Iroquois (Haudenosaunee), one such miraculously born (and reincarnating) spirit teacher has been known variously as the Pale One, Wotan, or the Peacemaker (Ywahoo 1987, 2, 18, 267–8). And then, of course, there is the most famous such story of all: that of Mary's divine birthing of Jesus.

Could, then, divine birth serve as the *siddhic* practice par excellence? Are these stories, like the many that have been explored in this volume, indicative of a worldwide female mystery practice—one that has been in front of our eyes yet escaped serious attention until now? How outlandish is it to consider such a possibility when we are now witnessing the appropriation of "parthenogenetic" power indeed by the biotechnology industry—through genetic manipulation, cloning, stem cell research, the specter of cyborging, and the creation of part-human, part-animal hybrid creatures known as chimerae?[6] Is it not odd that taking genes from one organism, violently splicing them into another, and creating mutant forms of life is considered rational behavior, while exploring the potential powers of the female reproductive system in a sacred context is deemed irrational?[7]

FUTURE AREAS FOR RESEARCH

Such provocative questions aside, on the scholarly level alone the theory presented in this book may well provide a useful template for reinterpreting and making sense of a wide variety of phenomena in archaeology, anthropology, religion, and folklore. The concept of pure daughter-bearing parthenogenesis as resulting in mother/ daughter "twins," for example, suggests that the numerous images of the "double goddess"—that is, identical goddesses depicted side by side or springing from the same torso, which have been found all over the world from the remotest of times (see, e.g.,

Noble 2003)—may merit further theoretical analysis. Obviously it also inspires a closer examination of the apocryphal literature surrounding the Virgin Mary and her mother Anne, who herself was said to have divinely conceived her daughter. Similarly, the theory points to the possible need for a reassessment of miraculous birth stories concerning other female figures in the Christian and Jewish traditions, including Elizabeth, mother of John the Baptist, and Sarah, mother of Isaac. Further, it suggests that much fruit may emerge from a new exploration of Gnostic texts with parthe-nogenetic themes. It also hints that an examination of the nature, origins, and original purpose of virgin priestesshoods in many historical traditions, among them the Vestal Virgins of Rome and the Catholic nunhood—in which women are posited as "brides of Christ" (Kalweit 1988, 142–3)—may be illuminating.

At the very least, this book should leave readers with an important new angle on Greek mythology. It is clear from the extensive analysis offered here that female figures were part of a critical piece of religious story in ancient Greece that has been ignored or glossed over. Besides the particular "nymphs" and "heroines" discussed throughout this volume, there are scores more whose tales of divine union prove foundational to the establishment of the legendary Greek state. The work yet to be done of bringing these stories to light fully, and properly reframing them as part of a larger practice of divine birth—even if, under the most conservative assessment, one that existed purely in the realm of "myth"—promises to lend agency and dignity to the female and the feminine, past, present, and future.

NOTES

INTRODUCTION

1. Trans. Mackail (1934, 275).
2. The literature that has come the closest proposes the existence of the *hieros gamos*, or rite of sacred marriage, in ancient West Asia and the ancient Mediterranean world. According to some scholars, the sacred marriage was a ritual act of sexual intercourse between a king and priestess as a means of guaranteeing abundance and fertility for the people. This idea has itself received its share of critique. See, for example, Nissinen and Uro (2008). The present work in part reframes the sacred marriage concept by considering women's agency in it, a much-neglected theme.
3. For a summary of current scientific thinking on parthenogenesis, see Chapter 8.
4. For feminist analyses of pre-Greek goddesses, see, for example, Spretnak (1978), Dexter (1990), Baring and Cashford (1991), and Downing (1992).
5. For further discussion of *hieros gamos*, see Chapter 1.
6. It is based closely on my doctoral dissertation, *Bearing the Holy Ones: A Study of the Cult of Divine Birth in Ancient Greece* (Rigoglioso 2007).
7. For mention of the parthenogenetic aspects of various goddesses, see, for example, Davis (1971, 33); Spretnak (1978, 20); Daly ([1978] 1990, 84); Dexter (1990, 172–3); Sjöö and Mor (1991, 27–30); Reis (1991; 34–53); Ruether (1992; 18); and, more extensively, Hwang (2005, passim). For claims of successful virgin births among indigenous tribes in Australia and Melanesia, see, for example, Roth (1903); Malinowski (1913, 1927, 1929); Montagu ([1937] 1974); Leach (1969); and Spiro (1968). For other, more controversial, claims, see Bernard (n.d.) and Melchizedek (2000, 2:282–5). For briefer discussions of virgin birth in ancient Greece, see, for example, Graves ([1875] 2004); Hartland (1894; 1909–10); Rhys (1922); Boslooper (1962); Warner (1976); Sissa (1990); Drewermann (1994); and Miller (2003).
8. Her work builds upon that of Ricoeur (e.g., 1965, 40–4; 1970, 32–6), who first articulated the concept of hermeneutics as an exercise of "suspicion" *(soupçon)*.

9. Although I am distinguishing here between *myth* and *legend*, I use the terms interchangeably throughout the book, along with *story*.
10. For a history of human diffusion, see, for example, Cavalli-Sforza et al. (1994).
11. For a modern consideration of gnostic epistemology, see Kripal (2007).

Chapter 1

1. For those not familiar with ancient Greek, I occasionally indicate where the stress should fall on certain key terms. *Parthenos* is accented on the second syllable: *parthénos*.
2. I refrain from using the term *immaculate conception* as a synonym for divine birth because it has a precise meaning in Christian doctrine that is in fact unrelated to virginal conception. There, it refers simply to the idea that the Virgin Mary was born "exempt from all stain of original sin" (Holweck 1910, 674). Its use as a reference to Mary's virginal conception of Jesus is incorrect.
3. This theory received yet another confirmation in the summer of 2007 by the Mount Lykaion Excavation and Survey Project, which uncovered evidence of the worship of a pre-Olympian deity in the archaeological layers under an altar to Zeus on the summit of Mount Lykaion in Arcadia in Greece (Wilford 2008).
4. For the classical exposition of matriarchy (one that is interesting but in many ways problematic from a feminist viewpoint), see Bachofen ([1861] 1897), portions of which can be found in English translation in Bachofen (1973, [1861] 2005). For a recent critique of theories of matriarchy, see Eller (2000). For a counterresponse to Eller, see Dashu (2000) and Marler (2005).

I rely on the definition of matriarchy proposed by Göttner-Abendroth (2001). A classical matriarchy possesses specific traits at four levels: the economic, social, political, and cultural. At the economic level, a matriarchy is characterized by reciprocity. Women have the power of distribution of goods, and inheritance is passed down through the mother's line. Yet, the society is egalitarian and includes mechanisms for distributing wealth to prevent goods from being accumulated by special individuals or groups. At the social level, a matriarchy is matrilocal; people live in large clans, and kinship is acknowledged exclusively in the female line. At the political level, a matriarchy is governed by communal and consensual decision making, and is characterized by leadership that is shared in complementary fashion between the genders. Decisions begin in the clan house and are carried out to the village level via delegates, who may be the oldest women of the clans or the brothers and sons they have chosen as representatives. On the cultural level, a matriarchy is characterized by religious traditions in which divinity is seen as imminent in the earth, nature, and the cosmos, and in which there is no separation between sacred and secular. Everyday tasks take on ritual meaning, the cycles of the seasons and other astronomical events are celebrated, and frequently the universe is conceived as a female or divine Mother. In short, the classical matriarchy is, in essence, an egalitarian society in which the female principle is considered foundational and central. This corresponds with Sanday's observation (1998, para. 2) that the term *matriarchy* itself should be redefined as "mother origin," since it derives from the Greek *mêtêr* (mother), and *archê*, which can mean "beginning," "origin," or "first principle." I contend that pre- and early Greek society evinced aspects of this type of matriarchal structure (if already partly patriarchalized, as I explain further below), and I provide support for this assertion throughout this book.

5. Occurrences can be found in Sophocles, frag. 310 (in Kerenyi 1975, 44 n14) and Plato (*Charmides* 153a).

6. While controversy surrounds Gimbutas's methods and conclusions (e.g., Goodison and Morris 1998; Hayden 1993; Meskell 1995; Tringham and Conkey 1998), the viewpoint I adopt is in accord with those of archaeologists and other scholars who are verifying and expanding upon various aspects of Gimbutas's theories (e.g., Nikolov forthcoming; C. Lazarovici 2008; G. Lazarovici 2008; Dergachev 2007; Yakar 1997, 2007; Brukner 2006; Christ 1996; Keller 1996; Spretnak 1996). Along with these scholars, I find that Gimbutas's theories have tremendous heuristic utility for the interpretation of not only archaeological artifacts, but also iconography, mythological motifs, and historical texts. That prominent classics scholars such as those cited earlier independently held to similar theoretical views puts, I believe, the assumption of an earlier matriarchal substratum in Greece, upon which my analysis is based, on firm, even if not conclusive, footing.

7. *Entheos* is accented on the first syllable: *éntheos.*

8. One ancient literary example of *entheos* is found in Euripides (*Hippolytus* 141).

9. Wasson et al. (1978) and Eyer (1993) argue that entheogens were used to stimulate the culminating experience of initiates during the Eleusinian Mysteries, for example. See also Hillman (2008) for a history of the widespread use of entheogens in the ancient world.

10. See Chapter 8 for further discussion of this topic.

11. On Egyptian terrain, this theoretical concept is supported in part by Troy (1986, 53), who notes that the roles of Egyptian royal women and priestesses were based on identification with the primary goddess of the pantheon.

12. Jerry L. Hall, ViaGene Fertility director, personal communication, August 19, 2004. One important exception is the honeybee, which I discuss at length in Chapter 7.

13. I contend this idea would have persisted even though, according to Hall (personal communication, August 19, 2004), theoretically a

parthenogenetically produced daughter would not in fact be a "clone" of the mother, given that each egg is genetically different and represents a unique combination of the mother's genes. What would have been stressed in the condition of daughter-bearing parthenogenesis was the symbolism of the mother essentially "creating (herself) out of herself," not technical scientific details (which may or may not have been understood). Moreover, given that, in the case of parthenogenesis, theoretically all genetic material would come from the mother, the parthenogenetic daughter would tend to look very similar to the mother, thus emphasizing the "twinning" aspect.

14. Space constraints preclude an analysis of the parthenogenetic aspects of the mythology and cult of Demeter and Persephone in this book. See my forthcoming *Virgin Mother Goddesses of Antiquity*.

15. The fragment is preserved in Plato:

> For from whomsoever Persephone shall accept requital for ancient wrong, the souls of these she restores in the ninth year to the upper sun again; from them arise glorious kings and men of splendid might and surpassing wisdom, and for all remaining time are they called holy heroes amongst mankind.
>
> (Plato *Meno* 81b, 1925, trans. Lamb)

I contend this references the sacrificial death and apotheosis of divinely born children that I am positing here.

16. My interpretation differs somewhat from that of Frazer, whose work has influenced the general understanding of the purpose of the divine king and his sacrifice. According to Frazer (e.g., 1905, 291–7; [1906–15] 1935, 2.1:318–23, 4:9–160), early communities regarded their kings as gods incarnate. The king was not supposed to grow old because his divine powers would dwindle with the decay of his body; therefore, he was put to a violent death at the first signs of aging. When he was killed, the divinity left his body to take its place in a younger person. Cook (1904 passim) similarly argues that the early Greek kings, honored as embodiments of Zeus and actually called by his name, were within traditional memory killed as soon as they began to exhibit old age. My point is that it was not old age that was the motivating factor in the death of the divinely born king, but rather the perceived need for periodic communal purification.

17. For a discussion of this feature of the Eleusinian Mysteries, see, for example, Harrison ([1903] 1957, 562–4). Again, this possibly late aspect of the cult of Demeter and Persephone will not be considered in this book.

18. The term is accented *hieròs gámos*.

19. The expression *hieros gamos*, as it applies to the marital/sexual union of a god and goddess (generally Hera and Zeus), does not itself appear in extant Greek literature before the Alexandrian period (i.e., c. fourth century B.C.E.). The Neoplatonist Proclus implies it originally had a place in certain mystical stories (Kerenyi 1975, 106–7).

However, the earliest references to it are in Plato (*Laws* 8.841d, *Republic* 5.458e), who uses it to refer to human marriage (Guthrie 1967, 54n1). The term also referred to private feasts held by certain families, and public marriage festivals in Athens, which were associated mythically with the union of Zeus and Hera (Avagianou 2008, 149, 158). In using the term, I support the early theories proposed by Frazer, Kramer, and others that acts of cultic sexual intercourse actually took place in various parts of the ancient world. See, for example, Nissinen and Uro (2008, 1–6) for a critical discussion of such literature. However, I restore what I believe is the missing piece in such theories. As I argue throughout this book, I submit that the purpose of *hieros gamos* was not just to generate "fertility for the land" in the abstract sense, as has been emphasized previously, but literally to generate a child from the union—specifically, what was considered a divinely endowed leader. *Hieros gamos*, then, was a means of engendering what was believed to be a divine bloodline. Rites intended to result in the divine conception of the pharaoh in Egypt as reported in ancient texts and on temple walls offer instructive parallels. See Rigoglioso (2007, 70–94) and Rikala (2008, 115–44). Cf. Avagianou (2008), who maintains that any ancient Greek story of a sexual liaison between a deity and human should not be called *hieros gamos*. I contend that our differences are a matter of semantics.

20. For evidence that Egyptian queen mothers similarly engaged in *hieros gamos* by surrogate to conceive pharaohs, see Rigoglioso (2007, 70–94).

21. More recently, Tyson (2000) has written of his own purported sexual encounters with disembodied entities, which he describes as intensely erotic.

22. See Griffiths (1970, 353 and n6) for a discussion of Isis as possibly having been understood to conceive Horus *after* Osiris died, when she constructed the artificial phallus. In short, lurking in some versions of the Isis story is the idea that, as Griffith comments, "having succeeded in reviving the dead Osiris, [Isis] was in a way responsible for both aspects of the sexual act."

CHAPTER 2

1. Various legends attributed Pythagoras's fatherhood to the god Apollo. See Rigoglioso (2007, 498–508). For expanded discussion on the orders of spiritual beings from the later occult perspective, including further classifications, see Iamblichus (*On the Mysteries* passim).

2. See, for example, Farnell (1921 passim and 403–26); Rhode ([1925] 1966, 115–55); Burkert (1985, 203–15).

3. In *Numa* (4.3–4), he says "that an immortal god should take carnal pleasure in a mortal body and its beauty . . . is hard to believe." Yet, in the next breath, he seems to consider "plausible" (*ouk apithanôs*)

the Egyptian belief that only women, not men, can be approached sexually by deities in order to be impregnated by them. Then, in the following lines, he seems to question such a distinction, stating, "But [the Egyptians] lose sight of the fact that intercourse is a reciprocal matter, and that both parties to it enter into a like communion." Finally, he seems to settle on the idea that the most "fit and proper" type of affection by a deity for a human "takes the form of solicitude for his character and virtue" (Plutarch 1914, 319, trans. Perrin). In *Table-Talk* (8.1.3/788A–B), speaking about the legend of Plato's divine birth from his mother via Apollo, he muses on the mechanism of divine conception, seeming to reject the idea that it could take place through the exchange of visceral fluids. Yet, he seems to support the possibility of divine conception through another means: "I do not find it strange," he says, "if it is not by a physical approach, like a man's, but by some other kind of contact or touch, by other agencies, that a god alters mortal nature and makes it pregnant with a more divine offspring" (Plutarch 1927–69, 9:117, trans. Babbitt). Cf. his *Advice to Bride and Groom* (48/145D–E), mentioned later in this chapter, in which he states, "It is said that no woman ever produced a child without the cooperation of a man" (1927–69, 2:339, trans. Babbitt).

4. For an extensive discussion of these divine birth stories, with a focus on the mothers involved (Parthenis/Pythais, Perictione/Potone, and Olympias, respectively), see Rigoglioso (2007, 498–539).

5. The implications regarding Jesus should be apparent.

6. Cf. the "daughters of humans" who mate with the "sons of god" in Genesis 6:1–4, and related stories in *1 Enoch* and *The Testament of Reuben,* discussed in Collins (2008, 259–74).

7. My interpretation here differs from that of Farnell ([1896–1909] 1977, 4:191), for example, who holds that *anairein,* "to take up," referred to one method of divination the Delphic prophetess used, the drawing of lots, which involved the picking up of beans.

8. That Greeks held the concept of the oracular "third eye" can be seen, for example, in Origen's comment (*Contra Celsum* 6.8) that Plato believed he possessed such an organ. Origen disregards Plato's purported claim as an "incredible tale," but it is clear that he has misunderstood the philosopher's meaning. In fact, what Plato no doubt meant was that he possessed the capacity of divine knowing. The idea of the oracular "third eye" is also suggested by the mythologem of Hera's giving the hero Argos an extra eye in the back of his head so as to guard Io from the predations of Zeus (Pherecydes frag. 22, in the scholiast on Euripides' *Phoenissae* 1123, cited in Cook 1914–40, 1:462). In his statue in Argive Larisa, Zeus also had a third eye on his forehead, although this was said specifically to refer to his triple dominion over sky, earth, and sea (Pausanias 2.24.3).

9. I wish to thank Josephine MacMillan, who provided me with the first seeds of this idea during one of her seminar paper presentations at the

California Institute of Integral Studies, San Francisco, in April 2001. MacMillan refers to the "third eye" as the "upper womb," and main- tains it has ontological correspondences with the "lower womb," or uterus. Others have also discerned the concept of the "upper womb" in the female body, but identify it as the mouth or throat region, for its numerous visual and symbolic analogies with the vulva/vagina. See, for example, Marler (2002, 18–9) and Sissa (1990, 53–70). Sissa (53) notes, in particular, that Hippocratic medicine analogized the mouth and uterus through its use of the same term for *mouth* (*stoma*) to describe the mouth of the uterus. However, as she acknowledges (58), "the association of the mouth with the genitals does not apply exclusively to the female body." Again, for the reasons I have argued here, I posit that the "upper womb" should be rightly identified as the "third eye."

10. See also Gilhus (2008, 501–8), who insightfully discusses the close conceptual relationship between "knowing" and sexuality, but does not fully consider the possibility that this abstracted "metaphorical" relationship, as expressed in patriarchal Gnostic and Judaic philoso- phy, may have much earlier roots in female reality, specifically, the female body. Speaking of the phenomenon of spirit possession in contemporary cultures, Sered (1994, 182) notes that women have long been thought to be particularly skilled at, or prone to, trance. Pointing out the "obvious parallels" between pregnancy and posses- sion, she posits that the ability of a woman to "share her body with a baby" is what prepares her for oracular reception (189–90). The thesis of this book takes such an argument a radical step further.

11. Again, however, Plutarch himself rejects this distinction, but his rea- son is not terribly clear. See *Numa* (4.4).

12. See Larson (2001, 65). Hesiod relates (*Theogony* 969–1020) that the following goddesses joined in love with mortal men and bore children: Demeter with Iason; Harmonia with Cadmus; Callirhoe with Chrysaor; Eos with Tithonus and Cephalus; Psamathe with Aiacus; Aphrodite (whom he calls Cythereia) with Anchises; and Circe and Calypso with Odysseus. The *Hymn to Aphrodite* (179–255) tells us that Aphrodite's birth of Aeneas from her union with the hero Anchises caused her great disgrace and a loss of status among the gods. Elsewhere, we learn that the moon goddess Selene loved the mortal youth Endymion and had 50 daughters by him (Pau- sanias 5.1.4), and that the Nereid Thetis bore the hero Achilles by the mortal Peleus (Homer *Iliad* 1.351–63, 495–543, 18.70–148, 38–467, 24.62). Nephele bore Phrixos and Helle to the mortal Athamas (scholiast on Aristophanes' *Nubes* 257, Apostolius 11.58, Eudocia *Violarium* 28, all cited in Cook 1914–40, 1:415 and n1). Plutarch (*Numa* 4.2) also reports a story that the legendary Roman king Numa engaged in a "holy marriage" (*gamos theios*) with a god- dess named Egeria, whom he met while communing in sacred groves

and meadows. The relationship was understood to have been sexual in nature.

13. Lyons (1997, 5), for example, defines a heroine as "a heroized female personage or recipient of heroic honors, and, secondarily, as a female figure in epic, myth, or cult." Larson (1995, 3) restricts *heroine* to "a cult recipient who, according to her devotees, was at one time a mortal woman," thereby eliminating from her purview any female figure for whom no cult is attested.

14. Even more intriguing, *Nephelai* has at least a superficial resemblance to the term *Nephilim* of the Hebrew Bible, which, in Genesis (6:1–4), refers to the "heroes of days gone by" who were born of women's unions with "sons of God." A linguistic analysis comparing the Greek and Hebrew terms is beyond the scope of this book, but at first glance the resemblance is certainly striking, particularly given the meaning of each in the context of the argument I am making here.

15. For other similarly suggestive uses of the various terms for *heroine*, see Larson (1995, 21–5).

16. According to Larson (1995, 3), by the third century B.C.E. in Greece, the terms for *heroine* apparently came to be used more routinely to refer to the ordinary dead, rather than to those deceased individuals who held special power or merited special honors.

17. Such a point of view may have had its analog in myths whereby goddesses' parthenogenetic offspring were depicted as deformed or monstrous. We see this in the case of Hera, discussed in Chapter 5, whose parthenogenetically produced son Hephaestus was, in one tradition, born lame, and whose other parthenogenetically born son, Typhon, was depicted as a troublesome, freakish winged creature. It is interesting to speculate about the degree to which the medical profession's assumption that parthenogenesis inevitably resulted in deformity may have corresponded with the theological "demotion" of the goddess's self-generative capacity under patriarchy, which I trace in detail in my forthcoming volume *Virgin Mother Goddesses of Antiquity*. I thank Marvin Meyer for drawing my attention to this theme.

18. Pindar (*Pythian Ode* 3); Pausanias (2.26.5–6); Apollodorus (3.10.3).

19. Dexter (1990, 167–70) further points out that, like Hera, various Hindu heroines were also believed capable of "renewing" their virginity either through ritual or at the conclusion of a marriage. In the United States, Nandu Menon, a contemporary spiritual teacher from Kerala, India, teaches about and conducts special rituals that he reports enable women to restore their "virgin" state energetically, particularly after traumatic events such as rape and abortion (personal communication, June 4, 2005).

20. Since *parthenos* is such a central term to this work, I mention again that stress falls on the second syllable: *parthénos*.

21. Again, a more extended discussion of the parthenogenetic aspect of these goddesses will appear in my future volume *Virgin Mother*

Goddesses of Antiquity. Given the multiple meanings attributed to the term *parthenos,* to avoid confusion I hereafter use *parthenos* in the more conventional sense to denote a prepubescent or presexual female, and "holy *parthenos*" to denote what I am proposing was a (usually virgin) priestess of divine birth. I subsequently capitalize the term "Holy *Parthenos*" to denote a goddess in her aspect as parthenogenetic creatrix.

22. For documentation regarding these aspects of the priestesshood, as well as a more comprehensive discussion of the role of sacerdotal women in Greece, see, for example, Connelly (2007), Dillon (2001), Turner (1983), Goff (2004), and Holderman (1913).

23. Writing much later, Strabo (17.1.46) mentions an Egyptian custom whereby a prepubescent girl of high birth who was dedicated to Zeus seems to have freely engaged in sexual relations with men until the time of her menarche and marriage. Budin (2003, 151–2) questions the interpretation that such a girl "concubined" herself, and suggests instead that she served as a handmaiden. Nevertheless, if the Theban maidens' role indeed was sexual, it may signal a devolving over the centuries of the original role of the virgin consort of the god into that of cult prostitute. For Herodotus, cited earlier, it is clear that the priestess of his day who was dedicated to Theban Zeus did not engage in sex with other men. On the other hand, it may be that a priestesshood of sacred prostitutes had (always?) existed alongside that of the virgins. I offer the conjecture that in such a case, each priestesshood would have had a separate function: the latter, to engender the divine child; the former to unite with him sexually to create his earthly lineage. A serious consideration of the cult of the sacred prostitute, of which Aphrodite was the tutelary goddess in the Greek context, is beyond the scope of this work. For suggestions of the practice of sacred prostitution in ancient Greece and West Asia, see, for example, Herodotus (1.199); Strabo (6.2.6, 8.6.20, 12.3.36). Cf. Budin (2008), who argues that sacred prostitution did not in fact exist in the ancient world.

24. Other priestesses may never have been required to be virgins. Among them was the priestess of Athena Polias at Athens, as attested by records of her priestess Lysimache, who served for 64 years and had children (Pliny *Natural History* 34.19.76; *Inscriptiones Graecae* ii[2] 3453, in Dillon 2001, 78). The priestesses of Hera at Argos similarly served for multiple decades and also had children (Herodotus 1.31). The priestess of Demeter at Eleusis could have children, as could the priestess of Aglaurus at Athens (*Supplementum Epigraphicum Graecum* 16.160, 32.115.10–1, in Dillon 2001, 77). Artemis also had a married woman priestess at her main Athenian sanctuary at Brauron (Hyperides frag. 199, in Dillon 77). The priestess of Nemesis at Rhamnous was married with children (*Inscriptiones Graecae* ii[2] 3462, in Dillon 77). It is not clear, however, whether such women

maintained chastity during the period of their service. See also Turner (1983, 215–28) for further examples, and cases of priestesses who were married to priests.

25. Athena, like Demeter, however, also had married priestesses as cult attendants (Turner 1983, 183).

26. As at Delphi, after the rape of one of the young virgin priestesses at Artemis Hymnia in Arcadia, the individual selected for the post was subsequently a woman who "had enough sexual intercourse with men" (Pausanias 8.5.11–3, 8.13.1, 5).

27. *Basilinna* is accented *basílinna*.

28. For a discussion of folklore (and, by extension, myth) as a repository for secret, subversive, and repressed religious beliefs, see, for example, Birnbaum (1993, 3–35).

Chapter 3

1. For a more in-depth discussion of Neith as a parthenogenetic goddess, see my forthcoming *Virgin Mother Goddesses of Antiquity.*

2. By the time of Plutarch's writing (first century C.E.), Neith at Saïs was also known as Isis (*On Isis and Osiris* 9).

3. The phrasing also implies, in particular, that she was never *violated* sexually. This connotation would have had meaning in Hellenistic Greece, where, as I demonstrate in this and subsequent chapters, the sexual predation of goddesses, nymphs, and mortals by gods was a regular part of religious story, pointing to the disempowerment of the feminine in the patriarchal era.

4. See, for example, Plutarch (*Cleomenes* 39); Pliny (*Natural History* 11.23); Aelian (*On Animals* 2.57).

5. Other locales in Greece, some of which had rivers or wells named *Triton* or *Tritonis,* subsequently asserted that Athena was born there, such as Alalcomenae in Boeotia, and Argos (Pausanias 9.33.5; Strabo 9.2.36). The bulk of the mythological stories and ethnographies, however, place Athena as originating in Libyan Africa. Nilsson ([1950] 1971, 484–500) argues for a Cretan origin for Athena, a view that seems to have been widely accepted (see, e.g., Guthrie 1967, 106). I am in strong agreement, however, with Bernal (1987–2006, 3:540–82), who uses historical, cultic, and linguistic evidence to support the argument for a Libyo-Egyptian origin for Athena, and for the transfer of her cult to Greek soil. My argument here overlaps with his to some degree, but goes further in looking at mythological and ethnographic evidence. Although they do not discuss Athena's Libyan roots, excellent feminist analyses of this goddess include Spretnak (1978, 97–101); Dexter (1990, 118–20); Baring and Cashford (1991, 332–45); and Downing (1992, 99–130).

6. Used rarely, the term *monogenês* is employed to describe two other goddesses who I suggest also represent daughter-bearing

parthenogenesis: Demeter and Persephone (Orphic *Hymn to Ceres* and Orphic *Hymn to Proserpine*). As Long (1992, 49) notes, the term is applied to Jesus in the prologue to the Fourth Gospel (John 1:14), and as such serves as "an early indicator of the process of [Female] Wisdom becoming absorbed" into the male godhead. That Jesus was one in a line of *parthenioi,* children of holy *parthenoi,* described in this work emphasizes the associations between the term *monogenês* and the concept of parthenogenesis.

7. Diodorus states he derives his own account from that of Dionysius of Mitylene. It is conjectured that the latter, surnamed Scytobrachion, lived either shortly before the time of Cicero (c. 106–43 B.C.E.) (and was instructed at Alexandria) or as far back as the fifth century B.C.E. Attributed to him were works recounting the military expedition of Dionysus and Athena, and a prose work on the Argonauts in six books. He may also have been the author of the historic cycle poems, lost epics recounting ancient history up to the twelfth century B.C.E. (Smith 1870, s.v. *Dionysius, literary* 34). One translator of Diodorus's history, C. H. Oldfather (Diodorus Siculus 1935, 246n2), dismisses Dionysius's purported account of the Libyan Amazons as a mere "mythical romance." However, that the work of Xanthus the Lydian, a source cited by Dionysius Scytobrachion, was once regarded as fictitious but is now thought to be both genuine and reputable (Brown 1946, 268 and n46) opens the door to the possibility that the latter's other sources could have reflected authentic historical material, as well. This may have included any source from which he obtained his information about the Libyan Amazons.

8. For a discussion of these and related customs as being indicative of matriarchy, see, for example, Göttner-Abendroth (1987, 2; 2001). Refer also to the definition of matriarchy I provide in Chapter 1, which is drawn from Göttner-Abendroth.

9. See, for example, Dodds (1951, 28–63) on the archaic tendency to assume that human misfortunes represented acts of justice by supernatural powers.

10. As Göttner-Abendroth (1987, 2) notes, in the social condition of matriarchy more broadly, "the relationship between the mother and daughter is the core relationship of the family."

11. The Great Panathenaia was celebrated with particular magnificence every fourth year. The Suda (s.v. *peplos*) says the *peplos* was prepared only once every four years.

12. Harpocration, s.v. *arrêphorein* (in Kerenyi 1978, 36 and n147). See also Connelly (2007, 31–2, 39 and n60) for differing scholarly views as to the age, role, and number of the females who served as *arrephoroi.*

13. Dean-Jones (1994, 98–101). Diocles, Empedocles, Aristotle, and Galen said all women menstruated with the waning (new) moon, for example. Correspondingly, one Hippocratic passage asserts that

most women conceived around the full moon (98–9), while another observes that the belief the moon itself was female was based on the fact that menses always occurred during the waning phase (100).

14. Harpocration (s.v. *Aglaurus*), and scholiast on Aristophanes' *Lysistrata* 439 (in Kerenyi 1978, 37 with n153).

15. See, also, Connelly (2007, 83, 104–15), who, in her masterful work on Greek priestesses, lends support to this idea.

16. The goddess's attempt to make Erichthonius "immortal" echoes the motif, which I discuss in Chapter 5, of Hera's breast milk making the sons of gods "immortal." This seems to refer to a ritual mechanism whereby the hero/son of a god, already considered a step above ordinary mortals according to the orders of spiritual beings discussed in Chapter 2, could achieve full godhead, as did Heracles.

17. The identification of the festival is given in the *Etymologicum Magnum* (s.v. *arrêphoroi*, in Kerenyi 1978, 56 and n250). It is not clear whether these two *arrephoroi* were the same as those who wove the *peplos* for Athena for the Panathenaia, or whether they were two different girls.

18. *Dialogi Meretricii* 2.1, para. 276 (in Kerenyi 1978, 57 and n257).

19. See, for example, Hesychius and Photios, s.v. *loutrides*, and *Etymologicum Magnum*, s.v. *kataniptes* (in Dillon 2001, 133); Cook (1914–40, 3.1:749).

20. See, for example, Herodotus (7.189); Plato (*Phaedrus* 229b–d); Apollodorus (3.15.1, 2).

21. For feminist analyses of Medusa, see, for example, Walker (1983, s.v. *Athene, Gorgon, Medusa*), Baring and Cashford (1991, 340–1), and Marler (2002). Walker considers Medusa's Libyan provenance, but posits her as a goddess, not a historical woman.

22. In all of these various legends, we may be able to discern a rough timeline for certain events concerning Athena/Neith's cult in both Greece and North Africa. Perseus was known as the great-grandfather of the Achaean Heracles, who was famed for his 12 labors (Diodorus 4.9.1–2). After his exploits in Libya, Perseus became the Achaean king of the ancient Greek cities of Tiryns and Mycenae, the latter of which he is said to have founded (Pausanias 2.15.4). Given that the Achaean Heracles' sons and grandsons fought in the Trojan War, which has been dated to approximately 1275 B.C.E., Perseus would have lived four or five generations before that. If we count a generation as 25 years, this would place his attack on Queen Medusa at approximately 1375 B.C.E.

23. Again, for the various means reportedly used in antiquity to induce trance in order to achieve *entheos* with divinity and/or *gnosis*, that is, profound or mystical knowledge, see Chapter 1, in which I cite Iamblicus's discussion in this regard (*Theurgia [Letter of Porphyry]* 1.3). For anthropological studies of the phenomenon, see, for example, Lewis (1971), Eliade (1964), and Kalweit (1988, 1992).

24. Here again I refer to the cross-cultural work of Lewis (1971, 57–64), who affirms that a belief that sexual intercourse is possible with spirits has been widespread across many cultures.
25. Pausanias (8.4.9, 8.47.4, 8.48.7); Apollodorus (2.7.4, 3.9.1); Diodorus Siculus (4.33.7–12); Strabo (13.1.69); Hyginus (*Fabulae* 99).
26. Jones (in Strabo 1950, 6:78–79n3) claims that the priestesses were replaced yearly and were forced to remain virgins when they returned home, but he does not offer a primary source for this assertion.
27. It should be noted that Strabo (13.1.40) claims the custom of sending Locrian maidens to Ilion (Troy) was not initiated to appease the goddess over Cassandra's rape, as no such story existed in Homer. Rather, he says, the custom was initiated well after the Trojan War, when the Persians were already in power. I find his statement unconvincing.
28. Roman legend held that the Palladium was brought from Troy to Rome, where the Vestal Virgins guarded it (Dionysius of Halicarnassus *Roman Antiquities* 1.68–9). I submit this indicates the Vestals comprised a divine birth priesthood, as well. A more comprehensive analysis of the Vestals as holy *parthenoi* is beyond the scope of this book but will find place in a future volume.

CHAPTER 4

1. See Apollodorus (E.3.21, E6.26), Pausanias (1.43.1, 9.19.6), and Euripides (*Iphigeneia in Aulis* and *Iphigeneia among the Taurians*) for the possible connection of Artemisian worship at Tauris and Boeotia with human sacrifice. Pausanias (9.17.1) similarly refers to a sacrifice of maidens to Artemis at Thebes.
2. Among them, for example, Guthrie (1967, 99–101); Harrison ([1903] 1957, 299–300; [1912] 1963, 502); Nilsson ([1950] 1971, 503; 1961, 16); Farnell ([1896–1909] 1977, 2:425–6); Rose (1959, 112–4). For feminist analyses of Artemis, see, for example, Spretnak (1978, 75–6); Dexter (1990, 115–9); Baring and Cashford (1991, 320–32); Downing (1992, 157–85).
3. Pindar (*Heracles or Kerberos for the Thebans*, Dithyramb 2.20), for example, depicts Artemis as yoking savage lions together during Dionysian revels, a likely reference to her identification with Cybele.
4. Artemis's identification with Britomartis can be seen, for example, in Pausanias (3.14.2), who notes that in Sparta, Artemis was "not really Artemis but Britomartis of Crete." Britomartis was a goddess of eastern Crete (Nilsson [1950] 1971, 510–1; Guthrie 1967, 105). Artemis is identified with Dictynna in Euripides (*Iphigeneia in Tauris* 126), Aristophanes (*Frogs* 1356), and Orphic *Hymn 35 to Diana*. Dictynna was a goddess of western Crete (Nilsson [1950] 1971, 510–1). For Artemis's identification with Eileithyia, see Orphic *Hymn 2 to Prothyraea*. According to Pausanias (1.18.5), the Cretans believed

that Eileithyia was born at Amnisus in the Cnossian territory and was also the daughter of Hera.

5. For Artemis accompanied by such creatures, see, for example, Pausanias (5.19.5, 8.37.4–5); Apollonius Rhodius (*Argonautica* 3.879); Suda (s.v. *Arktos*); Aelian (*On Animals* 12.4). For iconographic images identified as possible depictions of Artemis as Mistress of the Animals, see, for example, Harrison ([1903] 1957, 264–6) and Farnell ([1896–1909] 1977, 2:522 pl. 29).

6. See, for example, Hesiod (*Works and Days* 563); Aeschylus (*Libation Bearers* 127); Herodotus (1.78); Plutarch (*Table-Talk* 2.3.3/637B); Artemidorus (*Oneirocritica* 2.13); Pliny (*Natural History* 8.84); and Cicero (*De Natura Deorum* 2.26).

7. See, for example, Homeric *Hymns to Artemis* (9.1–2 and 27 passim); Homeric *Hymn 5 to Aphrodite* (15–20); Callimachus (*Hymn 3 to Artemis* 6–10); Orphic *Hymn 35 to Artemis*.

8. See, for example, Homer (*Odyssey* 6.100); Homeric *Hymns to Artemis* (9, 27 passim); Homeric *Hymn 5 to Aphrodite* (15–20); Callimachus (*Hymn 3 to Artemis* 10–5 and passim); Orphic *Hymn 35 to Artemis*.

9. For references to the Greek war against the Themadon Amazons, see, for example, Herodotus (4.105–19); Diodorus Siculus (4.16); Justin (2.4); Plutarch (*Theseus* 27–8); Isocrates (*Panathenaicus* 193, 194); Demosthenes (*Funeral Oration* 8); Lysias (*Funeral Orations* 4, 6; Aristides (*Panathenaic Oration* 83–4).

10. The placement of Artemis under an oak tree calls to mind the oracle of Dodona, which was centered around a large oak tree, and which was originally dedicated to a female deity, possibly an early version of Ge/Gaia. I return to the topic in Chapter 6.

11. For details about the Thermadon Amazons, see, for example, Bennett (1967); duBois (1982); Kleinbaum (1983); Sobol (1972); Tyrrell (1984); Wilde (1999); Noble (2003).

12. Hesiod (*Theogony* 346) writes that there were 3,000 such Oceanids.

13. See, for example, scholiast on Pindar's *Olympian Ode* 13.74; Pausanias (8.3.2); Ovid (*Fasti* 3.769, *Metamorphoses* 5.412, 9.651).

14. Nymphs were venerated, for example, at springs at Cyrtone (Pausanias 9.24.4), Olympia (5.15.4, 6.22.7), and Megara (1.40.1).

15. Nymphs accompanying Artemis: for example, Apollonius Rhodius (*Argonautica* 3.881–85), Callimachus (*Hymn 3 to Artemis* passim), Ovid (*Metamorphoses* 2.441–52, *Fasti* 3.155–9); nymphs assisting Artemis in hunting: for example, Callimachus (*Hymn 3 to Artemis* 162–7); nymphs joining Artemis in the bath: for example, Ovid (*Metamorphoses* 3.155–85; *Fasti* 2.153–74); nymphs and the footrace: for example, Ovid (*Metamorphoses* 4.297–9), Pausanias (2.30.3).

16. See, for example, Homeric *Hymn 27 to Artemis* (10–20); Callimachus (*Hymn 3 to Artemis* 170); Homeric *Hymn 3 to Apollo* (189–99).

17. Pausanias (5.7.8) names Opis and Hecaerge only.

18. Nymphs were sometimes portrayed as lascivious instigators of sexual activity with mortals, for example, in Homeric *Hymn 5 to Aphrodite* (5.256–63), Propertius (1.20.11–4), and Statius (*Thebaid* 4.329–30), but they were depicted in this way far less frequently.

19. For an extensive cataloging of nymphs, nymph children, their status as eponyms of Greek towns and cities, and cults associated with them, see Larson (2001).

20. The term was also used in ancient Greece as a synonym for "bride" or "young wife" (see, e.g., Avagianou 2008, 150). I suggest this usage served as a poetic reference to the original condition of the holy *parthenos*'s sexual union with the god, now extrapolated to the strictly mortal couple.

21. For an analysis of choruses of young women in ancient Greece in relation to Artemis and various other cults, see, for example, Calame (1997).

22. Orion again appears as a sexual predator of holy *parthenoi* in the story of the Pleiades, the seven virgin sisters who I argue in Chapter 6 were associated with a divine birth cult at Dodona.

23. In what follows, I frequently adopt the compound term nymph/priestess to underscore the possible historicity of the female figure in question.

24. My interpretation departs from other views on Greek metamorphosis, such as that the transformation story originated in an ancient belief in animal gods. See Forbes Irving (1990, 1–6) for a partial historiography of metamorphosis in Greek myth, and *passim* for his own more structuralist approach to such myths.

25. See, for example, Eliade (1964, 477–82); Kalweit (1992, 200); Villoldo (2000, 36–7, 102).

26. Forbes Irving (1990, 172); see, for example, Plato (*Republic* 2.380d, 383a) and Ovid (*Fasti* 140–3).

27. One story reports Artemis was in love with Orion and was tricked into killing him by Apollo (Hyginus *Poetic Astronomy* 2.34). However, given Artemis's clear preference for virginity and the companionship of women, as amply documented in this chapter, it seems likely this motif is a later patriarchal intrusion into her story. Elsewhere, Artemis and Orion are depicted as hunting companions and friends. See, for example, Pseudo-Eratosthenes (*Constellations* 32).

28. Callimachus (*Hymn 5 Bath of Pallas* 107–16); Apollodorus (3.4.4); Pausanias (9.2.3–4).

29. See Pausanias (5.7.2–3, 6.22.8–9, 8.54.3); Strabo (6.2.4); Ovid (*Metamorphoses* 5.577–641).

30. Contemporary Ortygia is located off the coast of the Sicilian city of Syracuse.

31. According to legend, Iphigeneia was indeed installed as a priestess of Artemis at Tauris by Artemis (Apollodorus [E6.26–7]; Antoninus Liberalis *Metamorphoses* 27).

32. Cf. Antoninus Liberalis (*Metamorphoses* 40), who relates that her name *Dictynna* derived from her having hid among fishermen's nets to escape Minos.
33. Nonnus (16.403–5) writes that Dionysus named the Bithynian town in Anatolia after Nicaea. According to record, some inhabitants of a small town of the same name near Thermopylae may have colonized it (Memnon in Photius *Library* 224, in Stillwell et al. 1976, s.v. *Nicaea*). That these towns were extant at least as far back as the Hellenistic period (see, e.g., Diodorus Siculus 16.59.2) indicates that the legend of Nicaea may originate farther back in antiquity. Cf. Strabo (12.4.7), who reports the military leader Lysimachus named the Bithynian Nicaea after his wife, the daughter of Antipater, in the fourth century B.C.E.
34. For evidence of the historicity of the *mainades*, see Dillon (2001, 139–53).
35. Elsewhere (1.28), Nonnus calls this Iacchus the "third" Bacchus/Dionysus, indicating that he may have been thought of as another "incarnation" of the god himself.
36. Pseudo-Eratosthenes (*Constellations* 1) reports that Artemis transformed Callisto into a bear. Apollodorus (3.8.1) relates it was Zeus who did so, and that Hera persuaded Artemis to kill the bear. Pausanias (8.3.6–7) says it was Hera who turned Callisto into a bear.
37. As a nymph who herself represents one of the seven stars of the Pleiades, Maia becomes important when I discuss the *peleiai/peleiades*, priestesses of Dodona, in Chapter 6.
38. Burkert (1985, 205) cautions that excavations have sometimes revealed that alleged hero graves were not graves at all, as they contained no bones. I suggest such "graves" nevertheless could have served as commemorative markers for actual deceased individuals whose bodies were interred elsewhere.
39. See also Aristophanes *Lysistrata* with scholiast (in Farnell [1896–1909] 1977, 2:564n32). The rite has been deduced based on the meager written evidence alluded to here as well as vase paintings dating to the fifth or early fourth century B.C.E. found in the temple in Brauron and the temple of Artemis Brauronia in Athens.
40. The very young maids on these kraters are depicted nude or dressed in short chitons, racing with torches toward or around an altar, or dancing, either in chains or circular formation. See, for example, Lissarrague (1992, 188–9, fig. 31).
41. Burkert (1985, 221), too, seems to intuit that gifts made to Artemis by girls before a marriage ceremony served as a means by which the maidens "ransom themselves, as it were, from her claims"—that is, her demand of girls' eternal virginity.
42. For the Boeotian tale, see Ovid (*Metamorphoses* 10.550–707); Hyginus (*Fabulae* 99, 185). For the Arcadian variant, see Aelian (*Historical*

Miscellany 13.1); Hyginus; Callimachus (*Hymn 3 to Artemis* 215–7; Apollodorus (3.9.2); Servius on Virgil's *Aeneid* 3.313.

43. In the Arcadian legend, Zeus metamorphosed them into lions (Apollodorus 3.9.2; Servius on Virgil's *Aeneid* 3.313). Given that lions were a symbol of Cybele, however, it is likely that the Boeotian story is the original.

44. Indeed, Servius on Virgil's *Aeneid* 3.113 (in Apollodorus 1967, 1:400–1n1) asserts that the apples Aphrodite delivered came from the garden of the Hesperides, which, as I demonstrate in Chapter 5, was the parthenogenetic realm of both Hera and Ge/Gaia.

45. Hyginus (*Fabulae* 99) says Parthenopaeus was Atalanta's son by the mortal Meleager. According to this version, shepherds who found and reared him named the child thus because Atalanta had exposed him on Mt. Parthenion. As Grant (in Hyginus 1960, 88) notes, however, this is a very late story, for in the earliest versions there is no connection between Atalanta and Meleager. Apollodorus (3.9.2) relates that Parthenopaeus was considered to be Atalanta's son by "Melanion or Ares." Such ambiguity points to the possibility that we are in the realm of *hieros gamos* by surrogate, as in the case of Aethra and her union with Poseidon and King Aegeus "on the same night."

46. All of these events indeed were said to have occurred during the legendary life of Asclepius. See, for example, Ovid (*Fasti* 6.733–62).

47. See Apollodorus (2.5.4) for the legend of Cheiron's accidental wounding by Heracles' poison-tipped arrow, which caused the centaur so much pain that he gave up his immortality in order to be surrendered to death.

48. Again, the case of the daughters of Cecrops and their mother Agraulus/Aglaurus, discussed in Chapter 3, similarly speaks of the existence of families in which all or several sisters were divine birth priestesses.

49. For lore and cult surrounding Asclepius, see, for example, Kerenyi (1959). For further discussion on Ascelpius's possible historicity, see Smith (1870, s.v. *Aesculapius*).

50. Leto's genealogy is also outlined in Apollodorus (1.9.2) and Diodorus Siculus (5.67.2).

51. For Leto's persecution, see, for example, Callimachus (*Hymn to Delos* 55–65); scholiast on Euripides *Phoenissae* 232; Hyginus (*Fabulae* 140).

52. This island is not to be confused with the aforementioned Ortygia in Sicily, where a cult to Artemis was also located.

53. Strabo (14.1.20) similarly places Artemis's birth in Ortygia, but says Leto gave birth to Apollo there, as well.

54. Whether Leto and Artemis in fact belong together or whether their "pairing" was also a manipulation of the patriarchal age is a valid question, but one I will not explore here.

55. Pindar (*Pythian Ode* 4.90); Callimachus (*Hymn 3 to Artemis* 110); Apollodorus (1.4.1).
56. Hesiod (*Theogony* 353); Hyginus (*Fabulae* Preface); Apollodorus (1.1.2–3).
57. Hesiod (*Theogony* 135, 901); Apollonius Rhodius (4.800); Apollodorus (1.4.1); Pausanias (10.5.6); Ovid (*Metamorphoses* 1.321).
58. Apollodorus (1.2.2, 1.4.5); Hesiod (*Theogony* 243, 930); Pseudo-Eratosthenes (*Constellations* 31); Hyginus (*Poetic Astronomy* 2.17).
59. Callisto: Apollodorus (3.8.2), Pausanias (8.3.6), Ovid (*Fasti* 2.175); Aegina: Hyginus (*Fabulae* 52); Othreis: Antoninus Liberalis (*Metamorphoses* 13); Iynx: Suda (s.v. *Iynx*); Side: Apollodorus (1.4.3); Io: (Apollodorus 2.1.3); Elare: Apollodorus (1.4.1); Semele: Apollodorus (3.4.3).
60. See Theoi Project (2000–7) (specifically, s.v. *Zeus: Zeus loves 1, 2, and 3*) for a comprehensive cataloging of Zeus's divine lovers. See also Apollodorus (1.3.1) for a partial list.
61. Hyginus (*Fabulae* 53) relates a later, presumably garbled legend that it was Zeus who cast Asteria into the sea after changing her into a quail, and that from her sprang up a floating island named Ortygia. There, he says, Leto gave birth to Artemis and Apollo while clinging to an olive tree. In this account, we have the conflation of Asteria/Delos with Ortygia, named as one of the birthplaces of Artemis.
62. Pindar (*Paean to Delos* 7b.43–52, 1997, 275); Callimachus (*Hymn 4 to Delos* 51–4); Strabo (10.5.2).
63. Zeno of Rhodes (in Smith et al. 1890, s.v. *Oraculum*); Diodorus Siculus (5.58.4); Virgil (*Aeneid* 3.73–120); Lucian (*Double Indictment* 1).
64. The earliest direct Greek reference to birth being "polluting" comes from the cathartic law of Cyrene of the fourth century B.C.E. (Dillon 2001, 252–3). Women also were not allowed to give birth in the sanctuary at Epidaurus (Pausanias 2.27.1, 6), and an Athenian decree of the first century B.C.E. stated that it was ancestral practice for no births or deaths to take place in sanctuaries (*Inscriptiones Graecae* ii2 1035.10–1, in Dillon). Yet, in Euripides' *Auge* (frag. 266, in Dillon), the virgin priestess of Athena, Auge, gives birth to her son by Heracles in the goddess's sanctuary at Tegea. Given the myths, discussed earlier, of Delos having been a site of sacred births, it seems likely that prior to the fifth century B.C.E., birthing may have been an integral part of its temple life.

CHAPTER 5

1. *Lexicon Rhetoricum Cantabrigiense* (s.v. *hieros gamos*, in Kerenyi 1975, 106).
2. Aristophanes (*Thesmophoriazusai* 970); Plutarch (in Eusebius *Preparation for the Gospel* 3 Preface, *Moralia* 15.157).

3. See, for example, Müller (1857, 249–55); Harrison ([1903] 1957, 315–21); Kerenyi (1975, 123, 132–6 and passim); O'Brien (1993, passim); Burkert (1985, 130–1). For feminist analyses of Hera, see, for example, Spretnak (1978, 84–7); Baring and Cashford (1991, 310–9); Downing (1992, 68–98).

4. "Queen of gods": Homeric *Hymn 12 to Hera* 2; seasons: O'Brien (1993, 116–7); earthquakes: Homer (*Iliad* 8.199, 14.285); atmosphere: Cicero (*De Natura Deorum* 2.26); rain: Pausanias (2.25.10); wind: Homer (*Iliad* 14.249), Apollodorus (2.7.1), Orphic *Hymn to Hera;* stars: Hyginus (*Poetic Astronomy* 2.3, 2.43). Hera's association with the moon was expressed in her connection with the cow, discussed below. As Kerenyi (1975, 127) notes, the horns of cattle were a symbol of the crescent moon in nearby West Asia. See also Cook (1914–40, 1:455–7).

5. Willow: Pausanias (7.4.4, 8.23.5); asterion: Pausanias (2.17.2); lily: Clement of Alexandria (*Christ the Educator* 72); pomegranate: Pausanias (2.17.4), Philostratus (*Life of Apollonius of Tyana* 4.28); wheat: *Etymologicum Magnum* (s.v. *zeuxidia*, in Farnell [1896–1909] 1977, 1:242n13a), which calls wheat "flowers of Hera."

6. Peacock: Pausanias (2.17.6), and see also O'Brien (1993, 38–9) regarding coins depicting Hera and peacocks at her central cult location of Samos; hawk: Aelian (*On Animals* 12.4); doves: O'Brien (229–30).

7. Callimachus (in scholiast on Apollonius Rhodius 1.87); cf. scholiast on Pindar's *Olympian Odes* 6.149. In Hermione, she was similarly worshipped as *Parthenos* (Stephanus of Byzantium, s.v. *Hermion;* scholiast on Pindar's *Olympian Odes* 6.149e).

8. See, for example, Aristotle (frag. 570, in Cook 1914–40, 3.2:1027n1); Pliny (*Natural History* 5.37); scholiast on Apollonius Rhodius 1.185–7; Callimachus (*Hymn 4 to Delos* 49); Strabo (10.2.17). Kerenyi (1975, 156) doubts *Parthenia* was the "original" name of Samos, but, regardless, the name came to be associated with Hera there at some early date.

9. See Strabo (10.2.17); Eustathius on Dionysius Periegeta 533, scholiast on Apollonius Rhodius 1.187, and scholiast on Homer's *Iliad* 14.295–6 (all in Cook 1914–40, 3.2:1027n1).

10. See, for example, Aelian (*On Animals* 9.26); Pliny (*Natural History* 24.33); Dioscorides (*Greek Herbal* 1.135, s.v. *Agnos* [1934] 1968, 73, ed. Gunther). Also see Galen (*De Simplicium Medicamentorum Temperamentis* 6.2), scholiast on Nicander's *Theriaca* 71, and Eustathius on *Odyssey* 1639, 2ff. (all cited in Cook 1914–40, 3.2:1030n5).

11. For Hera's wedding on Samos, see also Varro (in Lactantius *On False Religion* 1.17) and St. Augustine (*City of God* 6.7).

12. Hesychius and *Etymologicum Magnum* (s.v. *Heresedes*); scholiast on Pindar's *Olympian Ode* 6.149b, g.

13. Cf. Devereux (1982, 67–94), who approaches this idea in asserting that the restoration of Hera's virginity was a sign of her "unmarriage,

a periodic ritual interruption of her marriage" (*démariage, une interruption rituelle périodique de son marriage*).

14. Hesiod (*Theogony* 927–8); Chrysippus (frag 908, in Hesiod *Theogony*
925, 1959, 179); Apollodorus (1.3.5).
15. I will discuss Ge/Gaia as a parthenogenetic mother further in my
forthcoming volume *Virgin Mother Goddesses of Antiquity.*
16. Apollonius Rhodius (*Argonautica* 4.1390); Diodorus Siculus
(4.26.2); Hyginus (*Astronomica* 2.3); Apollodorus (3.5.11).
17. Herodotus (1.78); Artemidorus (*Oneirocritica* 2.13); Plutarch
(*Table-Talk* 2.3.3/637B); Pliny (*Natural History* 8.84).
18. Faraone (1990) discusses how apples, quinces, pomegranates, and
other fruit designated by the Greek word *mêlon* were used in ancient
Greek stories in connection with the initiation and preservation of
marriages.
19. For example, Pindar (*Hymn to Zeus Ammon?*, in Cook 1914–40,
1:366–7); Plato (*Symposium* 190b–1b); Plutarch (*Table-Talk* 2.3.3/
637B).
20. Again, for the hero cult of Greece and categories of heroes, see, for
example, Farnell (1921), Rhode ([1925] 1966, 115–55), and Burkert
(1985, 203–15).
21. Again, as Rhode ([1925] 1966, 141n23) points out, divine parentage was not necessarily a *requirement* for being made a hero.
Nevertheless, many heroes were believed to have had a divine parent,
as mentioned in Chapter 2 as well as in many of the myths discussed
throughout this book. Burkert (1985, 207–8) affirms that sons of
gods were regarded as heroes.
22. Alcmene's ancestral connection to Io can be traced through Perseus
back to Io's son, Epaphus, founder of a family from whom sprang
Danaus, Perseus's grandfather. See Smith (1870, s.v. *Io*) and
Apollodorus (2.1–4) to piece together this lineage.
23. See also Hyginus (*Fabulae* 29); Pindar (*Isthmian Ode* 7.6–7; *Nemean
Ode* 10.11–4); scholiast on Homer's *Odyssey* 11.266.
24. Pausanias (9.25.2); Pseudo-Eratosthenes (*Constellations* 44); Hyginus
(*Poetic Astronomy* 2.43).
25. Pindar (*Nemean Ode* 1.39–47); Apollodorus (2.4.8, 12); Euripides
(*Heracles* 914ff.); Pausanias (9.11.1); Hyginus (*Fabulae* 32); scholiast
on Pindar's *Isthmian Ode* 3.104.
26. In my forthcoming volume, *Virgin Mother Goddesses of Antiquity*,
I argue that a number of Heracles' so-called twelve labors were
attempts to dismantle or disrupt the earlier religion, particularly the
cult of divine birth.
27. Lucillus of Tarrha, frag. 10, and Linnenkugel on scholiast on
Apollonius Rhodius 1.187 (in Cook 1914–40, 3.2:1027n1).
28. *Greek Herbal* 3.164 (s.v. *Kannabis emeros* [1934] 1968, 390, ed.
Gunther).

29. Butrica (2002, 52). I was not able to verify Butrica's claim that *phalis* as the title of a priestess appears in Pausanias. Nevertheless, that asterion was in fact cannabis should, I believe, supersede Kerenyi's (1975, 121) identification of the plant as "a sort of aster." Moreover, the overwhelmingly dominant feature of the aster (in contrast to cannabis) is the flower, and Pausanias does not refer to any sort of flower in his description of asterion, only to the leaves. Finally, that asterion was twined to create garlands is in accord with the widespread use of cannabis for rope making in the Greek and Roman worlds (Butrica 2002, 53).

30. See, for example, Herodotus's (4.73–5) description of the Scythians inhaling cannabis vapors in special ritual tents and subsequently "howling" in a state of stupefaction. Later, Galen (*De Alimentorum Facultatibus* 6.549, in Butrica 2002, 61–2) confirms that cannabis seeds were enjoyed for their psychoactive effect.

31. Smith (1870, s.v. *Io*); see also Connelly (2007, 70). Hesychius (s.v. *Ió kallithuessa*) gives another variant of this title for Io, *Kallithuessa*, "She of the Fair Sacrifices." Yet other variants were *Kallithoé, Kallithué, Kallithea,* and *Kallaithuia* (in Cook 1914–40, 1:453 and n8).

32. Other daughters of Inachus were similarly considered "nymphs" (Robertson 1983, 153–62). This again may point to the possibility that Io belonged to a family of holy *parthenoi* sisters.

33. Hesiod (*Catalogue of Women* frag. 72, 2007, 145–6, ed. Most); Aeschylus (*Prometheus Bound* 589ff.); Callimachus (Epigram 58); Apollodorus (2.1.3); Euripides (*Phoenician Women* 676ff.); Hyginus (*Fabulae* 145, 155, 275); Ovid (*Metamorphoses* 1.570ff.).

34. The Greeks identified their own Dionysus with Osiris (Plutarch *On Isis and Osiris* 13/356A–B).

35. I return to the role of light in Chapter 7, when I analyze the mechanism whereby Apollo was thought to possess the bodies of his oracular priestesses at Delphi.

36. Cook (1914–40, 1:454 and n8) cites other sources that assert that in Argive dialect, *Io* meant "Moon," including Aelius Herodianus, Eustathius, and Suda, although he doubts such claims. Nevertheless, he agrees that the equation of Io with Isis supported Io's identification with the moon, given that the Greeks equated Isis with the moon. See also Hesychius (s.v. *Ió*); Macrobius (*Saturnalia* 1.19.12).

37. For scholars who see in her myth a confirmation of the belief in an ancient connection between the religions of Greece and Egypt, see Smith (1870, s.v. *Io*).

38. See also *On the Malice of Herodotus* (14/857E–F) and Herodotus (1927–69, 11:29 note b, trans. Babbitt), in which the author, possibly Plutarch, bitterly complains that Herodotus "abandons" consideration of what he assumes to be the "Greek" origin of Io and Epaphus in reckoning the ancestry of figures such as Acrisius, Danaë, and Perseus.

39. Pseudo-Eratosthenes (*Constellations* 23); Hyginus (*Poetic Astronomy* 2.21, *Fabulae* 84, 159, 250). As befits a child of divine union, according to the theory being put forth here, Oenomaus indeed possessed supernormal powers, specifically, the ability to control thunder and rain (Cornford, in Harrison [1912] 1963, 220).

40. See, for example, Diodorus Siculus (4.73); Hyginus (*Fabulae* 84); Pindar (*Olympian Odes* 1.69 ff.); scholiast on Apollonius Rhodius 17.52 (in Smith 1870, s.v. *Oenomaus*).

41. Tzetzes on Lycophron 156 (in Smith 1870, s.v. *Oenomaus*); Hyginus (*Fabulae* 253).

42. See also Meenee (2004), who argues for the precedence of the Heraia.

CHAPTER 6

1. Ancient Mt. Tomarus is contemporary Mt. Olytsikas. The ruins of Dodona lie 11 miles southwest of the present town of Ioannina.

2. Pindar, who lived even before Herodotus, refers to what may well be this same legend. See the scholiast on Sophocles' *Trachiniae* 170.

3. Other stories credit the founding of Dodona to either Deucalian, the Greek "Noah" (scholiast on Homer's *Iliad* 16.233, in Parke 1967, 44n16), or Hellus, the oak cutter (Philostrates *Imagines* 2.33).

4. That the "doves" at Dodona were held by the ancients to be priestesses is implied by the scholiast on Sophocles *Trachiniae* 171–2; Pausanias (10.12.10); Eustathius on Homer's *Odyssey* 1760; Strabo (7.7.10); Hesychius (s.v. *peleiai*); Servius and Probus on Virgil's *Eclogues* 9.11. Although Cook (1914–40, 1:443n2) points to ambiguity as to whether the "doves" mentioned in such instances were in fact women, I contend that the identification between the Dodonian "doves" and the priestesses is indeed implied by the ancient writers and I provide evidence throughout this chapter to support that idea.

5. Strabo (7.7.12) notes that the oracle at Dodona may have been transferred from Thessaly in the region of Scotussa, or from Epirus. However, he reports (7.1 frag.) the claim that after the oak tree burned in Thessaly, Apollo delivered an oracular pronouncement *at Dodona,* bidding that the oracle be relocated there. That the god would have given such a prophecy from Dodona itself implies the preexistence of an oracular site there.

6. The oracle at Dodona functioned with some interruptions by the Aetolians, Romans, and Thracians until the close of the fourth century C.E., when the temple to Zeus was destroyed and the sacred oak tree cut down (Dakaris 1971, 26).

7. According to others, Dione was the daughter of Uranus and Ge, or of Aether and Ge (Hyginus *Fabulae* Preface; Apollodorus 1.1.3).

8. See, for example, Guthrie (1967, 5). *Dione* is also related to the later Latin *Diana* (Cook 1914–40, 1:163).

9. I should acknowledge here that the topic of Egyptian influence on Greece has been controversial. The main ancient sources for such claims are Herodotus and Diodorus Siculus, who have received their share of ancient and contemporary critique (see, e.g., Lefkowitz 1996, 53–80). My approach, as should now be clear, is generally to accept the observations of both as containing a good measure of truth, and to attempt to cross-reference them with other literary and archaeological material. In this, I follow Birnbaum (2001) and Bernal (1987–2006), despite criticisms leveled against the latter (see, e.g., Lefkowitz 1996; Lefkowitz and Rogers 1996), which I find to be overzealous.

10. Later, he was known as Zeus *Ammon*, a name calibrated to 500 B.C.E., when the head of this god first appears on silver coins of Cyrene (Cook 1914–40, 1:351).

11. Cf. Sophocles (*Trachiniae* 170), who says there were only two and does not specify their age. In a late commentary, Servius on Virgil's *Aeneid* 3.466 relates a legend that it was an old woman named *Pelias*, in particular, who delivered the oracle at Dodona.

12. Epirus, the town in which Dodona is located, suffered disruptions by northwestern tribes migrating to the South during the twelfth century B.C.E., after the Trojan War, a trend that lasted throughout the Greek "Dark Age" until 700 B.C.E. (Dakaris 1971, 17–8). I propose this resulted in a number of patriarchal transformations of the priestesshood of Dodona.

13. Cf. Heracleides Ponticus (in Cook 1914–40, 2.1:214), in which a cauldron of boiling water is used.

14. Except, says Strabo (9.2.4), when oracles were being delivered to Boeotians, owing to their having murdered the priestess. In such cases, oracles were delivered by male priests.

15. See Parke (1967, 259–73) for examples.

16. Parke (1967, 17–8n25) disputes that dream incubation was a method of prophecy at Dodona.

17. See also the scholiast on Homer's *Iliad* 28.486.

18. Cf. Eustathius on *Iliad* 2.750 (335.44); *Etymologicum Magnum* (s.v. *Dôdônaios*). One legend relates that the site takes its name from the Oceanid Dodona, whom Deucalion, the Greek "Noah," married after consulting the oracle at the oak and hearing the dove tell him to settle in the spot (scholiast on Homer's *Iliad* 16.233, in Parke 1967, 44n16). For the story of Deucalian and the flood, see Ovid (*Metamorphoses* 1.348ff.).

19. Scholiast on Homer's *Iliad* 12.292; Herodotus (1.2.1); Apollodorus (3.1.1); Ovid (*Metamorphoses* 2.836ff.).

20. I disagree with Cook (1914–40, 1:524–26), who contends that Europa was originally a Cretan Earth goddess.

21. See the discussion in Chapter 3 of the "rape/abduction/seduction" of the holy *parthenos* as possibly having taken place during a trance state.

22. It is also worth noting here that Aeschylus (*Prometheus Bound* 732–4, 839–41) makes one of Io's stops in her wanderings as a cow the oracular center of Dodona, where the "talking oaks" of Zeus salute her as the god's "bride to be." Parke (1967, 52) dismisses the detail as Aeschylus's own invention, but it is interesting to the present argument that the playwright would think to have Io's "spousehood" with Zeus pronounced at Dodona, in particular. I contend he was drawing on an underground stream of folk belief in which Dodona was indeed seen as a place where priestesses served as the "spouse" of Zeus.

23. *Peleiades* is accented *peleiádes*.

24. Philostrates (*Imagines* 2.33); scholiast on Homer's *Iliad* 16.234; Servius on Virgil's *Aeneid* 3.466.

25. The rationale for possible cultural and linguistic transmissions between Greece and West Asia has been provided by Gordon (1962) and Bernal (1987–2006). Some have also posited a linguistic connection between *YVNH/ionah/ione* and the Sanskrit *yoni*, meaning vulva/womb (Wake 1870, 220, 223). If this is valid, and if one or both terms could be linguistically related to *Dione*, then the oracle of Dodona, with its dove goddess, could be read as the "oracle of the womb." Linguist Miriam Robbins Dexter (personal communication, August 28, 2008), however, says there is no direct connection between *Dione* and *yoni*, stating that "the Sanskrit equivalent to *Dione* would have been the masculine *Dyaus Pitar*," *Pitar* meaning "father."

26. This parentage, listed by Homer (*Iliad* 5.370–84), may be older than the more commonly known story of Aphrodite's birth in the sea from the severed genitals of Uranus (Hesiod *Theogony* 190).

27. Aelian (*On Animals* 4.2, 10.33); Plutarch (*On Isis and Osiris* 71/379D); Virgil (*Aeneid* 6.193). Doves frequently appear in association with Aphrodite, as they do, for example, on her temple in Cyprus (Baring and Cashford 1991, 358). A Greek vase painting shows Aphrodite holding a dove, and a terracotta plaque from Locri, Italy (c. 460 B.C.E.), shows her in a chariot led by winged cupids, one of whom holds a dove (Hansell 1998, 64–5).

28. Dakaris (2000, 20). Statius (*Silvae* 3.5.80) refers specifically to "Dione's dove." Mozley (in Statius 1928, 1:198 note a) assumes he means here "Aphrodite/Venus," but it is interesting that Statius specifically uses the ancient name of the love goddess's mother. This suggests an ancient understanding that the dove was indeed earlier the totem of Dione herself.

29. In this, I propose the dove was similar to the apple and pomegranate, which I argued in Chapter 5 were also likely parthenogenetic symbols before they became associated with heterosexual eroticism.

30. The Greek *peleia* translates as "wild-pigeon, rock-pigeon, stock-dove" and refers to a bird that is dark in color. Scientifically, there is no difference between a dove and a pigeon, although *pigeon* frequently

denotes a larger bird (Ardastra Gardens, Zoo and Conservation Center n.d.; and American Dove Association 2003–6).

31. Pausanias (8.42.4); Baring and Cashford (1991, 596, 42); Hansell (1998, 66–7).

32. Baring and Cashford (1991, 60, 396, 596); Hansell (1998, 14–24, 31, 33, 37–8).

33. Elderkin (1940, 49n5). Elderkin explains that another term for dove, *hê phaps/tes phabos*, became *hê Paphos* by metathesis of the aspirate.

34. See, for example, the annunciation scenes as depicted by Fra Angelico, Van Eyck, and the sixteenth-century French *Book of Hours.*

35. Boas (in Horapollo 1950, 91) notes arguments that the symbol had no Egyptian source and was purely Greek. Even so, the critical point is how the symbol of the "black dove" functioned in the Greek mind.

36. *Pleiades* is accented *Pleiádes.* In Greek texts, *Pleiades* also appears variously as *Pleias, Plêïadês,* and *Peleiades* (Allen [1899] 1963, 392, 395).

37. Minor legends say their mother was the Oceanid Aethra (Eustathius on Homer's *Odyssey,* in Smith 1870, s.v. *Pleiades*), or the queen of the Amazons (scholiast on Theocritus 13.25). Other parents named for them include Erechtheus (Servius on Virgil's *Aeneid* 1.744), or Cadmus (Theon on Aratus, in Smith).

38. Hyginus (*Poetic Astronomy* 2.21); scholiast on Apollonius Rhodius 3.226; Pindar (*Nemean Ode* 2.12); scholiast on Aratus 254; scholiast on Homer's *Iliad* 18.486. According to the scholiast on Pindar's *Nemean Ode* 2.19, the Pleiades fled in fear from Heracles. In another tradition, the Pleiades were placed in the sky on account of their grief over their father Atlas's being consigned to hold up the heavens (Aeschylus frag. 312, in Condos 1997, 254n2).

39. As mentioned earlier, the Pleiades were also said to be the half sisters (or sometimes full sisters) of the Hyades. See Hyginus (*Fabulae* 192); Ovid (*Fasti* 5.159 passim), in which the Hyades share with the Pleiades Atlas as father; Servius on Virgil's *Aeneid* 1.748. The Hyades, located in the "head" of the constellation of Taurus the Bull, announced rainy and stormy weather when they rose simultaneously with the sun (Cicero *De Natura Deorum* 2.43; Ovid *Fasti* 5.166; Virgil *Aeneid* 3.516).

40. Pseudo-Eratosthenes (*Constellations* 23). There was in antiquity, as now, ambiguity about the number of stars in the cluster visible to the naked eye. That number has ranged from 6 to 13 (e.g., Aratus *Phaenomena* 256–8). Sometimes, the Pleiades are counted as nine: seven sisters plus their parents Atlas and Pleione. In reality, the Pleiades comprise hundreds of stars. Estimates range from between 300 (Krupp 1991, 243) and 3,000 (Roy Miller 1988, 1), but the number seven seems to have stuck, most likely for its associations with virginity, as I discuss later. Ancient sources also variously located them in other parts of Taurus, including the bull's "tail" (Hyginus *Poetic Astronomy* 2.21) and "near the left knee" of the constellation of Perseus (Aratus *Phaenomena* 254).

41. Others include Hippocrates, Hipparchus, Ptolemy, Euripides, Sappho, and Simonides (see Allen [1899] 1963, 392–4, 401). See also Smith et al. (1890, s.v. *Astronomia*) for a comprehensive discussion of Greek and Roman astronomical references to the Pleiades.
42. See the scholiast on Aratus 254–5; Condos (1997, 175). Some ancient writers guess *Pleiades* was derived from the Greek verb *plein*, "to sail," because in the Mediterranean their appearance also coincided with the sailing season (Frazer 1921, 2:2–3n1; Servius on Virgil's *Georgics* 1.138). I contend the derivation from *pleiôn*, "more, larger, many," holds much greater esoteric import, particularly given that the Pleiades are in fact composed of hundreds of stars. Allen ([1899] 1963, 395) presents a similar idea.
43. Hesiod (*Works and Days* 383, 615–20). The "heliacal rising" of a star refers to its first visible, though brief, appearance as it rises on the eastern horizon before sunrise. The "cosmical setting" of a star marks the first day in which the star descends below the western horizon as the sun rises in the East. In 500 B.C.E., the heliacal rising of the Pleiades took place around May 17, and the cosmical setting around November 3 (Bickerman 1968, 143).
44. Again, for a discussion of Demeter and Persephone and pure daughter-bearing parthenogenesis, see my forthcoming *Virgin Mother Goddesses of Antiquity*. Chamberlain (2002, 28) (a.k.a. Laura Amazzone) similarly proposes that in ancient India and Nepal, where the rising of the Pleiades was also closely connected with the religious-agricultural cycle, the seven "Matrikas," or Mother Goddesses, represented the seven Pleiades. She posits that the image of seven female figures on seals of the prehistoric Harappan civilization (c. 3500–1700 B.C.E.) may in fact refer to these stars. Krupp (1991, 250, 142) notes that the Pleiades marked the beginning of the year in ancient India by virtue of their heliacal (predawn) rising in 4000 B.C.E. having marked the vernal (spring) equinox. The vernal equinox moon was known as the "Child of the Pleiades," an interesting name given that, as I discuss later, the Pleiades were conceived of as virgin mothers in Greek myth.
45. See Brumfield (1981, 148) for sources linking Demeter to the harvest; Foley (1994, 99–100) for myths attributing agriculture to Demeter.
46. See Hesiod (*Theogony* 517–20); Homer (*Odyssey* 1.52–54); Pindar (*Pythian Ode* 4.289).
47. Cook (1914–40, 1:754) affirms that astrology could have been a part of Greek tradition long before the third century B.C.E., when the borrowing and development of a complete series of constellations is first attested: "[A]strological notions of a sort are to be found in Greece long before the age of Alexander the Great—astrometeorology already bulks big in Hesiod, and even astrology in the strict sense of the term is presupposed by Greek mystic teaching of the sixth

century B.C. and by sundry passages of Heracleitus, Euripides, and Herodotus."

48. Euripides (*Phrixus* frag. 820, in Cook 1914–40, 1:549); Pseudo-Eratosthenes (*Constellations* 14); Hyginus (*Poetic Astronomy* 2.21); Ovid (*Fasti* 5.603–20).

49. My interpretation contrasts with one noted by Cook (1914–40, 1:548) that the seven stars on these coins represent Ursa Major, the Great Bear. However, these two interpretations ultimately may not be in conflict, as there may have been an esoteric relationship between the seven stars of the Pleiades and the seven stars of the Great Bear, which, as we saw in Chapter 4, were a symbol of Artemis and her divine birth priestess Callisto. Indeed, as I discuss later in this chapter, one of the Pleiades, Taygete, was herself a priestess of Artemis, having been temporarily saved by her from the embraces of Zeus.

50. Pseudo-Eratosthenes (*Constellations* 14); Hyginus (*Poetic Astronomy* 2.21); Ovid (*Fasti* 4.717–20, 5.619–20).

51. I thank astrologer Kalli Rose Halvorson for affirming the identification of Taurus with the goddess Hathor (personal communication, November 23, 2006). Dorothy Cameron's observation (1981, 4–5) of the striking correspondence between the shape of the bull's head with horns and the shape of the uterus with fallopian tubes may be of further interest here.

52. This image appears on the south wall of Queen Nefertari's tomb in the Valley of the Queens in Luxor. See Lamy (1981, 83).

53. Many centuries later, the Lithuanians called the Milky Way the "Road of the Birds," at whose end the souls of the good, which had flitted away like birds, would dwell in happiness (Cook 1914–40, 3.1:38). This calls to mind the symbol of the dove at Dodona.

54. The central motif of the later Roman religion dedicated to Mithras was the image of the god slaying a bull, an obvious Taurian reference given the prevalent zodiacal references in Mithraic iconography. The point at which his dagger enters the bull/Taurus's shoulder is precisely where the Pleiades are located (Ulansey 1989, 57). Might this suggest that Mithraism included an understanding of the ancient female-related importance of the Pleiades? Might the motif of Mithras's "stabbing" them have represented their "murder," that is, a shift in attributing the powers of *genesis* of souls/divinity from the feminine to the masculine sphere? That Porphyry (*Cave of the Nymphs* 24) refers to Mithras as the "creator and lord of *genesis*" indicates that Mithras absorbed what originally may have been considered the Pleiades' cosmic, generative role. That Mithraism was a male-only cult whose primary membership was drawn from the Roman army (Ulansey 1989, 6) underscores the female-suppressing nature of this religion.

55. Hesiod (frag. 89, 2007, 159, ed. Most). See also Apollodorus (3.1.2); Dodorus Siculus (4.60.3).

56. For this, the Pythagoreans apparently drew on the patriarchal story of Athena having sprung from Zeus's head.

57. The scholiast on Theocritus 13.25 (in Smith 1870, s.v. *Pleiades*) gives different names—Coccymo, Plaucia, Protis, Parthemia, Maia, Stonychia, Lampatho—but Apollodorus's are those most widely used to refer to the Pleiades throughout the ancient writings. It is interesting to note, however, that one of the names in Theocritus's listing is *Parthemia*.

58. As daughters of Atlas and Pleione (an Oceanid), the mythological Seven Sisters were "nieces" of the Olympian gods, among them Zeus. As in the case of my hypothesized "Leto II," that their stories more closely resemble those of legendary holy *parthenoi* than goddesses suggests their divinization was posthumous.

59. Psychopomp: for example, Homer (*Odyssey* 24.1, 9), *Homeric Hymn to Demeter* (379); Diogenes Laertius (8.31); Plutarch (*Greek Questions* 24; 296F); inventor: for example, *Homeric Hymn to Hermes* (51), Diodorus Siculus (1.16), Hyginus (*Fabulae* 277).

60. Plutarch (*On Isis and Osiris* 3/352A, *Table-Talk* 9.3.2/738E); Plutarch (1970, 263–4, ed. Griffiths).

61. See Barnstone and Meyer (2003, 495–523) for select Hermetic writings and the scholarly controversy over their authorship.

62. Hermes' tricking Hera into nursing Heracles to bestow immortality upon him, as mentioned in Chapter 5, becomes interesting in light of his own divine origins.

63. Electra is also said to have borne by Zeus Iason, who was killed by his heavenly father when he attempted to rape the goddess Demeter (Apollodorus 3.10.1, 3.12.3) (a possible reference to his attempting to violate a virgin priestess of Demeter?). In Hesiod (*Catalogue of Women* frag. 121, 2007, ed. Most), he is named Eetion.

64. Hyginus (*Fabulae* 192, *Poetic Astronomy* 2.21); Servius on Virgil's *Aeneid* 10.272.

65. Ovid (*Fasti* 4.77–8); Hyginus (*Fabulae* 192, *Poetic Astronomy* 2.21).

66. It was from this site that the Messenians are reputed to have abducted and raped maidens who had come to the celebration in honor of Artemis (Strabo 8.4.9; Pausanias 4.16.9).

67. Spartan maiden choruses are mentioned, for example, by Aristophanes (*Lysistrata* 1296–1315). For a thorough analysis of choruses of young women in ancient Greece, see Calame (1997).

68. Davenport translates *pharos* as "plow," but note the controversy regarding this interpretation, discussed below.

69. See Garzya (in Alcman 1954, 52–5) for other scholarly interpretations of the meaning of *Peleiades* in this passage.

70. This genealogy appears in Hesiod (*Catalogue of Women* frag. 130, 2007, 197, ed. Most); Porphyry (in Eustathius 281.41–4); Aristocrates (in Stephanus Byzantius, s.v. *Abantis*); and Hyginus (*Fabulae* 157), in which Arethusa's father is instead named *Herilei* or

Nerei. See Renner (1978, 287–8). Note that the "nymph" Arethusa whom Artemis turned into a spring, discussed in Chapter 4, seems to have been a separate individual, but the motif of both figures' metamorphoses may suggest some connection or identification between them.

71. Pseudo-Eratosthenes (*Constellations* 23); Hyginus (*Poetic Astronomy* 2.21, *Fabulae* 84, 159, 250). Cf. Apollodorus (3.10.1), who lists Sterope as the *wife* of Oenomaus, not his mother.

72. Ovid (*Fasti* 4.175); Servius on Virgil's *Georgics* 1.138; Pseudo-Eratosthenes (*Constellations* 23); Hyginus (*Poetic Astronomy* 2.21).

CHAPTER 7

1. Today, the site of Delphi is occupied by the modern hamlet of Kastri.

2. Cicero's statement (*On Divination* 1.36.79) that the Pythian priestess was "inspired by the power of the earth" indicates that even in the later period Delphi was still seen as partly under the jurisdiction of the chthonic goddess.

3. Pausanias (10.5.6) says at one time the oracle was thought to belong to both Ge/Gaia and Poseidon, but this seems to be a legend of lesser prominence. An inscription at Delphi also mentions a temple to Ge/Gaia at the site in historical times, well after Apollo was established as the oracular authority (Dempsey [1918] 1972, 4); Plutarch also refers to this temple (*Oracles at Delphi* 17/402C).

4. Aeschylus (*Eumenides* 1–4); Euripides (*Iphigenia in Tauris* 1259–83); Apollodorus (1.4.1); Pausanias (10.5.5–6); Ovid (*Metamorphoses* 1.379–83).

5. Apollodorus (1.4.1); Euripides (*Iphigenia in Tauris* 1259–62); Plutarch (*Greek Questions* 12/293C, *Obsolescence of Oracles* 15/417F–418A); Aelian (*Historical Miscellany* 3.1); Pausanias (2.7.7, 2.30.3, 10.6.5–7). Euripides (*Iphigenia in Tauris* 1259–80) also relates a legend that after Apollo sent Themis away from the oracle, Ge/Gaia transferred the gift of prophecy through dreams directly to those who slept on the ground. Apollo angrily appealed to Zeus, who took this power away from humans so as to make them dependent on oracles—and hence on Apollo. Strabo (9.3.11), on the other hand, says Apollo established the oracle *with* Themis "because he wished to help our race" by providing humans with divine counsel. The *Homeric Hymn 3 to Apollo* (285–99, 355–74) skips mention of earlier goddesses and claims that Delphi was founded outright by Apollo, who first had to rid the site of the serpent. Hyginus (*Fabulae* 140) relates that Python pursued Leto in response to a prophecy that she would bear a child who would kill the serpent. Pausanias (2.7.7) says Artemis joined Apollo in the slaying of Python, but, according to my argument in Chapter 4, given the pairing of Artemis with Apollo was likely a late development in the cult

of Artemis, this detail is probably a patriarchal addition to the story. Elsewhere, Pausanias notes (10.6.1) a euhemeristic legend that the name *Python* referred to a violent man, surnamed *Dragon*, who pillaged the sanctuary as well as homes. Apollo slew this Python at the request of the Delphians. According to Homer (*Odyssey* 8.80; *Iliad* 9.405), a more ancient name of Delphi seems to have been *Pytho*. The writer of the *Homeric Hymn 4 to Apollo* (3.370–74) explains that this derived from *puthesthai*, "to rot," because the dragon slain by Apollo rotted at the place of the oracle.

6. The sex of Python changed to male in Euripides (*Iphigenia in Tauris* 1245) and Pausanias (10.6.6). Other names for the dragon were *Delphyne* (female) (Apollodorus 1.6.3) or *Delphynes* (male) (Parke 1939, 12).

7. For another instance of oracular snakes in ancient Greece, see Aelian (*On Animals* 11.2), who reports a custom in Epirus whereby snakes' accepting or rejecting food offerings was taken as a good or bad omen. The Epirotes believed these snakes were descended from the Python of Delphi. Aelian (*On Animals* 11.16) describes a similar ritual whereby snake behavior was used to test the virginity of priestesses of Hera at Rome. Regarding the latter, he specifically notes, "This is the way in which I would demonstrate the faculty of divination in serpents." Thus, the idea of Python or a serpent "giving oracles" on Mt. Parnassus probably indicates that one early method of divination at the site was observing the behavior of a resident snake. Snakes in general were associated with the chthonic powers.

8. Herodotus (1.78); Artemidorus (*Oneirocritica* 2.13); Pliny (*Natural History* 8.84).

9. Interestingly, Apollo's violent appropriation of the oracle was something for which the Delphians said the god was compelled by Zeus to pay atonement by suffering nine years' exile in Thessaly (Plutarch *Greek Questions* 12/293C; *Obsolescence of Oracles* 15/417F, 21/421C). Such a mythologem indicating that Apollo's act was seen as a transgression contrasts with the view expressed, for example, by Plutarch (*Face of the Moon* 30/945B) that Python was an "insolent" and "violent" spirit who "confounded the oracle" at Delphi and occupied the site by force.

10. Plutarch (*Obsolescence of Oracles* 8/414B), who notes that, by his day, with the diminishment of visitors, one Pythia again sufficed.

11. Plutarch (*Greek Questions* 9/293A); Pindar (*Pythian Ode* 4.5); Claudian (*Sixth Consulship of Honorius* 28.25–30).

12. Fasting and bathing of Pythia: scholiast on Euripides' *Phoenician Women* 223; eliminating distractions: Plutarch (*Obsolescence of Oracles* 50/437D, 51/438C); officials and inquirers bathing: Euripides (*Ion* 94–104; *Phoenician Women* 222–5); male-only petitioners: Plutarch (*E at Delphi* 2/385D). For conflicting evidence regarding women as petitioners at Delphi, see Farnell ([1896–1909] 1977, 4:186a), who

concludes that, for consultation, women enjoyed the same privileges as the men. See also Connelly (2007, 78–9), who notes that in Euripides' *Ion*, maidservants are allowed into the Delphic sanctuary. She also mentions a decree in which Chrysis, a priestess of Athena Polias, was granted priority of consultation at Delphi. Finally, she notes that the fact that many surviving questions put to the Pythia related to fertility and childbirth argues in favor of women having participated as petitioners there.

13. Plutarch (*Oracles at Delphi* 7/397C, 21/404E, *Obsolescence of Oracles* 9/414E). Methods of divination at Delphi at one time also may have included dream incubation, as suggested by the legend, mentioned earlier, that Ge/Gaia granted the gift of prophetic dreams to those who slept on the ground (Euripides *Iphigenia in Tauris* 1262–6). Another method, to which I allude later, may have been divination by lot (Suda, s.v. *Puthô*).

14. Plato (*Phaedrus* 224b) refers to such possession as *mantikê entheos*, prophetic inspiration. As I discussed in Chapter 1, *entheos* literally means "full of the divinity," "having the divinity within," or "at one with the divinity."

15. Strabo (9.3.5); Plutarch (*Obsolescence of Oracles* 45/435D, 48/437F, 50/437C–D); Cicero (*On Divination* 1.19.38); Justin (24.6). A recent geological survey has revealed that a fault line beneath the ancient temple of Apollo at Delphi indeed could have been the source of hydrocarbon gases, including ethylene (Connelly 2007, 72 and n101). Ethylene is a potential entheogen.

16. Plutarch (*The Oracles at Delphi* 26–28/407D–8D). For a comprehensive discussion of oracles given at Delphi, see Parke (1939, 299–427).

17. Pythagoras: Diogenes Laertius (*Pythagoras* 8.8); Pindar: Pausanias (10.24.5); Socrates/Plato: Plato (*Apology* 20e, *Republic* 427b–c); Cicero: Cicero (*On Divination* 1.19.37–38); Plutarch: for example, Plutarch (*Oracles at Delphi* 29/409A, *Obsolescence of Oracles* 51/438A–D).

18. Among the more famous sayings were "Know thyself" and "Nothing to excess" (Pausanias 10.24.1; Plato *Protagoras* 343b; Plutarch *E at Delphi* 2/385D). For an extensive list of the Delphic "commandments," see Oikonomides (1987, 74–5).

19. Plutarch's statements that "the priests and the Holy Ones say they offer the sacrifice" (*Obsolescence of Oracles* 49/437A) and that "[the Holy Ones] do a great many things with the cooperation of the oracle interpreters" (*Greek Questions* 9/292D–E, Plutarch 1927–69, 5:493, 4:183, trans. Babbitt) indicate that the priests and oracle interpreters were distinct from the Holy Ones. However, he treats the priests and oracle interpreters as one and the same: for example, in one passage (*Obsolescence of Oracles* 50/438C), he calls Nicander an oracle interpreter, while in another (*E at Delphi* 5), he calls him a priest.

20. Guthrie (1967, 184) translates the maxim "*Gunaikos arche*" in this way. Oikonomides (1987, 74–5), identifying this as Delphic "commandment" no. 95, translates it more benignly as "Rule your wife," but the paternalistic meaning is still evident.

21. Plutarch (*Oracles at Delphi* 22/405C–D, *Obsolescence of Oracles* 51/438C). Inscriptions reveal that some Delphic prophetesses were married (Parke 1939, 32n7), but this most likely reflects their status prior to their assuming the mantle of the Pythia. Plutarch is clear that chastity was a requirement during the period of their service.

22. Herodotus (3.28.1); Aelian (*On Animals* 11.10); Plutarch (*On Isis and Osiris* 43); Suda (s.v. *Apides Isis and Osiris*).

23. For literary references to this image, see Aristophanes (*Plutus* 9); Euripides (*Orestes* 329); scholiast on Euripides *Electra* 980. For visual images, see, for example, Parke (1939, plate 3).

24. The three excerpts of Origen here are, respectively, from Origen (1953, 3–4, 143, 399, trans. Chadwick).

25. That women in ancient Greece gave birth sitting upright on special obstetric chairs can be seen on one dramatic Greek sculpture (see A History of Midwifery in Pictures n.d.). Artemidorus (5.73) mentions "obstetric couches," which may be a reference to such chairs.

26. Daphne as daughter of Ladon: Pausanias (8.20.1–3), Philostratus (*Life of Apollonius of Tyana* 1.16), Tzetzes on Lycophron 6; as daughter of Peneius: Ovid (*Metamorphoses* 1.452), Hyginus (*Fabulae* 203). See also Strabo (16.2.6).

27. Note Herophile herself claimed she had a human father who was from Marpessus (Pausanias 10.12.3), but this could be a reference to the man who merely reared her, not fathered her.

28. As mentioned earlier, ancient etymologies derived both names from *puthesthai*, "to rot," because the dragon was said to have rotted at the site of the oracle after Apollo slew it (e.g., Pausanias 10.6.5). It may well be, however, that these etymologies were later fabrications, and that the names *Pytho* and *Python* were pre-Apollonian.

29. See, for example, Aeschylus (*Eumenides* 22–3); Herodotus (8.36); Sophocles (*Antigone* 1126–30); Euripides (*Bacchae* 559).

30. See, for example, Plutarch (*E at Delphi* 21/939D, *Obsolescence of Oracles* 42/433E); Pseudo-Eratosthenes (*Constellations* 24).

31. See Aelian (*On Animals* 5.11–3); Xenophon (*Economics* 7.32–34); Varro (3.16.7–9); Virgil (*Georgics* 4.63).

32. Sexual intercourse is also a part of the bee community: once the drones mature, 10 to 20 of them copulate with the queen in midair. From this union, worker bees, or females, are produced. After the impregnation of the queen, drones, who do not perform other work in the hive, are driven from the hive to die of cold and starvation. For such details, see, for example, Steiner (1998, 11) and Milius (1999, 78).

33. That the "king" bee was really a "queen" apparently was not understood until the seventeenth century. See Ransome ([1937] 2004, 208).

34. See Pliny (*Natural History* 11.16); Aristotle (*History of Animals* 5.21 passim, 9.40 passim, *Generation of Animals* 3.10 passim). Hesiod (*Theogony* 594–607) also may assume drones are female when he (misogynistically) compares mortal women to these laziest creatures of the hive, who do no work and live off the labors of the worker bees.

35. Writing several hundred years before Pliny, Aristotle, who discusses bee reproduction extensively in his *History of Animals* (5.21) and *On the Generation of Animals* (3.10), was not able to reach a solution about its mechanisms that fully satisfied him. This is no doubt because he did not understand the function of the queen bee.

36. Plutarch (*Cleomenes* 39); Pliny (*Natural History* 11.23); Aelian (*On Animals* 2.57).

37. See also Philochorus (frag. 125, in Ransome [1937] 2004, 97).

38. Such an analysis supports Farnell's suggestion ([1896–1909] 1977, 4:193a) that the title *Melissa* was a remnant of the sanctuary's earlier cult association with Ge/Gaia.

39. Selene represented the moon and was identified with Artemis in the later period (Putarch *Face on the Moon* 5/922A; Farnell [1896–1909] 1977, 2:531).

40. That the Hebrew prophetess Deborah's name also means "Bee" in Hebrew similarly suggests an ancient origin for the title in connection with oracular priestesses in the lands bordering the Mediterranean.

41. Elswhere (24), Porphyry identifies the god Mithras as the "lord of *genesis*," which would seem to contradict the idea of the moon/Artemis as governing this process. However, since Porphyry does mention the moon/Artemis in association with incarnation, and since the cult of Artemis clearly predated that of Mithras in the Graeco-Roman world, I focus my commentary on this idea.

42. As I mentioned in Chapter 2, however, while children of holy *parthenoi* were considered to be in a special "divine" category, they were not necessarily expected to be especially elevated morally.

43. Once more, such an argument is beyond the scope of the present work.

44. As mentioned in Chapter 3, another daughter of Erechtheus was Oreithyia, the *kanephoros* who was (parthenogenetically) impregnated by "the North Wind."

45. Although Porphyry refers to other Greek and Roman beliefs that Cancer was the gate through which souls *descended* into human form, and that Capricorn was the gate through which souls *ascended* to the gods, he notes (20) the ambiguity in Homer's lines as to whether the southern/Capricornian gate was meant for descent or ascent.

All that is clear, he points out, is that Homer reserves this latter gate for the "immortals." Porphyry notes further ambiguity in this term, observing (23) that *immortals* may not necessarily have meant *gods,* but could have referred to human souls, on the basis that they, too, were considered immortal, according to Platonic philosophy. I propose these ambiguities are resolved by the argument I am putting forth here, that the southern/Capricornian gate was the portal by which *parthenioi,* the children of divine union, were thought to descend into incarnation. This does not contradict the idea that human souls could have been seen as "immortal," but rather again draws on the Greek concept, mentioned in Chapter 2, that varying orders of spiritual beings could incarnate in human form: divinities, semidivinities/*daimones,* heroes, and mortals.

46. Cf. Hesiod (*Theogony* 130–6), who does not include Dione as a Titan.

47. Egyptologist Arno Egberts (1997, 160) agrees that the phonetic correspondence between *Pr ṯḥn* and *Parthenon* (the term for the temple of the Virgin Athena, as we will recall) is excellent. He objects to such a correspondence on semantic grounds, however. Noting that the Egyptian name *Pr ṯḥn* is attested for the temple of Osiris at Saïs, he argues that the presence of the term *parthenos,* signifying "virgin maiden," would make no sense in association with this god. For what possible relation could virgins have with a god who was so virile that, as Bernal expresses it (1987–2006, 3:578), "he could even impregnate his sister/wife after his death"? The paradox is resolved if one accepts the meaning of *parthenos* as "holy priestess of divine birth." In this case, the posthumous "impregnation" of Isis by Osiris was made possible by virtue of her role as a holy *parthenos* who knew how to engage in *hieros gamos* with the spirit of her deceased spouse. This renders the connection between Osiris and *parthenos* entirely appropriate and meaningful. Again, I have not had space to discuss the Isis myth in this work, but merely mention it here once more given that the core of perhaps the most serious objection to the argument that *parthenos* was borrowed from *Pr ṯḥn* apparently hinges on this point.

Chapter 8

1. See, for example, White (1973); Mittwoch (1978); Farley (1982); Ezzell (1993); Lourenço and Cuellar (1995); Weidensaul (1997); Vrijenhoek (1998).

2. Urchins: Pauly (1987) and Cooper (2003, 14): turkeys: Olsen (1960, 1965) and Cohen (1998–9, 38).

3. Subsequent attempts to duplicate his work failed, however.

4. For a comprehensive summary of the evidence for extraordinary human phenomena, including *siddhis,* see Murphy (1992).

5. Murphy's (1992) otherwise excellent volume on extraordinary human phenomena, for example, ignores the topic entirely. He mentions unusual female reproductive events only in a pathologized context in his discussion of "false pregnancy" (238–40).
6. For intraspecies chimarae, see, for example, Mott (2008).
7. I wish to thank filmmaker George Langworthy for this insight.

REFERENCES

Adams, Douglas O. 1987. *Hrôs* and *hra*: Of men and heroes in Greek and Indo-European. *Glotta* 65: 171–8.

Aelian. 1959. *On the characteristics of animals.* 3 vols. Trans. A. F. Scholfield. Cambridge, MA: Harvard University Press.

Aeschylus. 1926. *Aeschylus.* 2 vols. Trans. Herbert Weir Smyth. Cambridge, MA: Harvard University Press.

Agrippa, Henry Cornelius. [1651] 2004. *Three books of occult philosophy.* Trans. James Freake. Ed. Donald Tyson. St. Paul, MN: Llewellyn.

Alcman. 1954. *I frammenti.* Trans. Antonio Garzya. Naples, Italy: Casa Editrice di Silvio Viti.

Allen, Richard Hinckley. [1899] 1963. *Star names: Their lore and meanings.* New York: Dover.

Allione, Tsultrim. 1984. *Women of wisdom.* London: Arkana.

American Dove Association. 2003–6. Frequently asked questions. http://www.doveline.com/faq.html (accessed June 3, 2006).

Andrews, Munya. 2004. *The seven sisters of the Pleiades: Stories from around the world.* North Melbourne, Australia: Spinifex.

Apollodorus. 1967. *The Library.* 2 vols. Trans. Sir James George Frazer. Cambridge, MA: Harvard University Press.

Archilochos, Sappho, and Alkman. 1980. *Archilochos, Sappho, Alkman.* Trans. Guy Davenport. Berkeley, CA: University of California Press.

Ardastra Gardens, Zoo, and Conservation Center. n.d. Pigeons. http://www.ardastra.com/pigeoninfo.html (accessed June 3, 2006).

Associated Press. 2003. Scientists eye virgin birth phenomenon. *CBS News* online (May 5). http://www.cbsnews.com/stories/2003/05/05/tech/main552408.shtml (accessed July 25, 2007).

Athenaeus. 1950. *The deipnosophists.* 7 vols. Trans. Charles Burton Gulick. Cambridge, MA: Harvard University Press.

Avagianou, Aphrodite A. 2008. *Hieros gamos* in ancient Greek religion. In *Sacred marriages: The divine-human metaphor from Sumer to Early Christianity,* ed. Martti Nissinen and Risto Uro, 145–71. Winona Lake, IN: Eisenbrauns.

———. 1991. *Sacred marriage in the rituals of Greek religion.* New York: Peter Lang.

Bachofen, Johann Jakob. [1861] 1897. *Das mutterrecht.* Basel, Switzerland: B. Schwebe.

———. [1861] 2005. *An English translation of Bachofen's mutterricht (mother right)*. Ed. David Partenheimer. Lewiston, NY: Edwin Mellen.

———. 1973. *Myth, religion, and mother right*. Princeton, NJ: Princeton University Press.

Baring, Anne, and Jules Cashford. 1991. *The myth of the goddess: Evolution of an image*. London: Arkana.

Barnstone, Willis, and Marvin Meyer. 2003. *The Gnostic Bible*. Boston, MA: Shambhala.

Bates, Oric. 1970. *The eastern Libyans: An essay*. London: Frank Cass.

Beatty, R. A. 1967. Parthenogenesis in vertebrates. In *Fertilization*, ed. C. B. Metz and A. Monroy, vol. 1, 413–40. New York: Academic.

Bennett, Florence Mary. 1967. *Religious cults associated with the Amazons*. New York: AMS.

Bernal, Martin. 1987–2006. *Black Athena: The Afroasiatic roots of classical civilization*. 3 vols. New Brunswick, NJ: Rutgers University Press.

Bernard, Raymond. n.d. *The mysteries of human reproduction*. Mokelumne Hill, CA: Health Research.

Bickerman, E. J. 1968. *Chronology of the ancient world*. Ithaca, NY: Cornell University Press.

Birnbaum, Lucia. 1993. *Black Madonnas: Feminism, religion, and politics in Italy*. Boston, MA: Northeastern University Press.

———. 2001. *Dark mother: African origins and godmothers*. San Jose, CA: Authors Choice.

Blundell, Sue. 1995. *Women in ancient Greece*. Cambridge, MA: Harvard University Press.

Boslooper, Thomas. 1962. *The virgin birth*. Philadelphia, PA: Westminster.

Brown, Truesdell S. 1946. Euhemerus and the historians. *Harvard Theological Review* 39(4): 259–74.

Brownmiller, Susan. 1975. *Against our will: Men, women and rape*. New York: Simon and Schuster.

Brukner, Bogdan. 2006. Possible influences of the Black Sea flood on the formation of Vinča culture. *Journal of Archaeomythology* 2(1): 17–26. http://www.archaeomythology.org/journal/read_article.php?a=0306_3_brukner.pdf (accessed July 14, 2008).

Brumfield, Adair Chandler. 1981. *The Attic festivals of Demeter and their relation to the agricultural year*. Monographs in Classical Studies. Salem, NH: Ayer.

Budge, E. A. Wallis. [1895] 1960. *The book of the dead*. New York: Gramercy.

———. [1904] 1969. *The gods of the Egyptians*. 2 vols. New York: Dover.

Budin, Stephanie Lynn. 2003. *Pallakai*, prostitutes, and prophetesses. *Classical Philology* 98(2): 148–59.

———. 2008. *The myth of sacred prostitution in antiquity*. Cambridge, UK: Cambridge University Press.

Burkert, Walter. 1965. Demaratos, Astrabakos und Herakles: Königsmythos und politik zur zeit der perserkriege (Herodot 6.67–8). *Museum Helveticum* 22: 166–77. Cited in Faraone and Teeter 2004, 198n55.

———. 1966. Kekropidensage und arrephoria. *Hermes* 94: 1–25. Cited in Goff 2004, 100.

———. 1985. *Greek religion.* Trans. John Raffan. Cambridge, MA: Harvard University Press.

———. 1987. *Ancient mystery cults.* Cambridge, MA: Harvard University Press.

Butrica, James L. 2002. The medical use of cannabis among the Greeks and Romans. *Journal of Cannabis Therapeutics* 2(2): 51–70.

Calame, Claude. 1997. *Choruses of young women in ancient Greece: Their morphology, religious role, and social functions.* Trans. Derek Collins and Janice Orion. Lanham, MD: Rowman and Littlefield.

Callimachus. 1975. *Aetia, iambi, lyric poems, hecale, minor epic and elegiac poems, and other fragments.* Ed. and trans. C. A. Trypanis. Cambridge, MA: Harvard University Press.

Cameron, D. O. 1981. *Symbols of birth and death in the Neolithic era.* London: Kenyon-Deane.

Cavalli-Sforza, L. Luca, Paolo Menozzi, and Alberto Piazza. 1994. *The history and geography of human genes.* Princeton, NJ: Princeton University Press.

Chamberlain, Laura Kristine (a.k.a. Laura Amazzone). 2002. Durga and the Dashain harvest festival: From the Indus to Kathmandu Valleys. *ReVision* 25(1): 24–32.

Chang, M. C. 1957. Natural occurrence and artificial induction of parthenogenetic cleavage of ferret ova. *Anatomical Record* 128(2): 187–9.

Christ, Carol P. 1996. "A different world": The challenge of the work of Marija Gimbutas to the dominant world-view of Western culture. *Journal of Feminist Studies in Religion* 12(2): 53–66.

Chrysostom, John. 1975. *The Nicene and post-Nicene fathers of the Christian church. Volume 12, Saint Chrysostom: Homilies on the epistles of Paul to the Corinthians.* Ed. Philip Schaff. Trans. Talbot W. Chambers. Grand Rapids, MI: Eerdmans.

Cohen, Philip. 1998–9. Like a virgin. *New Scientist* 2165 (Dec. 19/26–2 Jan.): 36–9.

Collins, John J. 2008. The sons of God and the daughters of men. In *Sacred marriages: The divine-human sexual metaphor from Sumer to early Christianity,* ed. Martti Nissinen and Risto Uro, 259–74. Winona Lake, IN: Eisenbrauns.

Condos, Theony. 1997. *Star myths of the Greeks and Romans: A sourcebook.* Grand Rapids, MI: Phanes.

Connelly, Joan Breton. 2007. *Portrait of a Priestess: Women and Ritual in Ancient Greece.* Princeton, NJ: Princeton University Press.

Cook, Arthur Bernard. 1895. The bee in Greek mythology. *Journal of Hellenistic Studies* 15: 1–24.

———. 1905. The European sky-god, III. *Folk-Lore* 16(3): 260–332.

———. 1914–1940. *Zeus: A study in ancient Religion.* 3 vols. Cambridge, UK: Cambridge University Press.

Cooper, Melinda. 2003. Rediscovering the immortal *hydra*: Stem cells and the question of epigenesis. *Configurations* 11(1): 1–26.

Corradini, Anna Maria. 1997. *Meteres: Il mito del matriarchato in Sicilia.* Enna, Sicily: Papiro Editrice.

Dakaris, S. 1971. *Archaeological guide to Dodona.* Trans. Elli Kirk-Deftereou. Ioannina, Greece: Cultural Society, The Ancient Dodona.

———. 2000. *Dodona.* 4th ed. Athens, Greece: Ministry of Culture, Archaeological Receipts Fund.

Daly, Mary. [1978] 1990. *Gyn/Ecology: The metaethics of radical feminism.* Boston, MA: Beacon.

Dashu, Max. 2000. Knocking down straw dolls: A critique of Cynthia Eller's *The myth of matriarchal prehistory: Why an invented past won't give women a future.* Suppressed Histories Archive. http://www.suppressedhistories. net/articles/eller.html (accessed July 25, 2007).

Davis, Elizabeth Gould. 1971. *The first sex.* New York: Penguin.

Davis-Kimball, Janine. 2002. *Warrior women: An archaeologist's search for history's hidden heroines.* New York: Warner.

De Sutter, P., D. Dozortsev, J. Cieslak, G. Wolf, Y. Verlinsky, and A. Dyban. 1992. Parthenogenetic activation of human oocytes by puromycin. *Journal of Assisted Reproduction and Genetics* 9(4): 328–37.

Deacy, Susan. 1997. The vulnerability of Athena. In *Rape in antiquity,* ed. Susan Deacy and Karen F. Pierce, 43–63. London: Duckworth.

———. 2008. *Athena.* London: Routledge.

Dean-Jones, Leslie. 1994. *Women's bodies in classical Greek science.* Oxford: Clarendon.

deGrouchy, J. 1980. Human parthenogenesis: A fascinating single event. *Biomedicine* 32: 51–3.

Demand, Nancy. 1994. *Birth, death, and motherhood in classical Greece.* Baltimore, MD: Johns Hopkins University Press.

Demosthenes [Apollodorus]. 1992. *Apollodoros against Neaira [Demosthenes] 59.* Ed. and trans. Christopher Carey. Warminster, UK: Aris & Phillips.

Dempsey, T. [1918] 1972. *The Delphic oracle: Its early history, influence and fall.* New York: Benjamin Blom.

Dergachev, V. A. 2007. *About scepters, horses, war: Sketches in defence of migrational conception by M. Gimbutas.* St. Petersburg: Nestor-Istorija.

Devereux, George. 1982. *Femme et myth.* Paris: Flammarion.

Dexter, Miriam Robbins. 1990. *Whence the goddess: A source book.* New York: Teachers College.

Dillon, Matthew. 2001. *Girls and women in classical Greek religion.* London: Routledge.

Diodorus Siculus. 1935. *Library of history: Books 2.35–4.58.* Trans. C. H. Oldfather. Cambridge, MA: Harvard University Press.

Dioscorides. [1934] 1968. *The Greek herbal of Dioscorides.* Ed. Robert T. Gunther. London: Hafner.

Dodds, E. R. 1951. *The Greeks and the irrational.* Berkeley, CA: University of California Press.

Dowden, Ken. 1995. Approaching women through myth: Vital tool or self-delusion? In *Women in antiquity: New assessments*, ed. Richard Hawley and Barbara Levick, 44–57. London: Routledge.

Downing, Christine. 1992. *The goddess: Mythological images of the feminine.* New York: Crossroad.

Drewermann, Eugen. 1994. *Discovering the God child within: A spiritual psychology of the infancy of Jesus.* New York: Crossroad.

duBois, Page. 1982. *Centaurs and Amazons: Women and the pre-history of the great chain of being.* Ann Arbor, MI: University of Michigan Press.

Egberts, Arno. 1997. Consonants in collision: Neith and Athena reconsidered. In *Black Athena: Ten years after,* ed. W. M. J. Van Binsbergen, 149–64. Hoofddorp, the Netherlands: Dutch Archaeological and Historical Society.

Eisler, Riane. 1995. *Sacred pleasure: Sex, myth, and the politics of the body.* San Francisco, CA: HarperSanFrancisco.

Elderkin, G. W. 1940. The sacred doves of Delphi. *Classical Philology* 35(1): 49–52.

Eliade, Mircea. 1964. *Shamanism: Archaic techniques of ecstasy.* Bollingen Series 76. Princeton, NJ: Princeton University Press.

Eller, Cynthia. 2000. *The myth of matriarchal prehistory: Why an invented past won't give women a future.* Boston, MA: Beacon.

Elworthy, Frederick. 1958. *The evil eye.* New York: Macmillan.

Eyer, Shawn. 1993. Psychedelic effects and the Eleusinian mysteries. *Alexandria* 2: 65–93.

Ezzell, C. 1993. South Pacific invasion of the sexual geckos. *Science News* 143(3): 38.

Faraone, C. A. 1990. Aphrodite's *kestos* and apples for Atalanta: Aphrodisiacs in early Greek myth and ritual. *Phoenix* 44(3): 219–43.

Farley, John. 1982. *Gametes and spores: Ideas about sexual reproduction, 1750–1914.* Baltimore, MD: Johns Hopkins University Press.

Farnell, Lewis Richard. [1896–1909] 1977. *The cults of the Greek states.* 5 vols. New Rochelle, NY: Caratzas Brothers.

———. 1921. *Greek hero cults and ideas of immortality.* Oxford: Clarendon.

Fehrle, Eugen. 1910. *Die kultische keuschheit im altertum.* Giessen, Germany: A. Töppelman. Cited in Turner 1983, 177.

Feng, Yan-Ling, and Jerry L. Hall. 2001. Production of neurons from stem cells derived from parthenogenetic mouse embryos. Paper presented at the annual meeting of the American Society for Reproductive Medicine, October 20–5, Orlando, FL. Abstract no. 575.

Foley, Helen P., ed. 1994. *The Homeric hymn to Demeter.* Princeton, NJ: Princeton University Press.

Forbes Irving, P. M. C. 1990. *Metamorphosis in Greek myths.* Oxford: Clarendon.

Frazer, Sir James George. 1905. *Lectures on the early history of the kingship.* London: Macmillan.

———. [1906–15] 1935. *The golden bough.* 3rd ed., revised and expanded. 9 parts in 13 vols. New York: Macmillan.

Fredriksen, Paula. 1979. Hysteria and the Gnostic myths of creation. *Vigiliae Christianae* 33: 287–90.

Gauthier, Henri. 1925–31. *Dictionnaire des noms géographiques contenus dans les textes hiéroglyphiques.* 5 vols. Cairo: L'institut français d'archéologie orientale.

Gilhus, Ingvid Saelid. 2008. Sacred marriage and spiritual knowledge: Relations between carnality and salvation in the *Apocryphon of John.* In *Sacred marriages: The divine-human sexual metaphor from Sumer to early Christianity,* ed. Martti Nissinen and Risto Uro, 487–510. Winona Lake, IN: Eisenbrauns.

Gimbutas, Marija. 1982. *The goddesses and gods of Old Europe 6500–3500 B.C.: Myths and cult images.* Berkeley, CA: University of California Press.

———. 1989. *The language of the goddess.* San Francisco, CA: HarperSan-Francisco.

———. 1991. *The civilization of the goddess.* San Francisco, CA: HarperSan-Francisco.

———. 1999. *The living goddesses.* Ed. Miriam Robbins Dexter. Berkeley, CA: University of California Press.

Goff, Barbara. 2004. *Citizen bacchae: Women's ritual practice in ancient Greece.* Berkeley, CA: University of California Press.

Goodison, Lucy, and Christine Morris, eds. 1998. *Ancient goddesses.* London: British Museum.

Gordon, Cyrus Herzl. 1962. *Before the Bible: The common background of Greek and Hebrew civilisations.* New York: Harper and Row.

Göttner-Abendroth, Heide. 1987. *Matriarchal mythology in former times and today.* Freedom, CA: Crossing.

———. 2001. Modern matriarchal studies: Definitions, scope and topicality. Paper presented at Societies in Balance, the First World Congress on Matriarchal Studies, September 5–7, 2003, Luxembourg. http://www.second-congress-matriarchal-studies.com/goettnerabendroth.html (accessed May 24, 2007).

Graves, Kersey. [1875] 2004. *The world's sixteen crucified saviors: Christianity before Christ.* Bensenville, IL: Lushena.

Griffis-Greenberg, Katherine. 1999. Neith: Ancient goddess of the beginning, the beyond, and the end. http://www.geocities.com/skhmt_netjert/neith.html (accessed December 19, 2006).

Guthrie, W. K. C. [1952] 1993. *Orpheus and Greek religion.* Princeton, NJ: Princeton University Press.

———. 1967. *The Greeks and their gods.* Boston, MA: Beacon.

Hagan, Helene E. 2000. *The shining ones: An etymological essay on the Amazigh roots of Egyptian civilization.* n.p.: Xlibris.

Hansell, Jean. 1998. *The pigeon in history: Or the dove's tale.* Bath, UK: Millstream.

Harrison, Jane. [1903] 1957. *Prolegomena to the study of Greek religion.* New York: Meridian.

———. [1912] 1963. *Themis: A study of the social origins of Greek religion.* London: Merlin.

Hartland, Edwin Sydney. 1894. *The legend of Perseus: A study of tradition in story, custom and belief.* 3 vols. London: David Nutt.

———. 1909–10. *Primitive paternity: Or the myth of supernatural birth in relation to the history of the family.* 2 vols. London: David Nutt.

Hawkins, Henry [H.A.]. [1633] 1950. *Parthenia sacra.* Aldington Kent, UK: Hand and Flower.

Hayden, Brian. 1993. An archeological evaluation of the Gimbutas paradigm. *The Pomegranate* 6: 35–46.

Herodotus. 1972. *The histories.* Trans. Aubrey de Sélincourt. New York: Penguin.

Hesiod. 1943. *Hesiod. The Homeric Hymns and Homerica.* Trans. Hugh G. Evelyn-White. Cambridge, MA: Harvard University Press.

———. 1987. *Hesiod's theogony.* Trans. Richard S. Caldwell. Cambridge, MA: Focus Information Group.

———. 2007. *The shield; catalogue of women; other fragments.* Ed. and trans. Glenn W. Most. Cambridge, MA: Harvard University Press.

Hillman, D. C. A. 2008. *The chemical muse: Drug use and the roots of Western civilization.* New York: Thomas Dunne.

A History of Midwifery in Pictures. n.d. http://www.geocities.com/ Wellesley/atrium/5148/history.html (accessed June 11, 2007).

Holderman, Elizabeth Sinclair. 1913. *A study of the Greek priestess.* Chicago: University of Chicago Press.

Hollis, Susan Tower. 1994–95. Five Egyptian goddesses in the third millennium B.C. *KMT: A Modern Journal of Ancient Egypt* 5(4) (Winter): 46–51.

Holweck, Frederick G. 1910. Immaculate conception. In *The Catholic Encyclopedia,* vol. 7, 674. New York: Robert Appleton Company. http:// www.newadvent.org/cathen/07674d.html (accessed March 29, 2007).

Horapollo. 1950. *The hieroglyphics of Horapollo.* Trans. George Boas. Bollingen Series 23. New York: Pantheon.

Hwang, Helen Hye-Sook. 2005. *Seeking Mago, the great goddess: A mytho-historic-thealogical reconstruction of Magoism, an archaically originated gynocentric tradition of East Asia.* PhD diss., Claremont Graduate University. *Dissertation Abstracts International,* publ. nr. AAT3159640, DAI-A 66/01 (July 2005); 218.

Hyginus. 1960. *The myths of Hyginus.* Trans. and ed. Mary Grant. Lawrence, KS: University of Kansas Publications.

Iamblichus. [1821] 1968. *On the Mysteries.* Trans. Thomas Taylor. London: Stuart and Watkins.

———. 1911. *Theurgia* or *On the mysteries of Egypt.* Trans. Alexander Wilder. New York: Metaphysical. http://www.esotericarchives.com/oracle/ iambl_th.htm (accessed November 27, 2008).

———. 1988. *The theology of arithmetic: On the mystical, mathematical and cosmological symbolism of the first ten numbers.* Trans. Robin Waterfield. Grand Rapids, MI: Phanes.

Johnson, Martin H., Susan J. Pickering, Peter R. Braude, Caroline Vincent, Ann Cant, and Janet Currie. 1990. Acid tyrode's solution can stimulate parthenogenetic activation of human and mouse oocyte. *Fertility and Sterility* 53(2): 266–70.

Jones, Ernest. 1949. *On the nightmare*. London: L. and Virginia Woolf at the Hogarth Press, and the Institute of Psycho-analysis. Quoted in Lewis 1971, 58.

Kalweit, Holger. 1988. *Dreamtime and inner space: The world of the shaman*. Trans. Werner Wünsche. Boston, MA: Shambhala.

———. 1992. *Shamans, healers, medicine men*. Boston, MA: Shambhala.

Keller, Mara Lynn. 1996. Gimbutas's theory of early European origins and the contemporary transformation of Western civilization. *Journal of Feminist Studies in Religion* 12(2): 73–90.

Kerenyi, Karl. 1959. *Asklepios: Archetypal image of the physician's existence*. New York: Pantheon.

———. 1975. *Zeus and Hera: Archetypal image of father, husband, and wife*. Princeton, NJ: Princeton University Press.

———. 1978. *Athene: Virgin and mother in Greek religion*. Dallas, TX: Spring.

King, C. W. 1887. *The Gnostics and their remains, ancient and mediaeval*. 2nd ed. London: David Nutt.

Kleinbaum, Abby Wettan. 1983. *The war against the Amazons*. New York: New Press.

Kripal, Jeffrey John. 2007. *The serpent's gift: Gnostic reflections on the study of religion*. Chicago: University of Chicago Press.

Krupp, E. C. 1991. *Beyond the blue horizon: Myths and legends of the sun, moon, stars, and planets*. New York: HarperCollins.

Lajoux, Jean-Dominique. 1963. *The rock paintings of Tassili*. Cleveland, OH: World Publishing.

Lamy, Lucie. 1981. *Egyptian mysteries*. New York: Crossroad.

Larson, Jennifer. 1995. *Greek heroine cults*. Madison, WI: University of Wisconsin Press.

———. 2001. *Greek nymphs: Myth, cult, lore*. Oxford: Oxford University Press.

Lazarovici, Cornelia–Magda. 2008. Symbols and signs of the Cucuteni-Tripolye culture. *Journal of Archaeomythology* 4(1): 65–93. http://www.archaeomythology.org/journal/read_article.php?a=0108_4_clazarovici.pdf (accessed July 14, 2008).

Lazarovici, Gheorghe. 2008. Database for signs and symbols of spiritual life. *Journal of Archaeomythology* 4(1): 94–125. http://www.archaeomythology.org/journal/read_article.php?a=0108_5_glazarovici.pdf (accessed July 14, 2008).

Leach, Edmund. 1969. *Genesis as myth and other essays*. London: Cape.

Lefkowitz, Mary. 1993. Seduction and rape in Greek myth. In *Consent and coercion to sex and marriage in ancient and medieval societies,* ed. Angeliki E. Laiou, 17–37. Washington, DC: Dumbarton Oaks Research Library and Collection.

————. 1996. *Not out of Africa: How Afrocentrism became an excuse to teach myth as history*. New York: Basic Books.

Lefkowitz, Mary, and Guy M. Rogers, eds. 1996. *Black Athena revisited*. Chapel Hill, NC: University of North Carolina Press.

Lesko, Barbara. 1999. *The great goddesses of Egypt*. Norman, OK: University of Oklahoma Press.

Lewis, I. M. 1971. *Ecstatic religion: An anthropological study of spirit possession and shamanism*. Middlesex, UK: Penguin.

Lezzi-Haftner, Adrienne. 1988a. *Der Eretria-Maler*. 2 vols. Rhein: Mainz. Cited in Avagianou (1991, 191–2).

————. 1988b. Anthesterien und hieros gamos. Ein choenbild des Methyse-Malers. In *Proceedings of the 3rd Symposium on Ancient and Related Pottery*, ed. Jette Christiansen and Torben Melander, 325–35. Copenhagen: Nationalmuseet. Cited in Avagianou (1991, 191–2).

Liddell, Henry George, and Robert Scott. 1889. *An intermediate Greek-English lexicon*. 7th ed. Oxford: Oxford University Press.

Lissarrague, François. 1992. Figures of women. In *A history of women: From ancient goddesses to Christian saints*, ed. Pauline Schmitt Pantel, 141–229. Cambridge, MA: Belknap.

Long, Asphodel P. 1992. *In a chariot drawn by lions: The search for the female in deity*. London: Women's Press.

Lourenço, W. R., and O. Cuellar. 1995. Scorpions, scorpionism, life history strategies and parthenogenesis. *Journal of Venomous Animals and Toxins* 1(2): 51–62.

Lyons, Deborah. 1997. *Gender and immortality: Heroines in ancient Greek myth and cult*. Princeton, NJ: Princeton University Press.

Malinowski, Bronislaw. 1913. *The family among the Australian Aborigines: A sociological study*. London: London University Press.

————. 1927. *The father in primitive psychology*. New York: W. W. Norton.

————. 1929. *The sexual life of savages in North-Western Melanesia*. London: Routledge.

Marler, Joan. 2002. An archaeomythological investigation of the Gorgon. *ReVision* 25(1): 15–23.

————. 2005. The myth of universal patriarchy: A critical response to Cynthia Eller's *The myth of matriarchal prehistory*. In *Prehistoric archaeology and anthropological theory and education*, ed. L. Nikolovna, J. Fritz, and J. Higgins, 75–85. Salt Lake City, UT: International Institute of Anthropology.

McDavid, Doss. 2005. Rosicrucian landmarks preserved in Greek isopsephia (Gematria). *Rose + Croix Journal* 2: 22–9.

Meenee, Harita. 2004. *The women's Olympics and the Great Goddess*. Athens, Greece: Eleusis Press.

Melchizedek, Drunvalo. 2000. *The ancient secret of the flower of life*. 2 vols. Flagstaff, AZ: Light Technology.

Meskell, Lynn. 1995. Goddesses, Gimbutas, and "New Age" archaeology. *Antiquity* 69: 74–86.

Meyer, Marvin. 2007. *The Nag Hammadi scriptures*. San Francisco, CA: HarperOne.

Milius, Susan. 1999. Do parasites explain female promiscuity? *Science News* 155(5): 78.

Miller, Robert J. 2003. *Born divine: The births of Jesus and other sons of God*. Santa Rosa, CA: Polebridge.

Miller, Roy Andrew. 1988. Pleiades perceived: Mul.Mul to Subaru. *Journal of the American Oriental Society* 108(1): 1–25.

Mittwoch, Ursula. 1978. Parthenogenesis. *Journal of Medical Genetics* 15: 165–81.

Mott, Maryann. 2008. Animal-human hybrids spark controversy. *National Geographic News* (January 28). http://news.nationalgeographic.com/news/pd/62295276.html (accessed July 7, 2008).

Montagu, Ashley. [1937] 1974. *Coming into being among the Australian Aborigines*. London: Routledge & Kegan Paul.

Muechler, Eberhard K., Margaret C. Graham, Ko-en Huang, Ann B. Partridge, and Ken Jones. 1989. Parthenogenesis of human oocytes as a function of vacuum pressure. *Journal of Assisted Reproduction and Genetics* 6(6): 335–7.

Müller, Heinrich Dietrich. 1857. *Mythologie der grieschisschen stämme*. Vol. 1. Göttingen: Vandenhoeck and Ruprecht. Cited in Harrison [1903] 1957, 315n1.

Murphy, Michael. 1992. *The future of the body: Explorations into the further evolution of human nature*. Los Angeles: J. P. Tarcher.

Neumann, Erich. 1963. *The great mother: An analysis of the archetype*. Princeton, NJ: Princeton University Press.

Nikolov, Vassil. Forthcoming. On the semantics of Neolithic altars. In *Signs of Civilization*, ed. Joan Marler. Sebastopol, CA: Institute of Archaeomythology.

Nilsson, Martin P. 1932. *The Mycenaean origin of Greek mythology*. New York: W. W. Norton.

———. [1950] 1971. *The Minoan-Mycenaean religion and its survival in Greek religion*. New York: Biblo and Tannen.

Nissinen, Martti, and Risto Uro. 2008. *Sacred marriages: The divine-human sexual metaphor from Sumer to early Christianity*. Winona Lake, IN: Eisenbrauns.

Noble, Vicki. 2003. *The double goddess: Women sharing power*. Rochester, VT: Bear and Company.

Oates, Whitney J., and Eugene O'Neill Jr., eds. 1938. *The complete Greek drama*. 2 vols. New York: Random House.

O'Brien, Joan V. 1993. *The transformation of Hera: A study of ritual, hero, and the goddess in the* Iliad. Lanham, MD: Rowman and Littlefield.

Oikonomides, Al. N. 1987. Records of *"The commandments of the seven wise men"* in the 3rd c. B.C. *Classical Bulletin* 63: 67–76.

Olsen, M. W. 1960. Performance record of a parthenogenetic turkey male. *Science* 132(3442): 1661.

———. 1965. 12-year summary of selection for parthenogenesis in Beltsville small white turkeys. *British Poultry Science* 6: 1–6.

Origen. 1953. *Contra Celsum.* Trans. Henry Chadwick. Cambridge, UK: Cambridge University Press.

Ovid. 1955. *Metamorphoses.* Trans. Mary M. Innes. New York: Penguin.

Parke, H. W. 1939. *A history of the Delphic oracle.* Oxford: Basil Blackwell.

———. 1967. *The oracles of Zeus.* Oxford: Basil Blackwell.

Pauly, Philip. 1987. *Controlling life: Jacques Loeb and the engineering ideal in biology.* New York: Oxford.

Pausanias. 1931–5. *Description of Greece.* 6 vols. Trans. W. H. S. Jones. New York: G. P. Putnam.

Pincus, Gregory. 1939. The comparative behavior of mammalian eggs in vivo and in vitro. IV. The development of fertilized and artificially activated rabbit eggs. *Journal of Experimental Zoology* 82: 85.

Pindar. 1997. *Nemean odes, Isthmian odes, fragments.* Ed. and trans. William H. Race. Cambridge, MA: Harvard University Press.

Plato. 1925. *Plato in twelve volumes.* Trans. W. R. M. Lamb. Cambridge, MA: Harvard University Press. Perseus Digital Library. http://perseus. mpiwg-berlin.mpg.de/cgi-bin/ptext?lookup=Plat.+Hipp.+Maj.+281a (accessed June 1, 2007).

Pliny the Elder. 1855. *The natural history.* Ed. John Bostock. London: Taylor and Francis. Perseus Digital Library. http://www.perseus.tufts.edu/cgi-bin/ptext?doc=Perseus%3Atext%3A1999.02.0137&layout=&loc=1. dedication (accessed August 3, 2006).

Plotinus. 1952. *The six enneads.* Trans. Stephen MacKenna. Chicago: Encyclopaedia Britannica.

Plutarch. 1914. *Lives: Theseus and Romulus; Lycurgus and Numa; Solon and Publicola.* Trans. Bernadotte Perrin. Cambridge, MA: Harvard University Press.

———. 1927–69. *Plutarch's moralia.* 14 vols. Trans. Frank Cole Babbitt. New York: G. P. Putnam.

———. 1940–1. *Über Isis und Osiris.* 2 vols. Trans. Theodor Hopfner. Prague: Orientalisches Institut. Cited in Plutarch 1970, 433.

———. 1969. *Plutarch's moralia.* Vol. 8. Trans. Paul A. Clement and Herbert B. Hoffleit. Cambridge, MA: Harvard University Press.

———. 1970. *Plutarch's de Iside et Osiride.* Ed. and trans. J. Gwyn Griffiths. Cardiff: University of Wales Press.

Porphyry. 1983. *Porphyry: On the cave of the nymphs.* Trans. Robert Lamberton. Barrytown, NY: Station Hill.

Ramsay, Sir W. M. 1985. *The cities and bishoprics of Phrygia.* 2 vols. Oxford: Clarendon. Quoted in Cook 1914–40, 2.1:288.

Ransome, Hilda M. [1937] 2004. *The sacred bee in ancient times and folklore.* Mineola, NY: Dover.

Reis, Patricia. 1991. *Through the goddess: A woman's way of healing.* New York: Continuum.

Renner, Timothy. 1978. A papyrus dictionary of metamorphoses. *Harvard Studies in Classical Philology* 82: 277–93.

Rhode, Erwin. [1925] 1966. *Psyche: The cult of souls and belief in immortality among the Greeks.* 2 vols. Trans. W. B. Hillis. New York: Harper Torchbooks.

Rhys, Jocelyn. 1922. *Shaken creeds: The virgin birth doctrine. A study of its origins.* London: Watts.

Ricoeur, Paul. 1965. *De l'interprétation.* Paris: Éditions du Seuil.

Rigoglioso, Marguerite. 2007. *Bearing the holy ones: A study of the cult of divine birth in ancient Greece.* PhD diss., California Institute of Integral Studies, San Francisco. *Dissertation Abstracts International,* publ. nr. AAT 3286688, DAI-A 68/10 (April 2008).

Rikala, Mia. 2008. Sacred marriage in the New Kingdom of Ancient Egypt: Circumstantial evidence for a ritual interpretation. In *Sacred Marriages: The divine-human sexual metaphor from Sumer to early Christianity,* ed. Martti Nissinen and Risto Uro, 115–44. Winona Lake, IN: Eisenbrauns.

Robertson, Noel. 1983. Greek ritual begging in aid of women's fertility and childbirth. *Transactions of the American Philological Association* 113: 143–69.

Rose, H. J. 1959. *A handbook of Greek mythology.* New York: Dutton.

Roth, Walter E. 1903. *Superstition, magic, and medicine.* Brisbane, Australia: Vaughan.

Ruck, Carl A. P., Jeremy Bigwood, Danny Staples, Jonathan Ott, and Gordon Wasson. 1979. Entheogens. *Journal of Psychedelic Drugs* 11(1–2): 145–6.

Ruether, Rosemary Radford. 1992. *Gaia and God: An ecofeminist theology of earth healing.* San Francisco, CA: HarperSanFrancisco.

Sandars, N. K. 1972. *The epic of Gilgamesh.* New York: Penguin.

Sanday, Peggy Reeves. 1998. Matriarchy as a sociocultural form. Paper presented at the 16th Congress of the Indo-Pacific Prehistory Association, July 1–7, Melaka, Malaysia.

Sappho. 1958. *Sappho.* Trans. Mary Barnard. Berkeley, CA: University of California Press.

Schüssler Fiorenza, Elizabeth. 1983. *In memory of her: A feminist theological reconstruction of Christian origins.* New York: Crossroad.

Sered, Susan Starr. 1994. *Priestess, mother, sacred sister: Religions dominated by women.* New York: Oxford University Press.

Shettles, Landrum B. 1956. Intrafollicular cleavage of human ovum. *Nature* 178(4542): 1131.

———. 1957. Parthenogenetic cleavage of the human ovum. *Bulletin of the Sloane Hospital for Women* 3: 39.

Shumaker, Wayne. 1972. *The occult sciences in the Renaissance.* Berkeley, CA: University of California Press.

Sissa, Giulia. 1990. *Greek virginity.* Cambridge, MA: Harvard University Press.

Sjöö, Monica, and Barbara Mor. 1991. *The great cosmic mother*. San Francisco, CA: HarperSanFrancisco.

Smith, William. 1854. *Dictionary of Greek and Roman geography*. London: Walton and Maberly. Perseus Digital Library. http://perseus.mpiwg-berlin. mpg.de/cgi-bin/ptext?doc=Perseus%3Atext%3A1999.04.0064 (accessed May 2, 2007).

———, ed. 1870. *Dictionary of Greek and Roman biography and mythology*. Boston, MA: Little, Brown. The Ancient Library. http://www. ancientlibrary.com/smith-bio/ (accessed April 18, 2007).

Smith, William, William Wayte, and G. E. Marindin. 1890. *Dictionary of Greek and Roman antiquities*. 3rd ed. London: J. Murray. The Ancient Library. http://www.perseus.tufts.edu/cgi-bin/ptext?doc=Perseus%3Atext%3A1999. 04.0063 (accessed September 18, 2007).

Sobol, Donald J. 1972. *The Amazons of Greek mythology*. New York: A. S. Barnes.

Sourvinou-Inwood, Christiane. 1988. *Studies in girls' transitions: Aspects of the Arkteia and age representations in Attic iconography*. Athens, Greece: Kardamitsa.

Spencer, Herbert. [1876] 1969. *Principles of sociology*. Hamden, CT: J. Archon.

Spiro, Melford. E. 1968. Virgin birth, parthenogenesis and physiological paternity: An essay in cultural interpretation. *Man,* New Series 3(2): 242–61.

Spretnak, Charlene. 1978. *Lost goddesses of early Greece: A collection of pre-Hellenic myths*. Boston, MA: Beacon.

———. 1982. *The politics of women's spirituality: Essays on the rise of spiritual power within the feminist movement*. Garden City, NY: Anchor.

———. 1996. Beyond the backlash: An appreciation of the work of Marija Gimbutas. *Journal of Feminist Studies in Religion* 12(2): 91–8.

Statius. 1928. *Statius.* 2 vols. Trans. J. H. Mozley. Cambridge, MA: Harvard University Press.

Steiner, Rudolph. 1998. *Bees.* Trans. Thomas Braatz. Hudson, NY: Anthroposophic.

Stillwell, Richard, William L. MacDonald, and Marian Holland McAllister, eds. 1976. *The Princeton encyclopedia of classical sites*. Princeton, NJ: Princeton University Press. Perseus Digital Library. http://perseus. mpiwg-berlin.mpg.de/cgi-bin/ptext?doc=Perseus%3Atext%3A1999. 04.0006 (accessed June 4, 2006).

Strabo. 1950. *The geography of Strabo*. Trans. Horace Leonard Jones. Cambridge, MA: Harvard University Press.

Strong, Eugénie Sellers. 1969. *Apotheosis and after life*. Freeport, NY: Books for Libraries.

Sykes, Bryan. 2001. *The seven daughters of Eve*. New York: W. W. Norton.

Theoi Project. 2000–7. http://www.theoi.com (accessed April 16, 2007).

Thornley, George, and S. Gaselee, trans. 1935. *Daphnis and Chloe by Longus; The love romances of Parthenius and other fragments*. Cambridge, MA: Harvard University Press.

Tringham, Ruth, and Margaret Conkey. 1998. Rethinking figurines: A critical view from archeology of Gimbutas, the "goddess" and popular culture. In *Ancient goddesses*, ed. Lucy Goodison and Christine Morris, 22–45. London: British Museum.

Troy, Lana. 1986. *Patterns of queenship in Ancient Egyptian myth and history.* Boreas. Uppsala Studies in Ancient Mediterranean and Near Eastern Civilization 14. Stockholm: Acta Universitatis Upsaliensis.

Turner, Judy Ann. 1983. *Hiereiai: Acquisition of feminine priesthoods in ancient Greece.* PhD diss., University of California, Santa Barbara. *Dissertation Abstracts International,* publ. nr. AAT8401758, DAI-A 44/10 (April 1984); 3135.

Tyrrell, William Blake. 1984. *Amazons: A study in Athenian mythmaking.* Baltimore, MD: Johns Hopkins University Press.

Tyson, Donald. 2000. *Sexual alchemy: Magical intercourse with spirits.* St. Paul, MN: Llewellyn.

Ulansey, David. 1989. *The origin of the Mithraic mysteries: Cosmology and salvation in the ancient world.* New York: Oxford University Press.

Valentis, Mary, and Anne Devane. 1994. *Female rage: Unlocking its secrets, claiming its power.* New York: Carol Southern.

van Niekerk, C. H., and W. H. Gerneke. 1966. Persistence and parthenogenetic cleavage of tubal ova in the mare. *Onderstepoort Journal of Veterinary Research* 33: 195–232.

Villoldo, Alberto. 2000. *Shaman, healer, sage.* New York: Harmony.

Virgil. 1934. *Virgil's works: The Aeneid, Eclogues, Georgics.* Trans. J. W. Mackail. New York: Modern Library.

———. 1947. *Virgil.* 2 vols. Trans. H. Rushton Fairclough. Cambridge, MA: Harvard University Press.

Vrijenhoek, Robert C. 1998. Animal clones and diversity. *BioScience* 48(8): 617–28.

Wake, C. Staniland. 1870. The influence of the phallic idea in the religions of antiquity. *Journal of Anthropology* 1(2): 199–227.

Walker, Barbara G. 1983. *The woman's encyclopedia of myths and secrets.* San Francisco, CA: HarperSanFrancisco.

Warner, Marina. 1976. *Alone of all her sex.* New York: Vintage.

Wasson, Gordon R., Albert Hoffman, and Carl A. P. Ruck. 1978. *The road to Eleusis: Unveiling the secret of the mysteries.* New York: Harcourt Brace Jovanovitch.

Weidensaul, Scott. 1997. The belled viper. *Smithsonian* 28(9): 96–104.

West, Martin L., trans. 2003. *Homeric hymns; Homeric apocrypha; lives of Homer.* Cambridge, MA: Harvard University Press.

White, M. J. D. 1973. *Animal cytology and evolution.* 3rd ed. New York: Cambridge University Press.

Wilde, Lyn Webster. 1999. *On the trail of the women warriors: The Amazons in myth and history.* New York: Thomas Dunne.

Wilford, John Noble. 2008. An altar beyond Olympus for a deity predating Zeus. *New York Times,* February 5. http://www.nytimes.com/

2008/02/05/science/05zeus.html?pagewanted=1&8dpc&_r=2 (accessed July 8, 2008).

Winston, Nicola, Martin Johnson, Susan Pickering, and Peter Braude. 1991. Parthenogenetic activation and development of fresh and aged human oocytes. *Fertility and Sterility* 56(5): 904–12.

Wolkstein, Diane, and Samuel Noah Kramer. 1983. *Inanna, queen of heaven and earth: Her stories and hymns from Sumer.* New York: Harper and Row.

Yakar, Jak. 1997. Did Anatolia contribute to the neolithization of Southeast Europe? In *From the Realm of the Ancestors: An Anthology in Honor of Marija Gimbutas,* ed. Joan Marler, 59–69. Manchester, CT: Knowledge, Ideas and Trends.

———. 2007. Interview with Jak Yakar. *Journal of Archaeomythology* 3(1): 25–31. http://www.archaeomythology.org/journal/read_article. php?a=0607_4_marler_yakar.pdf (accessed July 14, 2008).

Ywahoo, Dhyani. 1987. *Voices of our ancestors: Cherokee teachings from the wisdom fire.* Boston, MA: Shambhala.

Zaidman, Louise Bruit. 1992. Pandora's daughters and rituals in Grecian cities. In *A history of women: From ancient goddesses to Christian saints,* ed. Pauline Schmitt Pantel, 338–76. Cambridge, MA: Belknap.

INDEX

Breinigsville, PA USA
09 February 2011
255157BV00001B/2/P